Signifying Europe

Johan Fornäs

intellect Bristol, UK / Chicago, USA

Published with support from the Sven and Dagmar Salén Foundation and the
Publication Committee of Södertörn University in Sweden.

First published in the UK in 2012 by Intellect,
The Mill, Parnall Road, Fishponds, Bristol, BS16 3JG, UK

First published in the USA in 2012 by Intellect, The University of Chicago Press,
1427 E. 60th Street, Chicago, IL 60637, USA

A catalogue record for this book is available from the British Library.

Copy-editor: Macmillan
Cover design: Holly Rose
Typesetting: John Teehan

Cover image includes a detail of *Captain Euro*, reproduced here with the kind
permission of Nicolas De Santis.

ISBN (Hardback): 978-1-84150-480-3
ISBN (Paperback): 978-1-84150-521-3

Printed and bound by Latimer Trend & Company Ltd, Plymouth.

For Hillevi

Contents

LIST OF FIGURES AND ILLUSTRATIONS

With the exception of Figures 7.1–7.5, all figures appear in the colour section located at the back of this book.

INTRODUCTION

In January 2009, David Černý's sculpture *Entropa*, commissioned to mark the Czech presidency of the Council of the European Union, was unveiled in the Brussels headquarters (Figure 0.1). The work consists of satirical versions of national stereotypes, mounted in a framework looking like plastic model kits. For instance, Černý depicted the Netherlands as flooded, with only minarets visible above the water surface; France with a big 'strike' sign; and Romania as a Dracula theme park. A heated debate ensued, as it turned out that Černý had faked other artists that were supposed to have contributed to the work, and also since Bulgaria got their depiction covered over as it had the form of a standing toilet, which was considered insulting.

The artist declared a wish to provoke official European Union-speak, but also to express Europe's capacity of critical self-reflection. Through a playful analysis of national stereotypes, the intention was to expose the way Europeans tend to focus on differences between countries in terms of everyday habits: to 'show how difficult and fragmented Europe as a whole can seem' and to 'point at the difficulty of communication'.[1] The sculpture indicates that there is—and perhaps can be—no European unity. The name *Entropa* plays with the term 'entropy'—a thermodynamic term often used metaphorically to signify an unstoppably increasing level of randomness and disorder in a system. The artwork depicts each nation as a closed unity, effectively cut off from all others, unable to fuse into a unified whole, emptying the European Union (EU) project of any hope for success.

This is certainly in line with some apparent failures of the integration process. However, there is also a more problematic undertext in Černý's work: it seems to imply that European nations are well-defined and closed units—at least infinitely more so than Europe as a whole. This naturalisation of national identity is untenable. European nations are all 'imagined communities' (Benedict Anderson) that with shifting success have been consolidated by economic and political institutions. So Europe is not alone in being a sociocultural construction with strong imaginary elements, and more of a project than an existing empirical fact. Such imaginary communities are not necessarily mere illusions. Communities need not be natural or eternal in order to exist and have

1

an effect in the world. Ideas and discourses have a kind of 'reality effect' that makes people act differently and thus make the imagined communities come alive.

Politicians, philosophers or scholars have through the centuries drafted a European project, but they have not been alone. Various social strata have oriented themselves towards a real and imagined Europe, drawing up its contours in various sets of practices. Refugees and other migrants are attracted by imaginations of European welfare, social security, peace, human rights and liberties. Even as they react against the experienced shortcomings of harsh realities, their vernacular practices articulate certain recurrent elements of European identifications. Many are deeply disappointed by the deficits in how promises are (not) realised for them, but still the imagined European community remains in force—and it does not completely lack material basis. Other groups sustaining the European idea are exchange students looking for education, queer activists escaping homophobic threats, tourists appreciating European architecture and gastronomy, sports fans enjoying European football, and media audiences that in the Eurovision Song Contest (ESC) develop dialogues between the regions of this continent.

Contemporary migrants and travellers move along historic routes. Backpackers and Erasmus students cross Europe in the footsteps of pilgrims and journeymen. There are functional networks on various levels, not only for trade and banks but also for people in movement. Such links also transcontinentally cross the outer boundaries of Europe, but they are particularly dense within the European interchange that underpins the notions of what Europe means. In Africa, Asia and the transatlantic 'New World', there are also certain prominent ways to identify what is perceived as European.

Europe is no self-evident cultural or social unit. There is a deficit of channels for communication between its multinational citizens. A shared European public sphere is only in its infancy. But community may possibly not need to build on every member participating in exactly the same forum. Since the differentiation of television and other media forms into many divergent platforms and channels, this is not even true for any nation. Instead, Europe, like today's nation states, is crystallised by loosely combined 'spheres of publics'—networks of communication where no single medium or arena gathers all citizens but where their mutual exchanges produce a dynamic and heterogeneous totality, which is also not quite closed to the outside, but has permeable boundaries. This means that nations are not those self-sufficient enclaves suggested by *Entropa*: they are neither sealed off towards each other nor internally consistent units.

The complex diversity of Europe therefore need not necessarily annul the idea of a European identity. It only puts high demands on interpreting how elements of such an identity are spun around the symbols used for signifying what Europe means. This is the purpose of this study: mapping out the currently predominant meaning and identity of Europe—or rather the many *meanings* and *identities* linked to Europe through *symbols* developed for this purpose.

As Europe in particular undergoes radical transformations in its internal structure and global contexts, there is a renewed need to re-identify its meaning. A series of societal processes of transformation challenge inherited conceptions of identity. Historical processes of culturalisation and mediatisation make meaning-making more central in many social spheres, including the political and economic domains. This creates a situation where collective identities in general are renegotiated and reconstructed in several different arenas, both by established institutional actors and by practices and initiatives on a grass roots level.

In the EU, as well as in other institutions, organisations and movements, and among citizens who live within or move across the boundaries of this continent, a range of mediated symbols are used for signifying Europe—branding it 'from above', making it a home or critically problematising it 'from below'. New ways of signifying Europe are born in a time when collective cultural identities are in rapid transformation, under the pressure of geopolitical reconfiguration of power relations on a global scale; marketisation and economic restructuring; new dynamics of inequality in terms of class, gender, generation and ethnicity; migration linked to the spread of multiculturalism and cosmopolitanism; and culturalising mediatisation linked to the proliferation of digital networks. Such processes create an intensified symbolic work of identifying Europe through modifying or reinterpreting its key symbols. This study will focus on the meanings of a variety of symbols that today identify Europe as an idea, a geographical territory, a political–economic institution and a social community—highlighting the specificity of the five official EU symbols by selective comparisons with other federative, regional or national symbols.

Symbols proposed by Europe's own elites necessarily intend to represent the positive values and success of this unification. The interesting question is then *how* this is done: by which symbolic means is the success of the EU represented, and which specific qualities are ascribed to this union—in what way is this community described as strong and beneficial? Alternative symbols sometimes on the contrary critically depict Europe as weak or bad—as ridiculously fragmented or instead as dangerously powerful. They offer a useful sidelight that makes visible unintentional nuances in the official ones, helping to discern a range of hidden inner tensions and contradictions in the emerging European identity formation.

This study combines a cultural studies and a media and communication perspective, in an interdisciplinary mode of inquiry that combines tools from historical, political, sociological, media ethnographic, literary, visual and musical analysis in an interpretive framework where signifying and mediating practices form the main focus. This is motivated by a series of reasons. First, the meaning and identifying role of European symbols are the topic of an important discourse within the slowly emerging European public sphere. Second, European symbols are themselves integrated elements in widely disseminated European media texts. Third, European symbols may themselves be understood as media forms, even though media studies rarely regard for instance money as a medium.

Further research would more systematically investigate a wider range of symbols, the institutional actors and processes behind the formation of such symbols, as well as the interpretations and uses of these symbols by wider sets of citizens in various regions, settings and strata. The intention is to start exploring this fascinating terrain and propose new perspectives on the ways in which Europe and Europeanness are currently reconstructed.

The main questions dealt with in this study are:

> *How is Europe given identity through the meaning-making interpretive use of symbols in signifying practices?*
> - How are different *symbols* used, often in ambiguous or oppositional ways, to construct plural and sometimes contradictory sets of *meaning* that create an *identity* for Europe?
> - Which historical *roots*, experiences and values are central to the formation and continued existence of Europe as a political, economic, social and cultural community?
> - How is Europe identified through *differences* and similarities of its key symbols to those of other comparable geopolitical units?
> - How are these symbols integrated into multiple and sometimes competing founding *narratives* of Europe as a collective agency in the world?
> - Which main *conflicts of interpretation* may be discerned for each key symbol: which main meanings compete and are supported by which actors?

As an introduction to what follows, Chapter 1 scrutinises the name 'Europe', which is no official EU symbol but still has a primary identifying function, thus serving as a basis for all the subsequent symbols. This immediately leads to a series of myths that have been used for narratively expressing Europe's meaning. After a brief discussion in Chapter 2 of theoretical definitions of the kind of identifying symbols studied here, Chapter 3 then offers a general historical background to the European unification and introduces the official set of European symbols. These are then scrutinised one by one in the core Chapters 4–8, investigating the main symbolic domains used for signifying Europe today, revealing how they in turn add new dimensions to the identity of Europe. The concluding Chapter 9 makes an effort to summarise and compare the meaning clusters accumulated by combining the various symbols, and to sum up what they indicate concerning what Europe means today.[2]

1

Name and Myth

One of the most important symbols that identify an entity is its name. In many cases, names are often overlooked and taken for granted in ordinary usage. 'Europe' is a splendid example: it is never analysed or mentioned in official EU documents, as it can hardly be replaced—being inherited since antiquity, not seriously questioned or contested by any alternative name, and therefore not an object of political choice. Other geographic names may well be questioned—think for instance of Macedonia or Kurdistan. But there is an evident consensus on how to name this continent, even though its external boundaries are not fixed.

Even so, the name of Europe is an important verbal symbol that carries specific associations, though they are today a matter of naturalised habit rather than of conscious interpretation. Being much older than the official EU symbols, it deserves to be treated first, as the latter cannot avoid being intertextually affected by the meanings attached to it—and to the mythological figure of Europa, to which the name is intrinsically linked.

What's in a name—and in a myth?

> Juliet: 'What's in a name? That which we call a rose
> By any other name would smell as sweet.'[3]

It is not surprising that the first part of this famous quote from William Shakespeare's *Rome and Juliet* has been widely used in a variety of contexts—from Umberto Eco's philosophical detective novel *The Name of the Rose* to a range of contemporary texts on gender, race, nationality or other identity issues. Juliet's optimistic position is effectively contradicted by the fate of the two lovers, as their family names doom their love to tragedy. Even without engaging in detailed analysis of how naming has been

5

understood in cultural, social and linguistic theory, it is easy to see how two extreme positions have continued to struggle with each other.

At one end, 'nominalists' consider names to be arbitrary labels bearing no necessary relation to what they identify. Juliet's position suggests that names are only superficial conventions that do not affect the deeper meaning of existence. At the other extreme, 'realists' see names as strongly linked to objects and indeed crucial to their existence in the world. This is how Juliet's and Romeo's families might reason: for the Capulets and Montagues, names indeed meant everything, and at the end of the tragedy, the mortal fate of the lovers supports their position. By a strange twist, this is also what a third position would imply: 'constructionists' would argue that all social phenomena are the result of communicative discourses and have no separate existence outside them. Despite many mutual oppositions, a realist and a constructionist would agree that the question of what is a rose is impossible to even discuss without reference to the name of the rose: while one reduces language to a direct mirror of 'reality', the other in reverse reduces 'reality' to an effect of language use, whereas in contrast the nominalist understands name and reality as two separable entities.

In a general sense, names are words that in a given language denote and address something or someone, whether persons, collectives or things.[4] On some relative level, each name requires and constructs a degree of unicity in its reference. The word 'dog' is thus a name for a unique family of animals, while 'Dog' may be used as name of a specific dog individual. Similarly, 'association for cultural studies' names a specific kind of associations, of which only one bears the name 'Association for Cultural Studies'. The names discussed here are standardised and intersubjectively constituted condensed verbal labels identifying specific individuals, groups, institutions or other social or geopolitical entities (rather than for instance natural objects or abstract ideas). They do not provide full definitions or descriptions of what they name, but being widely used they contribute to rendering it meaningful, since they—as word combinations—semantically and pragmatically link the named phenomenon to certain sets of values and ideas. Interpreting a name therefore shows how people have interpreted or given meaning to someone or something.

Some human and social categories have such a prominent position that they not only get more or less unique names but also are surrounded by various mythical narratives that are sometimes wed to a particular name, forming a symbolic association between denoted subjects, names and myths that mutually identify each other in fascinating ways. Unique among world continents, this is the case with Europe, sharing name with the female protagonist of the ancient myth of Europa and the bull.

Tracing the cultural history of the concept of 'myth' is again at least as difficult.[5] A myth is a narrative of central value to a culture, binding people together in some way, and is linked to various rituals.[6] From Greek antiquity until today, together with neighbouring concepts like fable, legend, story and tale, myth has had a typically ambivalent status. It may be read in almost oppositional directions. In one reading, myths are thought to codify important truths about something—existential insights that cannot be expressed in other ways, transmitting through history a kind of inner essence of a community, linking it to universal or at least long-term human predicaments. The structural anthropologist Claude Lévi-Strauss sees myth as a transmittable symbolisation of virtually timeless structural truths of society's fundamental but unconscious laws.[7] Another example is when Karen Armstrong argues that 'mythology is an art form that points beyond history to what is timeless in human existence, helping us to get beyond the chaotic flux of random events, and glimpse the core of reality'.[8]

However, myth is on the other hand often taken as fiction describing impossible events and thus as the untrue antithesis of reason, history and factual knowledge. As Paul Ricoeur has noted, a long tradition of ideology critique and 'hermeneutics of suspicion' has worked to undermine mythical force, rather than affirmatively listening to it.[9] Myths may be seen as sets of utterances forming communicative systems that produce meaning. As signifying practices they can be interpreted, but they are particular kinds of signifying practices, forming a metalanguage that reflexively thematises 'ordinary' communication about reality. Roland Barthes argues that myth steals from language, and that critical interpretation therefore can steal back from myth to uncover its hidden truths.[10] This form of ideology critique has affinities with Karl Marx' views on the critique of religion and bourgeois ideology, with Sigmund Freud's dream analysis and not least with how Walter Benjamin understood the 'realization of dream elements, in the course of waking up' as the 'paradigm of dialectical thinking'.[11]

The fate of myth is thus to be revealing and/or deceptive: competing with rational understanding by either representing a deeper truth of reality than can be expressed in ordinary manners, or on the contrary a distorted ideology that hides that same reality. Indeed, one may even argue that it is this ambiguous position in-between reality and imagination that is the characteristic trait of mythical thinking and makes it capable of giving rise to an endlessly widening range of new interpretations.[12] In such a reading, a myth is not necessarily either right or wrong. It is a narration that mediates that which people believe is a central meaning for somebody and something, that is, a narrative key symbol that in temporally sequential and dramatised form expresses deep-seated shared meanings.[13] Mythical narratives symbolically transform and transmit memories of past events in ways that unify real and/or imagined communities, giving basic forms to their cultural identities.[14]

Introducing and interpreting the name and myth of Europe

Not all names are also myths, but some names either derive from mythical narratives or have subsequently had myths spun around them, elaborating their inherited meanings. This is the case with Europe. Neither name nor myth is mentioned as a European symbol by EU documents; this is because they are 'given' from the past, rather than a deliberate choice in the present. Today no political institution could, with any credibility, formally decide on a completely different name or founding myth of Europe. In other cases, such decisions are sometimes made, for instance when a city or nation state changes its name: think of Bombay/Mumbai or Burma/Myanmar. In Europe's case, the EU has named itself, but could only make a selection of the appropriate second term ('Union') and of the linguistic shape of the thus-composed name, while the concept of Europe itself has at this historical moment not been up for debate or had any serious competitors. It is always possible to reinterpret or deny a name or a myth, but in this case, no serious attempts have been made to invent or suggest a different name or founding myth.

As so often with old names, the origins of 'Europe' are unclear. It was used in ancient Greece, mentioned in writing in the seventh-century BC *Catalogue of Women* (falsely attributed to Hesiod); again in *The Histories* by the fifth-century BC Greek historian Herodotus; in *Library and Epitome* by Pseudo-Apollodorus in the first century BC; and in the Roman Ovidius' *Metamorphoses*, written before year 8 AD.[15] In the second century BC, the Syracusan poet Moschus clearly associated the myth of Europa and the bull to the continent.[16] Visually, the mythical couple was depicted in vase paintings at least from the seventh century BC (Figure 1.1 and 1.2). These early sources link the name both to the landmass to the northwest of the Levant and to a woman in a specific, but somewhat puzzling, founding myth of Europe.

Europa was said to have been a Phoenician princess or noblewoman who lived somewhere in the region of today's Lebanon in the Middle East. She was the daughter of Agenor, King of Tyre, who came from Egypt as the son of Libya and Poseidon.[17] Her mother was his Egyptian wife Telephassa, and Europa thus had a mixed Asian and African heritage. Agenor also had sons: Cadmus, Phoenix, Cilix and possibly also Thasus and Phineas. (*The Iliad* instead suggests Europa to be the daughter of Phoenix, which would link her to a theme of death and resurrection, but this may rather be a misinterpretation of her roots in Phoenicia.) Zeus, the king of gods, fancied Europa and disguised himself as a white bull to be able to come near her more easily than he would in his mighty godlike appearance. Ovid stresses this dichotomy between power and love, and underlines the mildness of this bull, as it mingles with her father's cattle. Gathering flowers with her female attendants, Europa noticed the bull, liked him and climbed onto his back. Zeus then ran away with her to the sea before she hardly noticed, and swam with her to the island of Crete. There, she gave birth to Zeus' three sons, Minos, Rhadamanthus and Sarpedon, after which she married King Asterius and became the first queen of Crete. Zeus gave them miraculous gifts: a necklace, the bronze giant Talos, the hunting dog Laelaps and a javelin. The gifts were handed over to Minos when he inherited the throne. Zeus also constructed the Taurus star constellation to commemorate his adventure.

Herodotus' more prosaic version just states that it was the Minoans who kidnapped Europa to Crete without any divine intervention, but in any case she remains linked to the sacred bull that was worshipped in the Levant and notably on Crete. It is not difficult to see how such a narrative could be understood as a mythical vision of the first settlement of Crete, and by extension, of Europe at large.

The identity of Europa is complicated, and linked to the meaning of the name itself, for which several layers of signification have been proposed. A contested but often repeated idea is that it goes back to a Semitic word for the land of the sunset, that is the Occident.

> It is plausibly argued that Europa was a goddess of the night, since her name relates to the Semitic verb 'to set'. A text from the Syrian city of Ugarit, a thriving commercial centre known to the Mycenaean Greeks before its destruction in about 1190 bc, speaks of 'our Lady, the goddess, the veiled bride […] entering the sunset'. In essence, this is the myth of Europa, who was carried away far westward to be married.[18]

Most sources allude to this reference to sunset and thus to the land of the West, but also to a place of evening and night. Some argue that Europa might be ultimately identical with the moon goddess. Support for this thought is supposedly given by the etymology of the Greek name that combines *euro* (wide or broad) with *op* (eye(s) or face) to mean 'broad-faced', presumably like the lunar cow. Lacking traces of any cult of Europa, one may doubt if she was herself really a deity. Later interpretations suggested the name implied that Europa was also open-minded, which is easy to infer from her fondness for the bull and the fearlessness with which she embarks upon the travel adventure.[19]

The origins of the name and myth of Europe are opaque, as are their core meanings. It is even hard to know for sure in which order the word, the myth and the identification of the specific territory appeared and were linked to each other. Was the myth spun around a spatial entity or did the latter evolve from the former? Did the myth crystallise out of a cluster of different myths in that region? Where and when was the name and/or the myth associated with the continent? These issues are difficult to assess, and actually not really decisive in this context. What is important here is rather which interpretations have been transmitted and used through history until today, as this speaks of the ways Europeans have constructed their collective identification.

Europa was the result of a combination of Asian (her Levantine father) and African (her Egyptian mother) sources, but the myth focuses on her union with the animal/ god, resulting in a mixed offspring. The intervention of Zeus to transport her to Crete recalls other divine interactions with humans: from Prometheus' gift of fire (to be further discussed below) and Zeus' many amorous disguises to those in the Old and New Testaments. It implies a higher spirit as the originating cause of Europa's settlement on European soil. The abduction and the subsequent founding of the Minoan dynasty is a move to the west, towards the European continent. Ovid stressed both the whiteness and the peaceful mildness of the bull. This gives a mythical explanation to the fair skin colour of Europeans and also lends a tranquil and peaceful aura to the abduction that can otherwise be understood as a violent kidnapping and raping of the poor princess. Instead, it is represented as an adventurous excursion, where both parties are in the older sources generally depicted as experiencing a kind of joy. Her position on top of the bull is depicted as giving her a certain degree of mobility and empowerment, complicating the element of violence and pain, as she is undoubtedly subjected to Zeus' power: he restricts her movements, as she is dislocated to Crete against her own will and cannot return home to Phoenicia. The myth implies that she is abducted from her home and family, but not by brute violence. Instead, her encounter with the bull is full of pleasure and desire, bearing traits of a passionate romance, which may also contain an element of transformative self-abandonment and persuasive power play. She is involuntarily dislocated but not deprived of her life, health, pride or honour. Instead her liberation from inherited family bonds may be read as a metaphor for the passage to adulthood and forming one's own destiny on a new territory, away from parents and siblings—all through the intervention of passionate relation with a foreign Other, in this instance Zeus as bull. Europa is a rather willing object of the god's desire and manipulation, as she caresses the bull and lets him sweep her away across the sea. He awakens erotic lust in her that carries her away: not into alienated exile but rather into forming new relations on new ground. Interpretations of the balance between lust and force in this story vary between versions: whereas a 1632 painting by Rembrandt shows Europa violently abducted from her company (Figure 1.3), a twentieth century sculpture by Carl Milles depicts her as engaged in a love-battle (Figure 1.4).

Myths of origin often imply a union of opposites, which may subsequently be articulated with later unifying projects, such as that of the EU. The form of union implicated by the Europa myth is that of a sexual love encounter where opposites join and are united in their diversity, to create a new social community. This can serve as a model for how European unification is conceived today. However, the image of her and the bull makes it difficult to decide with whom to identify as a European: is it Europa herself, the bull, their mutual union or the land of Crete to which they travel? In certain respects, male European elites may find it easier to identify with the combined whiteness, eroticism, strength and smartness of the divine bull, but it is not he who bears the name of Europa. One might construct Europeans as bull/god and Europa as the land he loves, following a common idea of feminising the inhabited land, but this comparison halts here, as she is obviously more human than he. One could therefore instead identify with her and see him as some kind of higher fate placing Europeans in Europe, equipping them with divine gifts. Also, she does not appear quite as maternally nourishing as motherlands and mother goddesses tend to be, instead her marked geographic mobility affirms a central aspect of European history, from the Greek and Roman networks, over Crusades and colonial empires to the modern European forms of culture and communication that have always tended to be restlessly on the move, up until the expansive EU itself.

Herodotus and his Greek contemporaries in the fifth century BC divided their known inhabited world ('ecumene') into three main parts: Asia (or Persia), Libya (or Africa) and Europe. Some time before the year 24 AD, the Greek geographer Strabo also used the term 'Europe', but for several centuries, Europe was more a geographical than a cultural (or even less a political) entity: 'The idea of a European identity had yet to be forged. Ethnoculturalism was in general focused on other reference points: Hellenism, Rome and the Christian church after the fourth century.'[20] The European idea was truly born as a political and cultural project in the eighth century AD, when the Christian church used it as a name for Charlemagne's Carolingian Empire. This identification closely linked Europe to Christendom in discourses constructing a genealogy that moved Europe another step to the west and made it the true but dislocated inheritor both of the biblical world and of Greek antiquity, as mediated through Hellenic and Arabic intermediaries. While Christendom was born outside Europe, it was there that its main developments subsequently took place, contributing Europe's key sets of ethical principles for social interaction, which are still cherished as human rights emanating from this continent, though since the French revolution mostly in secularised versions. Europe's main competitor had been Persia but now it was the expanding Islamic world, making it necessary to tone down mediaeval European culture's total dependence on Arabic sources for reconnecting to the greatness of ancient Greece.[21] While Europe had been a western borderland for the Greeks themselves, the emerging states inside the European continent had to translate the myth and its connotations in order to define themselves as the true heirs of the ancient golden age. 'Christianity was effectively "Europeanised" from the eighth century onwards', when the Carolingian Empire strived to build an 'Imperium Christianum'.[22]

Still, the word 'Europe' remained rarely used until the fifteenth century, as the continent was not a unified entity, but split in shifting fragments along several axes. Gerard Delanty argues that some kind of European identity became discernable first in the sixteenth century, as the idea of Europe was gradually liberated from that of Christianity and given a secular meaning. After that, there was a cumulatively strengthened feeling that Europe had a particular affinity with modernity, progress and civilisation.[23] The Christian theme in identifying Europe has little support in the name and the myth, as both are pre-Christian and make no references to biblical motifs; on the contrary, if Europa has affinities with Astarte, the myth is inscribed in a quite different Eastern Mediterranean and Oriental genealogy.

An extremist Evangelic website makes a range of wild speculations on the EU symbols, linking them to apocalyptic visions of the Revelations.[24] The combination of woman (Europa) and beast (bull) is seen as fulfilling St John the Theologian's prophecy of the appearance of the great harlot of Babylon: a woman sitting upon 'a scarlet coloured beast, full of names of blasphemy, having seven heads and ten horns'. A common interpretation is that ecclesiastical Babylon rides the political and commercial Babylon. These fundamentalists see several signs of this vision to be realised in the EU, where the female whore is identified with the Vatican and its allegedly corrupt Catholicism. The origins in pre-Christian and non-biblical mythologies thus seem to stir up interpretive uncertainties, and problematise any attempt to understand those European institutions that have made use of these mythical symbols to identify themselves.

The upsurge of nationalist movements and nation-building projects in the eighteenth and nineteenth centuries temporarily counteracted further geopolitical use of the concept of Europe, but after World War I, it was reinforced and channelled into the series of movements that will be described in a following chapter. German Nazism also integrated a European mission into its expansionist ideology—a hereditary chain that the EU is less keen on remembering.[25]

Today, the terms 'Europe' and 'European' are frequently used but rarely reflected upon. The activities of the Council of Europe and the EU have made these uses even more ambiguous. On the one hand, each association of interstate cooperation includes only a limited part of the geographic continent, while usually also including certain territories that are elsewhere generally thought to be outside its boundaries. The Council of Europe organises considerably more member states than the EU (currently 47 against 27), but Belarus stands outside both, the eastern boundary of Europe is notoriously vague, and several old French colonial territories in Africa and Latin America are at least partly integrated in the EU despite being geographically far outside the European continent as it is commonly understood. In spite of this, both these organisations have taken as their mission to represent the whole of Europe and not least to strengthen its cultural identity beyond their own formal membership area. As will soon be shown, the EU symbols are officially presented as 'symbols of Europe' rather than of the EU only. Even the euro currency, which is bound to the limited number of states partaking in the European Monetary Union (EMU), suggests a wish to symbolically represent the whole of Europe. Whether this expansive ambition has a wider legitimacy outside the EU as well remains to be empirically tested.

Luisa Passerini has shown how, in various phases of European history, the Europa myth has been activated to support efforts of peaceful unification, with elements of (courtly) love and desire as crucial elements.[26] The Europa myth has also been a recurrent motif in European art history, as well as on stamps, coins and caricatures up until the present.[27] Statues or illustrations presenting this striking event are found in many physical and virtual sites linked to EU institutions, for instance outside or inside buildings, or on websites. Outside the European Parliament building in Strasbourg, Nikos and Pandelis Sotiriadis have made the sculpture of *The Abduction of Europa* (Figure 1.5), and inside is Aligi Sassu's monumental ceramic mural of *The Myths of the Mediterranean*, in which Europa and the bull have the central place.

These depictions move between two main directions of interpretation of the myth, mirroring its inherent double character. This is a fundamental trait in strong myths, giving them a particularly wide and rich range of meaning, enabling them to function as key symbols, but sometimes also creating confusion. Stuart Hall finds this myth fascinating:

> This lunar goddess [...] symbolizes [...] the continuous movement westwards: the migratory drift from Asia, Egypt and the eastern Mediterranean, the diffusion of the alphabet and writing, the spread of agriculture into the fertile western European plain. Her very name derives from a Semitic root meaning 'western'. She is indeed a prophetic figure for Europe: richly suggestive but difficult to decode. If she represents Europe, why is she from 'elsewhere'? If this is 'an allegory of love', what has it to tell us about the European conception of the relation between love and seduction, sexual desire and marriage? And who or what, pray, is the bull?—deceptively white, but with a definite aura of 'otherness', of sexual power, male compulsion and patriarchal possessiveness, about him: something 'dark' and dangerous, who comes lumbering out of the European collective unconscious and steals Europa away to Crete?[28]

At one extreme, from Ovid's poem to Sotiriadis' sculpture, the abduction is depicted as a fun and victorious riding tour, where Europa enjoys the unexpected speed, length and adventurousness of the trip. Sotiriadis' bull even appears to have stairs in its back so that Europa could easily climb up and have her seat, and she looks like some happy acrobat demonstrating the newly found power that the bull has given her. She is united with the divine bull and together they ride the seas to conquer new territories. This conforms to several aspects of the myth, and can today easily lend itself to support optimistic visions of the contemporary unification process.

At the other extreme, from Herodotus to more critical current depictions, the event is rather understood as a kidnapping and even a rape, where Europa is a suffering victim, parallel to the rape of Lucretia or the kidnapping of the Sabine women. This interpretation mirrors EU-sceptical standpoints, as the bull might then be read as a symbol of European elites who mercilessly violate the will of common citizens. However, one should not forget the differences between Europa and the two other myths mentioned. The latter were violated by human males rather than a divine animal, and Europa is mostly depicted as welcoming the bull's courting with a pleasure of her own, both in the initial phase of seduction on the meadow and in the final stage of dynastic formation on Crete. Most images also show her as much more active than the Sabines, whose flesh is passively exposed to the gaze of men both within the picture (to the soldiers) and in front of it (to spectators of these artworks).

Michael Wintle shows that 'very early Hellenic examples tended to emphasize the violence of the abduction, while around the fifth century BC a "laicization" took place in the representation, with a more consenting (and therefore erotically charged) Europa on her bull'.[29] Later representations shift between these modes. As Europa becomes identified with the continent, her representations tend to confirm dominating understandings of this continent's political situation, either as helpless martyr or as privileged queen. As Europe has gradually grown into a leading global actor, most versions tend to illustrate this success story, emphasising the bold and pleasant aspects of the event and its dynastic consequences.

The myth activates an ambivalent male/female contrast. Zeus' bull displays a masculinity that wavers between power and lust, transforming divine power into a bodily beast force that in turn is performed as a sexuality that gives the woman pleasure in caressing the bull and riding him across the sea. The agency of the bull power therefore implies the emergence of an ordered masculine rule in the region, providing it with a phallic symbolic order that Europa on her own was not entrusted with, giving a political dimension to the myth.[30] Likewise, the older myth of the Cretan Minotaur tells us that this beast was the prodigy of Poseidon's white bull, seducing King Minos' wife Pasiphae, which shows that these themes had a widespread resonance in that period and region.[31] Europa combines positions of activity and passivity: she is conquered by the bull, but her links to Astarte and other Mediterranean fertility goddesses are reminiscent of a mythic prehistoric female power.[32] While the gender aspect is always visible and has been actively taken up in contemporary artworks on this motif, the potential ethnic aspect is less apparent in most depictions of this myth. The bull is sometimes made white, as the myth prescribes, but following the European tradition of 'Caucasianising' biblical figures, Europa's skin is generally also light, white or golden, rather than the darker colour that her mixed Egyptian and Middle East roots could have suggested.[33]

Among the official EU symbols, this myth is explicitly referred to only on the €2 Greek coin, even though one may find indirect associations to it elsewhere too, as will be mentioned in later chapters. The ambivalent obscurity of the myth complicates its use for self-asserting purposes, though this also makes it characteristic of Europe's real history and self-identity. After all, 'Europe' has in most historical periods experienced itself to live in times of decline, deep crisis and internal strife, expressing a kind of metaphorical dislocation of identity, not residing securely in itself. The first Europeans did move across the Mediterranean from Africa and Asia Minor to settle in the new territories, and the Europa myth may well be read as the prototype for a stereotypical image of the voyage, capable of being extended and varied to cover several different forms of travelling and dislocation, from exile and migration to trade and tourism.[34]

The genealogy of Europe as migrating to the northwest from the east and the south, and therefore being hereditarily linked to its Asian and African neighbours, implies a decentring and destabilising of Europe's own identity, which can then never be self-sufficient or firmly rooted in its own soil. Martin Bernal stresses the African roots of much of ancient Greek civilisation, with the Phoenician Europa and her brother Cadmus as examples.[35] George Thomson sees parallels between Europa and Demeter, 'both being emanations of the Minoan mother-goddess', and reads the myth as having a real background in Phoenician colonisation of Crete in the Middle Minoan period, supported by the existence of a parallel Phoenician myth of the bull god El and the mother goddess Asherat.[36] Robert Graves connects 'broad-faced' Europa not only to the bull but also to the full moon and Middle-East moon goddesses, linked to the willow tree and orgiastic witchcraft, possibly with mediaeval ancestors in the European witches.[37] This may be speculative, but testifies to an oppositional line of thought emerging from the historical settlement of the continent and symbolised by the Europa myth, though this thread is nowadays often repressed in dominant discourses.

Tzvetan Todorov has described Europe in the age of the American conquests as fundamentally dislocated:

> European civilization of the period is 'allocentric' rather than egocentric: for centuries its sacred site, its symbolic center, Jerusalem, has been not only exterior to European territory but subject as well to a rival civilization (the Muslims). In the Renaissance, this spatial decentering is linked to a temporal version: the ideal age is neither the present nor the future but the past, and a past that is not even Christian: that of the Greeks and the Romans. The center is elsewhere, which opens up the possibility for the Other to become, someday, central.[38]

Rémi Brague defines Europe as an 'eccentric culture', constituted by a series of divisions: Greeks/Persians, Christian/Islamic, Roman/Orthodox, Catholic/Protestant.[39] He argues that the early Romans and the Europeans who succeeded them shared a cultural and linguistic inferiority complex, which made them respect what they integrated from the outside, mainly from classical Greek heritage and from Middle East monotheism. Europe was formed as a fusion of 'Athens', 'Jerusalem' and 'Rome', with the latter contributing less content than a form of innovative transmission. Europe was less self-assured than the Arabs and other eastern civilisations, more aware of its own cultural shortcomings, and with a sense of self-defining dislocation, deriving its self-image from the outside. All cultures are of course indebted to their surrounding others, but Brague's thesis is that European culture has made this 'secondarity' essential to its own identity. With colonialism, imperialism and industrialism, the dominant European self-image has strived for a much more self-assured and xenophobic position, but Brague still believes that traits of the basic original eccentricity remain even today. Similarly, Zygmunt Bauman argues that Europe is a culture of restless anxiety that emphatically lacks a fixed identity and is always unfinished and on the move.[40] A similar belief is shared by many analysts of the current situation, including many who see the EU as an effort to get to grips with precisely such an experience of catastrophic self-destruction, and a wish to intensify rather than seal off communication with surrounding others.

Since at least a couple of decades, one of the official documents that uses the myth symbolically is the EU residence permit for foreign visitors. The permits are decorated with a bull, charging through five horizontal stars. This is a good example of how the myth lends itself particularly well to illustrate mobilities, as the bull here represents migration agencies making possible the travel into Europe, just like Zeus once helped Europa move to Cretan soil. The persistent presence of migration in the contemporary globalising world further links this aspect to the idea of cosmopolitanism.[41] Not only has Europe undergone waves of colonisation from east and south; these movements of people across the continent have continued to lend a mobile and diverse trait to European culture and identity, in spite of all efforts to reconstitute it in solid and unitary terms. Late modern identity discourses in the EU emphasise the value of flexibility, with nomadic diasporas emerging as avant-gardes rather than as discrepancies. One interesting example is the way Paul Gilroy and others have understood the 'Black Atlantic' diaspora as a vanguard for experiencing and expressing modernity, with structural affinities to the Jewish diaspora as well as to other more or less nomadic minorities.[42] European integration policies must link transnational unification to issues of multicultural citizenship and polysemic identification to which these mobilities give rise.[43]

Still, after thousands of years of European empire-building efforts, culminating in colonialism and world domination, Europe can hardly be identified as a homeless stranger. If anyone has abducted the treasures of other people, it is Europeans, having accumulated wealth by ravaging resources of other continents and having been, for almost a millennium, guilty masters rather than innocent victims of the abductions systematically organised by global slave trade. There still remains a tone of queer eroticism wildly crossing the borders between god, men and beasts, with echoes in the European anthem that are to be discussed below.

Comparisons

None of the other major continents have names equally strongly linked to any specific myth. Peoples dwelling in North Africa near Carthage were named 'afri', and the Roman suffix '-ca' denotes country or land. But the name may also have roots in the Phoenician 'afar' (dust), the Berber 'ifri' (cave), Abraham's grandson Epher, the Latin word 'aprica' (sunny) or the Greek 'aphrike' (without cold). In the late nineteenth century, an even more speculative etymology went back to the Egyptian 'af-rui-ka' (to turn towards the opening of the Ka, that is the womb or birthplace).[44] The first genealogies associate the name with geologic or climatic characteristics of North Africa, with its hot, sunny and sterile deserts, while the latter interpretation is inspired by how central African jungles underpin colonialist ideas of Africa as a dark continent of sexual fertility. Exoticising primitivist conceptions of Africa as the cradle of humanity have recently been revived by genetic findings locating the origin of homo sapiens in this continent.

In *The Iliad*, Homer mentioned both a Trojan ally and a marsh named Asios; the Greek word may derive from the fourteenth-century BC Assuwa confederation of states in Western Anatolia, possibly building on the Hittite word 'assu' (good). An alternative etymology goes back to the Akkadian '(w)asû(m)', meaning to go outside or to ascend, referring to the sunrise in the Middle East and possibly related to the Phoenician 'asa' meaning east. That would form a pair with Europe, but the explanation is far from universally accepted since it remains a mystery how 'Asia' could then be associated with Anatolia that is west of Semitic speakers, if they did not position themselves as Phoenician sailors on the Mediterranean. Around 440 BC, Herodotus used the name to denote Anatolia or Persia in contrast to Greece and Egypt, in a tripartite vision of the then-known inhabited world: Asia–Europe–Libya/Africa. In Greek mythology, Apollodorus in the mid-second century BC gave the name 'Asia' to the wife of Zeus' brother Iapetos. Among her children were Atlas and Prometheus, making her ancestor to humanity and linked to myths that will be further discussed below. However, she was previously and elsewhere known as Clymene; there was otherwise no influential mythical narrative linked to her, and several sources claim that she is not really related to the name of the Asian continent.

The other continents got their current names from European explorers much more recently. The terms 'Arctic' and 'Antarctica' began to be used in the second half of the fourteenth century. The Greek *arktikos* means 'of the north', but derives from *arktos*, meaning 'bear', referring to the northern star constellation called the Bear (Latin *Ursus*), while *antarktikos* then implied 'opposite the north'. There had been speculations of a southern continent since antiquity, but the first reliably reported observations were made in 1820. The northern Arctic region is not a continent but an ocean covered with ice, and sometimes also includes the northern tips of its 'shores' (i.e. northern Europe, America and Asia).

As a term for the American landmass, 'America' was first used in 1507 near Strasbourg by a cartographer linked to the Duke of Lorraine; the name was a Latinised and feminised version of the explorer Amerigo Vespucci's name, adhering to the praxis to let all continents have Latin feminine names. How this naming was established is unclear. 'Amerigo' is in turn an Italian form of mediaeval Latin *Emericus*, perhaps derived from Gothic Amalrich ('work-ruler') or Germanic Heinrich ('the ruler of the house'), together anticipating the current position of the United States as world-leading power.

'Australia' derived from Latin *Australis* (southern). There had, since Roman times, been legends of an unknown land of the south, though Europeans did not explore the continent until the sixteenth century, and the first English usage of the name was in 1625. The term 'Oceania' for the islands in the Pacific Ocean was coined in 1831, though the word 'ocean' has ancient Greek origins (*okeanos*), denoting the big sea surrounding the Earth disc, in contrast to the centrally located Mediterranean.

In general, indigenous peoples rarely had a name for the whole continent they inhabited, since naming is a differential game that presupposes conscious and reflected encounters between one community and another. The Middle East area where Africa, Asia and Europe overlapped was such an area, explaining their long-established names, while other continent names are rather modern inventions, abstracting from local specificities and striving to make totalising divisions of the whole world. Compass directions often play a decisive role in this naming game, indirectly indicating a specific point of reference in the centre of the ancient world in Asia Minor.

Europe thus differs from other continents by having its name also linked to a quite specific mythical narrative. Several nations around the world are likewise linked to important founding myths that provide narratives that can be activated to serve as key symbols for collective identification. However, as nation states are rather recent phenomena, these myths are elaborated long afterwards in response to later needs for legitimising nation building. They are modern fictions with clear political intentions, disguised as ancient myths but without any old mythical background, as elaborated by Benedict Anderson and Eric Hobsbawm through the terms 'imagined communities' and 'invented traditions'.[45] The etymological background to these names has shifting relevance to contemporary inhabitants, and few of them offer any particularly rich node for mythical or symbolic elaboration.

In the process of nation formation, particularly in the late eighteenth and nineteenth centuries, several nations were equipped with national personifications providing an anthropomorphic image of the mother- or fatherland in question. These could be used positively in national propaganda or negatively in critical cartoons and caricatures. Many were constructed on the basis of Greek Athena or the corresponding Roman Minerva, who represented a combination of wisdom and war that was suitable for characterising the birth and ambitions of these new nations. They tended to use the Latin name of the ancient Roman province that roughly corresponded to the modern nation in question, such as Britannia (a personification going all the way back to Roman times) and Germania or Helvetia (who became personifications of Germany and Switzerland from the 1848 national liberation events onwards). The effect was to intimate an imaginary foundation in classical antiquity that suited the bourgeois elites who sought to legitimate emergent nation states and cancel previous associations to primitive barbarism with which Antique Romans identified natives of these provinces.[46]

Parallel to these national personifications in classical style, other ones were also used, though they rarely had official status. Three examples are the British/English John Bull (created by Dr John Arbuthnot 1712), the French Marianne (popularised in the 1789 revolution, representing the republican values of the state) and Sweden's Mother Svea (1672). Each has a specific history and identifying characteristics, but they also share many traits and are mostly notoriously vague, mainly just standing for the strength and stability that the nation was supposed to guarantee for its citizens. The same is true for the American couple Uncle Sam (invented in 1812) and Lady Liberty (1886).

The majority of such national personifications are maternal or paternal figures, unlike Europa, whose main narrative—in spite of her three sons with Zeus and later offspring with Cretan king Asterius—depicts her as a daring young female, more akin to French Marianne than to Mother Russia. She is a much more complex figure than the others, with more complex layers of meaning accumulated, and thus symbolically contributing less to fixing than to destabilising of the concept of Europe. She does offer a comparably denser web of historically accumulated layers of signification than other continent myths. Already the very fact that Europe is the only continent with its name connected to an elaborate ancient myth narrative lends it a kind of magic aura, independent of the specific content of this myth.

The conflicts of interpretation surrounding Europe's name are thus confined to how to understand that name, rather than suggesting alternative names. However, new myths are created all the time, and in the future there may well be alternative candidates—if less for the name than for the myth.

Phoenix, Prometheus and post-World War II resurrection

A range of other myths also resonate with Europa's story and tinge the way Europe's current quest is mythically identified, symbolising what have been perceived as key facets of Europe. Here, only a few examples will be mentioned, those that have lately surfaced in EU-related discourses.[47]

Europe has in the modern era claimed to be the prime source in the global establishment of progress and modernity, with rationalisation, secularisation and individualisation as elements manifesting a growing human control over external and internal nature. Philosophers like G. W. F. Hegel have seen the Renaissance and the Enlightenment as major steps in a longer historical perspective of a civilising emancipation of humankind from an amalgamation of natural, mythic and authoritarian bonds. The European variant of modernisation has posited itself as a hegemonic model for the rest of the world, in a tradition of colonial and imperialist Eurocentrism. The Renaissance myth of Europe as true inheritor to classical civilisation and the Enlightenment myth of Europe heralding universal progress leaned on capitalist expansion in geographical and economic terms, with unprecedented costs that other continents were forced to pay. The globalising and universalising impetus implied that its inheritance was never exclusively restricted to Europe alone, and it can be argued that key facets of modernisation were even more evident at the colonial margins of the great empires than in their centres. Consecutive waves of counter-histories have also continued to question this success story by pointing at the high costs for this hegemonic growth and at the decentering sources of allegedly 'European' values in processes outside of itself.

The idea of Europe as carrying a unique global mission is deeply ambivalent: one understanding of expansionist colonial Eurocentrism leads to the Nazi myth of a reunited Third Reich, while another results in what could be named EU's founding myth of a united Europe as a peace project. Such European discourses have regularly mobilised and accumulated a number of mythical narratives that seem fit to anchor European culture in history and identify it either critically as marked by fateful destructivity or affirmatively as inheritor of unique empowering qualities.

The *phoenix* was in classical mythology 'a unique bird of the Arabian desert that burned itself on a funeral pyre every five or six centuries and rose from the ashes with renewed youth'.[48] Its name is related to Phoenicia (and to a red-purple colour), and its ancestry also represents the dislocation implied by the myth of Europa, as the phoenix symbol has both Egyptian and Asian origins and counterparts. Its Chinese counterpart, Feng-huang, is a combination of male and female, sun and moon. The phoenix is itself not specifically European, but its early Christian articulation with the resurrection and eternal life after death of Christ—and of the Christian congregation in spite of Roman persecution—has linked to it a European chain of meanings. Its own trajectory has thus to some extent resonated with the Europa myth's theme of dislocation from east to west.

There are a number of stories associated with the phoenix, but its most common use has been as a general image of the unstoppable life cycle. Its applications usually combine cyclical repetition with linear progress. It is significant that the phoenix must burn in order to be born again, hinting at a cathartic narrative of crisis and salvation (Figure 1.6). One may compare with tales in the biblical *Old Testament*, where Adam and Eve were driven out of Paradise so that man may in a distant future possibly be let in again, and where the Jewish people had to pass through great sorrows and pains to eventually reach salvation. This theme was again implicitly recalled in the Christian master narrative of death and resurrection in the Easter Passion of the *New Testament*. Early Christian congregations could re-articulate their own perilous destiny with that of Christ as well as with the phoenix myth.

With the gradual awakening of a sense of Europeanness, all these mythical narratives have in various phases, contexts and ways been articulated with the idea of modern Europe born through pain to victory. One example was Renaissance ideas of resurrecting classical greatness after centuries of Mediaeval darkness; another came with the French revolution as a resurrection after the dark rule of the absolute monarch. Heffernan speaks of 'Europe's optimists' in the nineteenth century who, despite having observed the many disastrous wars that divided the continent, had 'a remarkable capacity to imagine a golden future arising, Phoenix-like, from the ashes of each crisis'.[49]

A number of contemporary websites explicitly link the phoenix to Europe. In most cases, it is hard to discern any deeper meaning in the choice of names, for instance the French transport firm called Phoenix Europe Express S.A.[50] The phoenix seems particularly attractive in contexts of education and healthcare, probably as a means of calling forth the capacity of rejuvenation. For instance, Horizon Phoenix Europe is an Ireland-based healthcare provider, whereas Phoenix Institute Europe is a spiritually engaged Dutch foundation for 'education, leadership and friendship'.[51]

Elements from these stories echo what may perhaps be seen as the dominant myth of the EU itself, which is again and again repeated as an underlying theme behind the other symbols. This is the story of how European unity and dignity resulted from a specific kind of resurrection: a reconstitution of Europe after ages of internal strife and finally the catastrophic mid-twentieth century fascist rule and fatal wars. The EU consistently describes itself as a project of peace, security and welfare, to be built on the ruins of inter-European destruction. No wonder that the phoenix was issued on a Belgian-minted €10 coin in 2005, 'as a representation of a new Europe post 1945, celebrating 60 years of peace and freedom in the continent'![52]

The phoenix is understood as a metaphor for vital resurrection through destruction; this suits well for a continent where Christian traditions dominate and where a series of destructive catastrophes have finally given birth to a will to start again. Elevation through resurrection from disaster seems to be a lead motif for Europe: an elevation preceded by the deepest anguish and terror, suggestive of how the nymph Europa could found her own divinely legitimised dynasty after having suffered the violent abduction from her Middle East homelands. The theme of elevation is also associated to the fact that the phoenix is a bird: a species that can lift itself up into the sky. By its Egyptian, Asian or Arabic origin, the phoenix also confirms Europa's trope of dislocation.

In Greek mythology, *Prometheus* was a Titan who played a series of tricks against the main god Zeus, the last of which was to steal fire from the gods and give it to the human race (Figure 1.7). Zeus punished him severely by having him chained to a Caucasian cliff and letting a huge eagle eat his liver in a daily repeated torture.[53] There is a thematic affinity with the phoenix myth in Prometheus' eternal punishment, as his liver is thus magically 'resurrected' on a daily basis. Prometheus is a very ambiguous figure, a 'trickster' who mixes good and bad, standing halfway between gods and men. He has been seen as a benefactor of human civilisation, cleverly helping humanity master the civilising tool of fire, which gave humans an advantage over animals by enabling them to make weapons and tools. On the other hand, he was responsible for an irreversible rift between mankind and gods, since his activities stirred up anger among the latter and put an end to an era where boundaries between gods and humans were still permeable: a kind of Fall of Man from divine protection to having to rely mainly on his own capabilities.[54] No wonder the Enlightenment eagerly resurrected Prometheus!

There was also another mythical Prometheus '*plasticator*', who had created and animated mankind out of clay. These two myths eventually fused. The fire that Prometheus had stolen was then the fire of life with which he animated his clay models, and due to the 'creating' aspect, Prometheus became a symbol for the creating artist in the eighteenth century.

Prometheus' Greek name literally means 'fore-thought', and his cunning intelligence has been read as characteristic of a major stream in European industrial and scientific progress as well, thematised in shifting ways by, for instance, G. W. F. Hegel, Karl Marx and Max Weber. One might say that Prometheus was metaphorically set free from Zeus' mythical and traditional bonds by the Enlightenment and industrial revolution, when he came to symbolise both the engineering inventor and the creating artist. Percy Shelley's *Prometheus Unbound* (1820) advocated a Copernican shift to emancipate humanity from its self-inflicted tutelage, as in Kant's famous dictum.[55] In Shelley's lyrical drama, Prometheus says: 'He gave man speech, and speech created thought, / Which is the measure of the universe; / And Science struck the thrones of earth and heaven, / Which shook, but fell not.' This stirs up fears in the ruling god Jupiter/Zeus:

> The soul of man, like unextinguished fire,
> Yet burns towards heaven with fierce reproach, and doubt,
> And lamentation, and reluctant prayer,

Hurling up insurrection, which might make
Our antique empire insecure, though built
On eldest faith, and hell's coeval, fear.[56]

For this, both Prometheus and the humans are punished—the latter by excommunication with the gods, reminiscent of how Adam and Eve were driven out from Edenic Paradise after having tasted the fruit of knowledge.

The Prometheus figure became a common metaphor for western industrialisation's combination of technological and economic growth.[57] In a book typically titled *The Unbound Prometheus: Technological Change and Industrial Development in Western Europe* (1969), David S. Landes for instance stressed the links between technological change and a generalised creative human spirit of free-ranging imagination, with Prometheus as a bridge between these otherwise separate realms of hardcore technology and humanist arts. He saw the leap into Promethean modernity as irreversible, just like in the myth, adding yet another mythical layer by noting that 'the Industrial Revolution has been like in effect to Eve's tasting of the forbidden fruit of the tree of knowledge: the world has never been the same'.[58]

This irrevocability also heightens the sense of contradiction and danger in this new era: 'Change is demonic; it creates, but it also destroys, and the victims of the Industrial Revolution were numbered in the hundreds of thousands or even millions'.[59] Karl Marx also pointed at this double character of modern capitalist society as both civilising and catastrophic, and there were in the nineteenth century no lack of dystopic narratives seeking to come to grips with this flip side of modernisation. In his own preface to the lyrical drama, Percy Shelley mentioned that Prometheus had certain affinities with Satan, indicating the ambivalence of this figure, wavering between good and evil, generosity and evil self-interest. A dark sibling to Prometheus was created by Mary Wollstonecraft Shelley in *Frankenstein, or The Modern Prometheus* (1818), where Victor Frankenstein defied the gods by creating life himself.[60] Instead of just being the created, Victor takes God's place and becomes creator. He gets his punishment, but while Prometheus was punished by the god whose power he revolted against, Victor is instead punished by his own creation, who turns against him and ruins all his good ambitions. A creation of humanised Promethean spirit run wild, Frankenstein's monster came to signify the vices of technology that became increasingly obvious, echoed in the philosophies of Nietzsche, Heidegger, Adorno and Horkheimer, as well as in dystopian science fiction narratives.

The ancient and the modern Prometheus have merged and been reinterpreted by later technocritical philosophies, fictions and computer games. First bound by myth and traditional customs, then liberated by the modern revolutions from Romanticism to 'risk society', the modern Prometheus is understood as ambiguous, at once liberating hero and lethal villain. This reflexive insight often made culture and aesthetics the critical or even healing antidote to science and technology. Like a third, late modern Prometheus following the classical one of civilisation and the early modern one of technology, culture was long fettered in strict structures of spheres and sectors, but is now said to have escaped from its enclosed field and appears to be unbound, expanding across every border. After science, technology and industrialism, a new Prometheus seems to be unbound in the globalised, mediatised, late modern and post-industrial world. Linked to processes like modernisation, secularisation, urbanisation, aestheticisation, mediatisation and reflexivisation, each with its own genealogy and implications, claims of such changes may be termed 'culturalisation'. It too implies a kind of human hubris, where new forms of 'makeability' tend to understand almost everything as a controllable project rather than as fate or destiny. Such perspectives lend a dark shadow to the European self-understanding as a cultural mover in the world.

To this day, someone or something 'Promethean' is daring and skilful. The double-edged Promethean image has been used to characterise creative western 'geniuses', who struggled for high values against tough odds, whether in the artistic or the scientific arena. One often-cited example with particularly strong ties to later European identifications is Ludwig van Beethoven (see Chapter 7). In spite of his accelerating deafness, illness, loneliness and despair, and in a climate of conservative post-Napoleonic restoration, his musical work is heard as expressing high humanist values and hopes, for instance in the Third (*Eroica*) or Fifth (*Fate*) symphonies, the ballet *The Creatures of Prometheus* and the opera *Fidelio*, where revolutionary Leonore liberates her beloved from the dungeons of oppression, making great sacrifices to liberate humankind from its own tutelage, to quote Kant's definition of Enlightenment.[61]

Arbitrarily chosen examples of how Prometheus is today used in connection with European initiatives indicate a rather diluted sphere of meanings, where creative development is painted in much less complex terms than the myth itself may justify, mainly stressing the beneficial aspects of technological enterprise. For instance, the EUREKA Prometheus Project ('PROgraMme for a European Traffic of Highest Efficiency and Unprecedented Safety') was in 1987–95 the largest research and development project ever in the field of driverless cars.[62] Prometheus Europe Ltd declares as its mission to 'provide superior procurement, supply and advisory services to principals in all parts of the developing world on a strictly independent basis'.[63] PROMeTHEUS ('Health PROfessional Mobility in THe European Union Study') is a project based at the European Observatory on Health Systems and Policies, and founded by EU's Seventh Frame Programme from 2009.[64] 'Prometheus: European Union Studies' is the title of a course programme at the University of Tartu.[65]

In contrast, websites combining Frankenstein with Europe are—expectedly—fewer and mostly critical. While relatively more acceptable on other continents, genetically modified 'Frankenstein foods' have for instance raised considerable European fears.[66] The reception of these two narratives thus tends to split the ambiguous figure into a consistently good Prometheus and an evil Frankenstein.

Both Prometheus and Frankenstein fit into the theme of emancipating elevation that was reactivated by the Enlightenment, as they depict humans striving to rise above the animal world by conquering divine powers. As with Europa more than in the phoenix myth, there is also a strong element of desire, in this case for knowledge and power, and there is a kind of hybridity in the mixture of man, god and technology (fire or Frankenstein's robot).

Another line of quasi-mythical narratives that emphasise the ambivalence, and not least the dangers, inherent in western developments includes the legend of *Doctor Faustus*, developed in chapbooks from 1583 onwards, in plays by Christopher Marlowe (*The Tragical History of Doctor Faustus*, c. 1604) and J. W. Goethe (*Faust I-II*, 1808 and 1832), in Gounod's opera *Faust* (1859) and again in Thomas Mann's novel *Doktor Faustus* (1947). This story is less similar to the phoenix or Prometheus than to Frankenstein.[67] In *The Decline of the West* (1926–28), Oswald Spengler talked of Europe's 'Faustian culture', believing that just as Faust had sold his soul to the devil for power, western man had sold his soul to technology.[68] Such an interpretation obviously links Faust to Frankenstein, but there is little left to remind of the Europa myth, since Europa never had to pay any noticeable future costs for her intercourse with Zeus. Something similar may be said of Richard Wagner's 'ring' tetralogy (1869–76) and J. R. R. Tolkien's 'ring' novels (1954–55).

Faust shares with Prometheus and Frankenstein the desire for elevation and power. The 'ring' narratives (inspired by legends of the Holy Grail, with mixed Celtic and Catholic origins) additionally contain elements of dislocation and hybridity similar to those found in the Europa myth. They are all full of ambivalences. When used to construct a mythical narrative for Europe, this narrative is equally contradictory, and far from linear or univocal. The phoenix burns and is born again; Prometheus gives vital forces to humankind but is eternally punished for it; Frankenstein's monster is a masterpiece with fatal flaws; Faust achieves great success but to immense ethical costs; and the fatal ring comes with an equally grim prediction of where human, capitalist and in particular also European quests for universal power and riches may lead.

None of these myths has an officially acknowledged status as providing symbols of Europe. They have sometimes been mobilised for signifying Europe, but all have a more global or even 'universal' reach than that. It is easy to find examples of how the phoenix, Prometheus, Faust and Frankenstein are all used in American, Asian or African contexts as well. The phoenix is actually even more strongly anchored in Asia than in Europe, and it is for instance no coincidence that a Mandarin Chinese-language television channel based in Hong Kong and launched in 1996 by the Australian Rupert Murdoch in collaboration with mainland Chinese interests was named Phoenix Television (Figure 1.8). As for Prometheus, the Harlem Renaissance poet Walter E. Hawkins linked him to Africa: 'Hail, Prometheus, glad to meet you, / Fellow radical, I greet you; / We are comrades bound together / In the rain, and storm and weather.'[69] Asia has a leading role in Shelley's lyrical drama, and 'Prometheus Asia' is the name of a 'data mining' company.[70] However, as for example a biography of the atom physicist J. Robert Oppenheimer is named *American Prometheus*, this indicates that Prometheus normally is thought of as European.[71] A simple quantitative test on the Internet shows that the phoenix, Prometheus, Frankenstein and Faust are as often linked to America, Africa and Asia as to Europe, but in qualitative terms, they all appear to have a certain European bias. Still, only the Europa myth remains specifically bound to Europe's destiny, based both on the name and on the geographical setting. It cannot be applied to any other continent, and is also the only myth officially recognised as having a bearing on how to signify Europe.

Doctor Faust was based on a historically real person, and the ancient versions of myths such as those of Europa and of Prometheus may in prehistorical times possibly have been believed to have a reality substance. However, during the last few centuries of their use and elaboration, they have all been understood as in a strong sense fictional: as expressing some deeper layer of human existence but not as any precise description of what has actually happened. Other kinds of myths are considered to be more 'real', even though their truth value may well also be questioned. The ways in which 'real events' are recounted and interpreted strongly contribute to the formation of modern ideologies, as Roland Barthes has shown.[72] By being embedded in a dense web of symbolisms and legends like those mentioned so far, the memories and histories of the recent past also obtain a mythical quality.

One such 'real'—but precisely therefore no less ideological—myth is the EU master narrative that tells how Europe has been united. Its main outline is that Europe is a chosen continent endowed with the most extraordinary powers of the creative mind, giving her a strong and important task to benefit humanity at large, but at the same time also the capability to do much evil—yes, even to eradicate all humanity and potentially even all life on earth. Europe has risen from poverty and false beliefs, conquered intelligence and a unique artistic heritage, and used this to build just political and social institutions side by side with a capitalist economy that is able to spread welfare across the world and link it together by modern systems of communication. This double-edged capacity has led to an accelerating spiral that oscillates between positive achievements and the most terrifying disasters. Each revival after a dark period has brought new hopes for creating a solid and just social order to prevent future wars, and the most decisive of these historical turns was the end of World War II, which also brought the Nazi terror to an end. In a series of steps after 1945, most importantly the 'Schuman Declaration', Europe has finally made a firm decision to use its capacities for the common good, strengthening the mutual ties of friendship between European peoples and also opening up for peaceful dialogue with the rest of the world.

This is a brief summary of an historical narrative that is retold as a kind of foundational myth for the European Union. It is not necessarily all 'wrong', as there is an inner core of truth in most existing ideological myths, but it makes a specific selection from the many processes, forces and motives associated with the current European project—thus also silencing alternative perspectives. 'Myth does not deny things, on the contrary, it purifies them, it makes them innocent, it gives them a natural and eternal justification, it gives them a clarity which is not that of an explanation but that of a statement of fact.'[73] This particular myth gives the EU a universally emancipatory and empowering role, thereby blocking oppositional interpretations that might for instance instead emphasise imperialist expansion or efforts to control and regulate European space in the face of globalisation and migration.[74] By focusing on the will to peace as the core driving force behind the EU, and depicting economic and geopolitical strength as secondary means to achieve that goal, this myth consolidates a favourable perspective that in turn may be countered by critical readings based on reversed priorities. The tale of how Europe has united on the ruins of its own disasters has dramatic qualities that lift the political up to a universal and existential level, lending 'natural and eternal justification' to a political process which is badly in need of such an underpinning in order to legitimise decisions that have often turned out to be unpopular among citizens.

Yet, this does not reduce any of these myths to just ideological illusions or plain lies, constructed only to hide evil intentions and legitimise an oppressive social order. To Paul Ricoeur, there is no way to effectively destruct all myths, and myths continue to be worth interpreting, as they codify in symbolic form the key issues of any society. The symbolic language of myths is needed for people to share otherwise individual and mute experiences, and these mythical 'symbols give rise to thought', rather than prevent it.[75] Ricoeur argues that 'precisely because we are living and thinking after the separation of myth and history, the demythization of our history can become the other side of an understanding of myth as myth, and the conquest, for the first time in the history of culture, of the mythical dimension'.[76] Interpreting these myths not as immediate truths but as instructive narratives makes it possible to understand key mechanisms of cultural and collective identification.

Captain Euro

Among the more recent efforts to revitalise this mythical tradition in Europe, one quasi-mythical narrative is particularly instructive for understanding European signification in its very failure as a modern myth 'artificially' constructed for instrumental reasons (Figure 1.9). Inspired by the famous local resistance of Asterix and his brave fellow Gallics against the Roman Empire, the nationalist superhero Capitan Italia in the late 1990s had an evil enemy by the name of Euroman, from whom he defended Italian culture. No wonder that European institutions wanted to provide a positive counter-image. The superhero Captain Euro was a comic production aimed at children, with a plethora of signifying hooks.[77] The figure was created in 1998 on commission for the EU by the Spanish marketing expert Nicolas De Santis of the consulting firm Corporate Vision Strategists with its Twelve Stars Communications, whose blue logo has twelve yellow stars that do not form a circle but a rectangle. With a wide range of influential customers, this firm has made several projects for the EU. The idea was to construct a project that would test and improve young citizens' attitudes to issues of European identity and citizenship in the Union, as the firm's analysis had concluded that the official EU symbols failed to resonate with most Europeans, and some more popular alternatives were therefore needed to prepare for the introduction of the euro currency. Captain Euro was made to be a counterpart to Captain America (created by Joe Simon and Jack Kirby, and launched by Marvel Comics in 1941), and for a short while attracted media coverage but also critical attention from sceptics. It is interesting to scrutinise the ways in which Captain Euro was constructed as typically European, using the standardised genre of superhero comics to present for a young audience some key features of the European project.

The Captain Euro website offers two animated adventures, summary of lead figures and their various gadgets, plus a Euro currency converter tool and some meta-information on how this superhero is intended as a marketing device. This 'super-hero of Europe' is described as 'the protector of Europe who holds out for justice, who promotes peace and carries the message of goodwill around the world', his 'Twelve Stars' team 'bringing together millions of Europeans and protecting wildlife and the environment': 'Wherever they are, everyone recognises their distinctive European branding' that 'makes everyone proud to be European'.

The website paints the dawning twenty-first century as a 'world of change' where 'old structures are disappearing as new ones take their place, bringing with them uncertainty for the future': 'In this climate of constant change the European Union, a Union of prosperity and innovation, has emerged as a global superpower. The Twelve Stars organisation has been set up to defend the security of Europe and uphold the values of the Union.' The fictive organisation's emblem is 'a five-pointed yellow star in a clear blue sky with the 'E' of Europe at its centre—the shining symbol of strength through unity'. Captain Euro and his team are 'the new ambassadors of global peace [...] bearing the European message with them wherever they go [...] solving problems and averting the threat of danger'. Luckily 'Europe's most advanced technology is at their disposal', but there is a hidden threat: an evil organisation works against Europe's unity, led by the criminal Dr D. Vider who wants 'to divide Europe and create his own empire'. The battle takes place in areas such as sports and the arts, from where Dr D. Vider wishes to shut out the public.

The Twelve Stars team leader Captain Euro is dressed in a typical superhero costume, clearly reminiscent of Captain America but featuring European elements like the blue and yellow colours and the twelve stars of the EU flag. He is presented as Adam Andros, son of a famous European ambassador and a professor of palaeontology. Having travelled around the world, he is a polyglot with strong social skills. 'Captain Euro is a diplomatic hero—the symbol of European unity and values', who strives to use only 'intellect, culture and logic—not violence' to fulfil his benevolent mission. He has studied information technology so that he can combine 'language and technology skills with his international "savoir faire" and his natural investigative curiosity, to protect Europe and carry Europe's message of goodwill around the world'. He also has the relaxing hobby of painting European landscapes! A motor accident forced him to replace one knee with a metal joint, but otherwise he is 'in peak physical condition'.

His Twelve Stars team has its headquarters in the Atomium somewhere in Europe. It is fronted by Europa, alias Donna Eden (sometimes spelt 'Eaden'), an archaeologist and expert in ancient written languages. Her 'expertise in the Gaeia theory and her love of the natural world' made her a committed environmentalist and a scuba diving oceanographer who has explored 'the darkest depths of the oceans'. She forms a sporty pair with the Captain. All other sidekicks add new traits to the team. Blond, blue-eyed Erik the pilot manages space science and science fiction 'by Jules Verne and the whole school of European writers'. The dark-haired elite gymnast and dancer Helen coordinates the team's 'cultural, media and sport activities' and personally favours flamenco and waltz. The dark-skinned Marcus invents technological gadgets and is machine-like enough to almost never need any sleep. He plays chess with Pythagoras 1—a humanoid supercomputer that is surrounded by nine rotating balls and enjoys Greek philosophy, math and music (seventeenth-century fugues in particular!). Finally, the East Carpathian grey wolf Lupo uses his stunning intuitional skills to support the Captain. There is also a description of the team's gadgets, a play on the technological desires typical of young men, and of the nine areas of the Atomium, named the Conference, Control, Hi-Tech, Environmental, Space, Cyber, Media, Sport and Knowledge Spheres, roughly corresponding to main areas of cooperation in the European Union.

The bad guys are led by David Viderius, alias Dr D. Vider. He is a financier, speculator, curator and collector of ancient curiosities, but also an excellent cook: a multimillionaire in control of hundreds of businesses across Europe. His aim is to make money without any scruples, using the Global Touring Circus (GTC), a travelling company where he recruits new members from all over the world, as his base. Vider's son Junior is presented as an elegantly dressed sociopath and an expert on hypnosis and other circus tricks. The beautiful Mala Glamora has a showbiz background, collects jewellery and shoes, and is secretly in love with Captain Euro. Ninot, the human cannonball, also knows many tricks, collects hats and likes animals but fears Lupo. The Twins Castor and Pollux are contortionists and pilots who often quarrel, while the parrot Pappagallo can record conversations and has an advanced taste for foods. This nasty team also has a set of gadgets, and the GTC megacircus consists of five tents, one of which is secret and closed to the public, but all of them full of traps, cameras and other secret devices. There is a map engraved in the central smoked glass dome, 'representing a world without boundaries where no country is favoured—or spared!'

The first animated adventure, 'The Origins', starts when Swedish scientists in a ship on the frozen Baltic lake suddenly spot a Viking ship of steel coming out of an iceberg. Meanwhile on a sunny Greek island, the archaeology Professor Donna Eden searches for Agamemnon's last resting place but is surprised by two hands emerging from the underground. Among deadly spiders she finds an engraved stone when an earthquake almost makes her female colleague fall down into the abyss. Led by a dark-haired man who later turns out to be Adam Andros, a third team of explorers in the giant caves of Arta in Majorca are likewise endangered when a crack opens, and they almost drown in flooding water. Bikini girls sunbathing on a Mediterranean cliff-top are shocked when the Majorcan cave explorers appear from underground, having dug themselves out with a magic double axe they found in the depths, and which gives them superhuman powers. At home with his pet cat and exclaiming 'Merciful Minerva!', Adam tells his story over the phone to his father, who turns out to be the leader of the Swedish expedition. A week later, father and son visit the mysterious Baltic Viking ship by helicopter. A wolf has been watching them since the ship arrived, and the father says: 'He's a European wolf.' On a dog sled, Donna comes across the ice to help them solve their 'frozen mystery'. The dragon carvings on the axe handle show her that it is 'very early Celt, probably Welsh', as they bear the inscription: 'in Avagddu's name, Creiwry the Witch and Elfin the Prince shall be avenged!' (All geographic places exist in real life, and each name also links to an existing history or mythology. For example, in the Welsh myth of Taliesin, Avagddu is the son of Ceridwen and Tegid Veol, while Elfin is found in the Scottish tradition.)

In the next scene, the 'ruthless speculator, curator and ancient curiosity collector David Viderius' is informed by Mala and the rest of his 'surveillance team' of what the three good guys have found, including a message on the Baltic ship from Thor, the Norse god of death and destruction. When on that ship the three speculate about the 'three messages from the gods of Europe', suddenly the old stone plate bursts into fragments that form twelve stars: 'a magic number!' Adam falls into the Viking ship and discovers a sarcophagus that opens and releases a young golden goddess with a five-pointed star for a heart. She mysteriously speaks:

> I am the arms of your mother. The wood and earth walls of your
> first shelter… I am the stone of the home you left behind…! I am the
> hollowed trees and woven plants from which you tried to tame the seas
> and harness the winds… I am the pigment in your paintings, the paper

of the pages of past books, the pixels on your computer screens… I am art and truth… I am justice and knowledge and the warmth of love. I am all that is good.

Adam and Donna admire her beauty, but then she changes and becomes a dead skull:

And I am the dust thrown in another man's face. The flint fashioned to cut and kill… I am the poison that flows through every watery artery… I am the turbulence that sucks out your air… I am the fire that burns inside every blackened heart. I am all that is evil and I am all that is good. I am the spirit of Europe!

She points at 'the golden star of Europe' and before she melts away, she explains that whoever has it possesses the greatest power in the world: 'Take it and use it wisely!' A helicopter arrives with Mala and Dr D. Vider who start a fight where Adam's father falls overboard and Vider grabs the star. 'What power!', he exclaims, to a Black Metal soundtrack. The wolf attacks him and howls to the moon so that sharp icicles fall down from heaven and injure David. The evil couple escapes but threaten to be back for the star. Adam asserts that his father is now dead, and so are Adam Andros and Donna Eaden as well:

From now on we must fight for the memory of my father… We will fight for truth and justice… We must use the golden star of Europe as a force for good and use its powers for the benefit of humankind… From now on we shall be known as… Captain Euro, Europa & Lupo.

This ends the first adventure.

The second of the two adventures is called 'The Grand Canal'. It opens in the Twelve Stars' headquarters Atomium, where Captain Euro at work among European maps is visited by a figure with mask and red cape. It turns out to be Europa who says that Adam needs a break and is invited with her to the Venice carnival. They admire paintings in 'Galleria Dell'Accademia', where D. Vider is also present. He is 'more of a performance art man' and is about to stage some 'cultural sabotage!' In his penthouse, he explains his plans to Mala, 'my European beauty'. He sends Ninot to manipulate the water, so that gondolas get stuck in the mud. Adam, dressed in a blue T-shirt with 'European Sport Power' in yellow text, notes the sudden shortage of tap water in the hotel room. Marcus gives a scientific explanation of the drainage that will destroy tourism and jobs and thus kill Venice. D. Vider and his admiring son happily watch the Venetian despair through a telescope. In mediaeval carnival dresses, Ninot and Mala start shrinking museum palaces with a special gun, while Marcus with his scientific skills manages to figure out where the water is sucked out. Europa wins a fistfight with Castor and Pollux. Mala hides the now miniscule Venetian treasures as jewellery on her body. Next, Venetians are struck by panic by what appear to be UFOs from another world. From their big blue truck, Europa and Euro distribute 'weapons' that turn out to be blue umbrellas with the Twelve Star logo. Marcus explains that the UFOs were his invention to transport Antarctic ice to Venice 'and refloat the city in one rainy day!' The ensuing rain explains the need for umbrellas. Mala and Ninot continue to steal art treasures from the Palazzo Ducale. People shout 'Viva Europa' but it is too early to celebrate victory. Euro's team hunts the villains on water bikes. Mala is proud of having conquered 'million of euros of irreplaceable art' when Europa enters and starts a fight where Mala drops her palace miniature on the cobbled street, while Ninot escapes down into the sewers. Europa saves the miniaturised museum. Mala and Vider are both disappointed with their failure, and scenes from a toilet and the filthy underground finally show how Ninot is trapped in the sewers, crying out to his boss for help.

Captain Euro has been presented in detail here, not only because it is a little known and amusing phenomenon, but also because it testifies to difficulties in elaborating a modern European myth. It is easy to see how every inch of this superhero concept is full of references to identifying traits of Europe and the EU. The density of stereotypes in the comic strip narratives is partly related to the intended juvenile audience and partly to the branding purpose. This naive unidimensionality does not exclude a series of inner contradictions, some of which unintentionally result from inherent problems in the European identity project.

The most emphasised value suggested for Europe here is that of unity. The whole format is geared towards 'strength through unity', which is the expressed motto, and the enemy 'D. Vider' wishes to divide Europe, with even his name, when read as one word, sounding out his wish to be a great 'divider'. His evilness is also confirmed by the name's likeness to the dreadful Darth Vader of Star Wars. Besides unity and strength, the basic narrative composed by the website as a whole, including the two adventures and the side information, mentions prosperity, science and technology, security and environmental protection as key values. Favoured activity areas are technology, sports, arts and media, rather than political or economic practices. The heroes fight for culture and civilisation, as all action heroes as well as all politicians tend to do. A strong emphasis is put on communication and information technologies that link the social and artistic skills of language to the 'hard' capacities of natural science and technology. Each of the two heroes combines natural and cultural interests, physical and mental skills, with history and communication as bridging competence fields.

These featured values are well in line with the policies and symbolic practices of the EU at large. The twelve stars of the flag and the euro are repeatedly hinted at. The presence of a euro currency converter here links the fiction to the practical economic aspects of the EU, and one adventure also mentioned the euro currency several years before its real life introduction. The other EU symbols are notably absent. There may be many explanations for why the Atomium consists of nine spheres while the evil circus has five tents, including a very far-fetched reference to 9 May as Europe Day, but this is far from evident. The anthem is neither heard on the soundtrack nor alluded to in any other obvious way. As for the motto, it is implicitly present in the diversity of the Twelve Stars team, but the emphasis is clearly on unity rather than diversity, though elements of diversity persist and on several levels give rise to ambiguities. The adventures consistently demonstrate the strength of the united goodies as against the internally divided baddies. There is a higher degree of differentiation in the traits of the good guys than of the bad ones, but their actions contrast in the opposite manner, as the Twelve Stars are always united while the GTC members often quarrel among themselves. Each of the good guys possesses stereotypical characteristics that together represent a set of acceptable identity positions for Europeans, but never open up for any internal conflicts or even tensions within the team. It is also interesting to note how the 'Origins' adventure moves around the borders of Europe—Sweden, Romania, Greece, Italy, Spain, Wales—rather than into its centre around Benelux, France, Germany, Switzerland or Austria, but from all these parts of Europe's circumference comes the same divine message, once again confirming the unity rather than diversity of Europe.[78]

Captain Euro piles up so many references to the EU that it becomes hard to discern exactly which of them are supposed to be the key symbols: the Captain himself, his partner Europa, the whole Twelve Stars team, the Atomium or the golden star(s) inherited from the ancient European gods? Each of these elements can be said to contribute a different aspect of what Europe means: its agency, its territory, its social community, its institutions and its imagined immanent spirit.

The plots and the leading characters display a strikingly unproblematised male dominance, which is underlined by the names of the two heroes, when 'Andros' (Greek word for 'man') leads 'Donna' just like the evil David dominates Mala. This is different from the Greek myth where Europa has a key role and cannot quite be reduced to a passive 'feminine' position. Captain Euro's name combines military and financial associations, whereas his main sidekick Europa is linked more to civic culture and citizenship, in line with a rather conventional gender hierarchy.

The contrast between heroes and villains reinforces and specifies the image the former construct of European identity. Dr D. Vider is a businessman and his team combines global speculation with the nomadic showbiz of circus. This can easily be read as a struggle between EU politics against globalising forces that combine free market forces with equally borderless low culture.

Ethnically, the Captain and his main sidekicks are white: Caucasian or even Aryan; several critics have inferred and even found crypto-Nazi implications in this typical superhero trait. His black team member Marcus is dehumanised when described as being almost like a machine, needing no sleep and always talking in technical terms, making him more of a loyal tool for his white master than an autonomous subject. The villain twins look like Russian Cossacks or secret agents, adding a West–East tension. More importantly, critics have contrasted Captain Euro's Aryan traits with David's Jewish looks. His name also invites such a reading, and his interests in banking and collecting antiques easily fit a quite problematic genealogy back to an anti-Semitic tradition, from the Wandering Jew through Shakespeare's Shylock to contemporary racist caricatures. The megacircus and its artists can also be associated to Europe's traditional nomadic tribes, notably the Romanies (Gypsies).

This ethnic dimension is directly linked to a chain of other levels of interpretation, with anti-globalisation as one of its important facets. David as a kind of Wandering Jew then represents mobile finance capital, his circus and its artists are eminently global, and the tent dome map is described as 'representing a world without boundaries'. The good team is firmly located in Atomium, and they obviously defend the external borders of Europe and presumably also respect the national boundaries inside it, just like the EU is supposed to do. The fear of nomadism and borderlessness contrasts to the simultaneously emphasised uniting will. There are strong reasons to read the narrative as confirming the securing of a unified European fortress against the rest of the world, and rinsing this inner territory of the deviant nomadic elements, whether they are speculating sharks, showbiz artists or migrant ethnic groups.

The genre of childish superhero comics itself leans towards the low side of the high/low divide, but this narrative clearly favours high arts to popular culture. The Twelve Stars team has in many ways a higher cultural profile than the villains. It is often stated that the former prefer the arts: from chess to landscape painting and seventeenth-century fugues. The villains instead are all engaged in showbiz, Mala's surname is Glamora, and D. Vider characterises himself as 'a performance art man' who likes action more than works of art and engages in 'cultural sabotage'. They want to dethrone and level all high values, including aesthetic ones, never respecting any sacred ideals such as truth, justice or beauty. One can thus discern a distinction between the two camps: state power, stable and well-defined European roles and high culture on the good side and evil market forces, ethnic nomads and popular culture on the other. This conforms to a common stereotype of Old Europe's preference for high arts while the American New World stands for trendy popular culture. However, if Captain Euro was meant to offer European images with a potential to be more popular than the official EU symbols, this elitist content of the website does not seem to serve the purpose.

Most components of Captain Euro are structurally similar to other male, action superhero stories, such as Captain America. It is mainly the European references and the elements of high culture preference that seem slightly unique. The narrative focuses on protecting inherited values against cultural sabotage that wishes to divide Europe and steal its riches. It makes no obvious references to the myth of Europa and the bull. There are no abductions, nor any erotic play between the heroes. Instead, what dominates is the eternal struggle between good and evil, together with allusions to another widespread myth in popular culture and the high arts, notably in a range of Holy Grail myths in Celtic cultures and Mediaeval Christianity, and in Richard Wagner's and J. R. R. Tolkien's ring cycles. Captain Euro's 'ring' is the sacred and powerful European star, and like so many other good men, he inherits from past gods a quest and a force that is highly ambivalent. The intervention of the gods to help humankind has narrative kinship not only to Zeus' many interactions with humans but also to the Greek myth of Prometheus or Mary Wollstonecraft Shelley's *Frankenstein*. The guiding star can also claim a Christian heritage in the star that guided the wise men to the newborn infant's cradle in Bethlehem. There is thus a very mixed set of meanings in this symbolism, even though the narrative does little to differentiate or prioritise between them, or to further develop this 'archaeological' line of interpretation.[79]

The first adventure talks of 'the gods of Europe' and makes explicit references to Greek, Celtic and Nordic divinities. But there are also plenty of hidden but actually very important elements from biblical and Christian mythology and imagery. One example of this biblical-Christian subtext is found in the lead characters' names, *Adam* Andros and Donna *E(a)den*. Both Captain Euro adventures mention some kind of rain, which may also be associated with the flood.

As is already clear, many elements are hard to interpret. The reason for naming the evil twins Castor and Pollux is not altogether evident, neither is the signifying impact of this choice. Still, in a so carefully designed narrative, every element tends to become meaningful, which creates certain problems with the details that do not simply confirm established clichés. How come Dr D. Vider is a cook and why does Ninot love animals? Could this potentially stir up unwanted opposition among gastronomic lobbyists or those animal protection movements that have launched campaigns to point at deficits in EU's food production practices? The Venice adventure likewise invites unintended readings as the twenty-first century climate crisis has, since it was published, made the strategy of melting Antarctic ice rather problematic, to say the least, thus destabilising the story's strict borders between good and evil. This hints at the problems inherent in the construction of a specific content or narrative that expresses cherished values and provides key symbols and at the same time attempts to preclude any elements that contradict the intended values, or which may through historic developments soon come to do so.

In his emphasis on stability and uniformity, Captain Euro seems strangely old-fashioned. Many other popular narratives today make almost the opposite metaphorical construction of good and evil. One such striking example is the 2003–05 HBO TV series *Carnivàle* which chose the reverse roles: the 'good' camp being a touring funfair whereas 'evil' resided in a fixed church.[80] Depicting mobilities (of money and of people) as a threat to prosperity goes against late modern ideas of nomadic mobility as a progressive resource, cherished both by neo-liberalism and the radical left. One may indeed argue that it is the mobile (from markets to migrants) that contribute more to unification and equality than the static, who tend to strongly differentiate themselves from others, often in hierarchic terms. Captain Euro claims to defend the famous EU freedoms or mobilities of goods, services, people and money, but is constructed in a way that actually prioritises static stability, while it is his primary enemy who embodies precisely those mobilities. This striking contradiction to core European and EU values partly explains why the comic hero has failed. This deeply conservative, new 'pseudo-myth' contradicts both neo-liberal and leftist visions of Europe and is unable to empower practices, rituals and meanings that could make it a real, living myth.

It should of course be kept in mind that Captain Euro is geared towards children and not to be taken too seriously. Still, it was commissioned by the EU and motivated by a perceived need to develop more popular representations of what it means to be European, and to encourage future citizens to identify as such. Designer Nicolas De Santis himself argues that he and his team 'consider the project a total success for what we aimed at the time'.[81] A reception study would be needed to know whether this goal was reached in the intended target group, but evidence indicates a lack of lasting success. The website has not been updated much, and most commentaries seem to be negative.

Blog comments lend support to my interpretations. In the liberal left-wing *The Guardian* 1999, Dan Glaister was suspicious of Captain Euro's hidden agenda, arguing that 'Captain Euro is devoted to persuading all good young Europeans of the virtues of integration in time for the advent of the single European currency in 2002', and that 'with his strong jaw and clean-cut morals', Captain Euro may actually be 'a proponent of fortress Europe, an us-and-them world, secure for the haves and inaccessible to the have-nots', the latter notably including asylum-seekers.[82] A libertarian conservative blog by Scottish-American Aaron in 2003 found Captain Euro 'just too damn funny' and was annoyed by its flamboyant Eurocentrism: 'When will this crazy "United Europe" merry-go-round of international comedy ever end?!'[83] The British Tory MEP in 2006 Daniel Hannan considered the EU marketing efforts to reach out to children an utter failure, and pointed at the problematic Jewish traits of the villain Dr D. Vider.[84] Captain Euro seems to have failed both on the right and the left on the political spectrum, and one of the main points of criticism concerns the racial implications of the series. In

2007, the blogger Helen agreed that 'the intrepid and distinctly Aryan looking fighter for peace, harmony and European integration' has 'failed miserably'. She dislikes that the evil guy is a businessman: 'The man who creates employment, provides financial services and adds to the wealth of wherever he happens to be (incidentally, what is wrong with international business which breaks down national barriers?) is evil, evil, evil. The goodies are people who prat around as parasites on the body politic, financed by the taxpayer.' Luckily 'the idea did not take off', mainly because of the too clean looks of the characters, which both had racist implications and failed according to the generic rules of comic books: 'Captain Euro and his cohorts are superb specimens of physical attraction mostly on the Aryan side. Even the scientist is sexy and attractive. Their main enemy Dr D. Vider has a distinctly Semitic look and resembles the villains of cartoons in Der Stürmer of evil memory. He is assisted by "moustachioed, dusky-skinned cohorts". Ooops! Setting aside the political problem there, the creation shows a certain lack of knowledge. Comic heroes are not handsome.' The harsh conclusion is 'Maybe the creators of Captain Euro should have spent less time in focus groups and more time reading successful comics.'[85] Other blogs and discussion forums have also made fun of the implicit racism and even drawn parallels to Nazi dreams of a united Europe.[86]

This debate highlights the inherent problem in trying to construct symbols and myths supposed to be widely used and convey deep layers of meaning. It usually takes a long time and a series of interconnected collective experiences to chisel out such symbols that are deeply meaningful to people. When this is done in instant projects like this, it tends to fail because of inner contradictions and lack of legitimacy among citizens. This form of political correctness can be double edged, as it makes the representations too clean and neat, and thus boring. As soon as they dare do something extra that could make them memorable, like melting the Antarctic ice or preferring landscape painting or fugues, they risk creating an unintended and clearly unfavourable interpretation (as climate destroyers or elitist snobs) that effectively hinders their wider acceptance and just makes them ridiculous.

Conclusions

The Europa myth remains the primary symbolic resource of wide reach and validity today, but with an ambiguous status. On the one hand it gives Europe much more of a mythic background than any other continent, providing a narrative that plays with dislocation, desire, elevation and hybridity. On the other hand, it offers no clear direction to the European project. Still, its hidden layers and signifiers resonate interestingly with certain aspects of the newer symbols to be discussed below.

With Europa, Europe is at first glance identified as in some sense feminine. As has been mentioned in the section on comparisons above, it is common for national personifications in modern times to likewise be female rather than male, with Uncle Sam as an exception to that rule. One common instance of gender stereotyping depicts the soil of a geographically defined land area as a 'mother' of a male-identified culture and civilisation, a mothering source of existence and nurture but also a feminised object of metaphorically masculinised activities like ploughing, sewing, mining, travelling or exploring. Europa eventually becomes a mother of sons (and significantly no daughters) who found a civilisation, but the most cherished parts of the myth tend to portray her as a young and attractive mistress. The feminisation of Europe plays a role in the modern play of identifications between Europe and America, where gender stereotypes are often ambiguous.[87] One trope makes Europe old, elite and female, in contrast to America as young, popular and masculine, but with modernism's denouncement of mass culture as feminised and feminising, there are also reversals of these roles. Captain Euro is male, and has a female sidekick; among the baddies gender is balanced in the same manner, while identifying Europe as culturally elevated. In gender terms then, the old myth tends to feminise Europe, while the recent (failed) effort struggles to 'lift' her up to a more masculine status.

Which are otherwise the most striking identifying meanings that the myth has offered for contemporary Europe to nourish? The etymology of the word 'Europe' and the interrelated myth of Europa have attracted a number of interpretations of what Europeanness might mean. Four themes appear to be central. The recently fabricated Captain Euro narrative differs radically on all but one, indicating a set of inherent tensions in Europe's perceived identity today. The themes summarise the above readings of the myths, but also follow a rudimentary narrative structure, in a movement from past to future combined with a play on two levels, concerning both the position and the composition of Europe. The first theme thus relates to the positional origins of Europe, the second to the main driving force propelling its development, the third to its direction and aim, while the fourth concerns the result: what kind of being has Europe become?

1. Europa was forced into exile, abducted against her will from her family, even though she also turned out to have much to gain from it both in the beginning (lust) and in the end (founding her own dynasty on Crete). Europa's *origin* was clearly elsewhere, in a trope of 'eccentricity' that has been taken up repeatedly through history. The *dislocation* across the waters from east to west is a unique feature in this myth. The Europa myth is centred on horizontal movement, voyage and by extension migration, and these indeed remain essential experiences in today's Europe. Starting with Herodotus, this trait of the mythical narrative

has often been read as a symbolic representation of real, material movements of peoples and cultures in that same direction, since it has long been known that Europe was populated and its social and cultural achievements likewise developed through a series of westward transitions. The myth describes Europe's roots in Africa and Asia, and a will to be uprooted and move to the west. Both the myth and the proposed (though questionable) etymology of the name indicate a will to identify as a western outpost, a land of the future, to which civilisation moves and where it matures, rather than its original cradle. In this way, a key element of non-identity and alterity is firmly placed at the heart of European identity. This identity of Europe as western was in turn shaken by the conquest of America as the new 'New World', even farther to the west. But it still resonates with the innovative pioneering spirit of the Enlightenment, and with the idea of the intrinsic value of progress and mobility, which has in late modern societies become a global lodestar and that reappears in the euro currency, as will later be shown. But dislocation as a founding element also means that Europe is in essence a migrant culture: not with firm roots to its place of birth, but always on the move: mobile, transient. This element also has clear potentials in relation to late modern visions of empowering and liberating mobility that flourish in both neo-liberal and left-wing thought. However, one should bear in mind that Europa's mobility is restricted by the force of the god/bull: she cannot move freely but is forced by a higher power in a specific north-westbound direction. But then, late modern mobility too is not as free as neo-liberal ideologies portray it to be. Captain Euro speaks more of anchorage and a safe home than of dislocation, which is instead conceived as a threat embodied by the Global Touring Circus. Yet, dislocation is present there too, not only as a threat from the villains but also in the necessity for the heroes to always move around Europe's various corners in a quest for unity that demands never-ending mobility. Still, the difference indicates a contradiction deep in the European project, that between an inescapable dislocation and a strong wish for feeling at home in a given space—an inherent tension between values of mobility and of stability. After all, dislocation is also an opportunity to start anew—to make oneself at home on new ground, which even without any geographical travel suits well the self-image of a continent that wants to find a fresh basis for itself on a soil marked with ruins and blood from past atrocities.

2. A *driving force* of *desire* and pleasure is everywhere in this myth, and on both parts, lending a specific mood to the narrative. The abduction is often depicted more as lustful seduction than as violent rape, and Europa is often shown carried away in an apparently happy and adventurous mood. What propels Zeus as well as Europa has to do with passionate love, lust and desire. Europa is letting

herself loose in a daring and brave adventure where she throws herself out into the sea and is immersed in the water with the god, without any secure control. Her archaeological links to Astarte, the moon goddess of orgiastic fertility, play a role here, as does the carnal, animal eroticism of the bull in many Middle East traditions. The combination with the water element adds an oceanic dimension that on the one hand has a geopolitical aspect, as it combines the Middle East (and later European) land-based communities with the Phoenician and Greek sea-based civilisations, and on the other hand also has a deep mythical and experiential anchorage in the infant's earliest experiences as they are nourished in the mother–child symbiosis. The aspect of enjoyment might also resonate with the message of inter-human love and generosity in Christianity, based on the life and teachings of Jesus. The implicit result of eroticism and love is also significant, as the combination of this and Europa's fertility inevitably results in an offspring that by settlement can found a selected hereditary dynasty and a geographic community. To Captain Euro and his crew, instead of self-abandoning love-play, all seems to be about control and safety, whereas it is the villains who go for boundary-dissolving pleasure and entertainment. It seems as if Europe has to use much energy to wrestle with its inner impulses and desires, striving to reduce chaos and bring rational order and discipline in a messy territory. The good Captain's team fights for 'truth and justice' rather than love or happiness, using 'intellect, culture and logic' rather than care or compassion to reach their goals. In spite of his interest in information and high arts, he does not really seem to master the communicative ethos needed for developing the 'soft power' asked for in contemporary politics. This points at a deep ambivalence in European identifications between soft values of communication and love on one side and hard values of control and mastery on the other.

3. The myth also has a *direction* into the future, and this relates to a vertical exchange between god, woman and animal. There is the focal element of selectedness and *elevation* in that Europa is united with the mightiest and highest god Zeus; a selected human creature has intimate contact with divinity, resulting in a noble offspring where Minos founds a Cretan dynasty, and by extension, Greek and European civilisation. This elevatory element (that is further emphasised by Europa sitting up on the back of the bull) suits Europeans who wish to understand themselves as blessed with special gifts, just like those precious magic gifts Zeus gave Europa at the end: Europe as the cradle of high culture, intellectual life, education and enlightenment. This element of humans offered contact with divinity and elevation into sacredness again returns in the myth of Jesus as God's son, which the Christian tradition has found possible to reconcile with an idea of all-absorbing love and thus allowed for ways to reconcile the

element of erotic desire with that of divine elevation. The whiteness of the bull links to the purity and intellectuality of the high ideals and could in modern times simultaneously offer a racist celebration of the Caucasian male. This first aspect of the Europa myth is also found in that of Captain Euro, where past gods have left a treasure and a quest for Europe to inherit and be loyal to. This links to what was previously said about the comparative resource Europe has in having any founding myth at all, since it may strengthen the feelings of supremacy that Europeans, in line with their colonial heritage, can still cherish: convictions of possessing a special status in the world, a higher destiny or at least a place in the centre of global events. This links to the 'myth' of progressive perfection, cumulative regeneration and civilising development mentioned before, in resonance with the status of the bastion of high culture that seems to be a widespread attribute of Europe, both in the self-understanding of European elites and in the eyes of many external observers. Even though this is a point that the two myths (that of Europa and that of Captain Euro) seem to share, it has ambiguous implications, as Europe has to struggle to balance the hubris resulting from sacredness with a more humble secularity that is asked for since the Enlightenment but can also find support in Europa's vernacular play with the bull in the water.

4. The *result* of the recounted narrative can be discussed in terms of inner texture and character. In contrast to the other related myths, that of Europa is different in its many mixtures—of East and West, high and low, male and female. The result is a marked *hybridity*, not least in Europa's sons, where human, divine and animal traits combine into a new and versatile strength. The myth is on many levels full of otherness and mixture: of Africa and Asia; god, animal and human; male and female; white and dark; land and sea. The combination of animal and human produces three gifted sons, not the Minotaur monstrosity later born from another similar combination on the same island of Crete. It is particularly interesting to note how it depicts the East–West mixture of ancient Greek culture as the cradle of European civilisation. This aspect is often disguised and pushed into the background, in phases and camps where Europeans have wished to conceal and deny any dependence on that Arab culture and Islamic world that has in fact been essential in administrating, developing and transferring the rich tradition from ancient Greece into mediaeval European culture. The Europa myth is in many ways ambiguous and ambivalent, continually shifting perspectives between its characters. This has affinities with multicultural values of ethnic and national diversity, but like with the previous couple of traits, it is controversial and not universally accepted among Europeans, which may partly explain why this myth is after all rather marginal in today's European policy

landscape. Instead of hybridity, Captain Euro prefers to speak for a seamless unity, but he too remains haunted by ambiguities and tries desperately to integrate as many identity positions as possible into his team, so that diversity and heterogeneity continue to haunt his naive desire for strength in unity. The fact that Captain Euro prefers diplomacy to violence and loves language and communication is on the other hand at least a faint echo of the communicative elements in the Europa myth. There is again a clear tension in European identity, between diversity and unity. This is far from unique to Europe; it is in fact a problem faced everywhere, but as will be shown, Europe has found specific ways to deal with this tension.

Based in the Europa myth and highlighted by the other older myths linked to Europe's destiny, dislocation and mobility seem to be a unique spatial characteristic of Europa, while her mythical competitors tend to be more static. The driving force behind this process is lustful desire and passion, creating a mood of attraction and adventure, in contrast to for instance hatred, sorrow, longing or friendship that are encountered in other myths not related to Europe. Europe is mythically elevated, where the phoenix instead offers to Asia a more archaic, repetitively cyclical time process. Both Europa and Prometheus (as well as Captain Euro) emphasise a temporal and vertical element of lifting human beings up by communication with higher spirits. And Europa's mythical process charts a transformation from a female to a markedly hybrid identity, which is a fascinating trait that keeps the limits and boundaries of her human identity open to further hybridisations as well. Elevation combined with tensions between desire–welfare, mobility–sovereignty and hybridity–unity: these then appear to be key elements in the investigated mythical narratives of Europe. Which interpretation of each of these points is today closest to European identification remains to be seen when analysing the remaining symbols.

2

IDENTIFYING SYMBOLS

Before analysing symbols any further, it is necessary first to take a step back and consider the conceptual foundations of this enterprise. As tools for collective identification, symbols serve as clues to how communities are formed, though the symbolic realm is too often neglected by social research. Identities are here understood as meanings attached to human individuals or collectives, in interaction among themselves and with surrounding others. Identities are formed by signification processes spun around specific individuals or groups, where people in thought and action link somebody or something to a range of meanings representing characteristic traits and values for that person or collective.

Meanings and identities do not exist only as mental phenomena 'inside' people. They always arise and develop by the mediation of material tokens or signs of some kind: words, images, sounds or other perceptible external marks organised into various forms of artefacts, texts, works, genres and discourses. There are many possible vocabularies for these processes, depending on theoretical perspective. I will here use a range of theories, with the critical hermeneutics of Paul Ricoeur in focus, but also incorporating elements from the semiotics of Charles S. Peirce and early twentieth century works by Ernst Cassirer, George H. Mead and Susanne K. Langer. Along with Ricoeur, I will also make use of ideas from psychoanalytical hermeneutics (here primarily Hanna Segal and Alfred Lorenzer) as well as from structuralism and post-structuralist deconstruction. One obvious source of inspiration is social anthropology, especially the works of Sherry B. Ortner, Anthony P. Cohen and others. The conceptual analysis proceeds in a series of steps, each adding new aspects, by moving from meaning, signs and texts through identity to a multifaceted understanding of key symbols.

Meanings

Europe is given *meaning* by being understood as a meaningful text, that is, as an entity which means something, points at something else, not simply as its cause of existence (the way indexes do, for instance when a smoke indicates a fire), but due to a convention whereby people tend to associate Europe with certain ideas or values of some kind. Europe as meaningful implies that it is constructed and understood as a cultural entity: a text composed of signs, in the wide sense of both words, denoting any conglomerate of material marks used for carrying meaning. Europe is not (only) a text, but when people give it meaning, they approach it as if it was and thus construct Europe as a cultural category.

Meanings are not pure mental and subjective constructs. They are intersubjective, constituted by the interplay between people (subjects) in social settings where they ascribe meaning to various phenomena, from things to events and practices. As tools for signifying practices, these phenomena imbued with meaning then function as *signs*, and through discourses linking signs to statements, and statements to works of higher complexity, signs are combined into texts. Signs are 'expressions that communicate a meaning': 'Every sign aims at something beyond itself and stands for that something', says Paul Ricoeur.[88] These terms have been developed by a rich tradition of semiotic theory that will not be further explicated here, but which goes back to the semiotics of Charles S. Peirce: 'A sign, or *representamen*, is something which stands to somebody for something in some respect or capacity'.[89]

A first approximation of the concept of symbol ('symbol$_1$') is that it is a sign, something that points towards or stands for something else, by way of its meaning. A second specification is that a symbol ('symbol$_2$') is a particular type of sign, with a conventional rather than natural relation between the mark and its meaning.[90] A symbol$_2$ is then a basic material unit for making meaning by attaching meaning to it in socially contextualised interactive, intersubjective and interpretive practices. This is how Charles S. Peirce defines symbols as signs whose meanings are the result of conventional interpretation deriving from their use in social practices, rather than from any law of nature.[91] His other two categories of signs are the *icon*, which is in some way simply similar to what it represents, and the *index*, which is caused by what it represents. The first works by resemblance, the second by causation; by contrast, the symbol's relation to what it represents is wholly conventional, decided by social and historical processes that happen to link them. In a sense, only symbols have true meanings, since icons rather have similarities and indexes have causes.

Others who also use the term 'symbol' in a general sense as almost equivalent to 'sign' are Ernst Cassirer who talks of 'the universal *symbolic* function' and Susanne K. Langer who conceives symbols as all signs used 'not only to *indicate* things, but also to *represent* them', which she sees as a unique human capacity of formal abstraction.[92]

Norbert Elias has a similar perspective: 'Symbols are not pictures or mirrors of the world; they are neither windows nor curtains. They have not an imitative, pictorial, but a representational function.'[93]

Also, in the pragmatic and interactional tradition of social psychology, George H. Mead discusses 'significant symbols' as gestures that create meaning through being used in interpersonal interaction, thus constituting language.[94] Like the others, he also stresses that thinking and mental life is anchored in the ('inner') use of symbols: 'Actually, our thinking always takes place by means of some sort of symbols.'[95] This has been further developed by interaction-oriented psychological and psychoanalytical thinkers such as Hanna Segal, who links symbol formation to communication, wherein she includes not only communication with the external world but also 'internal communication' by means of symbols, such as 'verbal thinking' which uses words to, among other things, integrate 'earlier desires, anxieties, and phantasies into the later stages of development by symbolization'.[96] This particular function is of course derived from a psychoanalytical perspective on how individual human beings build their adult selves on remnants from their relational childhood experiences. But it may also be transferred to the collective domain, where for instance communities of Europe use symbolic processes in order to integrate historical experiences and ideals into their currently shared self-understanding.

In this sense, then, a symbol$_2$ (or a symbolic sign) is a conventional representation of something absent, making it virtually present ('re-present'): an object or a process that is recalled by signifying practices that forge interpretive chains of association. As core units in all webs of culture, signs are material marks that stand for something else (meaning) to some people (interpretive community) in certain settings (context). They are tokens that for certain people in certain settings (organised by daily practices) tend to 'point at' something outside themselves.

The word 'symbol' derives from the Greek *symbállein*, meaning 'throw together'.[97] Symbolic signs are indeed integrating, combinatory or linking devices in at least three ways: they join interacting people in a shared understanding of meanings, they integrate internal subjective experience with external material objects, and they join present signs and texts with absent but virtually re-presented meanings, thereby linking near and far as well as present and past. All symbols$_2$ are therefore mediating cultural phenomena, circulating through a wide range of communication media.

Taking inspiration from Ludwig Wittgenstein's 'language games' theory, Alfred Lorenzer stresses how symbols as constituents of language use mediate between physical nature and societal history as well as between consciousness and behaviour, by serving as tools for intersubjective coordination as well as for developing the individual mind.[98] Close to Peirce's sign concept, Lorenzer argues that symbols integrate language (cultural world) and practice (social world) by uniting three elements: body, situation and word, that is, interpreter, setting and signifier, or subject, context and text.[99] Material or 'external' symbols carry meaning anchored in 'inner' symbols that form a specific level of individual (as well as collective) subjects, mediating between sensory experience and mental imagination, as basis of identity.[100] I will soon return to this point, but for now conclude that symbols$_2$ are conventional or cultural signs.

Interpretations

What is then interpretation? It is an interaction between texts and their users ('readers'), where the meanings implied by the textual combinations of signs are reconstructed. Critical hermeneutics is the reflective theory of how such processes of interpretation develop in a dialectical interplay between understanding (tentatively approaching and appropriating the textual universe) and explanation (systematically testing interpretive hypotheses by analysing textual structures and other 'distancing' practices).

> The kind of hermeneutics which I now favour starts from the recognition of the objective meaning of the text as distinct from the subjective intention of the author. This objective meaning is not something hidden behind the text. Rather it is a requirement addressed to the reader. The interpretation accordingly is a kind of obedience to this injunction starting from the text. This [...] means that what has to be interpreted in a text is what it says and what it speaks about, i.e., the kind of world which it opens up or discloses. [...] This shift within hermeneutics from a 'romanticist' trend to a more 'objectivist' trend is the result of this long travel through structuralism.[101]

'The sense of a text is not behind the text, but in front of it. It is not something hidden, but something disclosed', Ricoeur continues in another text.[102] This is a welcome improvement of older, romanticist notions of interpretation, where textual meanings were seen as residing in the minds of authors. Ricoeur's development of critical hermeneutics thus productively responds to the structuralist critique of hermeneutics, including that voiced by Michel Foucault and others in his footsteps, making their 'anti-hermeneutical' critique largely irrelevant.

Several problems in this analysis of meaning, sign and text cannot be fully solved here. One such problem concerns the notion of 'convention'. Based on Saussure's linguistics, a strong version of structuralist semiotics has stressed that all links between signs and what they represent are totally arbitrary, and that all meanings only result out of the juxtapositioning of signs in a symbolic order that is thus in a way cut off from any 'real' world 'out there'. But it seems important not to totally reify this symbolic order, but remember how it is linked to concrete and situated histories of social experiences and practices. This means that at any given moment, signs in real everyday lifeworlds (as opposed to the technically specialised symbolisms constructed for instance in mathematics) are never totally arbitrary, but bound to human experience, combining biological-natural with historical-social elements. 'Thus in a variety of ways symbolic activity lacks autonomy. It is a bound activity', says Ricoeur. 'This bound character of symbols makes all the difference between a symbol and a metaphor. The latter is a free invention of discourse; the former is bound to the cosmos. [...] Symbols have roots. Symbols plunge us into the shadowy experience of power'.[103]

This also reminds us that it is important not to draw any line of division between interpretive and critical studies. Hermeneutics acknowledges the centrality of the signifying and interpretive practices of communication in human and social life, but this quest for meaning is not beyond the struggles of power and critique. Some proponents of structuralism and of critical cultural studies have constructed a polarity between understanding and resistance. In this, they distance themselves from an already outdated romantic version of hermeneutics. To Ricoeur, 'what is peculiar to modern hermeneutics is that it remains in the line of critical thought'.[104] It is true that he often seems to emphasise the element of restoration and tradition, for instance when arguing for acknowledging the tradition also of revolutionary ideas. But he repeatedly also asserts the necessity of a critical dissolution of founding myths.

> Thus, the time of restoration is not a different time from that of criticism; we are in every way children of criticism, and we seek to go beyond criticism by means of criticism, by a criticism that is no longer reductive but restorative.[105]

In fact, one may on the basis of a critical hermeneutics give equal weight to both sides. On the one hand, if an interpretation is to understand the meanings of any cultural phenomenon, it needs to make use of a series of distancing and critical detours that will enrich this understanding by highlighting how symbols, texts and myths are linked to various forms of power. On the other hand, no critique can be efficient if it does not proceed through an understanding of what the criticised phenomenon actually means; else it won't even hit its intended target. The present study of Europe symbols will strive to uphold an unreductive dialectics between moments of understanding and of critique, keeping different ways of using these symbols open as far as possible, exposing their links to problematic aspects of European history and identity without reducing their emancipatory potentials, however exaggerated these may be in official explanations.

Another problem concerns the priority of verbal language, based in speech. Much meaning theory is derived from linguistic or literary theory, and tends to see verbal language, especially speech, as the preferential symbolic mode, seeing other forms of expression (such as pictures or music) as fundamentally different. I will here not stick to such a model, but instead consider all symbolic modes as equally involved in signifying practices, even though they organise meaning-production in different ways.[106]

Meanings never exist a priori, but are always made and recreated in situated practices, in interpretive communities. Peirce expresses this in an almost poetic manner: 'Symbols grow. They come into being by development out of other signs [...]. We think only in signs. [...] A symbol, once in being, spreads among the peoples. In use and in experience, its meaning grows.'[107] In a similar spirit, Clifford Geertz argues that 'meaning is use, or more carefully, arises from use'.[108] The meanings of symbols and texts must therefore be interpreted by participating in the communicative practices and language games where they circulate. Cultural research therefore always demands moments of immersive participation into the symbolic worlds to be studied.[109]

Meanings—including that of Europe—are always constructed in an intertextual play with similarity and difference. Texts and meanings form—and are constituted in—networks that give rise to dynamic signifying systems. For instance, Europe's meanings are shaped by comparisons to other units, such as other continents (Africa, Asia, America), but also other artefacts that in myths, narratives or images are linked to Europe in terms of similarity or contrast: animals, flowers, etc. As Bo Stråth among others has understood, 'Europe is seen in the mirror of the Other'.[110] As Stuart Hall has shown, this interplay is unavoidable but entails certain trappings, including the risk of sticking to ideological combinations of polarisation (exaggerating contrasts between 'the west and the rest') and stereotyping (erasing internal differences on both sides of the divide).[111] This is important to remember when making comparative interpretations of European and other symbols.

Polysemies

All that is true for signs is also valid for symbols, since a symbol is a kind of sign. It has already been said that symbols$_2$ are conventional signs, constituting a symbolic order. But for the purpose of this study, the concept of symbol needs to be narrowed down still more, in three further steps. The first qualification was that a symbol$_1$ is a sign, the second that a symbol$_2$ is a conventional sign, which filters away those signs that are for instance merely physical traces or indices of something. The term 'symbol' is then reserved to those truly cultural signs that are dependent on human interaction and interpretation.

The third approximation of the concept of symbol is that a 'symbol$_3$,' may be defined as a particularly complex conventional sign that is charged with a '*double meaning*', to borrow Ricoeur's expression. Symbols$_3$ in this sense are emphatically polysemic and notoriously open to plural readings.

> Thus, contrary to perfectly transparent technical signs, which say only what they want to say in positing that which they signify, symbolic signs are opaque, because the first, literal, obvious meaning itself points analogically to a second meaning which is not given otherwise than in it [...]. This opacity constitutes the depth of the symbol, which, it will be said, is inexhaustible.[112]

'To mean something other than what is said—this is the symbolic function', says Ricoeur in another context.[113] 'I define "symbol" as any structure of signification in which a direct, primary, literal meaning designates, in addition, another meaning which is indirect, secondary, and figurative and which can be apprehended only through the first'.[114]

It should be noted that even in this sense, symbols$_3$ may still retain elements of iconicity and/or indexicality. For instance, if a drawing depicts a fire by combining some vertical wave lines, it has both an iconic element in that these lines are supposed to look like ascending smoke, and an indexical element in that smoke is supposedly an effect of fire.

Symbols$_3$ are therefore intrinsically linked to the need of interpretation through the 'hermeneutic problem' they pose, since 'there is something astonishing and even scandalous about the use of symbols':

1. The symbol remains opaque, not transparent, since it is given by means of an analogy based on a literal signification. The symbol is thus endowed with concrete roots and a certain material density and opacity.
2. The symbol is a prisoner of the diversity of languages and cultures and, for this reason, remains contingent: Why *these* symbols rather than any others?
3. The symbol is given to thought only by way of an interpretation which remains inherently problematical. There is no myth without exegesis, no exegesis without contestation. [...] Opacity, cultural contingency, and dependency on a problematical interpretation—such are the three deficiencies of the symbol as measured by the ideal of clarity, necessity, and scientific order in reflection.[115]

This outlines very well the task implied in trying to understand how various symbols identify Europe. It includes carefully reconstructing (1) the 'concrete roots' of these symbols—where they come from, historically as well as socially; (2) the various symbolisations found competing with each other in various cultural contexts; and (3) the possible critical and oppositional readings against the grain of the intended and official meanings suggested by dominant European institutions.

Identities

It is necessary to qualify the meaning of an entity like Europe by adding the concept of identity. What has been said so far may perhaps suffice to start interpreting the meaning of the word 'Europe', or of the corresponding geographic formation of the European continent as such. But this is not an issue here, or rather this is just a step towards understanding what Europe means as a political and cultural community—a collective of human subjects who identify themselves as members of this community. Texts have meanings, but the meanings of human subjects (whether as single individuals or as collectives grouped into communities) are different, as they are used for self-identification. They therefore deserve a special name: *identities*. In order to differentiate collective and symbolically mediated identities from personal or subjective ones, one often talks about 'cultural identities'.

In this sense, identities are meanings people attach to themselves and to others, to identify them as something characteristic. Individually as well as collectively, in constellations on every level, from intimate core groups to humanity as a whole, people identify as something, by interpreting themselves in terms of values or characteristics that are like meanings attached to acting subjects. This capacity of being 'inhabited' makes identities special. It is related to the fact that meanings are not pre-existing in any text, but always 'made' in signifying practices involving human subjects. In a reflexive mode, these subjects can turn their meaning-making capacity towards themselves (and others), and construct identities for selves and others, making them meaningful.

Identity does not suggest a complete unity, neither in time nor in space. This is true for individual as well as for collective identities. It is obvious that a person as well as a group is always to some extent internally divided, containing different sides. It is obvious that subjects are never in stasis, but always change and develop in various ways. The concept of identity only denotes and presupposes a relative coherence across time (stability) and space (coherence), and—borrowing an idea from Wittgenstein— there is more of a 'family likeness' than a total uniformity between what somebody is between moments.[116]

Ricoeur distinguishes two aspects of identity: 'on one side, identity as *sameness* (Latin *idem*, German *Gleichheit*, French *mêmeté*); on the other, identity as *selfhood*

(Latin *ipse*, German *Selbstheit*, French *ipséité*).[117] Only the former is characterised by numerical 'oneness' and 'permanence in time' in a strong and strict sense, and is applicable also to dead objects, whereas identity as selfhood is of key relevance to all forms of personal and cultural identity. These are constructed by narratives, by telling stories that locate individuals and groups in space and time, conferring meaning to them. Subjects are never given from the start but grow through their exchanges with texts of all kinds, used to identify the world, others and themselves. 'In place of an *ego* enamoured of itself arises a *self* instructed by cultural symbols, the first among which are the narratives handed down in our literary tradition. And these narratives give us a unity which is not substantial but narrative', says Ricoeur.[118] He underlines that

> the self does not know itself immediately, but only indirectly by the detour of the cultural signs of all sorts which are articulated on the symbolic mediations which always already articulate action and, among them, the narratives of everyday life. Narrative mediation underlines this remarkable characteristic of self-knowledge—that it is self-interpretation.[119]

All this also applies to collective selves, such as nations.

> It is at this radical level that ideology is constituted. It seems related to the need every group has to give itself an image of itself, to 'represent' itself, in the theatrical sense of the word, to put itself on stage, to play itself. Perhaps no social group can exist without this indirect relation to its own being through a representation of itself.[120]

On this basis, Ricoeur sums up the task of critical hermeneutics in regard to identities as combining three interrelated problematics: '1. the indirect approach of reflection through the detour of analysis; 2. the first determination of selfhood by way of its contrast with sameness; 3. the second determination of selfhood by way of its dialectic with otherness.'[121] Applied to the task of understanding European identity, this implies (1) that it must be approached by indirect way through analysis of its expressions in various symbolic realms; (2) that it needs to be outlined not by simple and univocal definitions but by tracing the narratives through which it is told and lived; and (3) that it always unfolds in a complex interaction with surrounding others.

In the last sense, identity adds to the interplay of unity and difference a dimension of (practices of) inclusion and exclusion, which has been discussed by Anthony P. Cohen. 'The most striking feature of the symbolic construction of the community and its boundaries is its oppositional character. The boundaries are *relational* rather than absolute; that is, they mark the community *in relation to* other communities.'[122]

People's sense of their Europeanness (or otherwise) is always intertwined with other identities, including those involving nationality, ethnicity, class, age, generation, gender, sexuality, religion and political affiliation.[123] European identity is also formed and must be interpreted relationally through differences to various 'others', notably Islam, Asia, Africa and the United States.

Cohen approaches social communities from an explicitly cultural perspective, in focusing on how people give meaning to social boundaries.[124] The use of the word 'community' implies

> that the members of a group of people (a) have something in common with each other, which (b) distinguishes them in a significant way from the members of other putative groups. 'Community' thus seems to imply simultaneously both similarity and difference. The word thus expresses a relational idea [...]. We are talking here about what the boundary means to people, or, more precisely, about the meanings they give to it. This is the symbolic aspect of community boundary.[125]

This interplay between meanings, symbols, identity and community is essential to the study of Europe symbols, since it makes the latter highly important to social action: 'People construct community symbolically, making it a resource and repository of meaning, and a referent of their identity'.[126] Benedict Anderson has studied the nation as precisely such an 'imagined political community', which is imagined since each of its members will never meet more than a minority of other members, but still nourish an image of their community—as a symbolic construction.[127] This is not to say that it is a pure fiction, since when people act according to such imagination, they make it as real as anyone can ask for, and also they underpin this symbolic construction by effective social institutions (customs and other border limitations, national state authorities etc.). In this study, it is the symbolic identification of Europe as a supra-, trans- or even post-national community that is at stake.

Identifiers

This leads to a fourth step, which narrows down the concept of symbol even further, especially in this particular study which looks at specific signs that are symbols of a particular social entity. The fourth approximation of symbols ('symbol$_4$') is that they are identity markers or *identifiers* in a more specific way than other signs. The Europe symbols to be discussed here are all of this particular kind: they are emblems of a community or group—in this case Europe. Europe as a thing, a word or a physically defined geographic area does not necessarily require such identifying symbols$_4$, since they have meanings but no identity in the sense discussed above. But Europe as a (political, social or cultural) community does, since such collective identities can only be constructed and understood through mediation, that is, via a detour through texts—and such identifying texts are symbols$_4$ in an even more qualified and precise sense than any of those mentioned so far.

Such symbols$_4$ not only have double but at least *triple meanings*. A symbol$_4$ is first a particular sign with a primary meaning ('meaning$_1$'), for instance a flag depicting a set of stars. Secondly, these stars are agreed to implicitly indicate a certain set of values or characteristics, for instance a harmonic relation between units ('meaning$_2$'). Third, as this sign with its double meaning is linked to a certain community, for instance Europe, it identifies this community as sharing these intended values, thereby knitting a third layer into its web of signification ('meaning$_3$'). For a European flag, meaning$_1$ is what it literally depicts; meaning$_2$ is its secondary meanings, that is, an implied set of values or characteristics; and meaning$_3$ is Europe. The signifying process involves linking the symbol to its primary meaning (deciphering what it is supposed to represent); then linking this to some secondary meaning which it indirectly and 'symbolically' represents; and finally constituting a bond between this secondary sphere of meanings and the entity for which the symbol is meant to serve as an identifier.

As is the case with the more simple meanings discussed above, all these complex operations—linking a symbol$_4$ to its triple meanings and thus ultimately identifying a community as something particular, constructing its identity—are dependent on socially situated interpretive or signifying practices, that is, on the practical uses of symbols$_4$ in discourses where meanings are tested and challenged. This signifying process is vulnerable and can be broken off in all steps. First, the symbol may lose its force by losing its capacity to indicate something specific and either be perceived as a meaningless bundle of elements or be misinterpreted to represent something else that is irrelevant to its uses. For instance, people could stop understanding the stars as stars, just experiencing them as irregular golden dots, or fail to think of the blue background as having anything to do with heaven. This way, meaning$_1$ gets lost or is reconstructed in ways that distort the initially intended significance of the symbol. Second, crucial elements of the customary secondary meaning$_2$ can be lost, for instance if people tend to interpret a circular form as implying not unified perfection but instead closure or narcissistic circularity. Third, if people fail to understand that the symbol is meant to identify Europe, its whole point again gets lost.

Whether individual or collective, identities are not fixed, stable or unified entities, as for instance Stuart Hall has repeatedly stressed:

> [I]dentities are never unified and, in late modern times, increasingly fragmented and fractured; never singular but multiply constructed across different, often intersecting and antagonistic, discourses,

practices and positions. They are subject to a radical historicization, and are constantly in the process of change and transformation.[128]

In a similar vein, Julia Kristeva talks of the 'subject-in-process', and Paul Ricoeur of 'oneself as another'.[129] Such an approach is common in literature on Europe, which is full of formulations such as this: 'Europe is not a fixed essence but labile and in a flux. European—and national—identities are always fluid and contextual, contested and contingent, and discursively shaped under various forms of inclusion and exclusion.'[130] This is also my position here.

Building on ideas from Antonio Gramsci and Ernesto Laclau, Stuart Hall elaborated on the concept of *articulation* in a way that seems applicable here.[131] He makes use of the intrinsic double meaning of this concept. On the one hand, it means to utter, to express and put into language, as when speakers articulate words. On the other hand, it is also used to denote phenomena where something is connected or combined with something else. This latter is for instance used by dentists for describing how the jaws combine, and Hall takes the example of an articulated lorry or truck that under specific conditions connects a cab to a trailer. 'An articulation is thus the form of the connection that *can* make a unity of two different elements, under certain conditions. It is a linkage which is not necessary, determined, absolute and essential for all time.' This idea directs the focus of attention to the circumstances that make possible for a discourse to articulate distinct elements that have no necessary, logical, natural or universal relation.

> Thus, a theory of articulation is both a way of understanding how ideological elements come, under certain conditions, to cohere together within a discourse, and a way of asking how they do or do not become articulated, at specific conjunctures, to certain political subjects.

This is a useful way of putting it, since it shows that while what the combination symbols make of elements (sign and meaning, or representation and reference) is always context-dependent, it need not be completely arbitrary in a strong sense, but conditioned by the historical and social circumstances where symbols circulate and are used. The concept of articulation invites studying how symbols are combined with plural meanings in socially situated signifying practices, and in particular to understand how those meanings that are attached to subjects as their identities also are context-dependent. This is highly relevant to the study of Europe symbols.

The symbols of Europe have—or are continuously ascribed—meanings. By being linked to Europe, they establish a shared set of interpretations of the identity of Europe. When a flag is used to identify Europe—for its own citizens, who thereby identify as Europeans, but also for outsiders who simultaneously associate European people with corresponding characteristics and values—the meaning of the flag is linked to that of Europe, and some properties of the flag are agreed to be similar to those of Europe. It is of course not every property of the symbol that becomes valid in this signifying process. The most concrete material traits of a flag, such as having a specific size or being made of cloth, is irrelevant to Europeanness, since they are the same for all flags and do not differ between flags. What is relevant is instead what the symbol signifies, its meanings. A certain design is understood to imply a certain set of values, and the use of such a symbol to identify a community then serves to establish an interpretation of that community as sharing those values.

The meaning of a symbol$_4$, like a flag, is then triple. The design of the symbol invites its users to construct its meaning: a star is not just a star but perhaps also stands for a member of some confederate unity. But through the use of the flag to identify a community, a third level of signification is added, by which the flag also means Europe, and through its own (second-level) meaning projects identity to that community. Through being used as a symbol for Europe, the flag links the characteristics of its own second-level meaning to Europe, so that the flag on this third level is said to both signify and identify Europe.

Compared to a simple thing or unitary sign, a full text or larger conglomerate both widens and narrows the range of interpretations. A complex composite unity like Europe can never have one single meaning/identity, not only because it (like all signs) as a totality is polysemic and can be understood differently from different perspectives, but also because it is a highly differentiated conglomerate of different elements that may be selected, combined and therefore also understood in various ways. On the other hand, a very simple unitary sign leaves large room for interpretation, while a complex text in many respects tends to fix and stabilise its interpretations. For instance, a short quote or motto may invite lots of divergent interpretations, but if it is read in a larger context, this contextualisation specifies which of these interpretations are most reasonable and legitimate.

Therefore, no symbols have once and for all a completely fixed meaning, and this openness to subjective or oppositional reinterpretation is actually part of their living force: 'Symbols are effective because they are imprecise', says Anthony P. Cohen.[132] This is particularly essential in relation to symbols$_4$ used for identifying communities, as all identities are always also (if in shifting ways and degrees) transient and multiple:

> Community is just such a boundary-expressing symbol. As a symbol, it is
> held in common by its members; but its meaning varies with its members'
> unique orientations to it. In the face of this variability of meaning, the
> consciousness of community has to be kept alive through manipulation
> of its symbols. [...] In this approach, then, the 'commonality' which is

found in community need not be a uniformity. It does not clone behaviour or ideas. It is a commonality of forms (ways of behaving) whose content (meanings) may vary considerably among its members.[133]

Studying the meanings of Europe symbols to see how they identify Europe as a community can therefore never result in a once-and-for-all explanation but is a continuing process where each interpretation can always be challenged by new events and reinterpretations, and where different actors—Europeans as well as outsiders—may construct this collective cultural identity differently.

Keys

Fifth, among these emphatic symbols one may discern some ('symbol$_5$') that are more crucial than others in a given society. Europe's meaning and identity is constructed by practices where it is linked to other and more simple and clear signs regarded as condensation of the core values of Europe, thus functioning as *key symbols* in a most distinct sense. Such key 'symbols$_5$' are particularly charged with many layers of meaning through their use as central tools of identification in practices of signification, and they are widely acknowledged as carrying values central to the whole community. A Europe symbol in this most strict sense would refer to a generally honoured condensed expression in any symbolic mode or genre of what is understood as characteristic of Europe and what it may mean to be European.

The social anthropologist Sherry B. Ortner has analysed the concept of key symbols, distinguishing between 'summarizing' and 'elaborating' symbols.[134] The first are often sacred, synthesising, standing for the social system as a whole, whereas the latter are analytic and have a more limited application. 'Symbols with great conceptual elaborating power' are 'root metaphors which provide categories for the ordering of conceptual experience', whereas 'key scenarios' 'provide strategies for organizing action experience'. There are thus two broad types of key symbols:

> Summarizing symbols are primarily objects of attention and cultural respect; they synthesize or 'collapse' complex experience, and relate the respondent to the grounds of the system as a whole. They include the most importantly sacred symbols in the traditional sense. Elaborating symbols, on the other hand, are symbols valued for their contribution to the ordering or 'sorting out' of experience. Within this are symbols valued primarily for the ordering of conceptual experience, i.e., for providing cultural 'orientations', and those valued primarily for the ordering of action, i.e., for providing cultural 'strategies'.[135]

Ricoeur also talks of 'root metaphors' that 'assemble subordinate images together' and serve as 'a junction between the symbolic level with its slow evolution and the more volatile metaphorical level'.[136] He comes up with a slightly different categorisation:

> I suggest that we distinguish various levels of creativity of symbols [...]. At the lowest level we come upon sedimented symbolism: here we find various stereotyped and fragmented remains of symbols, symbols so commonplace and worn with use that they have nothing but a past. [...] At a second level we come upon the symbols that function in everyday life; these are the symbols that are useful and are actually utilized, that have a past and a present, and that in the clockwork of a given society serve as a token for the nexus of social pacts [...]. At a higher level come the prospective symbols; these are creations of meaning that take up the traditional symbols with their multiple significations and serve as the vehicles of new meanings. This creation of meaning reflects the living substrate of symbolism, a substrate that is not the result of social sedimentation.[137]

Europe symbols are presumably to be found on all these levels. When taken up and accepted by a community a metaphor tends to become first trivial and then a 'dead' metaphor, while true symbols 'plunge their roots into the durable constellations of life, feeling, and the universe', achieving an incredible stability that gives the impression that 'a symbol never dies, it is only transformed'.[138]

The psychoanalyst Alfred Lorenzer differentiates between symbols as conscious representations and clichés as non-symbolic structures.[139] When experiences are repressed, they become unconscious but still continue to affect people's lives and behaviour. In that process, representations also become desymbolised or excommunicated, and degenerate into clichés working like irrational stereotypes or prejudices to distort communication. There is a two-way dynamics at play here, in that the formation of symbols in a symbolic order crystallises them out of a circle of what Lorenzer calls 'protosymbols', that is, a halo of vague and only partly conscious images and representations that form a nourishing ground out of which symbolic representations develop.

Ricoeur likewise alludes to a cloud of not-yet-crystallised meanings that enrich the significance of a symbol or a work and support its potential for plural interpretations:

> The secondary meanings, as in the case of the horizon, which surrounds perceived objects, open the work to several readings. It

may even be said that these readings are ruled by the prescriptions of meaning belonging to the margins of potential meaning surrounding the semantic nucleus of the work.[140]

This may also be applicable to Europe symbols, where it may be expected that formally acknowledged official symbols have core meanings that are also surrounded by open sets of secondary meanings inviting long chains of interpretations. There is no way to step out of this signifying crosscurrent. Responding to any text or symbol with silence will not diminish the force of the meanings that surround it, nor is there any fixed point of reference that would once and for all dissolve all differences of interpretation. With Ricoeur, I thus agree that the only way to go against bad or ideologically problematic readings is instead to suggest other and better interpretations, contributing to the endless *conflict of interpretations* that is basically what human culture is about: 'It is because absolute knowledge is impossible that the conflict of interpretations is insurmountable and inescapable.'[141]

In one of his last texts, Ricoeur returns to the role of symbolic mediation and representation for constituting social bonds and modes of identity:

> This connection between representations and social practices is expressed through the role of symbolic mediation these representations exercise when there is something specific at stake with regard to the social practices, namely, instituting the social bond and the modes of identity attached to it. Representations are not therefore abstract ideas floating in some autonomous space, but, as said, symbolic mediations contributing to the instituting of the social bond. What they symbolize is identities that confer a particular configuration on those social bonds as they are formed.[142]

This also reminds us that symbols may be increasingly important in times of historical change that challenges customary social bonds. This conclusion is drawn by Anthony P. Cohen as well: 'We have found that as the structural bases of the boundary become undermined or weakened as a consequence of social change, so people resort increasingly to symbolic behaviour to reconstitute the boundary.'[143] He believes that 'the diminution of the geographical bases of community boundaries has led to their renewed assertion in symbolic terms'.[144] This is certainly applicable to the current European situation, in face of the current transitions mentioned in the introduction.

Approaching European symbols

Analysing the 'values peculiar to a nation', Paul Ricoeur asks: 'What constitutes the creative nucleus of a civilization?' In many ways, this quest may be translated to the transnational level as well. Ricoeur concludes that they need to be sought out 'on several different levels', as a 'multiplicity of successive layers'.[145] Customs and traditions do not constitute this creative nucleus, as they represent inertia and reproduction.

> At a less superficial level, these values are manifested by means of traditional institutions, but these institutions are themselves only a reflection of the state of thought, will, and feeling of a human group at a certain point in history. The institutions are always abstract signs which need to be deciphered. It seems to me that if one wishes to attain the cultural nucleus, one has to cut through to that layer of images and symbols which make up the basic ideals of a nation. [...] Images and symbols constitute what might be called the awakened dream of a historical group. It is in this sense that I speak of the ethico-mythical nucleus which constitutes the cultural resources of a nation.[146]

There are thus plenty of good reasons to take European symbols seriously. By way of summarising what has been said so far, symbols are thus tools used in the fields where identities are cultivated through signifying processes of identification. But these fields are at the same time also battlefields where actors forge symbolic weapons to challenge others and promote their own interests. A first approximation is that a symbol is a *sign*, something that points towards or stands for something else, by way of its meaning. A second specification is that a symbol is a particular type of sign with a *conventional* rather than natural relation between the mark and its meaning; a conventional representation of something absent, making it virtually present, 're-presenting' it by signifying practices that forge interpretive chains of association linked to that which is signified. A third and more precise approximation is that a symbol is a particularly complex conventional sign that is charged with *multiple meanings*, notoriously polysemic and open to plural readings. Fourthly, the symbols discussed here are identity markers or *identifiers* that serve as emblems of a community or group. Collective identities can only be constructed and understood through mediation, that is, via a detour through texts, that is, through symbols in an even more qualified sense than those mentioned so far. Fifth and finally, among these emphatic symbols one may discern some that are more crucial than others in a given society: *key symbols* which are used to somehow embody a condensation of shared core values of Europe, for instance. A Europe symbol in this most strict sense would refer to a generally honoured condensed expression in any symbolic mode or genre of what is understood as characteristic of Europe and what it may mean to be European.

The Europe symbols to be studied here mostly move between the last two levels mentioned above, that is, the fourth and fifth approximation of the symbol concept (symbols$_4$ and symbols$_5$). The EU institutions strive to establish official symbols that will serve as key symbols for European citizens, while some other symbols discussed for comparisons are also in various ways emblems for some European community or organisation but do not possess that wide legitimacy that would make them true key symbols.

Contemporary Europe symbols are artefactual, textual, visual, aural or gestural compounds that serve as crystallisers of meaning around Europeanness; they are the polysemically charged nodal points in discourses and practices where Europe is constructed and interpreted. They are in a sense 'opaque', carrying contested and contradictory meanings, and deserve to be taken seriously by interdisciplinary cultural research that focuses on symbolic dimensions that otherwise often tend to be neglected in social science work on European identity formation. At the same time, such symbols should always be contextualised in relation to communicative practices and social contexts. Europe and Europeanness are contradictory, contested and dynamic concepts, involving issues of power and politics. There could never be one single identity for Europe, but always multiple and contested identities, developing in overlapping interpretive communities by means of interlacing communicative networks, underpinned by a growing range of digital technologies. Official efforts to consciously and intentionally define Europeanness from the top down intersect with bottom-up signifying practices of multifarious kinds. Also, Europe is internally divided between north and south, east and west, new and old nations and regions, making it essential to acknowledge the heterogeneous patterns of identification in play. For example, Europe may be depicted as male or female, old or youthful, globally strong or weak, linked to critical enlightenment or hyper-bureaucracy. Symbols across the different areas of cultural activity may refer to religious myths and rituals, historical events, political and economic practices and institutions, science and technology and the arts. There may be traces of Christian heritage, colonial history, Enlightenment ideas of progress, experiences of war, or reference to old and new transnational connections. These various representations have implications for people's understandings and experiences of being European.

3

Symbols of a Union

More than half of Europe's citizens are said to identify themselves as Europeans, and younger citizens increasingly so, alongside their sense of national belonging.[147] With a growing set of shared institutions, Europe is an increasingly relevant concept. Still, identification of and with shared European meanings seems to remain comparably weak, in the absence of effective cross-European public spheres, spaces of communication and cultural networks that allow for both diversity and commonality. The success of projects of economic–political integration depends on their being acknowledged as legitimate by an emergent wider European public with symbolic resources for signifying what Europe and Europeanness means. Studies indicate that the use of symbols may serve to strengthen a sense of civic and cultural European identity.[148] Cris Shore has described the cultural politics of European integration in the following terms:

> The role that symbols play in the articulation and formation of patterns of consciousness and identity is crucial to understanding how Europe is being constructed as a political community. Most of the fundamental categories and concepts pertaining to European integration, like those which gave flesh and form to the idea of nationhood, are represented through symbols. It is only through symbols that the meanings and 'reality' of ideas such as 'state', 'nation', 'citizenship' and 'Europe' itself can be rendered tangible and comprehensible. There is still a common tendency in much of the thinking and writing on European integration to dismiss symbols as 'cosmetic' and to argue that they are of secondary importance—or worse, simply window-dressing—in contrast to the eradication of those 'real' barriers to integration which involve legal and economic restrictions on the free movement of capital, goods and labour. Anthropologists would argue that it is a

mistake to underestimate the importance of symbols and the role they play in mobilising sentiment and public opinion. Indeed, symbols do much more than this.[149]

Shore goes on to argue that 'political reality is itself symbolically constructed': 'It is through symbols that people come to know about the structures that unite and divide them. Symbols do not simply represent political reality; they actively create it.'[150] Even though established symbols mostly play a marginal role in political as well as everyday life, they form a network of orienting and motivating meanings that guide this political and social practice. In the case of Europe, the expressions of such a collective identity in narratives, rituals and symbols have been found too few and too abstract to sufficiently underpin citizens' shared interests.[151] Michael Heffernan concludes that 'the EU has still not developed beyond a relatively narrow economic agenda and has also singularly failed to capture the imagination of the European peoples'. While every European nation has a plethora of symbols 'which mark out the cultural landscape of nationhood', there is as yet 'no such symbolic landscape for Europe as a whole'.[152] This is what the EU symbols were conceived to change. Have they succeeded, and, more importantly, what kind of identity do they together construct for Europe?

The 2004 draft Treaty establishing a Constitution for Europe referred to Europe as 'a continent that has brought forth civilisation', with inhabitants 'arriving in successive waves from earliest times', who 'have gradually developed the values underlying humanism: equality of persons, freedom, respect for reason'.[153] It drew inspiration from

> the cultural, religious and humanist inheritance of Europe, the values of which, still present in its heritage, have embedded within the life of society the central role of the human person and his or her inviolable and inalienable rights, and respect for law.

It was committed to a belief

> that reunited Europe intends to continue along the path of civilisation, progress and prosperity, for the good of all its inhabitants, including the weakest and most deprived; that it wishes to remain a continent open to culture, learning and social progress; and that it wishes to deepen the democratic and transparent nature of its public life, and to strive for peace, justice and solidarity throughout the world.

And it expressed a conviction that 'while remaining proud of their own national identities and history, the peoples of Europe are determined to transcend their ancient divisions and, united ever more closely, to forge a common destiny'. Thus 'united in its diversity', Europe was said to offer 'the best chance of pursuing, with due regard for the rights of each individual and in awareness of their responsibilities towards future generations and the Earth, the great venture which makes of it a special area of human hope'. With this background, the constitution founded the EU, 'reflecting the will of the citizens and States of Europe to build a common future' and based on 'the values of respect for human dignity, liberty, democracy, equality, the rule of law and respect for human rights' in a shared 'society of pluralism, tolerance, justice, solidarity and non-discrimination', with the main aim to 'promote peace, its values and the well-being of its peoples'. It offers its citizens 'an area of freedom, security and justice without internal frontiers, and a single market where competition is free and undistorted', while promising to 'respect its rich cultural and linguistic diversity', and ensuring that 'Europe's cultural heritage is safeguarded and enhanced'. The draft constitution explicitly specified five 'symbols of the Union':

> The flag of the Union shall be a circle of twelve golden stars on a blue background.
> The anthem of the Union shall be based on the Ode to Joy from the Ninth Symphony by Ludwig van Beethoven.
> The motto of the Union shall be: United in diversity.
> The currency of the Union shall be the euro.
> 9 May shall be celebrated throughout the Union as Europe day.[154]

These symbols were later deleted from the final version of the constitution, but are still widely used all over Europe, and have an official status after in several steps having been accepted both by the Council of Europe and by the EU, as will be specified below. Though the above was cited from a draft, similar formulations appear in lots of official documents, expressing a typical way of politically defining Europe's destiny.

Five symbolic keys to Europe, thus a flag, an anthem, a motto, a currency and a day. Not a very dense web of meanings to identify the EU project, but at least a start. They jointly identify the political, economic and cultural entity of Europe from the EU's top-level perspective. They are integrated in a standard stock of national symbols, and combine to work on several levels: one visual, one aural, one verbal, one economic and one temporal. While the flag, anthem, day and motto have a purely symbolic or discursive use, money has a double function as both a symbolic and a material tool of integration.[155]

Before scrutinising each of these symbols in greater detail, it may be useful to first briefly overview their immediate context in terms of the history of Europe and European identity from antiquity to the establishment and growth of the EU.[156]

The emergence of Europe

Europe is the second smallest of the continents, its 10,180,000 km^2 comprising only one-fifth of the Eurasian landmass and 6.8 per cent of all land on earth. Only Australia is slightly smaller, and Europe's area is roughly only half of that of either South or North America, and a third of Africa's. However, its population of 731 million (in 2009), corresponding to 11 per cent of the global population, is the third biggest (after Asia 60 per cent and Africa 14 per cent), making its population density the second largest, only slightly lower than that of Asia (70 and 87 people per km^2, respectively).

Europe has no strict borders to the east, and its southern boundary is also permeable. There were always numerous transitional links to the Asian landmass, while the Mediterranean was more of a communication network than a dividing moat, especially at a time when seas were easier to cross than most land areas. There are therefore an unlimited number of ways to visually map its geopolitical terrain, depending on from which perspective the mapping is done and which criteria it applies (Figure 3.1, 3.2, 3.3 and 3.4). There is currently a continuing expansion of the EU and other European organisations to the east but also to the south. Take for instance the *Eurovision Song Contest* (ESC), which currently includes Cyprus, Turkey, Russia, Georgia, Armenia and Azerbaijan, all of which often used to fall outside traditional maps of the continent.

Today, Europe consists of more than 40 independent nations, states or countries. These three terms have different but overlapping meanings. The *Concise Oxford Dictionary* defines a 'nation' as 'a large body of people united by common descent, culture, or language, inhabiting a particular state or territory'. American Indians or Nordic Sami people may thus form 'nations' within or overlapping the borders of a particular state, but still the most common usage of the term, for instance in forms like 'national', tends to identify 'nation' with the total population of a specific state. A 'state' is in the corresponding sense of the word defined as 'a nation or territory considered as an organized political community under one government', but may for instance also denote 'the civil government of a country'. A 'country' is 'a nation with its own government, occupying a territory', though this less strictly defined term may sometimes also be used for certain natural landscapes or for regional communities within nations. While the three concepts often cover roughly the same entities, at least within Europe, the composite term 'nation state', denoting 'a sovereign state of which most of the citizens or subjects also share factors such as language or common descent', indicates some of the correspondences, complexities and contradictions inherent in these terms, which will not be further interrogated here.[157]

The many countries or nation states of Europe use a great number of different languages, few of them being national language for more than one, and several countries subdivided into regions with populations who can hardly understand each others' mother tongues. This internal diversity has its counterpart in other parts of culture as well, where customs, tastes and traditions differ considerably across the continent. Unifying factors include the use of English language as a lingua franca, similar to how Latin functioned for parts of the European population in the Middle Ages, but then, this is almost a global rather than just a European glue, and it is surprisingly hard to pin down other truly common *and* exclusive denominators.

Contemporary efforts to establish a shared identity for Europeans tend to look back through history in order to establish the defining specificities of social life on this continent, as developed through a series of key historical moments with a unifying impact. Through such linking mechanisms, a mutually shared horizon of experience has germinated, with the Roman Empire, Christianity, the Renaissance, the Enlightenment, colonialism and industrial capitalism as bridging factors. Still, one cannot talk of any continuous existence of the concept of Europe, since even an embryonic European identity has only been a lived and acknowledged experience for some people in some regions during some time periods.[158]

Historically, Europe was distinct from the older advanced cultures formed around the Nile, Eufrat, Tigris and Ganges, in that its population was more mobile and thus had closer contacts with others across greater areas. This mobility was enhanced by climate and geography, as the many seas, lakes and rivers offered useful ways to connect by boat. This is one of the motors behind European powers' globally competitive and expansive character, laying the foundation for spreading universalising Enlightenment values as well as a colonial world market. The current diversity and communicative openness of Europe thus has a long genealogy. Heffernan talks of Europe as emerging from an 'intellectual palimpsest of competing geopolitical visions; a layering of differing meanings'.[159]

Little is known of cross-continental communications during the earliest time, except that the then sparsely populated area was scarcely accessible until the end of the last ice age some 12,000 years ago. There is no evidence of any strong prehistoric networks comprising larger parts of the area, and it is even less probable that there may have existed any self-understanding of its inhabitants as sharing any form of proto-European identity. The Phoenician culture and sea power that flourished from around 1200 to 800 BC is sometimes mentioned as an early impetus, with its invention of the alphabet and its trading links all across the Mediterranean. But it is three other fundamental pillars of early European civilisation that are mostly emphasised: ancient Greek culture, the Roman Empire and Christianity hold a privileged place in the currently dominant conceptions of its history and self-identity.

Classical Greek culture with its peak in the fifth century BC is considered the cradle of European democracy, culture, arts, philosophy and science. Roman culture during an equally long period around the first century AD contributed key elements of law and technology, but also an empire stretching over a great part of south and west Europe, thus for the first time binding considerable land areas together under a centralised rule. Christianity not only added the religion that still dominates the continent and today has a dominant worldwide presence (followed in size by Islam, Hinduism and Buddhism), but also built an effective network of churches, monasteries and other institutionalised practices that after the fall of Roman Empire continued to keep a growing part of the continent interconnected into and through mediaeval times. Though internally increasingly divided, first along the east/west axis (Orthodox/Catholic) and then between north and south (with the advent of Protestantism), Christianity continued to have a major unifying impact, for instance on the growth of schools and higher education, and with Latin used as the first transcontinental language.

The Church often worked hand in hand with secular state rulers, already from the last part of the Roman times, with the eighth century AD Carolingian Empire as a prime example. Charlemagne's *Imperium Christianum* from 800 AD was soon again subdivided, but the Holy Roman Empire survived at least nominally into the early nineteenth century. Charlemagne was sometimes referred to as 'Pater Europae', which is why the Carolingian time is often seen as a key moment when Europe started to exist as an at least imagined political community.[160] While there was still in effect little political unity across Europe in this period, the impressive transcontinental dissemination from the end of the Middle Age of artistic and intellectual movements such as the Renaissance, Baroque, Classicism, Enlightenment and Romanticism indicated the density of communicative networks that increasingly served to integrate European culture.

Heffernan agrees with most historians when stating that Europe did not really become a valid geopolitical concept until the modern era:

> The notion of Europe, or of any land continent, had little significance in classical or Medieval geography. [...] A concern with global continental divisions emerged only in the post-Roman, Christian era, particularly from the seventh century ad when any residual sense of Mediterranean unity was shattered by the first great wave of Muslim expansion.[161]

For centuries thereafter Europe remained subsumed under the idea of Christendom, and 'a sense of common "Europeanness" was still relatively weak', as new divisions split the continent vertically (Catholic/Orthodox) and horizontally (from Christian/Pagan to Catholic/Protestant).[162] Mediaeval Europe's feudal geopolitics still had a 'weakly developed sense of territoriality' and 'spatial fluidity' that made the identity of the continent a non-issue. It was in the early modern period that ideas of Europe started to emerge, with roots in the earlier Mediaeval ideas of Christendom, and the seventeenth century saw a new "'territorialisation" of power' and a "'fixing" of national spaces on the European map', says Heffernan.[163] The following centuries were filled with efforts to balance different local, regional and increasingly also national powers against each others, oscillating between violent wars and peace treaties from Westphalia (1648) to Vienna (1815) and onwards.

The bourgeois revolutions in the late eighteenth and early nineteenth centuries, together with the Napoleonic wars resulting in the 1815 Vienna Congress, gave new force to political visions of a less divided Europe, both among radicals and conservatives. A counteracting factor was the new system of competing nation states, whose strengthening and internal integration temporarily prevented further European cohesion, except through precarious treaties between independent national governments. European powers were simultaneously increasingly expansive in their worldwide quest for wealth and control, with exploration, mission, conquest and slavery as tools. Colonialism and imperialism accumulated resources in Europe while enslaving other peoples. By a kind of Hegelian master–slave dialectics, this brought change to the world and gave rise to independence movements that in the twentieth century further spread political, social and cultural resources and models of European origin. These processes took place through a close interaction between Europe and other continents, so that what may appear as a linear dissemination was actually a complex circulation and mediation of ideas and institutions in shifting paths and networks across the globe. Modern philosophy, science, technology, industry, parliamentary democracy, human rights and values are today recognised as global rather than European, as they all originated through dialogues between continents and are today relevant in most world regions, while their positively charged values are on the other hand far from secured in every European region.

Up until the mid-twentieth century, Europe seemed stuck in a rather strict division of fiercely competing nation states, using shifting alliances to combat each other rather than aim at any long-term association.[164] When most of the rest of the world had been cut up in colonial territories, the competitive thrust led to a series of disastrous wars, with immense loss of human lives and infrastructures, including the Franco-Prussian war of 1870–1 (almost 200,000 killed), World War I 1914–18 (over 15 million dead) and World War II 1939–45 (over 70 million killed). The terrifying escalation of unequalled human-made catastrophes fed renewed efforts of peace, disarmament, reconciliation and cooperation between the peoples of Europe.

The period between the two World Wars, 1918–39, saw the growth of a series of initiatives and movements nourishing new visions of a united Europe, both in right- and left-wing versions.[165] The Paneuropean Union founded in 1923 belonged to the former, looking nostalgically back to the imagined Christian unity of Middle Ages. In the socialist camp, the French Minister Aristide Briand in 1930 proposed to the League of Nations the organisation of a European federal union. In 1948, the Vatican Pope, wishing to defend western Christianity against Communism and restore the spirit of the Middle Ages, officially supported European federalism. This vision of a 'Vatican Europe' was heralded by the 1947 elevation of St Benedict to 'Patron Saint of all Europe'. This was not favourably received by socialists and social democrats, but soon the two camps converged in a more inclusive version of the unification programme.

The task of uniting Europe presented a difficult dialectic, as great wars tended to start with some large powers wanting control over the whole of Europe, and clashing with others with competing ambitions. Hitler's dream of the Third Reich was in an awkward way parallel to more peaceful visions of a united Europe. The form and method of unification was essential. In order to avoid new disasters, unification must respect the will of citizens in all countries, that is, be based on consensus and democratic decisions, where nation states were not erased but could retain a high degree of autonomy within the newly created totality. This task was urgent after the end of World War II, when Europe was in ruins, having been at once the cause, stake, perpetrator and victim of this global disaster. Time was ripe to start building forms of cooperation that would not once again cause a similar wave of destruction. Hence, the idea of a united Europe moved to the top of the agenda.

At least this is the official version: a favourite founding myth of the EU, repeated again and again in documents and public history. There certainly were (and still are) also several other motives and interests behind the unification process and the post-war wish for peace. Equally influential demands for economic welfare and imperialist power expansion are forgotten by the legitimating ideology of the EU as an idealistic peace project aiming for the happiness of everyone. On the other hand, this ideology is not just a false cover up for hidden real and less altruistic ambitions. The great twentieth-century European wars were no doubt enormous traumas, and there was a true and deeply felt need for concerted efforts to heal the wounds, among the elites as well as the masses, who experienced the devastating weight of the mass destruction Europe was capable of, and the need to find other ways to deal with mutual differences.

The European unification project had to avoid being inscribed into any more specific agenda, be it conservative, liberal or socialist, and instead forge a long-term alliance between a wide range of interest groups to the right as well as to the left. It had to be able to accommodate many different aspects without repelling any significant interest groups. Heffernan describes how the new European institutions built around the Council of Europe had to be compatible both with the US Atlantic system of the Cold War and with the interests of the national governments.[166] This made it impossible to copy US federalism, and necessary to respect the existing subdivision into autonomous nation states, so that the intergovernmentalist strategy continued to be hegemonic, with federalists functioning as idealist activists propelling integration forward but never being allowed to take over.

One keystone came to be the 'principle of subsidiarity' that guaranteed decisions being made on a lower, local or national level whenever there was no obvious advantage for federal institutions to take charge. A balance had to be struck between maximum and minimum ambitions regarding which areas to regulate jointly, for instance selecting if cooperation should include economic, political, military, social or cultural issues, or leave some of these outside, at least temporarily. As history came to show, it was also important to develop the federal resources in a reasonable order, so that each step could prepare for the next and breed a legitimate trust in the whole project among citizens and elites of all regions.

The principle of subsidiarity was related to another principle, which was only gradually established through experiences of the failures of unification proposals. It was never formalised or officially named, but could be called a 'principle of diversity'. Previous efforts often had an element of equalisation, of striving to make Europe one, with strong similarities between its constituents. Take the presumably universalising French ideals spread by the Napoleonic wars, the Germanic expansionism of the Third Reich, or the Christian resurrection envisioned by 'Vatican Europe'. In all cases, such homogenising efforts provoked hostile resistance. The post-World War II unifiers had learned the lesson; a more successful strategy was to avoid moving too fast towards sociocultural homogeneity. Instead, if Europe was to be united in a political and economic sense, it was pivotal that this unity had to respect the radical differences between its regions in other dimensions. Those unifying measures that did succeed offered specific pragmatic tools for enhancing welfare, communication and mobility across the continent, while not forcing everyone to become similar. Every time the elements of making Europe internally more homogenous sneaked in, there grew an immediate risk of failure. Unification had to start on a formal meta-level, unifying instruments for mutual exchange rather than the actual contents of public provisions in each country.

However, respecting subsidiarity and diversity were no easy principles, but a matter of precarious balance. Without any delegation of power whatsoever from regions and nation states to the federal level, nothing would ever change; and without at least some minimal kind of common social and cultural ground, the economic and political measures would encounter a deficit of legitimacy among European citizens. This was how European identity became a key issue.

There were several ups and downs in the unifying process, of which only some few milestones will be mentioned here. In a Zurich speech in 1946, Britain's former Prime Minister Winston Churchill spoke in favour of 'a kind of United States of Europe', navigating a third way between the United States and the Union of Soviet Socialist Republics (USSR). From 1946 onwards, a series of movements and organisations were formed in support of a European federation, having varying roles in the formation process. The Union of European Federalists (UEF, founded 1946) coordinated some 50 national federalist movements, with almost a total of 100,000 members, but was split in different fractions.

Against the Socialist Movement for the United States of Europe (MSEUE, founded 1946) stood the Christian Democratic Nouvelles Équipes Internationales (New International Teams, NEI, 1947; renamed European Union of Christian Democrats, EUCD, 1965), both marked by the emerging Cold War agenda. The European League for Economic Cooperation (ELEC, 1946) was a pressure group of industrialists and financiers bridging the economic, political and administrative elites. A series of federalist congresses were held in the late 1940s, including the Hague Congress in May 1948, which led to the formation of the influential European Movement (EM) where many of the other associations were brought together. The Brussels Political Congress in February 1949 proposed a European Charter of Human Rights and a European Court, while the December 1949 European Conference on Culture in Lausanne resulted in the establishment in 1950 of the College of Europe in Bruges and the European Centre for Culture in Geneva.

A particularly important step was the establishment of the Council of Europe, which came into existence on 5 May 1949 with ten founding countries. All European countries that undertake to 'respect human rights and the rule of law' are now welcome to join, and the Council of Europe today covers most of the continent. It functions as a highly active forum for dialogue and cooperation—a motor for strengthening European identity and furthering other and more substantial forms of unification.[167]

Economic cooperation was from the beginning a crucial task in particular, as much of Europe's material and industrial infrastructure was in great need of reconstruction after the war. EU's official founding myth places the Schuman Declaration, presented by the French Foreign Minister Robert Schuman in Paris on 9 May 1950, at the origin of this process. This was a carefully prepared and staged event, intended to initiate a series of key moves to establish the first keystones of an effective European cooperation. The peace question was explicitly in focus, promoting reconciliation between France and Germany—the two big powers that had repeatedly clashed so violently through the last hundred years. European peace presupposed a new friendship between those peoples, and it was important to avoid the fate of the post-World War I humiliation of the loser, Germany, which had fuelled the dissatisfaction that had only led to a new and multiply worse disaster. The significant idea was to build cooperation from coordinating precisely those industries that had fuelled the previous wars: coal and steel. This would create a crucial economic and material basis for European welfare, but also had a symbolic value in that it linked to mythical, almost biblical images of melting cannons to forge ploughshares, transforming destructive forces into nourishing sources of mutual solidarity and welfare.

> World peace cannot be safeguarded without the making of creative efforts proportionate to the dangers which threaten it. The contribution which an organized and living Europe can bring to civilization is indispensable to the maintenance of peaceful relations. [...]

Europe will not be made all at once, or according to a single plan. It will be built through concrete achievements which first create a de facto solidarity. The rassemblement of the nations of Europe requires the elimination of the age-old opposition of France and Germany.[168]

Schuman and the French Government proposed to 'place Franco-German production of coal and steel as a whole under a common higher authority, within the framework of an organisation open to the participation of the other countries of Europe':

The pooling of coal and steel production should immediately provide for the setting up of common foundations for economic development as a first step in the federation of Europe, and will change the destinies of those regions which have long been devoted to the manufacture of munitions of war, of which they have been the most constant victims.

The solidarity in production thus established will make it plain that any war between France and Germany becomes not merely unthinkable, but materially impossible. The setting-up of this powerful productive unit, open to all countries willing to take part and bound ultimately to provide all the member countries with the basic elements of industrial production on the same terms, will lay a true foundation for their economic unification. This production will be offered to the world as a whole without distinction or exception, with the aim of contributing to raising living standards and to promoting peaceful achievements. Europe, with new means at her disposal, will be able to pursue the realisation of one of her essential tasks: the development of the African Continent.

In this way there will be realised simply and speedily that fusion of interests which is indispensable to the establishment of a common economic system; it may be the leaven from which may grow a wider and deeper community between countries long opposed to one another by sanguinary divisions. By pooling basic production and by instituting a new higher authority, whose decisions will bind France, Germany, and other member countries, this proposal will lead to the realisation of the first concrete foundation of a European federation indispensable to the preservation of peace.

On this basis, Schuman suggested the creation of a 'common higher authority' to secure 'the modernization of production', a fair and equal supply of coal and steel 'to the French and German markets, as well as to the markets of other member countries', enhanced 'exports to other countries', and 'the equalization and improvement of the living conditions of workers in these industries'. Modernisation of production, economic balance between the European powers, a free trade market and a perspective towards secure welfare for European citizens—this was the prescription to cure the convalescent and still suffering continent.

It soon proved successful, as six core West European countries (Belgium, France, Germany, Italy, Luxembourg and the Netherlands) signed the Treaty constituting the Coal and Steel Community (ECSC) on 18 April 1951.[169] This treaty repeated the key elements of the Schuman Declaration, arguing for instance that 'world peace may be safeguarded only by creative efforts equal to the dangers which menace it'; that 'the contribution which an organized and vital Europe can bring to civilization is indispensable to the maintenance of peaceful relations'; that 'Europe can be built only by concrete actions which create a real solidarity and by the establishment of common bases for economic development', and so forth. Its double goal was 'the expansion of their basic production in raising the standard of living and in furthering the works of peace'. The ECSC was meant 'to substitute for historic rivalries a fusion of their essential interests; to establish, by creating an economic community, the foundation of a broad and independent community among peoples long divided by bloody conflicts; and to lay the bases of institutions capable of giving direction to their future common destiny'.

> The mission of the European Coal and Steel Community is to contribute to economic expansion, the development of employment and the improvement of the standard of living in the participating countries through the institution, in harmony with the general economy of the member States, of a common market [...].

Safeguarding 'the most rational distribution of production at the highest possible level of productivity', the 'continuity of employment' and economic stability were the key goals. The tools were to create a common market with equal access for all countries to coal and steel resources, furthering industrial modernisation and international trade. Again, 'the improvement of the living and working conditions of the labor force' was also mentioned.

A set of practical steps were selected and motivated to ensure acceptance and legitimacy for the Treaty. Explicitly ideological formulations were strictly limited to the almost universal basics of securing world peace with general and equal welfare. The provisions made concentrated on supporting rational modernisation and building a basis for stability and shared fortune. No blame was put on anyone, and no external or internal enemies were even indirectly identified, thus avoiding the trap of the Christian federalists who could never gain popular backing for any proposals for defending Europe against the Communist East or resurrecting a Catholic past.

By including provisions for improving workers' conditions, the Treaty could also be accepted by the Socialist Left.

In the international dimension, it is first characteristic that both these documents use American rather than British English, mirroring the crucial US support for the reconstruction of Europe, as codified in the Marshall Plan (1947). Second, it is interesting that Schuman, but not the Treaty, mentioned that Europe needs her regained strength in order to realise 'one of her essential tasks: the development of the African Continent'. This pointed towards the links of the modern European project to colonialism and decolonisation. This aspect is today rarely touched upon in official documents and histories, since it hints at a less dignified motor behind unification than the wish to secure peace and general welfare. Decolonisation was a difficult and often violent process where both symbolic and material interests clashed. All the main colonial powers were European, which meant that Europe could not be unified without in some way solving the colonial problem. Talking of 'the development of the African Continent' as one of Europe's 'essential tasks' could be read as a humanitarian care for an impoverished neighbour, but on the other hand also as an echo of the old imperial idea of the Third World as the 'White Man's Burden' (the infamous title of a highly Eurocentric poem by Rudyard Kipling, 1899). In such perspective, the talk of development, modernisation and civilisation was also a pretext for prolonged dependence, dominance and exploitation.

A series of independence wars, the most violent ones in Algeria, made grand-scale European colonial rule impossible, though its effects will last for long. The 1957 Treaty establishing the European Economic Community (EEC) had a Protocol on its 'relation to Algeria and overseas departments of the French Republic', stating a will to negotiate these problems in a peaceful spirit. Early maps of the community indicate that being formally a French overseas department, Algeria was part of the EEC. Its independence in 1962 brought an end to that, as with other former colonies, but up until today, the EU also contains a set of overseas territories that remain under French rule. Those with a good eyesight can discern them as microscopic dots in the margins of all EU maps, including the small ones on the euro coins.[170]

Some who worked for European unification surely had a hidden agenda to resurrect Europe's leading role in the world and also more specifically to save what could be saved of her decomposing colonial empires. This was particularly obvious in the case of France, but could also be seen among some of the other colonial powers such as Britain, Portugal, Belgium and the Netherlands. But these interests had to be balanced against the wish for stability and peace in the rest of Europe, and the independence wars showed that entertaining colonial rule had too great costs to be worthwhile in the long run. The European project was thus the outcome of a dynamic struggle between different camps, and cannot be reduced to either a prolongation of European imperialism or a pure peace effort.

Going back to the establishment of the Council of Europe (1949) and the ECSC (1950), the former became an important ideological force to push integration forward, while the second was an example of what could be achieved by economic cooperation. Together, the two initiated a series of steps towards a geographically as well as sectorially more comprehensive cooperation. Only the main traits of this process will be briefly summarised here. The EEC was funded by the Rome Treaty in 1957 by the six ECSC countries ('the inner six'), while the less far-reaching European Free Trade Association (EFTA) was funded by seven other countries of Western Europe in 1960 ('the outer seven': Austria, Denmark, Norway, Portugal, Sweden, Switzerland and the United Kingdom). Finland and Iceland also soon joined the EFTA, and from the 1970s onwards, the United Kingdom, Denmark, Ireland and Portugal moved from EFTA to the EEC. In the 1980s, mutual cooperation between the two organisations gradually deepened, until the EU was finally established by the Treaty of Maastricht 1993. Its original twelve member states were the 'inner six' plus Denmark, Greece, Ireland, Portugal, Spain and the United Kingdom. In just a couple of years, Austria, Finland and Sweden entered as well, and with the integration of the former Eastern Bloc after 1989, the number has grown to 27, plus further candidates eagerly waiting their turn.

This rough outline of European unification history has several deficits. First, it underplays the influence of the United States, which was simultaneously political, military, technological, economic, social and cultural. For instance, the military bloc of the North Atlantic Treaty Organization (NATO) was since its establishment in 1949 also an important factor for European development. In 1955, a proposal to install a European army, named the European Defence Community (EDC), failed, and instead a much weaker Western European Union (WEU) was formed to establish rudimentary military cooperation. Second, the description is seriously biased, with a western perspective, as there was a parallel unifying movement in Eastern Europe as well, though with more coercive means and controlled by the USSR. In January 1949, responding to the Marshall Plan, the USSR created a programme of economic cooperation between Soviet bloc countries, called the Council for Mutual Economic Assistance (CMEA or Comecon). NATO's military counterpart was the Warsaw Pact, signed in 1955, comprising Albania, Bulgaria, Czechoslovakia, Hungary, Poland, Romania and the USSR, with the German Democratic Republic entering one year later. Both Comecon and the Warsaw Pact disintegrated in 1991, and many of its states have subsequently become EU (and in several cases even NATO) members.

The impetus for European integration thus came from many directions. It had shifting motives in east and west, north and south, in political and economic terms. From the first germs of the idea soon after World War II, it took roughly half a century until the greater part of the continent had developed a reasonably firm common platform in the enlarged EU. The expansion has so far primarily been directed to the east, besides efforts to make singular remaining non-members like Norway or

Switzerland join too. This reflects the notoriously unstable geographic and political division between Europe and Asia, with no easy method to decide to which continent countries like Russia or Turkey belong. The other particularly contested border, to the south, has remained relatively constant. In 1987, Morocco's application for membership was rejected as it was not considered a European country. On the other hand, the remaining French and Spanish colonial tentacles in northern Africa and Latin America continue to blur the continent's geopolitical boundaries.

The EEC aimed to create a common market and draw up common policies, notably in agriculture and transports, securing the free movement of goods, services, people and money (or capital). These 'four freedoms' remained a focal concern of the EU, and will prove important for how the European symbols were designed. The EU was constructed around three 'pillars' or areas of responsibility: (a) the primarily economic European community policy; (b) a common foreign and security policy; and (c) cooperation on police and judicial matters. The former was most important for supranational integration, while the other two were in practice more intergovernmental. The goal of the EU was 'an ever closer union among the peoples of Europe'—a vague expression used already in 1949 in the Statute of the intergovernmental Council of Europe. The United Kingdom managed to avoid any explicit references to a 'federal purpose', though several Treaty goals had such overtones: single currency, citizenship, common foreign and security policy. While talking of abolishing internal frontiers, the Treaty also stated that the 'Union shall respect the national identities of its Member States'. The principle of subsidiarity prevented the community from intervening when the objectives of the union could as well be attained by a member state acting on its own. Democratic reform gave more power to the directly elected European Parliament. A European passport had been introduced already in 1985, and the 1993 Treaty of Maastricht established European citizenship not to replace national citizenship but to supplement it by granting the right to vote and to stand as a candidate in European and municipal elections in the member state in which a citizen resides (not only in the country of origin), the right to petition the European Parliament and to submit a complaint to the Ombudsman, etc. These European citizenship rights aimed at heightening the public awareness of European identity and thus strengthening identification with the European unification project.[171]

The 1993 Treaty of Maastricht was not yet a full EU constitution, but just a preamble of a more complete and binding regulative document. Then followed the complicated integration of East Europe into the EU, and then after the millennium shift the efforts intensified to construct a constitution for Europe that would make the union both efficient and more democratic in its functioning. This has so far turned out to be difficult, and the result remains an open question. In 2004, the 25 EU countries signed a Treaty establishing a European Constitution, designed to rationalise decision-making and management in the radically expanded union. However, referendums in France and the Netherlands rejected the new Constitution, forcing a temporary halt in the process. Intense negotiations resulted in a revised version formulated in the 2007 Treaty of Lisbon, which was finally ratified by all member states in 2009.

Introducing the EU symbols

The issue of a shared European identity has proven to be one of the key obstacles to success. Social and cultural issues were often placed on a national rather than supranational level, by a combination of the subsidiarity and the diversity principles. There were for instance only feeble efforts to create joint European policies concerning the arts and the cultural industries. Still, cultural aspects were never far away. There were symbolic aspects already in the grounding of a community in precisely the coal and steel industries. The establishment in 1950 of a College of Europe and a European Centre for Culture, resulting from the 1949 European Conference on Culture, was another example, and since the Eurobarometer published its first data in 1974, it has had multiple functions, enabling practical economic coordination but also offering a tangible representation of Europe as a unity, thus with a cultural function as well. On many levels there was thus a cultural and symbolic dimension present even where decisions on the surface just talked about trade statistics or governing bodies. The explicit regulation of identifying symbols of Europe was just the tip of an iceberg, but as such, it draws attention to a wider set of cultural facets, with far-reaching roots and implications.

Federalist movements had flags expressing in condensed form how they conceived the meaning of Europe. For instance, the Paneuropean Union had since 1923 used a golden sun on a blue background with a red cross in the middle of the sun, while the European Movement, founded in 1947, used a big green 'E' on white background.[172] Even though the ECSC and the EEC emphasised economic and legal aspects, there were always also cultural or symbolic elements involved. Selecting names and logotypes for associations is one such cultural act that is far from innocent, since such symbols propose an interpretation of Europe for Europeans to identify with.

Inheriting some of its spirit from the agenda of the federalist movements, the Council of Europe served as a testing ground for new ideas and was from the start particularly interested in matters concerning European identity and citizenship rights, helping to prepare the ground for effective measures later taken by other bodies on a political, economic and military level. The Council of Europe has therefore been the main motor behind the formalisation of the current symbols of Europe, which will in turn be presented and analysed in the following chapters.

In 1951, the Secretariat General of the Council of Europe produced a memorandum on the European flag, opening with the characteristic words: 'There are no ideals, however exalted in nature, which can afford to do without a symbol.' In 1955, the Committee of Ministers adopted a blue flag with a circle of stars, and in 1972 an anthem followed. In the 1970s and 1980s, there was much talk of widening the 'Traders' Europe' of the EEC common market into something considerably more far-reaching and complex: a 'People's Europe' for which the issue of a European identity was essential. At a 1973 Copenhagen Summit, the then nine Foreign Ministers of the EEC published a 'Document on The European Identity', where they 'decided to define the European Identity' and clarify the EEC members' responsibilities in relation to other countries.

> The Nine wish to ensure that the cherished values of their legal, political and moral order are respected, and to preserve the rich variety of their national cultures. Sharing as they do the same attitudes to life, based on a determination to build a society which measures up to the needs of the individual, they are determined to defend the principles of representative democracy, of the rule of law, of social justice—which is the ultimate goal of economic progress—and of respect for human rights. All of these are fundamental elements of the European Identity.[173]

Several similar formulations returned in the 2004 draft Treaty establishing a Constitution for Europe. Speaking of 'the' European identity as a given and unproblematic unity was an idealisation with little support in European realities. The document emphasised Europe's political will to strengthen relations to the rest of the world as well as the value of diversity:

> The diversity of cultures within the framework of a common European civilization, the attachment to common values and principles, the increasing convergence of attitudes to life, the awareness of having specific interests in common and the determination to take part in the construction of a United Europe, all give the European Identity its originality and its own dynamism.[174]

Measures were taken to remove obstacles for mobility and improve life conditions for European citizens in everyday life. At the Fontainebleau European Council meeting on 25–26 June 1984, the idea of a 'People's Europe' was further specified: 'the Community should respond to the expectations of the people of Europe by adopting measures to strengthen and promote its identity and its image both for its citizens and for the rest of the world'. Among the specific measures suggested was to create 'symbols of the Community's existence, such as a flag and an anthem', but also 'European sports teams' and 'a European coinage'. A report to the European Council in Milan on 28–29 June 1985 by a Committee on a People's Europe, led by Pietro Adonnino, presented a much more detailed list of measures to enhance European integration in the cultural domain, including citizens rights; culture and communication (with a focus on television); information; youth, education and sport; volunteer work in the Third World; health, security and drugs; twinning of towns and cities; and 'strengthening of the Community's image and identity'. This last point is particularly relevant here. European stamps were mentioned as a possibility, but the two main symbols discussed were the flag and the anthem, to which later chapters will return.

In June 1985, the Milan European Council approved the adoption of the flag and the anthem as official emblems of the European communities, and also agreed to establish a Europe Day. A key moment was when the 2004 draft Treaty establishing a Constitution for Europe recognised the flag, motto, anthem, day and euro as being official in the EU. The Treaty only listed the symbols without any further ideological explication or provisions on how they were to be used.

On 12 January 2005, the European Parliament approved this Constitutional Treaty by an overwhelming majority of 500 votes in favour, 137 against and 40 abstentions. Communists, the European People's Party and the far right were against, though it was clearly more the rationalisation and strengthening of EU's institutions than the symbols that provoked resistance. The Czech Republic, Poland and the United Kingdom had a majority against the Treaty. However, all member states had to ratify the Treaty before it was valid. This process was scheduled so that the Constitution would have entered into force on 1 November 2006. As referendums in France and the Netherlands voted against it, the process was halted, resulting in a deep crisis through which the Constitution was revised in a prolonged negotiation process.

In articles I:1–2, the resulting 2007 Lisbon Constitutional Treaty states that 'inspiration from the cultural, religious and humanist inheritance of Europe' has made it possible to develop 'the universal values of the inviolable and inalienable rights of the human person, freedom, democracy, equality and the rule of law':

> The Union is founded on the values of respect for human dignity, freedom, democracy, equality, the rule of law and respect for human rights, including the rights of persons belonging to minorities. These values are common to the Member States in a society in which pluralism, non-discrimination, tolerance, justice, solidarity and equality between women and men prevail.[175]

'The Union's aim is to promote peace, its values and the well-being of its peoples', offering its citizens 'an area of freedom, security and justice without internal frontiers'. It is these kinds of values that the EU system wishes its symbols to express and anchor among citizens. Even though the symbols were never the main issue, the effort to constitute a shared cultural identity through official symbols was not favourably received. The revised version in the Treaty of Lisbon only mentions the euro as the official currency but not any of the other symbols. In spite of this, they continued to be used roughly as before, just like so many nations use flags and other insignia without any legal consolidation of them. After all, they had in turn been approved by both the Council of Europe and the EU. In 2007, sixteen member states also signed a declaration on the symbols, which was included at the end of the Treaty of Lisbon:

> Belgium, Bulgaria, Germany, Greece, Spain, Italy, Cyprus, Lithuania, Luxemburg, Hungary, Malta, Austria, Portugal, Romania, Slovenia and the Slovak Republic declare that the flag with a circle of twelve golden stars on a blue background, the anthem based on the 'Ode to Joy' from the Ninth Symphony by Ludwig van Beethoven, the motto 'United in diversity', the euro as the currency of the European Union and Europe Day on 9 May will for them continue as symbols to express the sense of community of the people in the European Union and their allegiance to it.[176]

Note some of the absences: it is not surprising that the Czech Republic, Denmark, Estonia, Finland, France, Ireland, Latvia, the Netherlands, Poland, Sweden and the United Kingdom did not sign up, since they have been hesitant about the new constitution and/or less enthusiastic about inventing European symbols. A working hypothesis that goes way beyond the scope of what can be shown here might be that scepticism towards symbols may be strongest in northern areas with a quasi-iconoclastic Protestant heritage and a high degree of secular individualisation, whereas icons and other symbols are more respected in Catholic and Orthodox regions.

In spite of these reservations, there are strong interest groups that favour these symbols. Also, the European Parliament has in the process repeatedly expressed a will to use the symbols more often, presenting the flag at all meetings and in all rooms, playing the anthem regularly, printing the motto on official documents and formally recognising Europe Day. 'Symbols are vital elements of any communication process', according to the EU Parliament, as they 'convey an emotional image of the underlying values of the organisations they represent'.[177]

On 9 October 2008, an overwhelming majority of European Parliament members (503 to 96 with 15 abstentions) voted for continuing to use the EU symbols.[178] Even though their legal status remains unclear in the EU, they are thus in practice accepted and used everywhere, and their importance is repeatedly stated in public EU documents. For instance, the *European Navigator* website has a large section on 'The Symbols of the European Union', which depicts the importance of these symbols:[179]

> The purpose of the political symbols of the State (flag, emblem, motto, anthem, currency, national public holiday) is obviously to provide an identity.
>
> They crystallise national identity by making it tangible; in other words, they codify the subjective nature of the nation. The nation is in practice an invisible concept and therefore has to be symbolised if it is to be seen and acclaimed if it is to be loved. It is precisely in this way that the symbol provides identity: it shows citizens what is theirs and encourages them to be loyal (*affectio societatis*) to the sign representing the nation. The use of symbols consequently has a unifying and federating power.
>
> When they sing the same anthem, honour the same flag, use the same currency or celebrate the same public holiday, citizens are all sharing a common sentiment. Every political symbol is therefore a tangible sign of identity which codifies the shared values which the symbol represents and which are generally detailed in a constitution.
>
> The purpose of political symbols is to provide an identity for the European Union as well as for its Member States. They are the external signs of that constitutional patriotism—to take up Habermas—through which European citizens, aware of their belonging, can be influenced to leave aside their differences and act in the common public good and, therefore, to perceive the European Union as their home or Heimat.
>
> Understood in this way, symbols may help to consolidate the fledgling European demos. They should undoubtedly not do so in opposition to the national demoi but as a synthesis of the specific and shared values of a highly integrated area such as the European Union. The Community methods and participative democracy launched by the Constitutional Treaty could help the European Union to emerge as a new post-national political system based precisely on shared values where the national interest coincides with the European interest. The political symbols such as the flag, the anthem, the motto, the currency and Europe Day may therefore help, by creating emotive images and rites, even subliminally, to make the European Union more legitimate in the eyes of its citizens and help them to identify with the plan for a common destiny. In other words, they help to construct a political

identity, where a set of values which identify us as belonging to the same community are felt to be binding. [...]

The role of the symbols in forging an awareness and an identity of the European Union as a political community is therefore crucial. It is in practice true that most of the basic categories and concepts relating to European integration and, in particular, those breathing life into the notion of belonging, are represented by symbols which make the very notion of citizenship tangible, real and comprehensive. [...]

The symbols therefore, far from playing a 'cosmetic' function, secondary in importance to the function of the four freedoms or of Community policies, express the deep-seated values of the European Union. They are also able to mobilise the sentiments of European public opinion. They do not just breathe life into the notion of belonging, but help actively to support it, thereby helping the fledgling European demos to put down roots.

Even fierce opponents of the EU and/or the proposed symbols of Europe tend to put considerable faith in the force of symbols—perhaps it is actually this faith that makes them so fiercely critical. A nationalist Danish website for instance argues as follows:

Identity is inextricably connected with symbolism of some kind. [...] Symbols are the first things we connect with identity—and the last things to perish—even when ideology has removed any contents of the word. [...] So, there [are reasons] to take the EU symbols very, very seriously: They are the New World Order's intermediar[ies] conveying to us [...] a New international identity to replace our ancient, Christian national identities.[180]

Other critics do not fear any 'European statehood sneaking in again through the back door' together with these symbols; according to these critics they do not result from dangerous ideological manipulation but rather from stupid 'managerialism' and 'second-rate branding consultants':

What we're seeing isn't a threat, but a self-regarding waste of time and public money. You can manage taxes and borders and subsidies and rebates and bureaucratic structures, fine. But you can't manage the collective unconscious. [...] People cleave to the symbols that arise out of political identity; but you can't start with a set of symbols and hope to reverse-engineer an identity from them.[181]

Many believe that European symbols are meaningless, unrelated to any European identity or feeling of community, unanchored in any pan-European public sphere or any wider public of citizens, and in several cases (particularly with Europe Day) unknown by most citizens. Aware of these criticisms, Hartmut Kaelble still argues that European symbols have a history that is well worth studying, that they are not at all meaningless, that they tend to evoke a European citizenship and a European identity, and that they are communicated in a (multilingual, multinational and yet incomplete but still emerging and growing) European public sphere.[182] The symbols can be seen as tools for developing and strengthening the shared pan-European public sphere that has for years been an important goal for EU's communication policy, aiming to close the gap between the union and its citizens, with inclusiveness, diversity and participation as key values.[183]

Though the symbols were withdrawn from the final Treaty of Lisbon, they obviously continue to be widely used and debated. However, their failure to be included in the European Constitution has cast some doubt on the efforts of ratifying a handy set of symbolic signifiers for shared values and a sense of European identity giving Europe 'a soul' that would help citizens to better identify with the union, as EU officials used to argue. In itself, this indicates that the issue is a difficult and contested one.

Against this backdrop, it is well worth scrutinising these and other official Europe symbols, in order to investigate what meanings they attach to European identity, which inner and mutual tensions they present, how they have been interpreted and which alternative symbols circulate in various contexts. Sources will include websites presented by the EU itself, by nation states inside and outside Europe, and by citizens, groups and movements in civil society. The aim is to uncover conflicts of interpretation in each symbolic realm. While the EU and its member states seek to provide official symbols to bind citizens together in Europeanness, there are equally important unofficial, 'bottom-up' cultural practices that contribute to the emergence of European identities and communicative spaces, if often in a critical vein.[184] Comparisons will also be made with symbols of entities other than Europe, but with Europe symbols deriving from elsewhere than the EU too, as well as some of those competing symbols that were rejected as the EU selected its official set. This is a way to outline the meanings of Europe through comparative interpretations that consider a wider cloud of meanings that surrounds it.[185]

Identifying symbols depict Europe as something, and there are two main sides to this signification. Formally, they must signal and prescribe in which symbolic genre they are to be inscribed. They are designed in ways that cause them to be interpreted as signifying a geopolitical unit rather than anything else, such as for instance a private company, a social movement or a clan. It is interesting to see how they indicate that they signify a union of member states, and how do they through various formal arrangements characterise the particularities of the ways in which Europe (and in this case the EU) unites its constituents into a specific kind of social community.

At the same time, the contents of the symbols indicate in many other ways what it may mean to be European. It is interesting to look for other themes that do not simply express the formal union trope but strive to characterise this entity as such: what it means to be European. The two are not strictly distinct, since Europe's inherent qualities are inseparably linked to the way it is formally constituted—and the form of unification indicates how Europe and Europeans are supposed to be. Each symbol combines the two sides with a shifting balance and in a specific manner.

The order of presentation will not follow the historical chronology, but instead move from the most abstract to the more concrete symbols, thus adding in each chapter wider and more specific layers of meaning: day—motto—flag—anthem—currency.

4

Day

It is common for nations and communal causes to have a particular day in the calendar. These are intended to be used to each year recall and cherish the entities, events or causes in question, and are therefore closely linked to ritual activities enacted on these dates. A Europe Day has been decided upon, occasioning celebrations that aim to strengthen the feeling of community and collective identity. However, this day is relatively little known or venerated among citizens, particularly in north, west and central Europe. This chapter will scrutinise its development, uses and meanings.

What's in a day?

A day may seem simple enough, but actually is both an abstract and a complex phenomenon. In itself, it is just a unit of time, but it is charged with meaning by signifying practices that name and relate it to other, surrounding or contrasting, dates within an organised calendric structure.[186] According to Paul Ricoeur, the practice of dating events is one of the cultural tools that create a 'third time', bridging lived (subjective, experiential, concrete) and universal (objective, cosmological, abstract) time, and that thereby 'cosmologizes lived time and humanizes cosmic time'.[187] This mediating historical or cultural time is shaped by techniques, narratives and rituals that connect lived and universal time: the calendar, the successions of generations, archives, documents and traces.

Calendars are media for storing as well as narratively 'storying' time. By choosing and ritually celebrating specific dates, people make the flow of time meaningful, both by just constructing the particular node in their shared calendar and by enacting a set of collective rituals each year on that specific date. A day thus opens up not only issues of time consciousness and the writing of history, but also those of understandings of the social and cultural meaning of rituals.[188] Anniversaries such as national days are built around a specified date in the annual calendar that organises the flow of time on the basis of cultural interpretations that humanise time and mediate between the individual and the cosmological. When a thus marked date occurs on a given day in a year, people who respect that date organise ritual activities (meetings, marches, festivals, concerts etc., on sites decorated with flags and emblems) to manifest their mutual recognition of the importance of whatever the date is meant to celebrate—past events, historical experiences and shared values.

Annually recurrent days of commemoration and celebration thus add a cyclical element to time experience and construct a temporal universe of collectively shared identifying values tied to specific events: the historically unique celebrated event as well as the regularly repeated celebrating events that are staged every year, with ritualistic components but also each time with new variations that express the dynamics of the unfolding interpretive community that thereby celebrates itself.

These ritualised activities linked to a day of celebration exemplify those 'invented traditions' that over time tend to get naturalised and regarded as more ancient and original than they actually are. Eric Hobsbawm defines 'invented tradition' as 'a set of practices, normally governed by overtly or tacitly accepted rules and of a ritual or symbolic nature, which seek to inculcate certain values and norms of behaviour by repetition, which automatically implies continuity with the past'.[189] Anette Warring shows how days of commemoration are used to form a shared interpretation of the past among what she calls 'communities of memory'.[190] But such days are also directed towards the present and the future, in gathering those communities around contemporary activities that reinforce social cohesion and constructing a moment in time for reflecting on one's shared tasks and potentials.

John R. Gillis distinguishes three broad periods of national commemorations: the pre-national era, the national era from 1789–1960, and the current post-national era.[191] Hobsbawm sees Europe 1870–1914 as a mass-producer of such traditions, which were closely bound to the consolidating system of nation-states that had become the ultimate focus and arena of political life: 'State, nation and society converged'.[192] However, the key European symbols discussed here would belong to the post-national period, where there is supposedly a shift from national to new combinations of local and global frameworks. The persistent returns of national and nationalist sentiments have problematised such simplistic schematics, but there seems to be at least an element of truth in that diagnosis. Even where national identifications seem as strong as ever, this could well be the defensive response to a more fundamental weakening of the national system that came into being in the nineteenth century. In general, one may assume that times of intense historical transformation would increase citizens' needs for actively constructing memory and continuity.[193] Modernity at large is an era constituted on the basis of continual transformation and change, so this is true for all of the modern era. It may be particularly true of decades where economic, political, social and cultural change was felt to be intensified. For various reasons, this was true for many Europeans in the 1960s as well as around 1990. William M. Johnston talks of a current 'cult of anniversaries' that is underpinned by a 'commemoration industry', operating on local, regional and national levels.[194] No wonder that determining a Europe day became a prime task for the expanding pan-European institutions in the expansive 1960s and then again after the 1989 fall of the iron curtain.

Dating is a way of inhabiting time and giving it meaning. The celebration of a day signifies a geopolitical community like Europe in three main ways. (a) First, looking backwards, a celebratory day that is reminiscent of something that once happened, commemorating a unique *past* event of founding importance to a community or an institution. (b) Second, looking forwards towards the *future*, such a date expresses how a social collective intends to direct its joint action along a set of cherished core values. (c) Third, in the *present*, as the day returns every year, through the cyclical aspect of the calendar, it gives a community the occasion to jointly celebrate and display its unity and its values in specific ceremonial rituals enacted that day, offering annually ritualised time for communal activities that serve as a symbolic model for collective practices to unite people and integrate them in a shared social and cultural sphere of meaning. Through such mechanisms, celebrations of jubilees, memorials, festivals and anniversaries stabilise collective memory and strengthen cultural identity. Annual commemoration days serve to remind of important past events, often of a foundational character, but also to regularly manifest a persisting community through the enactment of various ceremonial rituals that help constructing the meaning and thus identity of that community. This is evidently true of national days, but also of religious holidays and various kinds of anniversaries. David McCrone and Gayle McPherson stress that as regularly recurring dates, 'National Days give the nation a heartbeat—a calendric rhythm of self-awareness and pride', but also that this universal mechanism is the basis for great variations between different national days, testifying to the flexibility of these practices, serving different functions for different people.[195]

This is how the *European Navigator* explains the general function of such days:

> As we know, with the advent of monarchies, feast days of a civil or dynastic nature began to be celebrated, although many included a religious element (coronations, sovereign's weddings, birth of the heir to the throne, etc.). These feast days were generally accompanied by tournaments, jousts, cavalcades and hunting parties. After the French revolution, however, civil feast days of a popular and national type began to become important with a view to celebrating the achievement of liberty from domestic privilege (France) or from subjection to foreign rule (in the case of the Americas). In the Member States, one day is set aside for national celebrations. Civil holidays are a significant

way of preserving memory, and help periodically to naturalise an eclectic heritage, to keep awareness of the past alive and to unify relational networks. The national public holiday is often the day on which the State became independent, and in some cases it celebrates the patron saint or another event that is particularly meaningful for the nation.[196]

Europe is no nation or nation state, nor has it stated any wish to become one. Still, European policy-makers saw a need for a day to celebrate the emerging transnational community of Europe, and called for determining a Europe Day.

Introducing Europe Day

The European Union's *Europe Day* is 9 May. It is supposed to commemorate 9 May 1950, when the French Foreign Minister Robert Schuman presented the Schuman Declaration, in which he expressed a wish to maintain peaceful relations in light of the grim experiences of two disastrous European wars. He therefore proposed that European countries, with France and Germany as the central axis, should pool together their coal and steel production as 'the first concrete foundation of a European federation'.[197] It was precisely this industry sector that formed the basis of military power, and for those countries that had recently fought a horrible war against each other, resulting in vast material and moral desolation, this was an important step towards an organised Europe.

From 1955 to the early 1960s, there were several proposals and recommendations that called for the institution of a Europe Day to strengthen the 'feelings of fellowship among Europeans'.[198] Some proposed the first Wednesday in March; others 21 March. The need for such a day was 'psychological and educational', as it was supposed to be a tool for teaching Europeans to feel European through awakening a mass movement for the unification of Europe. That such movement may well have been needed or at least missing seems obvious from the insight that the leading institutions—in spite of the strong ideological will—had about a lack of support for these ideas in the public opinion of many countries, which made it hard to come to any decision. It remained difficult to choose a specific date, and a European Conference on Local Authorities in March 1962 advocated the institution of a Europe Day but could only propose 'a provisional date' for it. That same year for instance, the Consultative Assembly of the Council of Europe stated that the date chosen must have 'a symbolic and historical significance'. At that moment, some day in early May seems to have been the first option. Both 1 and 5 May were mentioned on various occasions, but soon the latter date became the main alternative, for instance when the Committee of Ministers in

1964 recommended that governments of member countries should 'arrange for Europe Day to be celebrated, *if possible*, on 5 May' (my emphasis). Brochures were distributed widely, and every year, renewed efforts were made to establish the day properly, but under the celebratory surface, documents hint at a certain disappointment at the lack of enthusiasm in the general public of many member states—and probably also among several of their leading politicians. A European Committee for Europe Day set up in 1970, chaired by Jacques Chaban-Delmas, proposed to 'organise in the week of 5 May great demonstrations of popular support for the European cause', asking the people of Europe to use the opportunity to stop for a moment, 'to think of their common heritage, of their joint interests, their shared hopes and destiny'.[199] In spite of all these efforts and declarations, the Committee of Ministers again and again found reason to repeat its solemn commitment to make the Europe Day celebration 'a major event in the lives of the peoples of Europe'.[200]

The process was thus slow, partly because there was no real consensus on which date to choose. However, the European Council in Milan 28–29 June 1985 decided to adopt the flag, the anthem and the day, by confirming a report from an 'ad hoc Committee on a People's Europe', the so-called Adonnino Committee, which proposed 9 May as Europe Day.[201] Since then, this is Europe Day according to the EU, even though the Council of Europe continued to have other preferences. 9 May was among the official EU symbols included in the 2004/2005 Constitutional Treaty and was also mentioned by the sixteen member states who in 2007 wished to express a loyalty with the symbols that had after the defeat of the draft been expelled from the Lisbon treaty. This means that 9 May is today the main candidate for Europe Day, with an at least semi-official status within the EU.

Europe Day remains a contested symbol, as the dating issue is still not quite resolved. The 9 May Europe Day has been seen by some critics as 'a unilaterally French act', 'politically calculated, and not resulting from the overwhelming will of the European peoples'.[202] In 1997, French history and geography teacher Yves Depoux proposed 25 March as an alternative date, in order to avoid collision with the 8 May celebration of the end of World War II. 25 March is also Annunciation Day, which Depoux found suitable for symbolising the calling of Europe to its elevating cause.[203] This Christian sphere of association has a certain rootedness in large parts of Europe, but has for decades been avoided in the name of building a secular political order that fully respects the separation of church and state. Still, as will be shown, there are echoes of this religious universe in some of the other symbols.

More importantly, the Council of Europe has since 1964 continued to celebrate 5 May as Europe Day, celebrating its own founding on 5 May 1949. It is striking that different print and web sources choose to present either 5 or 9 May as the only existing and obvious one, without mentioning the other alternative. Those who do mention them both often make an ideological distinction between the two. For instance, the

Wikipedia article on 'Symbols of Europe' informs that 5 May 'is still observed by some Europeans because of the CoE's role in defending human rights, parliamentary democracy and the rule of law, whereas the Schuman Declaration was merely proposing the pooling of French and German coal and steel'.[204] This seems to lend 5 May a more idealistic, ethical and social aura, while 9 May would then rather lean towards economic and industrial aspects of the European project. However, this is not quite as simple as it may sound, as the opposition can be read as either one between idealistic elites and down-to-earth pragmatists, or on the contrary between democratic ideals and market-based capitalist power. The issue is further complicated by the idealist aspects found also in the Schuman Declaration, which combines industrial pooling with a wish for international peace and social welfare. Here is an interesting case of conflict of interpretation where two alternative and mutually excluding dates compete. Such discord between leading European institutions certainly does not make it any easier to anchor any Europe Day among European citizens!

Interpreting Europe Day

The 9 May commemoration is clearly meant to celebrate the historical foundation of the unifying project while simultaneously expressing its future-oriented core values:

> The celebration of 9 May is not just the celebration of the founding document of the process of European integration. It also provides an opportunity to reflect on the current and real situation which changes daily. The reality of life in a European Union based on the principles of the rule of law, which possesses a democratic order based on popular sovereignty and on values which are now accepted and shared by the vast majority of European people. The meaning of the celebration lies in its commemoration of the path that had to be taken to consolidate these principles and values, without taking for granted the victories won.[205]

The Adonnino Committee report that the European Council supported in Milan 28–29 June 1985 had proposed

> confirming 9 May of each year as Europe Day with a view to creating awareness and giving information in schools in particular as well as on television and in the other media. The date of 9 May, which is of great significance to the Community, will fit in with similar initiatives taken by the Council of Europe.[206]

The Milan Summit thus emphasised the foundation of the EU in values of peace and solidarity that 'find expression through economic and social development embracing environmental and regional dimensions which are the guarantees of a decent standard of living for all citizens'.[207] In agreement with the Schuman Declaration, the EU continues to believe that in order not to repeat the tragedies of history, and instead of building on the conquest and domination of one group or power, there is a need to unite Europe around rules and institutions that respect 'freedom and the identity of all of the people which compose it', in order to 'control the mastery of its destiny and develop a positive role in the world'. 'The European Union is at the service of its citizens. While keeping their own specific values, customs and language, European citizens should feel at ease in the "European home."'

This talk of Europe as a 'home' for its citizens can be employed by both a conservative paternalistic and a socialist or social democratic welfare state model. In Sweden for instance, it was the Social Democratic PM Per Albin Hansson who in a famous 1928 speech formulated the influential political ideology of the *folkhem* (people's home), referring to society and the state as a shared home for all its citizens, where all were both held responsible and taken good care of, and which was based on community, equality, care and cooperation, breaking down social and economic divisions. This egalitarian but slightly paternalistic vision of an all-encompassing social contract echoes in the Schuman Declaration as well as in several EU policies.

Europe Day thus has a direct link to the EU foundation myth, of which the Schuman Declaration is a key example. Its stress on replacing internal differences with mutual peace and unity that guarantees stability places it closer to Captain Euro than to the Greek Europa myth. Europe Day is meant to cherish the foundational values of peace and mutual solidarity 'through economic and social development embracing environmental and regional dimensions'.[208] It thus aims to combine several spheres of values, from high ethical standards to more material values related to economic prosperity, social welfare and ecological sustainability. These value spheres are clearly interconnected. For instance, the 'blue' (liberal or conservative) values of economic strength have in modern European history been productively combined with 'red' values of social welfare (anchored in a socialist or social democratic tradition), the two mutually boosting each other, and to this alliance have recently been recruited the 'green' values of the ecological and environmental movements. These sets of values can certainly often clash and contradict each other, but efforts are made to see how they instead may be linked to and support each other, for instance by making climate attention a tool for strengthening and modernising industrial and post-industrial production. It is evident from the Schuman Declaration that Europe Day is meant to celebrate a combination of economic prosperity, social welfare, political unity and mutual understanding across different nations and cultures—a combination which is not easily accomplished and gives rise to a series of political tensions that the other symbols often strive to bridge.

William M. Johnston has found that the vast majority of European anniversaries celebrate modern secular figures and can therefore be seen as celebrations of modernity itself, rather than being traditionalist.[209] This is relevant for Europe Day too. Even though it is not an anniversary celebrating a particular individual, it commemorates a high-modern event that was enacted by a forward-looking and secular politician. Johnston further argues that while most anniversaries in the United States concern specific events, those in Europe tend more often to celebrate 'creative geniuses', explaining this by the overwhelming number of such great individuals that have accumulated through the centuries.[210] The effect is to forge a 'Golden Chain of Genius, stretching back through the Renaissance and Middle Ages to antiquity', and thereby constructing a distinctly European heritage, highly useful to boosting its shared but unique cultural identity, particularly in the presently ongoing process of integration that 'encourages commemorating pan-European luminaries' who 'personify pan-European heritage', so that this cult of anniversaries function 'as a modern substitute for the cult of ancestors'.[211] Robert Schuman is just one example; others will be mentioned later, from patron saints to the personalities honoured on euro coins. Europe Day belongs to that category of anniversaries that respond to the fact that today 'Europeans need emblems of uniqueness'.[212] In 1991, Johnston predicted that this process would become increasingly transnationalised, which has since been confirmed.[213]

Michael E. Geisler argues that national days are 'unstable signifiers': while other national symbols work through 'over-determination', establishing a complex web of signification by being integrated into everyday life practices, national days happen just once a year and are then instead meant to be explicitly noticed.[214] They are never examples of the 'unwaved' symbols of 'banal nationalism' that Michael Billig has shown to be so effective, since they are not 'time-in culture', to borrow a phrase from Klaus Bruhn Jensen, but rather 'time-out culture', separated from the ordinary flow of history.[215] Europe day has another kind of function than most symbols analysed in later chapters, as it organises focused activities that tend to combine all those other symbols in a dense node of experience for citizens. The meaning of the day will therefore also evolve through its actual use, making it difficult to interpret in isolation from all those annually renewed practices.

Comparisons and commentary

There is a kind of 'intertextual' interference between both the European Days and the dates for celebrating the end of World War II in Europe. 9 May coincides with Victory Day, celebrating the end of World War II in East Europe, while Victory Day happens to be celebrated either on 5 or 8 May in West Europe. This collision can be a negative competition that contributes to the neglect of Europe Day, particularly in East Europe where Victory Day remains important, but there may (in both cases) also be gains in connecting the two, as it may give the celebration a polysemic meaning that strongly identifies European unification as a peace project.

Another intertextuality is of course with national days: those specific dates that are often national holidays and on which celebrations mark the nationhood of a country. They tend to be most intensely celebrated when they go back to not too distant dates of liberation, independence or other key constitutional events that have made national sovereignty important for the citizens of a nation. The Irish St Patrick's Day of 17 March, the US 4 July and the French 14 July are all connected to key moments in their national histories and are usually celebrated on a grand scale, whereas for instance the UK countries England, Scotland and Wales pay scarce attention to their patron saints' days and do not even have any shared national day.[216] This reflects the diminished role of the Church for modern nation's identity, as well as the importance for a people of having sufficiently recently gone through a process of liberation from oppression, whether by foreign imperialist colonisation or by domestic autocracy. This is for instance why Norway celebrates its sovereign constitution after liberation from Denmark on 17 May 1814 (though followed by a royal union with Sweden until 7 June 1905) much more emphatically than Sweden marks its 6 June, which did not become a holiday until 2005 and which relatively few Swedes recognise as a commemoration of how Swedish nobility in 1523 made Gustav Vasa their king and thus in a sense marked the foundation of Sweden as a modern nation state. It is also relevant to note that celebrations of Denmark's National Day were intensified in periods where European integration and migration were problematised by emergent nationalist movements in the early 1970s and again in the late 1990s.[217] In Spain, one may almost talk of a reversed celebration, as the Hispanic Day of 12 October marks when Christopher Columbus first set foot in the Americas in 1492, thus commemorating an event that certainly vastly expanded the territory and wealth of Spain, but as this colonial empire has since long collapsed, it gives the Spanish National Day an ambiguous aura of nostalgic loss and—from a postcolonial perspective—rather problematic overtones.

With two exceptions, neither of the two Europe Days seriously collides with another well-known celebration. The British Channel Islands use 9 May as their national day, commemorating the liberation from Nazi German occupation in 1945. In a similar spirit, besides their Queensday on 30 April, the Netherlands celebrates Liberation Day on 5 May.

Among the other continents, Australia is the only one that is also a nation state. Since 1808, Australia Day 26 January celebrates the proclamation of British sovereignty over Sydney and the east coast of Australia in 1788, but is controversial and since 1988 opposed by aborigines who rename it 'Invasion Day', which has resulted in debates whether to instead find another date.[218] There is also an Africa Day, commemorating the 25 May 1963 founding of the Organisation of African Unity (OAU), which in 2002 transformed into the African Union.[219] Considering the cultural and political divisions of Asia and the Americas, it is unlikely that they will follow the same path in the near future. The US federation may be seen as the closest comparison, but while EU's Europe consists of sovereign nations, the United States is one single and considerably more homogenised nation, even if it consists of separate states—but then so does Germany, for instance.

The whole Europe Day discourse shows how closely it links the past to the future: the meaning of the 1950 Schuman Declaration has a bearing on the shared values, hopes, promises and goals that the EU and presumably a majority of Europeans are supposed to strive for. However, every such memorable day also, and most importantly, has a third dimension: that of the present—the actual event that unfolds each 9 May. A day of celebration is of course nothing without celebrations. It is made to be actively used for recurrent ritual practices, and its full meaning only develops through such use. Europe Day has little meaning if it is not actively used for ceremonial collective activities. Confusion between contesting dates and lack of knowledge or interest is therefore an obvious problem in this case. The actual uses of Europe Day—or indeed of any of the other official symbols—have not been precisely regulated in any binding treaty, though a set of practices has been established over the years.

EU sources thus explain that Europe Day is intended to be used for 'activities and festivities that bring Europe closer to its citizens and peoples of the Union closer to one another', celebrating its basic values.[220] This was why a date with symbolic significance was to be selected, and already in the early 1960s, the Council of Europe suggested that governments and local authorities should use the new European flag colours for public decorations that day.[221] It was during the following decade also proposed that other European events, such as the release of Europe stamps, should be focused around early May, and even that 'great demonstrations of popular support for the European cause' should be organised that week, so as to create a momentum around Europe Day.[222]

> Europe Day on 9 May offers a yearly opportunity to bring Europe closer to its citizens. It is a day of information, guidance and discussion of European Union themes, especially, but not just, in schools and universities, with events of a particular cultural and educational content. Europe Day must also be an opportunity to forge closer ties between the citizens of Europe and overcome the sense of distance, indifference and even disaffection that they feel for the European institutions. It is a time at which the most can be made of the Union's symbols. As in the case of a national day, what is needed is a good

showing of European flags, not only at places at which events are being held but also, and in particular, at windows. Lastly, 9 May should be a day of public holiday where men and women from different cities, regions and countries of our Europe can meet.[223]

9 May is an official public holiday in only a handful of smaller nations, including Kosovo. Celebrations have in most regions remained rather limited and few European citizens are aware of them or indeed of the significance of this date, as even the official EU website has to admit.[224] In some places and some years, there have admittedly been a considerable wealth of activities that day, for instance in France 2006, which was the twentieth time Europe Day was celebrated, and therefore a great number of festivities were organised all over Paris.[225] However, that tends to be an exception, and it is difficult to describe the reception and use of this day as a success story. It is interesting to note that the only mention of Europe day in a recent volume on European national days is that it is 'an invented supra-national tradition' that is 'dubious and not popular'.[226] One difficulty derives from the confusion around which date to celebrate, but there is also a more general and problematic difficulty of constructing a really suitable ritual practice to gather European citizens around shared values. Some examples from recent years indicate the main issues involved in operationalising the day to boost European identification.

In 2009, websites reported rather small-scale celebrations, mainly by officials and politicians, both in Europe and outside, with scattered speeches, conferences and concerts. Reports came from EU member states but also from Turkey, Palestine, Armenia, Canada, US, Caribbean Dominica, Gambia, New Zealand, China and Taiwan, where EU delegations and/or local organisations for Europeans organised minor events, stressing Europe's positive role for the country in question. Celebrations were more actively reported in regions where EU issues were high on the agenda, as for instance in Ukraine 2009, where the EU is used as a kind of shield against Russian domination. A news agency reported that 'Ukrainian Prime Minister Yulia Tymoshenko has congratulated Ukrainian citizens on Europe Day', with the following words:

> It is pleasant to note that celebrations of Europe Day have already become a tradition in all of the country's regions, both in the west and the east. The Ukrainian people is united in its being an integral part of European civilization.[227]

The article then concludes by telling that Ukraine since 2003 celebrates Europe Day on the third Saturday of May, which is a bit paradoxical considering the divergence from EU's established date.

In 2009, a British pro-Europe web magazine, *European Lifestyle*, asked a dozen people in the street and none knew that 9 May is Europe Day or what it is meant to celebrate. 'The problem is the European Union never actively promotes it very much to those whom its rules directly impact.' The argument here was that too little was done to advertise this actually quite important event: 'It all comes down to image'. This website was one of the few that really spoke of the EU symbols: 'The symbols, which Europe has adopted to promote itself with, makes the EU far more obvious than any background organisation ever has, save the UN.' With more information, there would be a better understanding of the importance of the European project: 'When that happens we can all expect the flags, celebrations and parties of Europe Day to become second nature'.[228]

An Irish pro-EU blogger likewise wished for more people to take the day seriously:

> So next time that the 9th of May is the day, you do not have to sing the 'Ode of Joy', you do not have to be dressed in blue from head to toe or wave the EU flag, but simply go to any happenings for the day near your area, meet and talk to people from all over Europe living there, share ideas, express your disappointment if you wish and tell where EU has failed you, exchange and discuss topics about your culture, your country, what you love about the country you live or come from, what you love about living in EU and how it has helped you and your country, what must be done for EU to be better and what vision do you have for it for the future. That is what the 9th of May should be all about, that is how you must celebrate it, and I am sure that it will make a difference for you if you do so.[229]

In 2009, most others were considerably more sceptical. On 9 May, an amusement park in Helsinki, Finland, was the stage for a couple of speeches and a panel discussion among MEPs. 'Only one was missing—the audience', a blogger ironically reported and mentioned that another Europe Day event in Helsinki got more visitors—one with the theme of European Wine Culture: 'Also here the "Europeanization" of Finns got some setback as in cold weather the participants desired a bit stronger drinks. Also some Wine experts missed more Wines from Australia, America etc instead of Wines from Europe.' The gloomy experience led to the conclusion that EU is not on the top of the average Finnish taxpayer's priorities.[230]

A Lebanese website reported on celebrations in Brussels, interviewing visitors from a range of countries and focusing on the 'lack of engagement between EU institutions and the European public'. Thousands of people were reported to stream through the doors of the EU institutions in Brussels, but 'the crowds seemed blissfully unaware' of what Europe Day is. A Belgian MEP complained that it is 'very difficult to get people interested in European issues', since 'they are interested in their own problems': 'People say that Europe is too complicated.'[231]

A cosmopolitan blog with a 'European perspective' agreed that 'most people in Europe are not aware of it', and considered 'if it would make sense to have 9 May as a public holiday throughout Europe, in order to raise awareness and celebrate the European project', but added that 'EU symbolism is not very popular at the moment' and found the main obstacle to be that this would be too expensive in the current economic crisis: 'Nobody wants to get rid of "National days" in favour of a European one.'[232]

On the same occasion, Swedish EU commissioner Margot Wallström published a text about 'The subtle pleasures of Europe Day', where she tried to portray it as an event worthy of serious consideration and suggest its importance without forgetting the difficulties in making it a meaningful event. She argued that Schuman's vision of how to prevent further European wars 'seems to have worked' and that 'all those authoritarian governments' with their 'dictators, communists and colonels' are now gone:

> So what? Many people say. They see a blue flag with 12 stars. Does it evoke passion? In a small minority, perhaps. Some see it as a symbol of good, a tiny minority detest it, but to most, it is a symbol that is just not relevant to them. The EU is a bit like the insulation in your house—it's useful and good to know it's there but the average person does not go around thinking or worrying about it all the time. And yet, maybe that is its greatest success.
>
> The EU doesn't really do passion. If anything, the EU flag stands for boring reason over passion [...]. And yet the EU does stuff that is highly relevant to us. [...] No need to wave a flag. But when you think about the positive and useful everyday work that European countries now do together, maybe it's a nice idea to remember the day in 1950 when one man, looking out over a continent that had been the world's greatest battlefield only five years previously, suggested that he might have a way of making sure it never happened again.[233]

Wallström thus emphasised the small steps to a better life that the EU makes possible, but is sceptical towards the value of its symbols: 'No need to wave a flag.' It is notable that Wallström's chronicle was not very successful even in her Swedish homeland, where there was in the largest Swedish newspaper, the liberal *Dagens Nyheter*, on that same day 9 May 2009 not a single mention of Europe Day, even though the imminent European Parliament election was mentioned in various places. The single exception was in a comic strip expressing a regret on Europe's inability to defend the local, regional and national values against Americanisation through the media. The same was the case in 2010, with lots of information about the Russian World War II memorial day and the ongoing financial crisis but no word on Europe day except in that same comic strip (Figure 4.1).[234]

It has already been mentioned that for historical and political reasons, attention to Europe Day tends to be greater and more positive in East Europe, where occasions to celebrate European values play a pragmatic role in efforts to reinforce progressive Europeanisation, not least in those countries that continue to aspire for EU membership. However, even for the ex-Yugoslavian region, a 2010 report offers a mixed picture. The report refers to High Representative for Foreign Affairs and Security Policy of the European Union, Catherine Ashton, having 'noted that Europe Day was a symbol of new beginning, free and successful cooperation between sovereign countries, on basis of common values and interests—democracy, peace, solidarity, welfare and rule of law'.[235] On this by now well-known basis, the report mentions the complicating issue that there are actually two European days (5 and 9 May), and that they collide with celebrations of victory over fascism. Examples from each country in the region are then given of how state institutions organise events but also how sometimes civil society organisations 'join the band-wagon'. Formal events included public speeches by government officials, presentation stands by EU member states or brass concerts where presumably the European anthem was performed. Less formal celebrations were often marked by activities that would possibly have happened anyhow, but that were now linked to Europe Day, such as students' sports tournaments or openings of youth centres. Here is a typical example of the mixed activities that people participated in:

> In Macedonia, the Government Secretariat for European Affairs (SEA) organized the multimedia event 'The More the Merrier', in cooperation with the Municipality of Centar (Skopje), to inform and educate Macedonian children, through games and fun, what EU was about and what values it stands for. The traditional 'Skopje Marathon' was held on Europe Day, with participation of over 2,000 runners, who completed the distances of 5000 metres, half-Marathon and full Marathon race. EU Ambassador to Macedonia Erwan Fouere was present at the traditional 'Waiter's Race' in down-town Skopje, and at the performance by the Orchestra of the Youth Cultural Centre in front of the Memorial Home of Mother Theresa.[236]

Creativity was also striking in Bosnia and Herzegovina (BiH), with awards for 'European Friend of BiH for 2010' and 'The Most-European Citizens of BiH for 2010', as well as 'setting the new Guinness Record for most people simultaneously dancing the waltz in Tuzla'. In Sarajevo, a 4 km 'Race to Europe' was held, as well as a European Film programme. In some countries, anti-fascist organisations took the opportunity to organise events linking Europe Day to Victory Day, and in Albania and Macedonia, the report noted that oppositional groups staged mass demonstrations demanding democratic reforms and propagating accelerated integration in the EU. But these Balkan phenomena on both sides of the current EU border are exceptions to the general rule. It is only in 'new Europe' that Europe Day(s) has (have) a presence and even urgency for at least some state bodies and sections of the public sphere and civil society, with an emphasis on activities for children and young people, and often cleverly combining the European theme with other events that thereby become articulated with Europeanness without being by any means necessarily bound to it. Citizens of the old and more sceptical west and north tend to be considerably more ignorant.

Conclusions

In the beginning of this chapter, it was mentioned how identifying days have three main directions: anchoring a socio-political unity in a historic past, expressing its orientation towards the future, and giving occasions for collectively celebrating its community in the present. These dimensions are always interwoven. This is true for Europe Day as well. It is similar to many other such days, in that it connects to a founding moment in the (recent) history of the European unification project, with links back to the fateful experiences of the two world wars. The release and liberation is here thus not so much from external or illegitimate autocratic rule, as is the case with a majority of the most intensely celebrated national days. The autonomy and sovereignty commemorated each May is rather a kind of liberation from internal division and strife.

Commemorating particular heritage also motivates what is perceived as the specific calling and thus acknowledged goal and task of a unified Europe. This constructs a meaning for Europe that identifies it as a project of peace and prosperity, of unity and welfare. The Schuman Declaration and its many elaborations so often repeated in official explanations all underline this overcoming of mutual conflicts and the building of a safe, responsible and successful joint future as the core of the EU project. It was shown how the EU discourses strive to make Europe Day link to a set of strong political ideologies, by constructing a kind of alliance between what was here called blue, red and green values: liberal and conservative aims for solid prosperity, socialist demands for equal social welfare, and ecological values of sustainable development that does not disrupt the ecosystem. These values are co-articulated in the discourses around the other EU symbols as well. It is yet difficult to clearly discern their priority order or relative strength, as they are differently articulated in different settings, and there is an ongoing process where different social groups struggle for their interests to take the lead. Public and official proclamations tend to first of all emphasise issues of peace and solidarity, taking Europe Day to reinforce unity and community, forging closer ties between peoples but with full respect for their national, regional and individual identities. Rule of law, sovereignty and democratic order is to be the way for Europe to achieve mastery of its own destiny in the world. Economic and social development for securing a solid and increasing living standard is the second priority in rhetorics, whereas critical readings may well suspect that in fact economic expansion may for many influential actors be the hidden core interest, with peace, democracy and social security as means of global competition rather than as goals in themselves. Likewise, environmental sustainability is to some groups in civil society the top priority, while for others it can rather be seen as a currently efficient tool for renewed economic development.

However, for the day of Europe, the main difficulty that has been generally acknowledged and discussed lies in the third dimension: that of the present. This is the aspect that most evidently fails in many West European nations today. The intention is that it should serve as a recurring occasion to ritually reconstruct social bonds in empowering, community-reinforcing practices. In practice, local activities and communal rituals celebrating Europeanness happen that day all over Europe, but attendance and attention is scarce, and the media coverage they get is mainly negative these days, focusing on the deficits or even failure of Europe Day itself, whereas only a limited number of enthusiasts continue to try and reconstruct this as a success story.

It is thus possible to deconstruct various contradictions and hidden implications in the historical and teleological dimensions of Europe Day, and discern even more evident problematics in its contemporary pragmatic uses. Its signifying aspects may thus be summed up as follows, in comparison with the corresponding interpretation of the myth and name.

1.   The ancient Europa myth was characterised by multiple dislocations, homological with the historical origins and continual development of European settlements and culture. The more recent Captain Euro alternative on the contrary stood for a safe rootedness. My conclusion was that there is a persistent tension between values of mobility and stability. Here, Europe Day is not that clear, even though sovereignty, autonomy and control appear to be more central than dislocation. By not explicitly foregrounding dislocation or mobility, taking the fixed localisation and settlement of Europeans in Europe and its various nation states for granted, it tends to favour the opposite and take for granted that Europe is (in) a fixed place. However, the Schuman Declaration can also be read to hint at another kind of dislocation: an historical (rather than geographic) disjuncture whereby Europe at a given moment decides to do things otherwise—a promise to change irreversibly by being open to the differences of the other within and outside itself, respecting diversity and building solidarity on that respect rather than by conquering the

other. The day does not specify an origin involving geographic migration or transport, but it does convey a sense of not being comfortably at home and thus of metaphorical or mental dislocation. Still, the day makes a centring movement, by building one united Europe from its previously divided core. *Spatial fixity* in the spirit of Captain Euro is thereby combined with *temporal disjuncture* and a kind of enlightening awakening which has certain affinities with the Europa myth.

2.   There was a striking polarity between the two myths in terms of values of communication and of control. There is little pleasure in the motivation for the day, except that the desire for world peace is in itself a kind of loving and caring pleasure, opposed to aggression and domination. From the Schuman Declaration to current EU practices, cool rationality is more characteristic of the celebrations than hot passion, even if some intensity can be noted in a few formulations. Welfare and prosperity tend to be more focused upon on Europe Day than pleasure as such, which is left to citizens to fulfil in their lifeworlds. Some efforts are made to introduce fun and enjoyable elements in its annual celebration. Commissioner Margot Wallström's formulations on the honourable lack of passion in the EU project hints at a hidden tension between on the one hand the more pragmatic north European standpoints, perhaps rooted in Protestantism and reformist popular movements, and on the other more demagogic South European ideologies, with links to Catholic ideals which in this respect may be closer to the Europa myth. Here, the overall tension between the two facets remains in play. The prominent *desire for peace* theme echoes Europa's pleasures, though the main emphasis is on *calculated control*, as a means to fulfil a wish to make change in history by putting an end to suffering.

3.   The theme of *elevation* was the only one that was central to both the analysed myths, and it is present in Europe Day as well, as it is implies a kind of lifting of Europe and its peoples from greedy and violent self-interests to higher ideals. Europe Day's past and future dimensions signify a wish for ethical and political elevation from war and destruction to tolerance and cooperation, but also a material elevation from ruins to a prosperous welfare society. However, the lack of imagination, in inventing ways in which to realise and symbolise this elevating thrust in annual rituals for community-building in the present dimension, and the many ironic or even ridiculing comments, which existing efforts receive in various media, disclose a difficulty in realising this aspect of identity in actual practice.

4.   Europe Day is once again closer to Captain Euro's preference for homogeneity than to the hybridisation signified by Europa. In the past and present, it focuses on the lack of *unity*, with unity as a future goal: a unity to be accomplished,

with unification as an ongoing project and task rather than a fact. The balance weighs towards overcoming division, forgiving past grievances and joining hands to peacefully build unity, but the efforts to uphold tolerance and respect for national, regional and individual identities shows that the tension again persists—as least as much as in other comparable socio-political units. The emphasis is on the unifying thrust, with diversity more as a starting-point or even an obstacle to be overcome: introducing a higher level of unity and shared efforts across internal differences.

Europe Day thus connects to the characteristic tension of values that was discovered in the combination of the myth of Europa and that of Captain Euro, reinforcing the dominance of the latter, that is, of elevation, rationality, fixity and unity, with relatively subordinated supplementary values of desire for peace, mobility and diversity.

5

MOTTO

Among EU's symbols, the motto 'United in diversity' (Latin: *In varietate concordia*) is the most abstract and maximally condensed form of verbally expressing the idea of Europe as a union. Mottos are formulated by many social actors, such as royalties or businesses. Before approaching the content of the EU motto, one should consider what a motto is used for.

What's in a motto?

Standard lexicon definitions state that a motto (sixteenth century Italian for 'word') is a short phrase meant to formally encapsulate the beliefs, ideals, motivations or intentions of a social group or organisation, generally linked to some kind of heraldic design. In more traditional contexts, it is often formulated in Latin, and is typically used in heraldry (combined with a symbolic image) but also in literature (usually in the form of a quote that signals the essence or key ideas of the following main text). Germanic languages also have access to synonyms such as those that might be rephrased as 'elected saying' (German *Wahlspruch*, etc.), which emphasises that a motto is something individuals or representatives of a social group or institution actively choose to stand for their main goals. A motto thus conveys an active will, the future-oriented intentions of an agency: a word of wisdom that somebody has chosen to represent certain leading ideals or goals. A motto is a kind of verbal key symbol for a community or an individual, which differs from other verbal expressions (such as descriptions, laws, poems, novels) in that it formulates a promise or an intention, often in a striking manner. A motto is closely related to a slogan (the word derived from the Gaelic *sluagh*, 'army' + *gairm*, 'shout'), which is a short and memorable (written or chanted) phrase used for propaganda or marketing to socially express an idea or unified purpose of some kind of collective.

The relation between a myth and a motto can be seen as one of archaeology versus teleology. While a myth is inherited and binds to the past, a motto is emphatically *not* inherited but consciously and intentionally constructed or at least selected among a stock of standard formulations in this peculiar genre, in order to convey the goals of an agency—a subject such as the ruler of a nation or an institution like the EU. A motto is not primarily a description of its bearer's past achievements and present characteristics, but a promise for the future. However, while mainly presenting the future-oriented promise of an agency, a motto always nods to the past and the present as well—directly or indirectly. First, mottos usually also tend to describe how that agency understands itself, that is, its own self-image. Second, they always also indirectly hint at the character of the agency, in the same way as any future vision, for instance in science fiction narratives or in political utopias or dystopias, discloses key current traits and tendencies in the agency and time of its author. The intentions of any (individual or collective) subject are always mutually implicated in its background and character, due to the crucial link between agency and intentionality. What somebody declares as her will does after all say much about who she is, 'positively' by the style in which she formulates her intentions, which bears the mark of her identity, as well as 'negatively' by her wish to in the future come to grips with her past shortcomings. For instance, a strong will to unite can hint *both* at community formation as a long-term characteristic of a region, *and* at a current internal division that is felt as problematic and in need of decisive counter-measures.

Monarchs, warriors, sports teams and business firms are some of those agencies that sometimes tend to put up significant mottos. In times of intensified competition, mottos and slogans are multiplied as symbolic weapons in the struggle for recognition and proliferation, for instance when increasingly many towns today develop more or less successful slogans as aggressive marketing tools of city branding. For instance Stockholm has for some years now marketed itself as 'the Capital of Scandinavia', predictably provoking the rivalling Danish and Norwegian neighbours Copenhagen and Oslo. As tools for branding, mottos are today abundant, being used for publicly showing that a particular institution is a major player in a specific field of activity. Some gain widespread recognition and are often cited; others are ridiculed or quickly forgotten. Coca Cola and other firms have been successful examples, whereas the efforts by smaller cities often have scant success.

Introducing the European motto

The European motto 'united in diversity' is the youngest of EU's five symbols. Though little known among ordinary people, it appears on official EU websites and is increasingly often used or at least implied in the official EU rhetoric.

'United in diversity' had actually been used by the European communists from 1964 until the rise of Eurocommunism in the late 1970s, as a way of reconciling national parties' autonomy with the support of the Soviet Union.[237] This forerunner seems not to have been directly referred to in the new EU usage. Mostly in a slightly different form—'unity in difference'—the slogan had been used in the EU sphere at least since the mid-1960s, as a way of recognising both the plurality of independent nation states and their shared general interests.[238] It had for instance since the 1990s been the official slogan of the European Bureau for the Lesser Used Languages (EBLUL). If any formulation was used to identify the EU, that was it, but it had yet no formal status for the EU system as a whole.

In 1998, French journalist Patrick La Prairie at the newspaper *Ouest-France* started organising a competition among school pupils, engaging 40 newspapers from EU member states. September 1999 to January 2000, some 80,000, 10–19 years old pupils sent in more than 2000 different proposals to a website (www.devise-europe.org). Fifteen national juries each selected ten mottoes. Selecting among them, a European media panel in April 2000 presented a shortlist of seven alternatives. On 4 May 2000 in Brussels, 'unity in difference' (proposed by Luxembourg school kids) was selected by a grand jury consisting of fifteen 'eminent European personalities', chaired by Jacques Delors, and aided by a lexicometric survey.[239]

It is a bit strange to note that such a complex selection process resulted in precisely that motto that had already been most used among European institutions. But the history of all these symbols is full of similar 'coincidences', related to the need for each decision to be in a certain manner 'overdetermined', that is, anchored at once on several different levels and by divergent mechanisms that together may ensure a kind of consensus or at least legitimacy of the chosen motto.

A second curiosity is that the selected motto was then modified into 'united in diversity', before it was accepted by the President of the European Parliament, Nicole Fontaine, and officially written into the European Constitution draft of 2004, with an authorised translation into all the 23 official EU languages, as well as in Latin: '*In varietate concordia*'. It is striking that publicly available EU sources do not offer any substantial explanation of the motives behind this modification. Research is needed in order to clarify this interesting change, and explain how the change could be so swiftly made without disturbing the legitimacy effect. It is not difficult to imagine a range of *possible* reasons. The change from 'unity' to 'united' might possibly reflect a wish to emphasise that Europe's unity is no initially given fact, but the outcome of a painful historical process. The change from 'difference' to 'diversity' could indicate a wish to connect more strongly to the politically anchored discourse around ethnic multiculture. Finally, the whole modified construction seems able to stress a more crucial interdependence of unification and diversity: where 'unity in difference' *could* be understood to signify a unity *in spite of* internal differences, 'united in diversity' more clearly leans towards the interpretation that it is diversity that is the very basis of unity. This interpretation will be analysed in greater detail below.

Interpreting the European motto

Europe can be conceived in many different ways—as a geographic continent, a politico-economic actor or a sociocultural community. However, the EU is primarily a union of nation states, and its symbols will therefore necessarily express an understanding of what it means to be such a federation. It is almost self-evident that a union needs a motto that in some way expresses its character of being precisely a union, overcoming differences. But nuances are therefore of essence. European *Union* symbols (but not necessarily every other European symbol) will always elaborate on the theme of uniting different constituents into a strong whole. The question is *how* this is done.

A first observation is that it is not always quite obvious whose motto this actually is. It is put forward by the EU, which is the major economic and political actor in this continent, but it does not organise all the countries and states in this geographic area. Even so, the union is obviously strong enough to dare to propose symbols that are supposed to be valid for the whole continent. Like the other symbols, the slogan is officially presented as 'the European motto', rather than 'the European Union motto'. This invites an empirical investigation of how Europeans who are not in the EU relate to this motto, which falls outside the scope of this study.

A second and related problem concerns what kind of unification is implied. From the EU perspective, the unification is primarily political and economic, but the whole involvement with symbols indicates an effort to also extend this unification to include cultural elements, in particular communicative resources that may build a common European public sphere where citizens and networks can interact and form a truly transnational polity.

A third question asks which diversities are intended. One possible interpretation relates to the plurality of EU structures, but two other, more plausible, meanings are relevant. One is to the maintenance of the relatively independent national identity and mutually exclusive political authority of each member state. The diversity would then be national and political. The other reading focuses on the more inclusive ethnical diversity of cultures that need not coincide with nation states but may either be sub-national or transnationally regional, all relating to the protection of minority rights.[240] The EU as a political and economic institutional project activates the first topic, while Europe as a cultural and social community may equally well make the second one relevant.

Gerard Delanty and Chris Rumford distinguish four ways to conceive the relation between unity and diversity: (1) diversity as derivative of unity (as in ideas of a historical heritage of Greek-Roman and Christian culture); (2) unity as derivative of diversity (in the cultural policy project of overcoming differences through intercultural understanding and cosmopolitanism); (3) unity as diversity (where diversity itself is not to be overcome but rather to be acknowledged in a postmodernist fashion); and (4) a self-limiting unity (a post-national position where a minimal kind of unity is formed out of an active engagement with diversity).[241] Position 1 was in the mid-twentieth century common among Christian conservative circles but is today more often encountered among right-wing extremists, while EU policy-makers tend to waver between positions 2 and 3, none of which seem to have much popular support, according to Delanty and Rumford. Position 4 is what for instance Habermas proposes, when emphasising the role of communicative mechanisms rather than any underlying cultural identity.

> Current thinking seems to point towards a view of unity in diversity as an accomplished fact and that therefore the only unity possible is that which is built on the basis of whatever common values can be found in the various European identities. A European identity is then not an over-riding identity but only the common expression of those values that presently exist. This might suggest that it is unlikely that European identity can rest on stronger values, in a way comparable to, for example, American values.[242]

Delanty and Rumford are deeply sceptical towards 'the unity in diversity myth' that 'denies the possibility of a European identity since this will always be in danger of undermining national diversity'; they even argue that it is 'close to a legitimation of xenophobic nationalism'.[243] Instead, they see (political, class, gender and lifestyle) differences within nations as greater than those between nations, and argue for creating new spaces for communication that do not fix identities but rather open up for an unfinished project of social justice, cosmopolitan identity and dialogue.[244]

The validation of diversity may be seen as a necessary concession to the antifederalist sceptics who in many nations slowed down the integration process, but it still has important signifying consequences. When it became a leading EU policy keyword, it had been updated by a series of theoretical ideas on hybrid identity and multiple citizenship that gained impetus from the mid-1980s, not least in central Europe.[245]

A commentary text on the European motto, published by the *European Navigator*, offers an insight into how leading EU authorities think about the motto. Quoting Jack Lang, Ortega y Gasset and Valéry Giscard d'Estaing, it spends considerable effort on arguing for the need to avoid both fragmentation and implosion. There is on the one hand a perceived need for convergence, standardisation, integration and unification. On the other hand, there must also always be a necessary respect for the national sovereignity of each member state:

Striking a balance between unity and diversity is crucial. Too much unity would run the risk of standardisation and therefore of the destruction of national identities. Too much diversity could easily prevent intentions from converging and, in the long term, undermine the construction of a re-united Europe. […] It therefore seems crucial to seek unity in basic values and the combined presence of unity and difference.

The 'dominant culture within the institutions in Brussels systematically underestimates diversity, viewing it as an obstacle to the further standardisation of Europe', *European Navigator* continues. But a key lesson from a difficult historical experience is that 'diversity is the genetic heritage of our continent in which unifying factors such as a single language, a common religion or a central power able to impose a uniform European model are lacking'. Differently from China or the United States, Europe cannot build its identity on any dominant uniformity, whether linguistic, religious or ethnic. 'Europe has to be organised from its diversity and not against its diversity. A reasonable balance therefore has to be struck between the needs of diversity and the need to form a coherent whole.'[246] This is the pronounced motivation behind the selected motto, in concordance with the EU Constitutional Treaty, based on principles of subsidiarity and proportionality, meant to carefully respect the sovereignty of each national member state. No wonder the motto is increasingly often used in official documents and declarations. It can also be found quoted or indirectly alluded to in other European websites, songs and other kinds of texts that thematise Europeanness today.

Comparisons and commentary

It should first be noted that there is a strong homology between the motto and the day, and also the myth. The intercourse between Europa and Zeus-as-bull is a form of unification in diversity, as the theme of hybridity expresses: human-woman travelling together with divine-animal-man and creating an offspring whose strength supposedly derived from precisely that diverse genealogy. Also, when 9 May celebrates the first formation of a European union, it does so by emphasising how enormous internal differences could not only be overcome but also preserved and respected in this new entity that was to develop into the EU.

The meaning of the motto can be further elaborated through a detour over a comparison with other mottos. Across previous periods, it is difficult to speak of any clear motto for Europe. 'The Senate and People of Rome' ('*Senatus Populusque Romanus*', abbreviated SPQR) pointed back at the two main bodies constituting the Roman Republic and the Roman Empire in which this motto was used. Today, nobody would be satisfied with a motto that just named the institutions and people of Europe, without offering a sense of direction forward. Charlemagne's motto was 'renewal of the Roman Empire' ('*renovatio imperii Romani*'), which is much too backward-looking or even reactionary to be reused in modern times, where future-oriented progress is the main narrative. Later actors striving to create a transnational European power—for instance Napoleon or Nazi Germany—had several different mottos linked to them, none of which really got any general status in the larger territory.

The African Union still has no official motto, though the need for creating such pan-African symbols has been discussed in that union. Both Indonesia and South Africa use an almost similar national motto as the EU, 'unity in diversity'. In their case, the word 'unity' stresses the goal of unity more strongly than the more processual 'united' of the EU, and—as these states are no federations of formally separate states (though South Africa was a 'Union' until 1961)—'diversity' refers not to different nationalities but to the subnational plurality of ethnic groups. In the EU case, the latter term is intended to be much broader, including not only cultural and ethnic but also and prominently political and national diversity, since the Union is bound to respect the relative autonomy of each member state.

Since 1956, the official US motto is 'In God We Trust', derived from the lyrics of the American national anthem: 'The Star Spangled Banner', written in 1814. However, since before that, and still in widespread use today, has been the more secular '*e pluribus unum*' ('out of many, one', 'one for many' or 'one from many [parts]'). It is said to derive from a Roman poem called 'Moretum', sometimes attributed to Virgil, and where it describes how different colours are blended into one. It was included on the 1776 Seal of the United States, adopted by an Act of Congress in 1782 and used on US coins since 1786. As it was never codified by law, the Congress in 1956 decided to instead officially adopt 'In God We Trust', but it has still remained in use until recent times, for instance on dollar coins.[247] Like the motto of most federations, the US one states that many different merge into one single, united whole. It was actually used by European politicians in the late 1950s for stressing the necessary balance between individual states and a common identity. In the 1993 De Clercq report, it was modified into '*In uno plures*' in order to strike a distance from the US melting-pot approach.[248] The US motto conforms to the melting-pot image of the US federation, where plurality disappears for the benefit of unity. It refers to the welding of a single federal state from a group of individual political units—originally colonies and now states. The EU motto instead makes a key point that it is precisely diversity that is the main resource for the ongoing process of unifying European nations, more in line with a multicultural 'salad-bowl' interpretation of diversity, though transposed from ethnic to national relations.[249] It is more explicitly diversity-friendly, stressing that it is the internal plurality of the union that is its defining characteristic. This also corresponds to the extraordinarily many linguistic and cultural differences within Europe, which have been seen as an obstacle to unification, but which the motto explains being rather a positive source of strength. 'Whereas the US motto aims at [a] unity created from a diversity of states, the EU puts any further unity under the condition of a maintained diversity amongst the states', as Toggenburg formulates it.[250] An interpretation would seem to indicate that the motto expresses a kind of balance between the polarities represented by the two myths mentioned before, making the combination of diversity and unity a key resource of Europe.

Few criticisms of the motto are found on the Internet. Most seem rather happy about it. For instance, someone at the Leicester Intercultural Communication and Leadership School (ICLS) found this motto helpful:

> For a start, the EU's motto is 'United in Diversity', a motto I can fully relate to working for ICLS in Leicester. It helped me start to overcome a few of my prejudices. Like many Brits, I had not considered myself a European, mainly because of media influences and our 'island mentality'. However, after speaking with my new friends from Rotterdam, Berlin and Rome, I realised that Europe is a strong coalition that can exert pressure (for better of worse) when engaged in international negotiations. It seems to me that this is the best reason to remain and become more engaged in the EU, because as a democratic institution we can encourage it to use its power in a globally responsible way.[251]

Some websites question if there is any real unity, if it is at all possible, or if it is a welcome vision for the future. Some have made fun of the abstract and slightly paradoxical character of the motto, and of the way it was created:

> That, of course, means no more than 'diversity through unity' would mean. Or 'sameness through difference', 'white through black' or 'one through zero'. And it will have exactly as much effect as any of those slogans would on our 'identification of or with' and 'emotional attachment to' Europe. [...] This slogan is the bland expression of an abstract contradiction. It was arrived at through a quasi-democratic process; and then unilaterally altered by people who decided they knew better in order to get a result they preferred. It is, as the Committee on Constitutional Affairs so elegantly puts it, 'the perfect definition of the essence of the European project'.[252]

This is witty, but at least the accusation of being contradictory is basically flawed: 'United in diversity' is not synonymous with 'white through black' or any other paradox, as the analysis here should already have made evident. Compared to the fate of the flag and the anthem, to be discussed in following chapters, the motto has met strikingly little strong substantial opposition or fewer alternative proposals, except that some still after so many years refer to the EU motto in its initial form, 'unity in difference', and others passingly mention various other slogans that circulate in Europe, including shifting combinations of keywords like 'freedom', 'justice' and 'solidarity'— or some other variation on the French Revolution's *liberté, égalité, fraternité*—but without really confronting the official one.

Since back in 1958, the Council of the European Union has a presidency that rotates among member states every six months. This 'EU Presidency' often comes with a particular motto and logo that aim to reflect the particularly important current tasks, but also shed some new light on how Europe is identified. For instance, in spring 2006, Austria used 'Partnership for a social future', and in spring 2007, Germany used three different slogans: 'Europe—succeeding together', 'Living Europe safely' and 'Europe—a partner for sustainable global development'. Portugal in autumn 2007 had 'A stronger Union for a better world', Slovenia in spring 2008 talked of 'Si.nergy for Europe', France in autumn 2008 promoted the considerably more controversial and Captain Euro-like 'a more protective Europe', and the Czech presidency in spring 2009 opened up again with 'A Europe without barriers', which Sweden in autumn 2009 connected to by its 'Openness, effectiveness and dialogue'. Sweden also made use of a 'Me-We' formula striving to balance and link an individualised perspective to a collective belonging and institutional underpinning in formulations like 'Me-We: Your contribution times half a billion—what a force!' All these slogans are clearly conjunctural and bound to particular tasks deriving from the situation of that specific period. Together, they indicate that in these last years, the widening and strengthening of the Union has been a primary goal, where different countries and/or periods put emphasis either on openness or on safety.

Many nations have mottos that promote the individual country in question, highlighting its strengths or formulating a task to make it stronger in relation to others. A typical example is the current Swedish king Carl XVI Gustaf with his 'For Sweden—With the times' (*'För Sverige—i tiden'*). Some nations include a certain measure of transnational orientation, such as Turkey who since Atatürk's time uses 'Peace at home, peace in the world' (*'Yurtta sulh, cihanda sulh'*). In comparison, the European motto is turned more inwards. It acknowledges plurality within itself, but does not in any way thematise its relations to the rest of the world.

One may find several variations on the European motto in use by different associations and companies. To take just one single example of the latter, the WSP Group, established in the United Kingdom in the 1970s, is today 'a global business providing management and consultancy services to the built and natural environment' with 9000 employees worldwide.[253] Its presentation material uses a plethora of visionary formulations, including the typical 'core values' of 'trust', 'support and sharing', 'pride and passion', 'sustainability' and 'innovation'. Their main slogan leans heavily on EU rhetoric:

> We don't suppress individuality or the different needs of our clients and our teams. Though we are united by our shared pride, passion and desire to collaborate, we have very different areas of expertise, specialism and innovation. Put it all together and we can be the very best to work with and work for. We call it: 'United by our difference'.[254]

This repeated slogan carries a similar message as that of the EU, only more openly and simply stated: 'Ultimately being *United by our difference* means our people flourish in an environment that allows them to produce and be their very best.' This is presumably also the intention behind the EU, and the ideological transfer shows how compatible such a motto is not only with interstate collaboration but also with corporate marketing.

Conclusions

The motto is a highly abstract and compressed verbal symbol of Europe. It is framed by a genre of mottos that express the intended goals and responsibilities of a social actor. This actor is in this case a union of sovereign nation states, and even though the EU claims to represent the whole of Europe, it is therefore not surprising that its motto focuses on the form and process of unification itself, rather than on any other aspect of European identity. Each term in the motto is crucial. 'United' indicates an accomplishment resulting from a process rather than given by definition: a decisive step has been taken, namely, the formation of the EU that has united Europe's nations into something stronger than a simple gathering, without eradicating their mutual differences by fusing them into one single state. 'Diversity' signals a cultural and political plurality rather than an inner contradiction or polar otherness. And the word 'in' seems to combine aspects of a 'through' and 'by', making diversity a sustainable and respected feature of the accomplished unification, rather than just an initial condition or starting point. Here, the four aspects analysed in the previous symbols seem only partially valid.

1.   The motto is rather neutral in relation to the first aspect, involving the polarity of *dislocation* and *fixity*. The processual term 'united' instead of 'unity' does contribute a certain sense of dislocation, namely from a state of inner division and fragmentation to another situation where diversity remains but does not any longer block and prevent unification, since unity has been redefined so that

it does not demand standardised uniformity. This is apparently possible in the present, late modern time where individualisation and flexible specialisation have enabled new and more open ways of connecting, also alluded to in terms like glocalisation (combining globalisation and localisation).[255]

2. As for *desire*, it is possible to conceive the unification of diverse agencies as something that creates joy and satisfaction, whether allusions are made specifically to (hetero)sexual intercourse or just to intersubjective or intercultural communication in general. The motto talks of a *desire for otherness* or for internal difference, with affinities to the Zeus–Europa encounter. The talk of unification at the same time has a loose affinity with the complementary value of rational *control*. The motto can therefore be said to—equally much as the day—balance these two poles that Europa and Captain Euro represented.

3. The motto has a very faint connection to a theme found both in the Europa myth and in Europe Day: that of *elevation*. The processual character of the term 'united' may indicate some kind of civilising historical accomplishment (or task ahead). This would have been more evident had the formulation been more like that of the United States, which depicts plurality as developing into unity. In the EU case, diversity is never abandoned, so that unity and difference remain equally valid for Europe today. It is therefore hard to point at a clear elevation to some kind of higher level, in the way that princess Europa was temporarily lifted up by the god Zeus. Still, one may possibly stretch the interpretation a little bit and consider the depiction of inner diversity, as the main and identifying asset of this union, to be a kind of uplifting self-image: Europe is supposedly to some extent unique (a) in containing such a vast number of ethnicities, religions, languages, cultural communities and political nation states, and (b) in regarding this inner division as a positive resource, which carries over to the fourth aspect below. Still, these embryonic meanings seem rather weak, and on the whole, the motto appears to be rather neutral and does not to contribute much along this dimension of elevation.

4. The motto thus only faintly takes up the first three themes found in the previous symbols. However, the fourth aspect of *hybridity* may well be seen as almost synonymous to the motto. In a way, hybridity is another term for precisely the fusion of unity and diversity: differences that persist even though they are unified into one new kind of body. Harmonious unity and diversity compete, with shifting balance, in all the different symbolic domains. From this perspective, the complex diversity of Europe need not defeat the idea of a European community. To unify a social body that lacks any generally shared or unitary life form—

language, religion, ethnicity or political rule—is a challenge that demands an intense building of bridges in all directions, but it is no final contradiction of the European project as such. The EU motto 'united in diversity' suggests that the irreducible plurality may be the strength of this project. Instead of substituting diversity with unity, it is the diversity itself that forms the basis of Europe: in Étienne Balibar's words, Europe's dense history of superimposed differences has lent it a particular capacity to act 'as the *interpreter of the world*, translating languages and cultures in all directions'.[256]

6

Flag

The most prominent visual symbol of the EU is its flag with twelve golden stars in a perfect circle on a blue background. This is probably also the most familiar of these symbols to most people inside and outside Europe, since it is widely visible both on flagpoles and in various print and electronic material related to the EU. In this way, it is a kind of logotype that fulfils a quite traditional role of flags.

What's in a flag?

A flag is a piece of cloth, usually attached to a pole and designed to identify and symbolise a community or an office. The term may fall back on the verb form 'to flag', which is probably derived from an old Nordic onomatopoeic expression of something flapping in the wind. It is actually used both for the piece of cloth itself, and for the graphic design or emblem that it shows, and which may also be depicted in print, on the Internet or in any other visual medium. Flags may have widely different shapes and sizes (from standards and banners to pennons or streamers), but most are oblong and carry an easily recognisable colourful design. Wording and verbal elements are often avoided in flag design, since they are linguistically limited and tend to disturb the need for simplicity and symmetry, especially since flags are made of thin cloths.[257] The most relevant type here is the national flag, but there are also flags for provinces, cities, organisations and businesses, as well as flags used for signalling or decoration. A flag thus works like a kind of logo—a graphical emblem or icon forms a trademark or brand of a company, together with the designed typeface that is its logotype. But whereas commercial logos have a rather recent history, flags go several millennia back in time.

The earliest forms of flags were used at sea and as insignia of leadership in warfare. They developed from what in vexillology (the study of flags) is called 'vexilloids', or proto-flags: prehistoric decorative signs (but not yet coloured pieces of cloth) that serve as marks of office for a leader of a community, for instance those used by the classical Romans as well as by the Mongolian invaders. Before that, the Chinese invention of silk between 6000 and 3000 BC enabled the introduction of cloth flags, probably in that same period. Most Chinese flags were monochrome, but some showed birds, tigers or dragons. Flags were equally important in India, and were probably brought to Europe by the Saracens, whose more abstractly designed military banners used by Muslim Arabs in battles inspired the crusaders to make similar flags, often based on crosses with specific colour combinations. Their designs became increasingly organised with the development of heraldry in the tenth century AD. The first national flags were introduced at sea by the Italian city republics of Genova and Venice in the early eleventh century AD. The Danish flag 'Dannebrogen'—red with a white cross—derives from that time and is thereby the oldest national state flag still in use. A more extensive use of national flags with a fixed and elaborate system for their use (for instance raising flags on fortresses) was developed with the journeys of discovery in the fourteenth and fifteenth centuries.

Even though flags thus have a long history, some elements of their uses that are today experienced as quasi-natural actually are rather recent 'inventions'. Flags were for instance traditionally used as signs for state authority, and it was only with the French revolution in 1789 that a national flag, the Tricolour, became used by citizens in movements of liberation, both in European and in Latin American countries' struggle for independence in the early nineteenth century. And it was not until around 1900 that national flags started to be generally flown by individual citizens. All this implies that even though flags in general have an ancient history, the focus on flags as national symbols used by ordinary citizens for identification with their country is something relatively recent, which may explain that it became quite a difficult issue in the European unification process after World War II.

European national flags are intertextually related to each other, forming a kind of traditional 'flag families', of which the Christian cross banners (the Nordic countries, Greece, Switzerland, England and the United Kingdom) are the oldest; coats of arms of royal houses (Liechtenstein, San Marino) or at least their colours (Belgium, Germany, Hungary, Luxembourg, Monaco, Poland and Spain) survive particularly in monarchies, while countries with stronger republican traditions usually have a tricolor inspired by the Netherlands (horizontal) or France (vertical).[258] The EU flag is of a different kind.

What flags mean depends not only on their design but also on their uses: which values and emotions are invested in them varies a lot between nations (or other organisations whom they symbolise). Some are consciously used as strong and sometimes controversial identity markers, while others are more routinely used in the background, 'unwaved' bearers of 'banal nationalism', according to Michael Billig.[259] Thomas Hylland Eriksen has argued that the most influential flags fulfil three demands: they symbolise a shared identity that is based on more than just the flag; they are empty vessels that allow people to fill them with many different meanings; and this ambiguity vanishes at the boundaries of a nation, where their contrasts to surrounding others must be clear.[260] As will soon be shown, the European flag easily lives up to the third criterion, as it is rather unique in the world, but it has greater problems with the first two ones. As it is still most actively waved from above, by central institutions rather than by committed citizens, the existence of a shared European identity to back it up remains uncertain, and many seem to feel that its signifying power is too fixed. However, it may not hopelessly have lost this battle for recognition, and a closer interpretation will open up a number of options for how to read it.

Introducing the European flag

Whereas the motto is a newcomer, the European *flag* has been used for quite long (Figure 6.1). It was instituted in a series of steps starting in 1951 and ending with its establishment by the Council of Europe on 8 December 1955. Its heraldic description declares that it shows 'on an azure field, a circle of twelve golden mullets, their points not touching', and with an official symbolic description stating that 'against the background of blue sky, twelve golden stars form a circle representing the union of the peoples of Europe; the number of stars is fixed, twelve being the symbol of perfection and unity'.[261] It is instructive to scrutinise how this flag was established, even though the minute details of inventors, copyrights and datings will not be discussed here, and alternative designs used earlier or in parallel will be discussed later.

During the period from the convocation of the Congress of Hague 1948 and the formation of the Council of Europe in 1949 to its 1955 adoption of the final flag design, a complex process took place through which this design was established. In the beginning, there was no simple consensus, but several different designs were proposed by various European organisations and activists, in particular by the Paneuropean Union with its red cross on a yellow sun with a blue background, and by the European Movement with its green 'E' on white (these designs will be further discussed below). In a July 1951 memorandum from the Secretariat General of the Council of Europe on the European flag, a wide range of proposals were summarised and discussed. The rivalry between existing designs was mentioned, as was the fact that they remained 'private emblems' of organisation and had no official status or even use in practice within the emerging European institutions. A flag was needed as a tool 'to make the peoples of Europe more directly aware of their unity', but there was no existing design ready for use. 'It would seem wiser not to adopt any flag already existing', the memorandum argued. 'A completely new flag must be designed', meeting some basic requirements: '(a) Sufficient symbolical significance; (b) Simplicity; (c) Legibility; (d) Harmony; (e) Pleased appearance; (f) Orthodox heraldic design'.[262]

A range of proposed symbols were classified: a cross; the letter 'E'; a white star in a circle (used in 1944–5 by the armies of liberation); multiple stars equivalent to the number of member states in the Council of Europe (green stars on white, or white on red ground); the coat-of-arms of the Town of Strasbourg (symbolising the seat of the Council of Europe); a sun (dawning hope); or a triangle (representing culture). Various conflicting arguments were made concerning the main colours green, white and blue. Priority was given to visual recognition, excluding too intricate designs, clashing colour combinations and multicoloured emblems on the diagonal (as being too reminiscent of shipping companies' house flags). No less than twelve different 'main proposals' were outlined, but none of them was even remotely similar to the eventual outcome four years later; none had blue background, and the only one with multiple stars, suggested by Lucien Philippe, presented fifteen green stars in three rows on a white ground, which was indeed far from the current EU flag.

An intense discussion went on for a couple of years, where the Paneuropean Union's sun-cross was increasingly questioned, since it could not be accepted by Muslim members—and Turkey was since 1949 member of the Council of Europe. In December 1951, Salvador de Madariaga, Spanish founder of the College of Europe in Bruges, proposed an azure flag with a constellation of stars representing European capitals, with Strasbourg as the Council of Europe seat having a larger star. In 1952, Arsène Heitz, working for the Council's Mail Service, started developing the flag design that was to be the final official choice.

In September 1953, the Consultative Assembly of the Council of Europe adopted as its emblem a blue flag with a circle of fifteen stars, corresponding to the number of member states at the time. 'The complete circle symbolises unity, whereas the stars shining in the firmament symbolise the hope of our nations', said the report by Mr Bichet, who had prepared the proposal. However, this demanded that Saar was counted, which Germany could not accept. Also, it was foreseen that the future expansion of the union would cause recurrent redesign problems. It took a new round of negotiations and redesigns by Arsène Heitz, so that in January 1955 the two remaining alternatives were those of Madariaga and Heitz. It was the latter that won, and the flag was finally adopted by a Council of Europe Assembly decision on 25 October 1955, confirmed by the Committee of Ministers on 8 December that same year. The number of stars had then been reduced to twelve, and they were not anymore (like for instance the stars in the US flag) linked to the number of member states, but intended to signify perfection and harmony in a more general sense.

The flag was thus to represent the whole of Europe, but it was only formally adopted by the Council of Europe. For three decades it remained not yet officially sanctioned by the rest of the EU system, but that did not prevent it from being widely used. The Adonnino Committee report to the European Council meeting in Milan on 28–29 June 1985 suggested the establishment of a visual image identifying Europe:

> There is clearly a need, for both practical and symbolic reasons, for a flag and an emblem to be used at national and international events, exhibitions and other occasions where the existence of the Community needs to be brought to public attention.

The Committee proposed that the European Community emblem and flag should be 'a blue rectangle with, in the centre, a circle of 12 five-pointed gold stars which do not touch, surrounding a gold letter E'—corresponding to the final result adopted later, except that the 'E' was again omitted, possibly conforming to the general rule of avoiding wording in flags, but also in effect suppressing the name of 'Europe' and purifying the visual imagery. With the 1955 shape and design, the Flag of Europe was finally adopted by the EU institutions in 1986.[263]

The European flag thus evolved through a complex interplay between top politicians, European movements and designers. Like with Europe Day, key decisions were taken in the relevant EU bodies, but there was never any Europe-wide competition or voting as was at least to a limited extent the case with the European motto.

The flag functions as a logo, and it is not only found on pieces of cloth hanging on flagpoles outside official buildings in the EU member states, but also on websites and printed material related to the union.[264] Wherever infrastructures or regional backwaters are improved with EU support, the logo is visible to remind people that this welcome development could only be done by shared efforts, spreading badly needed goodwill around the emergent community-formation. One may also find the star circle on various tourist items and destinations, again to express transnational linkages, but much still remains to be done before it is as widely spread and used in popular media culture as for instance the US stars and stripes or the Union Jack. The logo is also displayed at number plates on all member states' cars. This secures wide distribution of the symbol all over the union, along its roads and autostradas, almost like blood circulation with the roads as veins and arteries, and Brussels as the pumping heart. The mobility of cars has been a key symbol for the mobility of modern life, ever since the early and mid-twentieth century. Today these mobile carriers of the EU symbol help symbolising the single market and at least the first three of the four key mobilities or freedoms of the EU itself—the free movement of goods, services, people and money—as EU-marked trucks, buses and cars carry goods and people across the continent.

Interpreting the European flag

Various EU texts declare that the flag is meant to symbolise 'Europe's unity and identity', through a circle of gold stars representing 'solidarity and harmony between the peoples of Europe' or 'the ideal of unity among the peoples of Europe'.[265] In order to investigate its layers of meaning, I will here in rather arbitrary order discuss its main features: the blue and golden yellow colours; the stars; the number twelve; and the symmetric and circular shape of the star constellation.

The choice of the colours *golden on blue* is far from arbitrary. It is often said that blue is traditionally used to represent the European continent, and it is true that blue is included in several European flags since at least the nineteenth century (see below). Conventional classification, inspired by racist thinking, has linked Africa to black colour, Asia to yellow and (north) America to red while Australia has been associated with green.[266] With a similar race metaphor, Europe could actually as well have been conceived as white, but this has in practice rarely been the case, perhaps indicating that the dominant 'race' does not see itself in racial terms, but as universal man. Seen from the earth through its nearest atmosphere, blue is the natural background to stars: 'the colour of the sky and the universe'.[267] Blue is used symbolically to represent sky and water, and by extension as the background to symbols for nations or continents surrounded by seas, such as Australia or Europe. However, this argument is rather weak, since all continents are, by definition at least, surrounded by water, so this does not explain why Europe could have a special affinity to the colour blue. Actually Europe and Asia are the continents with least sea boundaries, as their shared land boundary takes up much higher percentage of their total periphery than for any other continent. But blue has also come to represent the West, in contrast to the red East. In medieval Europe, it became associated with the Virgin Mary, being the colour of her mantle and of her sapphire stone. In the twelfth century it became a royal colour.[268]

Another argument has been that all colours other than blue were already occupied by some widely recognised special meaning: red for socialism and communism, green for Islam, black for mourning, yellow for quarantine and white for capitulation. In contrast, blue was free to use, as it has not been used to signify any other continent or been to tightly linked to any specific but unsuitable general concept. A website summarising popular perceptions of colour meaning states that dark blue represents 'knowledge, power, integrity, and seriousness':

> Blue is the color of the sky and sea. It is often associated with depth and stability. It symbolizes trust, loyalty, wisdom, confidence, intelligence, faith, truth, and heaven. [...] Blue is strongly associated with tranquility and calmness. In heraldry, blue is used to symbolize

piety and sincerity. [...] As opposed to emotionally warm colors like red, orange, and yellow; blue is linked to consciousness and intellect. [...] Blue is a masculine color; according to studies, it is highly accepted among males. Dark blue is associated with depth, expertise, and stability; it is a preferred color for corporate America.[269]

The cited EU sources display a politically and socially biased perspective in interpreting the red colour as evidently socialist and thus problematic for general use, while the blue colour is seen as sufficiently 'neutral'. The royal and aristocratic uses of the blue colour are homological with its associations of the sky and heavens with highness in general, and also with the modern link to male gender identity—with pink as the female counterpart, according to a widespread cliché, for instance in children's dress. This ideologically 'dominant' relative positioning of blue may in turn explain its current associations with institutional stability, high nobility and elites with liberal or conservative ideas. It is no wonder that it is a favoured colour when political and economic elites wish to symbolise reliable institutions.

Expressions such as 'blue eyed' or 'out of the blue' critically express the weak spot of such self-elevation, by materialistically underlining the emptiness of the upper stratosphere. The use of blue for a kind of melancholic feeling, for instance in the blue notes and moods of jazz and blues, is an exception to the rule, forming an alternative genealogy of interpretation that also has long historical roots, as already Chaucer in the late fourteenth century had used 'blue' for 'sad' and the seventeenth century had its 'blue devil'. There may be a connection to the skin colour of people in fear or depression, but the main understandings of blueness in modern times sticks with the other, dominant line of identification with highness and stability.

Not forgetting any of the other implications mentioned so far, I conclude that a main reason for—and effect of—the choice of blue and golden colours is that they allow the signification of some kind of elevation, since they remind of (a) heavens and stars and also to some extent of (b) the precious metal of gold, which for ages has been an ultimate image of refined wealth and nobility.

This is then also the main explanation of the fact that the objects appearing on the blue background are *stars* and not for instance just dots or circles, or arrows, flowers, trees or anything else. Not all flags depict specific objects: some are monochrome, while some others just contain a couple of contrasting colour fields. But when objects are shown, stars are the most common ones. The star constellation lends the flag a 'cosmic dimension' representing the 'hopes and elevated values' of these European peoples, EU sources agree.[270] The stars 'light the night sky and orbit around the polar star and are therefore perceived as symbols of the cosmic order':

In flags, the star illustrates independence, unity, liberty, renewal and hope. It is not by chance that the flags of many former colonies contain stars together, in many Islamic countries, with the crescent. [...] One of the features of the stars of the European flag is that they have five points which do not touch one another, also known as a pentagram or pentacle. Since five-points stars can be drawn with a single, interwoven closed line, the Pythagoreans gave them a mystical meaning of perfection. In the European flag, the pentagram fits in well with the circle which is also a symbol of perfection. The five-point star is also the symbol of man as an individual possessing five fingers and toes, five senses and five limbs.[271]

This interpretation offered by EU sources stresses the meaning of a star with five points as a specific kind of individuality: a perfect subjectivity or spirit that is at once cosmic and human. Six-pointed stars would have given unwanted Jewish associations, four points would remind too much of a Christian cross, while fewer points are more difficult to see as a star, so that five points work as the simplest geometric version of a star with rays around a central body, and the star shape also has a long history in European heraldry. Stars are incredibly hot and lucid, full of intense energy, hinting at Europe's states and citizens being supposedly likewise strong, enlightened and dynamic agents in the world. At the same time they are incredibly fixed in the sky, in the same manner as the EU wants to be a guarantee of stability, and Europe as a whole to be seen as a global fixpoint and reliable basis for enlightenment. Again, this confirms the theme of human elevation or even divination or sacralisation. The stars are intended to stand for Europe's constituents—peoples and nations—and they are thus depicted as if they are all by themselves perfect creatures stretching out into the sky and shining like superb stars.

The latter 'if' is perhaps not quite innocent. Most interpreters seem to take almost for granted that the stars stand for European member states, since a flag of a union is generally supposed to contain symbols of the basic entities that are united, and the EU is after all still more a union of member states than for instance of regions or of citizens. But a star constellation in a blue sky could also signify a guiding ideal, like the star over Bethlehem in the New Testament of the Christian Bible directed the three wise men to the stable where Jesus was born. This would make the flag more like the motto, an expression of the will and intent of the EU: a wish to strive for elevation or perfection perhaps. Still, it is difficult to avoid the interpretation of the stars as symbolising the basic entities that this union unites, that is, the European nation states that are members of the EU.

So, why are there precisely *twelve* stars, and not just one, three, or for instance as many as there happen to be member states in the EU?

When there is more than one star, they generally represent a unit of measurement, i.e. they number federal states (United States), provinces (Costa Rica, Venezuela), geographical areas (Philippines), parishes (Grenada), islands (Comoros, Cape Verde, São Tomé and Príncipe) and peoples (Burundi, Burma).[272]

But the number of stars in the EU flag has nothing to do with the number of member states. The number twelve was chosen as a traditional 'symbol of perfection, completeness and unity', the EU information sites explain. Twelve is the number of months in a year and the number of hours shown on a clock face, thus connoting the dynamism of time.

> Twelve is considered to be an ideal number. It provided the foundation of the Babylonian numerical system (called duodecimal for that reason). There are 12 signs of the zodiac which therefore represent the universe. There are 12 months of the year, 12 hours of the day and 12 hours of the night, 12 Egyptian gods, 12 Olympian deities which formed the Greek pantheon from the 5th century B.C., 12 laps in the chariot races of ancient Greece, 12 labours of Hercules in Greek mythology, 12 tables making up the first codification of Roman law, 12 knights of King Arthur's Round Table in Celtic tradition and 12 gates of Paradise in Scandinavia.
>
> Twelve is also a number in Judaeo-Christian symbolism. The tree of life has 12 fruits; there are 12 sons of Jacob, 12 patriarchs, 12 tribes of Israel and 12 gates of the New Jerusalem. Moses sent 12 explorers to the lands of Canaan, the bread multiplied by Jesus was placed in 12 baskets and Jesus talks of 12 legions of angels after the kiss of Judas; lastly, there are 12 apostles. The number 12 is also the product of multiplying three, always a divine number (the trinity), by four, the number of the earth with its four cardinal points; 12 is therefore the symbol 'of the union between the divine and the terrestrial world' which, as we know, embodies the central mystery of Christianity.[273]

This speaks again of perfection, but combined with a more specific reference to time, and to a temporal aspect of Europe as an historical project rather than a static fixpoint.

Finally, what does the particular circular, symmetric and uniform shape of the star constellation imply? The choice of a perfectly symmetric *circle* of stars where each star is exactly identical, of equal size and shape, is meant to signify en egalitarian union of peoples or nations. 'The complete circle symbolises unity, whereas the stars shining in the firmament symbolise the hope of our nations' said the report that in 1953 established the first version of the EU flag.

> A circle has no beginning or end, no direction or orientation and is
> homogeneous, perfect and indivisible. A circle leads back to itself and is
> therefore a symbol of unity, of the absolute and of perfection. In a circle,
> all the points of the circumference are equidistant from the centre. For
> this reason it is a good illustration of the union of the peoples of Europe
> to which the official symbolic description refers. However, it is just as
> good an illustration of the parity of the Member States.[274]

The circle is often used as a symbol of unity, and the circular pattern reinforces the
already mentioned association of the stars to perfection and elevation. It was previously
said that each star could be seen as an individual constituent of Europe. Alternatively,
the symbol could depict Europe itself, though absent in the centre of the circle,
stretching up into the heavens and being encircled by stars. Star images have ancient
roots and therefore a wide resonance around the world, but it has often been pointed
out that there is also a more specific Christian subtext here, in that the star circle looks
like a halo or nimbus around a saint. The design of the star circle is often said to have
been inspired by—or at least reminiscent of—the nimbus of a Catholic St Mary image,
possibly in a church of Paris or Strasbourg.[275] This would be consistent with the choice
of the blue colour that is also since medieval times associated with the Virgin Mary, and
thus with the human being that becomes elevated through an intimate contact with the
divine being—in resonance with the mythical fate of Europa in her encounter with
Zeus, and thus strengthening the symbolic ties between Europe and the flag design.

The flag's main designer Arsène Heitz himself, looking back in 1987, admitted that
his design had Christian inspiration, claiming that 'the flag of Europe is the flag of
Our Lady', and it is often thought that the precise inspiration stemmed from a fresco
by Pietro Berrettini da Cortona in the Grand Salon of Palazzo Barberini in Rome,
where a huge figure of Immortality holds a crown with twelve shining stars (Figure
6.2). However, Carlo Curti Gialdino is sceptical towards this theory:

> Even though this is an attractive theory, as it would enable the design
> of the European flag to be associated with fundamental human rights,
> it seems a somewhat unlikely solution, dreamed up after the event and
> perhaps just a 'trick of memory'.[276]

Curti Gialdino's own alternative (but admittedly unsupported) hypothesis is that the
design was instead inspired by an early US flag with a circle on stars in the blue canton,
adopted in 1777 (Figure 6.5). This flag may in turn have been inspired by the halo of
stars in Giovanni Battista Tiepolo's painting *The Immaculate Conception*, painted a
decade earlier (Figure 6.3).[277] Curti Gialdino points at the difficulty with admitting
any US inspiration at all, since it could risk stirring up an accusation of federalism

that remains a highly controversial issue in the EU. One may also add that the EU is unwilling to admit any inspiration from its so far main global competitor. So many saints have traditionally been depicted with a star halo that the detour over the United States may not be needed: see for instance the many popular 'médailles miraculeuses' featuring the Madonna thus illuminated (Figure 6.4).

Irrespective of its credibility, the Catholic connection is often repeated in comments to the flag design. A UK website for fundamentalist Christian but anti-Catholic Bible prophecy caters to those who find a deeper meaning in that the flag was supposedly inspired by the halo of twelve stars around Catholic Madonna pictures, representing either her son's twelve disciples or the twelve tribes of Israel, relating to a passage in *Revelation* 12:1: 'A great and wondrous sign appeared in heaven: a woman clothed with the sun, with the moon under her feet and a crown of twelve stars on her head.'[278] The *European Navigator* also confesses to that inspiration: 'Twelve together with stars, the crown of stars, reflects, as has been said, the vision of the Virgin Mary of the Revelation (12,1) and is the symbol par excellence of popular Marian iconography.'[279] In all interpretations, an almost sacral elevation seems to be a main implication of the twelve star circle.

The Virgin Mary connection can also be generalised in that the circular shape with the central 'hole' in several ways connote femininity, far from any phallic masculinity. Julia Kristeva has used Plato's concept of the rhythmically pulsating '*chora*' (receptacle) to analyse a maternally derived pre-semantic level in language use, working like a void container and lending the origin of communication a gendered dimension.[280] Both in a material and a metaphorical sense, the open circle seems to construct Europe as female gendered, in tune with the Europa myth.

A partly related association that has been made to the star circle is Jesus Christ's crown of thorns, as mentioned in the Bible Gospels and depicted in endless numbers of sculptures and paintings since then. Thorns in Christian symbolism represent sins and trials, and the martyr crown of thorns is a strong symbolism for many saints' victory over torture and death. Making a crown out of something so painful creates a double meaning: supposedly intended by the evil to mock the martyr, but inverted by Christians as a sign of elevation from the deepest agony to eternal sacredness. The association of the star circle to the thorn crown is not purely accidental, since Christian interpreters have also argued that Mary as Queen of Heaven and Mother of Sorrows (Mater Dolorosa) symbolically wears her son's martyr crown in a kind of refiguration, transposed from painfully bodily thorns to heavenly lucid stars. Already in the artworks that originally may have inspired the Europe flag design, the twelve five-pointed stars together form a shape that may well remind not only of cosmic dignity but also of being raised through the most fearsome material disaster to this sacral position. This would then be perfectly homologous to the key post-war narrative that legitimates the European unification project: the way Europe after having almost perished from internal strife and catastrophes is now rising in peace and unity. This almost mythical turn from the deepest darkness up to blessed light is a classical one, well in tune with how the European Enlightenment regarded itself as a climbing up from Mediaeval darkness to universal rationality, so the thorn/star image can well also be transposed to a secular level. This interpretation certainly adds to the complexity of the initially simple visual symbol.

Another possible association of the golden circle is to the ring motif, famous from Wagner's and Tolkien's already mentioned quasi-mythical narratives. In such a reading, the golden ring of stars could be reinterpreted as a rather mixed blessing: an object of immense desire that brings a fatal curse to its owner. This would confirm the suspicion among sceptics that the perfect harmony sought for by the EU is in reality a too heavy burden to carry for its member states, an alluring image that fools politicians astray into some kind of catastrophe. This is of course not the intended or preferred reading of the flag, nor is it often actualised in the debates I have found.

The harmonious perfection of the circle at the same time has the disadvantage of appearing closed and self-sufficient, not opening up very much to the external world, and also being quite static.[281] This symbol of unitary harmony leaves little space for difference. The closed form appears like a wall around an empty void in the middle, with each star shining as a perfect, separate individual shape, each exactly same as the other. The flag in this reading thus presents the EU as a monolith, with no space for real multicultural diversity. What speaks against this critical reading might perhaps be the fact that the circle is not a fully closed ring but an open circle of stars with permeable space in between:

> If the points of the star do not touch, this means that the circle is open. Symbolically, therefore, the European Union is not a closed society; it is not, as is often said with a negative connotation, a fortress; in contrast, the European Union is above all open to the accession of the States of Europe and is also an active member of the international community, is open to the outside world and plays its part in the life of international relations.[282]

In this reading, it is thus crucial that the star circle is not a closed ring: there are openings between the stars, which thus do not form an inaccessible fortress but perhaps a hospitable space. Also, the crown of thorns reading mentioned above contradicts any fortress-interpretation, as such thorns are primarily delivering pain inward to the bearer of the crown, while the edges of a fortress wall are turned outside. The star points are as sharp in both directions, making either interpretation possible, but it is difficult to univocally pin down the flag's meaning to just the closed circle metaphor.

In this interpretive direction, there is a key secular and political aspect to the star formation. The uniformity and equidistance of the stars may be understood to symbolise the basic equality needed for a just democratic rule. Such an argument may be based on Jean-Pierre Vernant's studies of the circular metaphor in ancient Greek cosmology and politics, in *Myth and Thought among the Greeks*.[283] Carefully analysing the close links between a geometric cosmology, urban space and political life, Vernant shows how Anaximander's (c. 610 BC–546 BC) circular cosmology, reorganising physical space in a circular fashion around an immobile earth, systematically corresponds to Kleisthenes' constitutional reform of the city of Athens 508–507 BC, where the *agora* as a kind of common or 'public hearth' likewise became the centre around which all citizens of the *polis* were placed at equidistance (Figure 6.6 and 6.7).[284] In this first democratic and secularised organisation, all parts 'were clearly similar, symmetrical, and fundamentally equivalent in their common relationship with the single center', which 'expressed in spatial terms no longer the notions of differentiation and hierarchy but rather those of homogeneity and equality'.[285]

This rather abstract circular metaphor may well be applied to the EU flag. It may be interpreted as depicting European political space as an open and egalitarian *agora* (of member states or, by extension, of individual citizens), parallel to how civil society can also be understood as structured by modern public sphere. The term 'public sphere' is particularly suitable here, as a 'sphere' is likewise a circular metaphor: it constitutes a perfectly symmetric and egalitarian abstract space where all surface points have the same distance to the void centre. The public sphere has a centre, but, unlike the role of the absolute monarch in the feudal representative public domain, nobody permanently occupies it. The centre around which modern democratic citizens are ideally and in principle equidistantly placed is a stage for interaction and dialogic exchange of ideas and opinions. This normative ideal is never fully realised in practice, as hierarchies remain in full force, along several dimensions of identity, but it is a key symbolic norm against which modern societies tend to be measured. The 2011 events on Tahir Square in Cairo (at the start of the Arab revolutions) and Syntagma Square in Athens (protesting against the financial crisis) indicated how the symbol and space of an open square is still fundamental to late modern democratic ideals. In this reading, the emptiness of the centre is no accident but a deliberate choice. It is an image of a civil society centered on a communicative network that does not allow single individuals to place themselves as fixed autocrats in the middle. This is at least one possible interpretation of the circular symbol, based on an important line of European history.

Egality is in this reading thus a 'higher', more civilised and refined political order than the authoritarian societies that a hierarchic pyramid would signify. The circle would then imply a secular form of perfection, suitable for the democratic system that Europe strives to defend.

Besides the rather obvious aspect of (sacral or geometric) elevation, then, the circular constellation also seems to indicate some sort of openness, which in turn may be understood either negatively or positively. To sceptical critics, the empty circle may represent Europe as a void, a nothingness, a chiasm, indicating that something is missing in its centre, conforming to the problematisation of the allegedly alienating abstractness of all EU symbols.

But the circle could on the other hand equally well signify the opening of a space, a stage for actors to enter, an agora for interaction, a kind of new public sphere to be filled with communication. An early idea when the flag design was discussed was that each European institution could later insert a specific symbol inside the circle, just like the Paneuropean Union has in later years combined the EU flag with its own sun-cross (see below). The circle is sometimes also filled by other actors, when the EU collaborates with for instance national institutions in a specific project. The circle invites precisely this kind of symbolic practice, and this is also something that was approved in the discussions leading up to the adoption of this design.[286]

Comparisons and commentary

The polysemy of the flag design opens it up to a comparably wide range of interpretive conflicts. Two main lines of interpretation may be discerned. On one hand, the blue colour, the stars, the number twelve and the nimbus shape all are associated with the sacred perfection of Christian inspiration. On the other hand, the perfect but open circle of equal stars is a symbolism that connects to classical democratic ideas of egality, the public sphere and political life at the agora. In both cases, Europe stretches up into the sky, is lifted up to a higher level and spreads a light of hope or enlightenment, in either a sacral or secular form of perfection. The open void in the middle may or may not invite some kind of dislocation or mobility, but the flag still tends more towards fixity and uniformity than mobility or hybridity.

In several senses then, the flag links up to important facets of the Europa myth: elevation and a dislocation in the sense that the empty centre suggests that something or someone has been taken away or is alternatively invited to step in and make Europe a home. On the other hand, it allows very little diversity, and its fixed perfection is also easily accommodated to the stress on unity and stability foregrounded by Captain Euro.

The Flag of Europe looks familiar but is still unique in many ways. Single stars, or a shifting number of stars in various formations (either geometrical patterns or star constellations), are combined with other colour elements in a number of national flags, including those of China, Ethiopia, Rwanda, Kosovo, Turkey, Uruguay, Venezuela and Vietnam, but nowhere is there a sky-blue background combined with such a symmetric composition of stars. For instance, Kosovo's flag is since its independence in 2008 blue with six white stars, one for each ethnic group, forming an arc above a golden map of the country (Figure 6.8). Turkey has since 1844 a red flag with a white crescent moon beside a five-pointed star—a motif going back at least another millennium to pre-Islamic symbols of the moon goddess Dianna, perhaps distantly related to Europa (Figure 6.9). Though a similar stellar combination of moon and star is commonly used in the Arabic region, it has no Muslim origin but rather symbolises the land and region itself. The People's Republic of China since 1949 has a flag with five stars on red background (Figure 6.10). While the red colour since nineteenth century symbolises communism and socialism in Europe, it has an older resonance in China, where it was cherished in the Zhou Dynasty (1045–256 BC), symbolising good fortune and joy, and remains widely used in New Year celebrations.[287] While the European stars are equals, the Chinese form a clear hierarchy with one big (standing for the Communist Party) and four small (symbolising the four main social classes: working class, peasants, petty bourgeoisie and national bourgeoisie), expressing an hierarchical relation between one dominant ruler and four humble subjects.

United States' stars and stripes are globally well known, but the formation of those stars, equalling the number of states in the federation (while the thirteen stripes correspond to the original numer of states), has more an aura of rational protocol than of a cosmic heaven, and there are no further official meanings attached to the design. In 1920, the Universal Negro Improvement Association and African Communities League (UNIA) adopted the 'Pan-African' or 'Black Liberation' flag, with three horizontal bands in red, black and green, which was also used in African-American movements (Figure 6.11). The red was supposed to stand for blood (i.e. race) and liberation, black for skin (race again), and green for Africa's natural resources. Compared to many other flag symbols, this is a heavily race-oriented one, in line with certain primitivist tendencies to focus on the human body, ancestry and links to pre-historic nature. In 2004, the African Union (AU) decided to adopt the flag of its predecessor, the Organisation of African Unity (OAU), which existed from 1963 to 2002 (Figure 6.12). It was a green flag with a wide white horizontal band in the middle, narrow gold bands separating the white from the green, and in the middle the circular emblem of the AU, consisting of a golden map of Africa without borders, placed inside two concentric yellow, green and red circles, with palm leaves on either side. The AU explains that green stands for African hopes, the gold circle for Africa's wealth and bright future, white for pure friendship and red for solidarity and blood shed for the liberation of Africa.[288]

This rather complicated design seemed to demand an equally complex interpretation, far from the apparent simplicity of many other comparable symbols. No wonder therefore that the AU at its meeting on 30 January 2010 decided to instead adopt a much simpler design: a green flag with a circle of no less than 53 small golden five-point stars encircling a silhouette of the African map that covers a large sun whose

53 beams each end at one of the stars (Figure 6.13). The green background is said to symbolise 'African hopes and aspirations', the stars represent member states of the AU and the golden circle stands for 'Africa's wealth and bright future'.[289] It is fascinating how colour coding shifts: the green colour is now said to stand for a general principle of hope, but was previously supposed to signify Africa's grand jungle nature, and may have in a third interpretation symbolised Islam. The latter reading may have been welcomed by Libya's Muammar El Gaddafi who as outgoing Chairperson of the AU had the honour of presenting the new flag to the world, but would surely be rejected by Africans with a different confession. Similar redefinitions of colour codings are common. For instance, Srirupa Roy shows that for the Indian flag, the green, white and saffron colours were either understood to signify the religions of Muslims, Hindus and Buddhists or the universal values of hope, purity and sacrifice.[290] In such cases, however, the old interpretations are hard to obliterate and tend to linger on, giving established symbols an increasing richness of meaning. Africa = hope + nature + Islamic religion: each reading has highly different implications, but together they add to a dense but polysemic identification of Africa as a developing region serving as the Other of Europe and the western first world. It is certainly no mere coincidence that the simplified design with the star circle has obvious similarities with the EU flag, as the relative success of the EU model is something AU states desperately wish to imitate. One may perhaps wonder how to interpret the way the African continent seems to shade and darken the sun: presumably the idea has been to show how the sun starts shining bright from the heart of Africa, but the image may also (presumably unintentionally) hint at the old colonialist metaphors of Africa as the dark continent, for instance in Joseph Conrad's novel *Heart of Darkness* (1899). The new African flag is in any case a more suggestive and evocative emblem than the one it replaced, and it will be interesting to see how it is received inside and outside its continent.

A look at some older European flags and previous proposals sheds light on continuities but also divergent trajectories. If any symbol was typical of the classical Roman Empire and its resurrection as a Holy Roman Empire by Frederick Barbarossa in 1155, it was probably the *eagle*, originally a symbol of Jupiter. However, in modern times, it has become most used by continental Europe and finally much associated with Germany, and then also been almost monopolised by the United States, making it less useful to European unification. The Carolingians never really had a formal emblem, but shared with the crusades a variety of crosses, including the so-called Carolingian cross, composed of circles and developed from the triangular 'triquesta' that was in itself a Celtic and pagan symbol that was reinterpreted in Christian terms by relating it to the Holy Trinity (Figure 6.14). Besides the cross, there were few symbolic elements for the EU to take up from ancient history. Therefore it was no wonder that an intense creative process was initiated as the European project started rolling for real in the twentieth century.

Some symbolic elements repeatedly turned up in the various proposals that were put forward as the new European community sought to identify itself after World War II: (a) One was the capital letter 'E' for 'Europe', testifying to the identifying power of the name itself. (b) Another was the rising sun, which could as well be the descending sun, as Europe has from its main point of origin sometimes been identified as the land of the sunset or the west. (c) The cross has often been proposed, with a wide range of associations, but those to Christianity are hard to avoid and also to accept for a secular political rule, which for instance also Turkey should be able to idenfiy with. (d) A fourth and today almost forgotten one was the triangle, which supposedly represented culture, but with an unfortunate freemason touch. (e) Finally, the coat of arms of Strasbourg—diagonal red stripe on white background—as the seat of the Council of Europe has sometimes been up for debate, but was deemed as too closely linked to a particular place, town and nation.[291] It was two main designs that with minor variations were particularly much used to signify Europe: on the one hand the letter 'E' (a), on the other hand a cross in a sun (b+c). Each of them was promoted by one of the two leading pan-European movements at that time, and both designs differed considerably from what later became the EU flag.

The federalist movement called the Paneuropean Union has since its inception in 1923 used a blue flag with a yellow sun-cross in the centre, that is, a golden-yellow circle that is divided by a thin red cross (Figure 6.15). The blue and yellow colours and the stellar associations (only with a sun instead of stars) remind of the EU flag, but the difference is large enough to result in rather different signifying implications.

In a July 1950 memorandum on the European flag, Richard Coudenhave-Kalergi proposed that the Council of Europe adopt the flag of the Paneuropean Union, of which he was the President.[292] His principal criteria was that the flag must (1) be 'a symbol of our common civilization', (2) present 'a European emblem', (3) 'not provoke any national rivalry', (4) 'represent a tradition', and (5) 'be beautiful and dignified'. In his own interpretation, the blue sky was 'the natural background of the Sun' and 'a symbol of peace'. The sun was 'the eternal symbol of light, of spirit, of progress, of prosperity and of truth' and the red cross 'recognized by the whole world, by Christian and non-Christian nations as a symbol of international charity and of the brotherhood of man'. Coudenhave-Kalergi spent considerable energy to defend the cross as 'the great symbol of Europe's moral unity':

> The crushing majority of European Christians will not admit the cross being removed from the European flag—while the non-Christian minority cannot oppose this symbol, inseparable from our history and civilization; as the Christian minorities in the Near East do not oppose the national symbols of the Crescent and the Star of David.

He emphasised that the cross was 'a pre-Christian symbol of world-harmony, on Celtic and Germanic monuments', and that the red cross was 'the first European Flag at the time of the Crusades'. However, precisely that kind of Christian image was clearly not acceptable for the majority who strongly defend the secular basis of this political union, not wanting to alienate for instance Muslim immigrants, nor those republican nation states for whom a strict separation of politics from religion was an essential value. Already in the early 1950s, Turkey was against this design when it was discussed in the Council of Europe. The cross symbol in any case signals a rather conservative interpretation of European identity, which is also problematic for the socialist left, as it connotes conservative institutions such as the church and also (since the crusades) the aristocratic nobility. Also the rising sun image itself was a bit difficult to reconcile with Europe as the 'occident' or land of sunset, which is inherent in the name of Europe/Europa, as explained in a previous chapter.

In recent years, the Paneuropean Union has added the circle of twelve stars around its 'sun', thus incorporating European flag into its own design and emphasising an affinity with the EU (Figure 6.16). But already the original sun logo did have a certain semiotic proximity to the EU symbol, in the combination of centrally placed and symmetric yellow shapes on blue background, indicating some astronomic or cosmic phenomenon: something abstract, universal and almost eternal; something high and elevated; something grand and powerful; and something luminous that offers enlightenment to the earth.

The European Movement, formed at the Congress of Hague in 1948, has on its flag a big and geometric green 'E' on white background (Figure 6.17). The Congress of Hague was organised by the International Committee of the Movements for European Unity and witnessed divisions between unionists (who wanted a loose union) and federalists (working for a United States of Europe). The flag is sometimes also called the 'federalist' flag. The flag used by the Congress itself had an 'E' in red on white, but the European Movement changed it to green when they subsequently adopted the design at their own first meeting in September 1948 and started using the flag the following year. Probably the red colour was perceived to be too closely related to communism to be acceptable. The 'E' of course stands for 'Europe', and the green colour supposedly signifies youth and more importantly hope, which in Latin-Romance languages is denoted by a word also starting with an 'e' ('espérance', 'esperanza' etc.). The flag was intended to symbolise the hope for peace and unity in Europe.[293] Associations could also be made to ecology and sustainability issues.

This even more abstract and rather anonymous geometric design is hard to associate to any specific content, and that was also partly intended. It reminds us more of flag signals than of national emblems. Most sources suggest that the design was proposed by British Conservative and leading European Movement spokesman Duncan Sandys, son-in-law of Winston Churchill, and the design was therefore sometimes nicknamed

'Churchill's underpants', which did not exactly invite the respect wanted for the European project. The green and white colours were deliberately chosen not to make any problematic political associations (such as blue for conservatism, red for socialism etc.). However, the symbol had much less mythological or emotive resonance and has not at all been taken up by the EU, for a combination of reasons. Green and white are not deemed to be practical for flags, since the white tends to get dirty and the green is not so easily visible. There was also a general scepticism about using verbal symbols. The green 'E' also leads to some unwanted risks of misunderstanding. A rather discrete association may be made to the Irish colours, and even the three fingers of the letter 'E' could perhaps remind of the Irish Shamrock. Like the three leaves on the Shamrock, used by St Patrick to symbolise the Holy Trinity, the three 'E' fingers could then also be considered a symbol for magic power and completeness. However, the technical design gives little food for such mythical thoughts, and it is most likely that the main association is just to the word 'Europe' (compare the European road system numbers E1, E2, E3, etc.), thus possibly falling back onto the semantics of that name itself, analysed above. Another possible reason for avoiding the green colour is that it is in many world regions pretty intimately linked to Islam, which would potentially cause the opposite political problems from those caused by the cross. The intense usage by federalists could finally also have scared unionists away from accepting it, and it now stands for a more radical political struggle for a European federation, while the EU flag has come to symbolise the real existing European unity of today.

It is also worth having a look at other flags, logos and various identifying visual symbols that have been used by pan-European authorities and institutions over the years.[294]

The Central Commission for Navigation on the Rhine (Commission Centrale pour la Navigation du Rhin, CCNR) is the oldest extant European institution, and allegedly even the oldest still running international organisation of the whole world. It dates back to agreements at the 1814 Congress of Vienna that restored European peace after the Napoleonic wars. It is based in Strasbourg, but was originally seated in Mainz (1816–61) and then in Mannheim (1861–1920). Its function is to 'encourage European prosperity by guaranteeing a high level of security for navigation of the Rhine and environs', and its five member states are Belgium, France, Germany, the Netherlands and Switzerland, through which the river flows.[295] This institution has a light blue flag with four horizontal dark-blue lines across the lower half (Figure 6.18). A yellow anchor is placed in the centre of the bottom half, while a circle of six yellow stars is placed immediately above, in the centre of the top half of the flag. The yellow star circle on blue background has certain affinities with the EU logo, though the much lighter blue colour of the upper half gives a different overall impression, with not so much of that combined royal and cosmic aura that lends weight to the EU flag. The light and dark horizontal stripes across the lower half look like flowing water, but the overall effect is also to make the flag slightly parallel to the original US flag with its thirteen horizontal stripes and a circle of thirteen stars. There are only six stars in the CCNR flag, and the naval associations of the anchor and the horizontal water lines make it reasonable to understand the stars as navigational aids, so that the states help ships to find their way through Europe. The primary meaning of the flag is to represent stars, anchor, sky and water; its secondary meaning has to do with perfected guidance across difficult waters by wise and harmoniously cooperating states; its third meaning being to identify the CCNR as an international institution. The star formation can be seen as representing a navigation aid doing service to mankind from above, in a span from safe guidance to governance control. The number six transfers this sense of power from above onto the collaborating states themselves, forming a protective ring, in an articulation of different signifying layers. For today's Europe, the literal sense of navigation is no longer viable, but the sense of giving directions from an elevated position may well be. The European flag is sufficiently reminiscent of the CCNR one to confirm the circle of stars on blue as a European tradition, since it is not equally common outside Europe.

The European Coal and Steel Community (ECSC) was founded through the 1951 Treaty of Paris, inspired by the Schuman Declaration of 1950 that is celebrated on Europe Day. The ECSC got its own flag in 1958 (Figure 6.19), which was used until 2002 when the ECSC was finally dissolved and merged into the European Community, as an integrated part of the EU, by which it had for a long time effectively been replaced.[296] Its flag was thus created in roughly the same period as the EU flag, so it is little surprise that they have certain similarities in the use of stars on blue. The flag depicted over the years six to twelve yellow or white stars centrally placed in two rows on a horizontally divided background in blue and black. However, the ECSC flag used a divergent background, placed the stars very differently, and also had one star for each member state, forcing it to add stars when the number of member states grew from the original six in 1958 to twelve in 1986, no further stars were added in spite of the continuing enlargement. The corresponding decision had been taken for the Flag of Europe that was used by the Council of Europe and other sister organisations in the expanding European family, where the choice of twelve was meant to represent perfection and unity. At the same time, a modification was made in the colours used. The stars that had originally been golden yellow were made white, while the blue of the upper half was modified from dark to light blue, making it more similar to the colour coding of the CCNR flag than that of the EU. Like the CCNR flag, that of the ECSC divided the background horizontally, but the fields had a completely different meaning, as the blue upper half stood for steel, the black lower half for coal—the two natural resources that had once in a way caused and fuelled the catastrophic European wars but were now to form the core of a new and peaceful cooperative effort. Formally the colours look somewhat similar, but coal and steel are of course quite different from rivers and skies, the latter two evoking the classical elements of water and air, while the former correspond to fire and earth.

The WEU is a relatively unimportant intergovernmental military association for defense and security issues, established on the basis of the 1948 Treaty of Brussels, and with ten full member states.[297] The original members were Belgium, France, Luxembourg, the Netherlands and the UK; West Germany and Italy joined in 1954, Portugal and Spain in 1990 and Greece in 1995. The WEU flag makes another variation on the same theme as the preceding ones (Figure 6.20). Its design is derived from the Flag of Europe. And even though the WEU is formally independent of the EU, all WEU members are also EU member states. The background is dark blue, with a semicircle of ten yellow five pointed stars, broken at the top, and with the two official abbreviations of the Union's name in the centre: WEU placed horizontally and UEO (the French, Portuguese and Spanish form) vertically across the centre, so that the key letter 'E' (for Europe!) is shared by both and placed in the centre of the symbol. The similarity with the EU flag is evident and deliberate. The current version was introduced in 1993, before which there were only nine stars (before Greece entered), and the stars in the bottom were progressively larger than the upper ones. The change was in line with the EU flag symbolism, where equality among stars/states is essential. Initially the organisation had a five-links chain forming an upside-down pentagon, with a thick red-gold-black-white border, filling roughly half the total area, and referring to the colours of the flags of the original member states. The imagery of chain links has security/military connotations, as has the pentagon that is reminiscent of the famous headquarters of the US Department of Defense in Arlington, Virginia. The WEU by necessity cooperated closely with the US-dominated NATO, but the subsequent design modifications reflected a growing European wish to be respected as a major and fully autonomous world power. Besides combining the (halved) star circle with the name of the organisation, the current flag invites many different interpretations, including perhaps a telescope or a shield protecting the union, or some kind of starship with the acronym as sails, or a bowl or open hand protecting a cross: the way the letters are arranged forms a cross shape with religious connotations that are otherwise avoided in official European symbols.

There are many other more specific flags and logos used by various European institutions, including specific joint forces and operations of EU countries. Today these units often use variants of the main EU flag, modifying the composition of the stars and/or adding some other design element that connotes the particular area and objective of that unit.

An interesting example is the EU Presidency logos that sometimes experiment with combining national and European elements, often with blue as a basic colour. For instance, in the autumn of 2006, Finland used an abstract bird wing in green-blue, possibly suggestive of the migratory birds found on Finland's euro coins (see

Chapter 8). Portugal in the autumn of 2007 had an abstract light blue flower, whereas in autumn 2009, Sweden presented a 'three-dimensional' blue sphere crossed by a flowing yin-and-yang-like yellow 'S' (for 'Sweden').[298] The globe shape could have been meant to symbolise the importance of global climate issues in that period, with a crucial climate conference to be held during that term.

Other European logos include those of partly independent but Europe-wide organisations in various sectors of society. For selective comparison with the EU flag rather than offering any comprehensive overview, only a few of these will be briefly scrutinised here.

The European Broadcasting Union (EBU) is formally unrelated to the EU, but is one of the oldest, strongest and most successfully operating transnational media ventures in the world. It was formed on 12 February 1950 by 23 European and Mediterranean radio and television broadcasters, and today boasts of 75 broadcasting organisations from 56 (mostly but not exclusively European) countries and 43 associate broadcasters from another 25 countries (spanning from Canada, Mexico and the US to India, Hongkong and Japan). Most of the active members are public service providers in the wider geographic area covered by member states of the Council of Europe. EBU's Eurovision Network organises the famous ESC, but also the Eurovision Dance Contest, the Junior Eurovision Song Contest and other competitions for young creative and media artists. Other areas of cooperation have concerned the production of documentaries and programmes for children, the European transmission of the Olympics and FIFA World Cup, and the Vienna New Year's Concert event.[299]

The first EBU logo was designed in 1954 by Timothy O'Brien of the BBC, and was first broadcast on 6 June that year to launch the Eurovision summer season (Figure 16.21).[300] It was based on the then new Flag of Europe with its circle of twelve stars on blue, but here the stars were white rather than yellow, and looked like floodlights with rays radiating out from each star/light, while the blue background was also a little bit lighter than in the European flag. Between each star/spotlight, the letters 'EUROVISION' were spelt out, and in the open centre, each participating national broadcaster could enter its own logo (both the sending and the receiving one). It was sometimes nicknamed 'the pine-needle design', but of course rather aimed to associate to footlights or limelight around an open stage, and by extension also the broadcasting radiation of radio and television from cooperating national public service units. The logotypes of both the sending and receiving company were shown in the middle.

Since 2000, the EBU instead uses a more catchy and modern logo, designed by Lambie Nairn of London, and derived from a similar version designed in the 1990s by Swiss broadcasting (Figure 16.22). A modern version with 3D-animated treatment was launched on 1 January 2009 for the New Year's concert from Vienna. In either version, it almost looks as if it is made by hand: a tilted thin yellow ring where three 'V's (or perhaps flying birds) in shifting blue nuances 'radiate' out across a golden ring, or perhaps it is arrows moving into the centre? The abbreviations EBU and UER (the corresponding abbreviation in French for *L'Union Européenne de Radio-Télévision*) are placed underneath. A difference from before is that there is no more a blue but a white background, and that the colour ordering is almost reversed in that now it is blue rays that seem to move across an open space with golden-yellow border. Another difference is that the number of elements around the circle is reduced from twelve to only three. A third difference is the avoidance of putting any other symbols (for instance national broadcasters' logos) inside the circle, as the new design really does not make this possible any more, instead letting the three blue figures fill up most of the open space, just like Eurovision broadcasting presumably is supposed to flow around and fill up the communicative space opened up by the emergent European public sphere.

> The three blue elements create a movement of convergence, joint forces
> focusing on the same goal, the shapes differ slightly symbolising the
> union of different cultures. The colours hint at the European colours
> and the arrangement of the motif suggests a star.[301]

Both these EBU logo designs allude precisely to that public-sphere mixture of dialogue and dissemination, of agora and mass communication that was also hinted at in the Flag of Europe. But the current EBU logo more obviously links to the 'united in diversity' motto than both the old pine-needle design and the EU flag.

The ESC, initiated in 1956, is nowadays the most well-known EBU activity, unique to Europe even though more and more other continents have started to try and organise something similar. In this context, the stars of the EBU symbol may well add another meaning of not only TV channels' transmitters but also individual singing stars on Europe's musical heaven. The ESC has each year also had its own, separate logo. They were highly varying and only rarely took up elements from the general Eurovision or EBU imagery, until the Istanbul final in 2004, when they became standardised, in order to display a consistent visual identity for the ESC (Figure 16.23). The logo now has 'EUROVISION' (or perhaps 'EUROVISion') in a free layout with an impression of it being 'handwritten', stylistically slightly reminiscent of the EBU logo, above the words 'SONG CONTEST' in strict block letters. The 'V' is designed as a heart, which each new country that organises the finals fills with its national flag and adds the city and year at the bottom. The heart may be read both as the hub of communication for the whole European 'body' and as a traditional symbol of warm friendship, affection and love, but there are otherwise few associations to the EU symbols.

The Union of European Football Associations (UEFA) is another example of a pan-European institution independent of the EU, being the administrative and controlling body for European football. As football is enormously popular in Europe, where it has great significance as a public ritual, it is particularly instructive to look at its symbolism, in relation to similar logos from other continents.[302] UEFA was founded on 15 June 1954 and has since then grown from 25 to 53 national associations. It is the biggest and probably the strongest of the six continental confederations of the International Federation of Association Football (FIFA, for its French name: *Fédération Internationale de Football Association*). UEFA represents its national associations, organises competitions and controls prize money, regulations and media rights, and not least the latter issue has led to a series of conflicts over regulations with the European Commission. As with the media, Europe appears to be an influential brandname that attracts borderland nations such as Armenia, Georgia, Kazakhstan, Turkey, Israel, Cyprus, Russia and Azerbaijan to participate in UEFA rather than in the Asian Football Confederation (AFC).[303]

The UEFA symbol is not rectangular but circular (Figure 16.24). Inside a thin golden circle is a thicker red circle with 'UEFA' in white inscribed in the upper part. Then come two very thin circles, a white outside a golden one. The innermost circle, with a diameter roughly half of the whole symbol, is a map of Europe, where the waters are blue and the land areas white with a blue checked (or pixelated) screen pattern. The gold, white and blue colours and the circular shape may perhaps remind one a little bit of the Flag of Europe, but the symbolism is quite divergent. The circle is of course suitable for all ball sports, and the design is reminiscent of several older and more recent team badges, not least the one used by the German team FC Bayern since the early 1980s. (FIFA also has a motto, 'For the Good of the Game', and its symbol consists of two footballs with white stitches and filled with a world map with land in red and waters in blue.) The red colour in the UEFA symbol radiates competitive energy and activity, and in sports, the golden colour cannot but signal victory. The map only includes the European part of Russia and excludes Greenland for instance. Its pixelated quality could for example remind that association football is locally anchored or that television is of key importance to all sports in this mediatised era of mediated communications.

The Champions League is UEFA's annually organised European Cup for association football, and it also has its own logo in black and white (or silver), with the main element being a 'football' or a globe constructed by stars, where eight such stars can be seen (Figure 16.25). One might think that it may well take twelve stars in all to compose the whole ball, including the invisible backside, but the number eight is no coincidence, as precisely eight teams played in the first Champions League competition, and eight clubs still count as the leading ones.[304] Introducing these stars is clearly a way of linking to the Flag of Europe, and it shares with the flag also the strict symmetry and unified colour scheme.

This so-called starball was commissioned in 1991 from UEFA's commercial partner, Television Event and Media Marketing (TEAM), who also came up with the 'house colours' of black and white or silver, as well as an anthem (to be discussed in Chapter 7).[305] Interviewed by Anthony King, the TEAM representative Richard Worth explained that this design was deliberately chosen as a way to differ from the youthful and colourful style that otherwise dominates in sports, and to demonstrate that Champions League 'has tradition, history, and sets itself apart from the ordinary', representing 'the quality, prestige and heritage of top European football'.[306] The silver is supposed to stand for something rich, precious and valuable, indicating that European football has a long and strong tradition of highest quality, but also for solidity and high class that simultaneously connotes sociocultural elites and the fine arts: it 'denotes nobility'.[307] King sees this effort as motivated by a need to legitimise some radical changes made in the rules and organisation of the game at that time, by convincing fans and critics that European football remains true to its traditional heritage in spite of these modifications.[308] Something similar may be said of the EU too: its rather conservative and high cultural symbolic policies may likewise be understood as a way to convince the public of the union's deep rootedness in a long tradition, against accusations that it is just a contrived gadget.

King also shows how additional new televised designs used by the Champions League from 2000 onwards further confirms this interpretation, as it adds contrastingly colourful club badges that are subsumed under the classical European black/silver rule, symbolising a mutually beneficial synthesising power balance between the clubs as 'dynamic commercial forces' and 'the tradition embodied by UEFA and the European Cup which are represented by "classical" black, white and silver'.[309] The confinement of the brash coloured crests within the starball tames these new market forces under UEFA's pan-European hegemony.

> Only allied to the traditionalism of UEFA do the clubs enjoy their market power. In turn, the traditionalism of the competition is itself invigorated, not compromised, by the clubs and by commercial forces. The black, white and silver become more precious in contrast to the bold reds, blues and yellows.[310]

The televised sequence develops the stark contrast between the two sides 'from antagonism into symbiosis', providing 'an alibi for UEFA' by pointing at the need for the tradition of which it is the guardian, thus representing 'an idealized reconciliation of the clubs and the federation'.[311]

This visual symbol is thus an effort to virtually transform a threatening inner tension into a mutually strengthening contrast, almost in the same way that the 'united in diversity' motto makes a virtue out of necessity and magically transforms threatening fragmentation into a unique resource. King's critical reading of how this symbol produces ideology can easily be extended to the EU at large: 'The starball defuses the politics of this relationship with a utopian image of solidarity. It transforms history into nature.'[312] At least this may be the intention, but King finds deep contradiction under this ideological surface. In spite of such intentions, the symbols do not manage to conceal the deep gaps: 'On the contrary, these symbols signify a continent which is in ever greater internal competition with itself.'[313]

> The starball implies that supranational institutions like UEFA can provide a broad regulatory framework for this dramatic struggle but the future of Europe will be primarily determined by dominant market institutions, such as major football clubs. In this way, the starball may be a new symbol not only of European football but of Europe itself. The European Union may be characterised less by political cohesion than by increasingly ferocious market competition.[314]

It may be discussed whether this inner tension is always traceable also in the symbols used. Like the 1991 Champions League logo, the Flag of Europe appears to be quite solidly united in its impact. However, by relating it to other European images, elements of such inner contradictions may well be discerned.

Many more organisational European logos could be scrutinised, to show how certain elements of a shared visual imagery—notably the twelve star circle, often also the blue colour, as well as a general symmetric balance in design—are used in shifting combinations with area-specific elements. But EU's core symbol can also be contrasted with a couple of alternative and rather different images that have in recent years been proposed for the EU and for Europe as a whole.

In May 2001, after Brussels was by the Treaty of Nice formally made the capital of the EU, EU leaders had a series of meetings with intellectuals on how Brussels could be made to live up to this eminent task. Among the invitees was the Office for Metropolitan Architecture (OMA), an international design firm for 'contemporary architecture, urbanism, and cultural analysis', running a Rotterdam-based design and research studio called AMO.[315] Leading Dutch architect Rem Koolhaas was the most famous of its six key figures, working with a staff of more than 200 persons and 35 nationalities. AMO raised the issue of Europe's representation at large, including its symbols and its media presence, criticising the former for being 'mute, limp, anti modern and totally ineffective in an age dominated by mass media', and suggesting that there was 'a direct relation between the absence of a visual language, described as "Europe's iconographic deficit," and a widespread ignorance about Europe's causes among the general public'. To inspire the discussions, AMO presented a set of images, in particular the so-called barcode (Figure 6.26):

> The barcode merges the flags of current EU member states into a single colourful symbol. It intends to represent the essence of the European

project, showing Europe as the common effort of different nation states, with each state retaining its own cultural identity while sharing the advantages of acting together.[316]

Whereas the Flag of Europe always has twelve stars, the barcode expands horizontally when new members join the EU, with one vertical colour line for each national flag colour of EU members, presented roughly in a west–east order. It was proposed not as an alternative but as a parallel supplement to communicate the European idea in new ways and new contexts. The barcode was used as EU Presidency logo by Austria in spring 2006 and was thus given at least a semi-official status. It has also been printed on various merchandise and used at summit meetings. However it has far from replaced the official EU flag, and it should also be noted that not only has the barcode been extended when new members enter the union, but the order and shape of the previous stripes have also been modified. While serving as a visually and symbolically attractive supplement, the barcode is difficult to remember or reproduce faithfully. A minor BBC poll indicated a clear preference of 71 per cent people for the old flag with only 29 per cent preferring Kohlhaas' barcode, and all but one of eight posted individual comments were also unfavourable to the latter.[317] Another negative response is from a webpage that argues that the barcode invites parody, and therefore presents four satirical variants, including a fussy mix of colours that assumedly 'speaks to the rationality of official EU policies' and another that 'signals the clarity of EU bureaucratic proclamations'.[318]

The signifying effect of the barcode is again totally different from all the previous logos. Designs related to the Flag of Europe open up an agora, an open space illuminated by stars, an elevated stage for performance. The barcode has none of this, but is instead a cumulative addition of national contributions to a kind of European web, extending indefinitely from left to right, west to east. It is clearly in line with the European motto 'united in diversity', as the many individual colours mix and blend into one colourful whole: an open-ended totality that always welcomes further additions but still presents itself as one entity. Both symbols are in a way egalitarian, but the cosmic elevation of the former is totally absent in the latter, whose colourful bar lacks any vertical dimension, graphically as well as metaphorically. The European Flag seems to focus on the institutional frameworks for inter-European communication, while the barcode highlights the contents added from each member state (and presumably its citizens). Also, the complete uniformity of the EU stars stand in sharp contrast to the diversity of the fused flags of the barcode. To the three contrasts between elevation and horizontality, form and content, and uniformity and diversity, one may also add a fourth polarity, between fixity and dynamics, in that the barcode grows with each extension of the EU. The two symbols therefore seem to supplement each other in interesting ways, combining to give Europe and its union a more complex meaning.

Likewise originating in the Netherlands, 'Picobelleuropa!' was the humoristic Dutch designer Hans Kruit's proposal from June 2005, after France and the Netherlands had voted against the new Constitution (Figure 6.27). Kruit had designed a couple of the previous Dutch banknotes, and was frustrated by the confusing arguments behind the failure of the new constitution, arguing that feelings were now more important than reasoning: 'A new élan begins with a new, okay flag', since the star symbolism is too indistinct and vague. His alternative proposal was thus to change the stars into one single hollow circle that could also be used as the basis for a hand gesture, inspired by Winston Churchill's V-sign for victory, but choosing the so-called picobello or 'all clear' sign where the thumb and forefinger are joint to form a circle indicating top quality. Kruit argued that this would send much more positive feeling to Europe, and could possibly be used by ordinary citizens in everyday life, not only by official institutions. He emphasised that this was a citizen initiative, 'not sponsored by any government or stakeholder': 'Because it's not only about the money, it's also about the feeling!' An additional idea was to make it possible to combine it with national flags in varying size proportions depending on how much one identified as European. The proposal was ironic but in essence positive: 'That looks much better, a clear symbol, a beautiful round eurO, with a hole in the middle. A zero, yes, but who cares. Large amounts have lots of zeros. It simply looks good, nice and robust.'[319] The combination of a simplified image with a well-known positive gesture was thus one of several efforts meant to compensate for the lack of grass roots legitimacy for the official EU symbols, but also critically hinting at the emptiness of the whole venture. However, a further association to the fateful ring motif is a possibility that is never even hinted at by Kruit.

The perfectly symmetric star circle has obviously been a key obstacle to the reception of the EU flag. Precisely the harmonious balance and perfection intended by many EU politicians has been seen to contradict the motto's stress on diversity and to conform too much to a problematic image of Europe as a closed and rigid fortress. This has inspired several counter-images. For instance, Maarten Vanden Eynde's flag for the 2006 Europe Day represents the EU's geographical space by placing one star for each member state capital (Figure 6.28). It was part of a larger project called *Europe2006–2014* (2005) consisting of five flags reconstructing the evolution of the EU and intended to celebrate its utopian goal of global freedom and equality. The flags were shown in 25 EU countries on 9 May 2006, as a way to celebrate unification by 'creating an abstract sky full of stars'. The flag for 2006 (Figure 6.28) had one star for the capital of each of the fifteen full member states up to the 2004 enlargement, based on the argument that the latest newcomers had not yet become fully equals. That for 2008 included all the current members, the one for 2010 added all European capitals of potential member states and that for 2012 showed all the world capitals, while the last one represented a light blue sky. 'If you zoom out far enough you see no stars anymore, no more capitals, no more borders. What is left is an open sky, the flag of our blue marble, planet Earth. It is a visualisation of a unity of diversity and questions both the relevance of closed borders and the constant geographical expansion.' Again, the uniformity of the star circle has provoked the artist to this alternative design, intended to better represent the diversity and openness of the European project. Instead of Kruit's ironic joke, and more like the barcode, this flag was seriously intended and has actually been used in various places, particularly as a pan-European political art event on Europe Day in 2006.[320]

Since designed by a British lesbian in 2005, a gay European flag colours the stars in the six standard colours found on the LGBT (lesbian, gay, bisexual and transgender) movement 'rainbow flag' invented in 1978 but with its current design fixed in 2008 (Figure 6.29). There are many layers of meaning in this colouring, including possible references to sexual diversity, to more abstract values such as life (red), nature (green), sunlight (yellow) and harmony (blue), or to the colours of the triangles that Nazi victims had to wear.[321] Like the Picobelleuropa!, this kind of symbol in a positive spirit suggests a kind of improvement that adds precisely the element of diversity so clearly lacking in the official EU flag. It may indirectly be seen as a critique against such uniformity, but the alternative image proposed does not attack European unification. Instead, it is in principle loyal to it, and revises its visual symbolism to respond to the demands of this movement.

Cartoonists and political movements have at various occasions constructed critical versions on the European flag, in order to communicate some kind of counter-message, mostly directed against the EU. In 1999, Yugoslavians put a swastika in the centre of the EU star circle, in order to protest against EU involvement in the NATO bombings there. In 2002, Polish protesters carried the EU flag with the stars crossed over in red. In June 2008, there were manifestations in Göteborg against new Internet surveillance laws, where the PRC flag with the EU blue replacing the Chinese red was used to imply that Sweden and Europe had growing undemocratic traits. The Portuguese *Público* newspaper on 22 August 2002 had a cartoon where the EU stars had eyes in them, illustrating a Danish proposal for enhancing electronic communication surveillance in Europe. A British cartoon in *The Times* on 20 May 2005 substituted the stars with question marks to hint at the unpredictable post-referendum future of the European Constitution; the day after *The Economist* illustrated the deficient integration of Europe's banks by replacing stars with arrows pointing outwards in obvious disunion.[322] All these examples show ways to question the target of criticism, but also implicitly indicate the symbolic efficiency of the European flag itself.

Also, artists have made pictures that rework the EU flag. Here, the intention is often equally critical as in the cartoons, but sometimes with a less clear direction and hence greater openness of interpretation. One example is Romanian Vlad Nancă's installation *I Do Not Know What Union I Want to Belong to Anymore* (2003), with two flags, one depicting a hammer and sickle in yellow on blue placed above the star circle in yellow on red (Figure 6.30). The constellation seems to express a confusion of identity resulting from the EU eastward expansion, whereby West European liberal values collide with those of the former communist bloc, creating a strange transfer of associations where polarities such as freedom/coercion, individuality/collectivity, market/state or civil society/systemic institutions tend to be turned upside down. Another similar example is Croatian artist Nemania Cvijanović's *The Sweetest Dream* (2005), showing a blue flag with seventeen golden stars arranged to form a swastika (Figure 6.31). Such a strong symbol is at the same time open to an extreme variation of interpretations, depending on the perspective taken, for instance if the idea is that the EU institutions have fascist traits or that fascist and neo-Nazi movements pose a threat to Europe.

In January 2009, Czech artist David Černý's art installation *Entropa* was unveiled in the Council of Europe's building in Brussel, marking the Czech Republic Presidency in spring 2009 (Figure 6.32). It showed Europe as a giant DIY construction kit, where each bit was one nation, and each nation was presented through some funny stereotype. This linked up with a common critique of the EU project as being a failure, since the pieces were completely separate and could never join into any coherent whole. *Entropa* caused great debate since some nations protested against the way they were depicted. Notably Bulgaria protested against being identified by squat toilets, and even succeeded in getting their caricature hidden by fabrics. However, the artist argued that the piece was inspired by other satirical art such as the Monty Python team or Sacha Baron Cohen, and that with its subtitle 'Stereotypes are barriers to be demolished', it was fully in accord with the Czech European Union Presidency's motto of 'Europe without barriers'.

As argued in the introduction to this study, this artistic critique of the European unification project is thought provoking but rather problematic. European identity is of course a discursive and highly ideological construction that often covers up deep divides. But so are national identities. It is problematic to insist that any other identification is more 'natural' or 'authentic'—or 'better' in an ethic or political sense. 'Efforts at constructing *inter*national identities have had as long a history as the attempts to create *national* identitites', as Matthias Kaelberer notes.[323] Also, even though European identity has many flaws and limitations, it still is in many ways effective. Being constructed does not prevent it from existing and having a certain influence on history.

The Danish anti-Islamic EU-blogger Anders Bruun Laursen complains that the EU symbols propose 'a new international identity to replace our ancient, Christian national identities'.[324] He particularly fears the loss of the Danish flag cross, as explicit Christian motifs are consistently avoided in the official EU contexts. More than the day or motto, the flag has attracted hostility from EU sceptics and nationalists, not least in Britain, where a minor war of interpretation has been waged. There have been less of suggestions for alternative images, or debate of its current design, but more of criticism against the EU's adoption of a flag at all, and its use of it to manifest its presence all over Europe. Being much exposed and visible, it comes to symbolise an intrusion of federalist ideas into political everyday life, to the annoyance of those who want to minimise the reach and role of the EU. A more specific critique has been that an ambiguity is built into this flag, as it is both launched as an inclusive symbol of all European peoples and at the same time protected as an exclusive property of the specific political bodies that control its design, distribution and usage.[325] Another problematic issue lies in the allegedly Roman Catholic bias or at least inspiration of the star halo, which has forced officials to repeatedly emphasise the lack of any religious intention behind the design.[326]

Let me just mention a few examples. In 2006, the Dutch Socialist Party organised an 'alternative EU logo competition', where the winning design by J. Sanders had the star circle around a flying duck, with the words 'United States of Europe' underneath, to illustrate the soft way in which the EU politicians mimic the US with its strong eagle.[327]

'What Story Should Europe Tell' is a website for European debate, organised by Timothy Garton Ash. On 22 October 2008, the British administrator and Portuguese user Gheryando had a brief but illuminating discussion on European symbols.[328] The critical voice preferred national symbols to the European ones: 'The EU cannot have a "national" anthem, flag or animal because it is not a nation. These symbols only mimic national ones and so are artificial'. The idea was that the only symbols that really count are those for nations, supported by full citizenship. 'The Institute of Directors has a flag, the BBC has a flag, BP has a flag, everybody has a flag. These flags mean as much to people as the EU flag does, basically nothing, a fluttering logo and that is all'. Again and again, criticisms seem to alternate between denouncing the flag as empty, meaningless and irrelevant to European citizens, and fearing that it might take over and deteriorate the more historically grounded national symbols of the EU member states. Very few arguments are ever made about the specific design and meaning of the flag. The main objection seems to be that it is too vague and abstract to attach any significant meanings at all, possibly indicating a warning that the interpretations elaborated above are far from established by any collective tradition. It is probably still an open question how much of the potential meaning range of the flag can ever be developed and realised in practice.

Conclusions

With the visual symbol and the additional range of significations suggested by the other European icons analysed here, the polysemy of Europe widens. At the same time, it also narrows, by adding signifying specifications to those implied by the name, myth, day and motto. A visual image is in a sense not a discursive but a 'presentational' symbolism, presented not in linear order (as the name, myth and motto) but as a simultaneous, integral totality that can be perceived in a number of different ways, and therefore seems particularly rich in protosymbolic content: meanings that are not yet fully crystallised but shimmer as a halo around the intended main interpretation. It is even harder to pin down the meanings of the various logos than those of the motto, but some core elements have at least been discerned so far.[329]

1. The symmetric stability of the flag design, and the apparent cosmic timelessness of star constellations in general, give an impression more of *fixity* than of mobility. The only element of dislocation may be the empty centre of the star circle, which is a marked absence, unclear of what: a void to be filled by something unknown, or perhaps left open after something has disappeared—been dislocated. Still, the main impression is of stability and stasis. The barcode is instead to be continually updated and thus mobile, while *Entropa* is a bit unclear, fixing the nations in strict frames but still inviting Europe to be thought of in constructivist rather than essentialising ways.

2. In terms of driving force, the sublime perfection presents a measured, 'Apollonian' pleasure that combines *desire* and *control*. The flag design invites others to fill its central void and thus calls forth a measure of desire for others to enter, while simultaneously offering joy in the rounded and sublime perfection of the star ring. In counterpoint to that image, *Entropa* expresses an unfulfilled desire for joining the disparate national pieces into a coherent whole.

3. The theme of *elevation* is strongly supported by the Flag of Europe, as well as several of the other symbols discussed here, including Picobelleuropa but not the barcode. The stars strongly suggest something high up in the sky, pulling Europe up and above more mundane competitors. The nimbus shape further adds an aura of sacredness that points in the same direction, as does the 'perfection' of the symmetric circle as well as the number twelve. There are Christian echoes of the nimbus around Virgin Mary and other saintly figures, and there is certainly an amount of sublime elevation in conceiving a human institution as a perfect star circle. On the other hand origins (and intentions) do not determine meanings forever. Many symbols have religious origins, or rather religious periods on their routes through history, and not least secular republicans and socialists have often reused and reinterpreted such imagery in a 'Promethean' manner, stealing images from the gods and inserting humanity in the space previously occupied by divinity. With its abstract and clean style, the flag links Europe to high culture and classical aesthetics, rather than to popular culture—which was also one reason to experiment with the Picobelleuropa

and barcode alternatives. The latter lacks any explicit reference to elevation, instead emphasising egalitarianism, but it is also important to note that the flag likewise constructs an egalitarian relation between the twelve stars, so that a specific combination of elevation and equality is added as a new characteristic to the previous symbolic meanings. The critical *Entropa* instead profanes the European puzzle by depicting it as a hopeless childish game.

4. Finally, Europe's function as an empty container to be filled by various activities and actors evoke a rather vague character of this communicative space, which may be deemed to be just formal and abstract, but at the same time evades more precise interpretation, escaping out to the pre-semantic or protosymbolic, which may also be a condition for symbolic creativity (and civil society interaction) inside the formal frames marked out by the twelve stars (or by the European institutions). The uniformity and equidistance of the stars may also allude to the basic equality needed for a just democratic rule, where the empty inner circle would then signify the opening of a space, a stage for actors to enter, an agora for interaction, a public sphere to be filled with communication. The circular harmony can then indicate a secular kind of democratic egality, and the way it is sometimes used in combination with other symbols that are allowed in to temporarily fill its centre in practice supports that understanding. This arrangement of stars thus has quite different implications than for instance the arithmetic filing of the US flag or the hierarchic relation between one ruling star and four humble subjects in China's case. The flag definitely prefers *uniformity* or *equality* to hybridity. Equality and justice are the foregrounded values, and there is no explicit trace at all of diversity. Far removed from the EU motto, the EU flag could rather illustrate the caption 'united in equality'. The abstract design, and the void in its centre has been seen as symptomatic of a lack of substance in European identity, which Picobelleuropa makes fun of. The empty circle of stars represents Europe as a nothingness, a chiasm, indicating that something is missing in its centre. The absolute uniformity and equidistance of the stars seems entirely to miss the diversity aspect expressed by the motto. Alternative designs with rainbow-coloured stars, as well as the barcode and *Entropa* all indicate a desire to balance this tendency.

As a star nimbus, the European flag sacralises, as Europe stretches up into the heavens and is encircled by stars. It implies an elevation, a reliable fixity and an egalitarian uniformity among these thus selected nations, lacking any evident link to ideas of mobility, transformation, diversity or hybridity, which may be one reason why so many efforts have been made to supplement it with other images. As the oldest and most well-known functioning EU symbol, the flag has more alternatives and variants than any of the others. It is interesting to see that its strong expression of almost sacral elevation, fixated stability and strict uniformity has obviously been challenging and has provoked many comments in the form of other visual symbols that strive to present other images that are intended to better represent the fundamental European values, not least the diversity that is so much in focus in the motto but totally invisible in the official flag. Between these symbols, it is now clear that a kind of struggle is going on over European identification: a conflict of interpretations that indicates that the definition of Europe's meaning is an issue that many actors find important in the contemporary situation.

7

Anthem

One official EU symbol is musical: the European anthem, based on the 'Ode to Joy' theme from the final movement of Ludwig van Beethoven's Ninth Symphony. This has a parallel history to that of the flag, stretching even longer back in time but with a rather different position and way of being used. The idea is that people need some joint activity when they are gathered to celebrate European unity. Silently waving flags is then not enough: this is a classical case where music and singing tends to play a key role, just like it has for so many nation states, not to forget ritual chanting, sing-along, karaoke, ecstatic moments in pop concerts and other examples of how joint singing is used to reinforce feelings of belonging and community, as individuals gathered in a space actively express some kind of shared identity in sounds and lyrics.

What's in an anthem?

A hymn is a song of praise, the term deriving from the Greek *hymnos*: a song or ode praising gods or heroes, possibly related to *hymenaios*, wedding song, derived from 'Hymen', the Greek god of marriage. It has from the Middle Ages acquired a sacral accent, mostly denoting some kind of religious song or praise. The term 'anthem' derives from Greek *antiphona* (against + voice), a song performed in a responsorial fashion. In the late fourteenth century, the term came to apply to any sacred composition or a song of praise, and became used for the British national song 'God Save the Queen/King'. This was the first national hymn, with unknown authorship and a complicated genealogy, was published in 1744 and has been in public use since 1745. From there the term came to be applied to all subsequent national hymns, without any remaining link to its original responsive meaning: 'a rousing or uplifting song identified with a particular group or cause'.[330]

An anthem as well as a hymn is a song of praise made for communal singing. It should preferably be reasonably easy to remember and to sing, making it tempting or even irresistible to join in singing, and this activity of participation is intended to spill over into some level of identification with what the anthem stands for. In this way, anthems are constructed to emotionally boost collective identification, through the medium of voice and sound. Peter J. Martin sees the unprecedented demand of popular music today in the light of its capacity of forming communities: 'The close-knit communities of Romantic mythology have given way to the quest for a sense of belonging', where individuals 'seek to identify themselves with symbolic entities'. Here 'popular music becomes a useful commodity', offering 'a sense of who you are and where you belong'.[331] Popular songs help construct a wide range of different collective identifications, while anthems are made for underpinning those that have a more official character, being supported by formalised institutions, such as nation states.

Malcolm Boyd has analysed a great number of national anthems and divided them into five main categories, of which the two first are most common: (a) *hymns* with a solemn pace and melody (for instance the British 'God Save the Queen' or the European anthem); (b) *marches* (such as the French 'La Marseillaise'); (c) *operatic tunes* (exemplified by El Salvador and some other Latin American countries); (d) *folk tunes* (mainly used in Asia, for instance by Japan and Sri Lanka); and (e) *fanfares* without text (found in Kuwait, the United Arab Emirates and other oil states in the Middle East).[332] Just like the idea of a nation was established in Europe, this is also true for the sound of national anthems. Except for the few, mainly Asian, examples of folk anthem category (d) that build upon a Herderian notion of '*specific* musical nationalism', expressing a particular ethnicity, Martin Daughtry has argued that most national anthems tend towards a '*generic*' musical nationalism, as they by musical means signal that they are precisely that by adhering to the classical European musical conventions that have established musical nationalism as a kind of specific supranational genre, where they are perceived as sounding familiarly 'anthemic', rather than specific, to a particular nation.[333]

As a mode of communication, music has several peculiarities advantageous for communal celebration.[334] First of all, it is based on sounds that involve the ear and the human voice, but organises these sounds differently than in speech that is based on a verbal logic of relatively late origins in the history of mankind. What is seen of a person is primarily the outside surface, while what is heard tends to derive from the interior of that person's body, in particular the sonic organs in and around the throat. The combination of physiological constitution and genetic origin lends to music an extraordinary emotional reach and subjective involvement that have led many to understand it as a unique and privileged mode of expression, reaching beyond or underneath the more conscious modes of visual and verbal communication. Swearing an oath, proposing to a beloved, crying or laughing—such strong subjective expressions normally need to be made orally in order to fully convince of their authenticity and sincerity, and music is a way of organising such expressions in a more direct way than in the linguistic system built on words. Susanne K. Langer thus characterised music as a presentational symbolism, which is experienced in a holistic way, in contrast to the discursive one of verbal language, where clearly distinct elements are added in a sequence.[335] Psychoanalytical theorists have similarly linked music to pre-verbal psychic strata, as hearing is developed earlier in the infant than seeing, and thus has mental roots that go back to before language acquisition, to more archaic strata that are closely linked to deep-seated bodily and pre-rational emotions. Such specificities have led some semioticians and cultural theorists to argue that music is a form of communication without meaning.[336]

This whole line of thought has been brought under critical scrutiny by theorists like Jacques Derrida, who questions the linear developmental logic and essentialist romanticisation behind the idea that sound and voice are more primordial than sight and vision.[337] I see no reason to believe that musical sounds are any less meaningful than words—only the precise signifying procedures differ.[338] The particular kind of bodily activity involved in the use of voice and ear in making or listening to music do not prevent them from communicating meanings, but may at least partially explain why music is so often experienced as a vague and emotional mode of expression. Whether art music or popular music, with or without words, foregrounded or for instance in film soundtracks—music certainly is able to invoke meanings that are determined by interpretive communities of listeners and music makers, in geographically and socially situated communities that evolve historically, but it never escapes the cumulated networks of signification that constitute the traditions of musical genres. Parallel to verbal and visual modes of communication, pieces of music mean something to people in shifting contexts, and these meanings are polysemic and negotiable, inserted in the never-ending stream of conflicts of interpretation that is extended by every new usage and discourse.

While eyes may deliberately be directed and closed, this is not as easily done with ears. Music therefore has an almost intrusive material force on human bodies, and can be perceived even when people strive to focus on something else. Music is hard to block out but at the same time often out of focus, serving as a background to other activities. These qualities also make it difficult to focus on discursively, and most people find it much harder to find words to clearly describe music than images.

Music is itself a multimodal form of expression, as a full musical experience does not only emanate from abstracted sounds but also involves sight and other human senses. Music is further easily combined with other modes, not least verbal and visual ones. Music also often exists in combination with lyrics in song and with gestural or cinematic visuality in opera or film. Besides such multimodal genres and art forms, many people enjoy reading, writing or working with something silent while simultaneously listening to music in the background that boosts their energy or soothes their nerves. They may of course also have a nice picture on the wall, but lifting eyes to really look at it demands a break from desk work that is not in the same way required, at least on a subliminal level, to enjoy music while working.

These traits also combine to make music particularly suitable for collective interaction, to a higher extent than most other modes of communication, except possibly for dance (with which it is as a rule fused, as silent dancing is a rarity). Music lends itself to be made collectively not only *for* but also *by* groups, in heterophonic or polyphonic modes of communal expression, while for instance images or words tend to demand exclusive momentary concentration and thus function in a more monologic or dialogic way.

Visual symbols are typically integrated in lots of settings, both solemn and vernacular. Flags can be sighted all year round, and logos may appear on car number plates as well as on printed and electronic documents, for instance. Anthems are drastically different. Few people hum them several times a day: instead they are brought forward on festive occasions. They are less 'banal' or 'unwaved' in Michael Billig's sense. Other kinds of music may well be heard in the background, as soundtracks to everyday life, but anthems have too strong a symbolic force to lend themselves to such banalisation. Being actively performed at distinct ceremonial events, they are often the focus of attention, performing a kind of sacralising function of consolidating a kind of communion. Benedict Anderson has talked of 'a special kind of contemporaneous community' suggested by poetry and songs, for instance national anthems as sung on national holidays, when they give rise to 'an experience of simultaneity', an image of 'unisonance' and a 'physical realization of the imagined community', as 'people wholly unknown to each other utter the same verses to the same melody', connected by nothing but 'imagined sound'.[339] Among the main symbols discussed so far, one may argue that the flag is the most integrated and vernacular one, followed by the motto, then the anthem, with the day at the other extreme, as the whole point with Europe Day is to be a unique annual event supposed to be consciously celebrated, even though it may in this respect largely be seen as a failure so far. While a motto can be hinted at often in political discourses, and a logo may be integrated in a large number of settings, an anthem is more apt to be used on special occasions, when there is cause for a common celebration of shared matters, for instance on national holidays. In Klaus Bruhn Jensen's terms, anthems belong to ritualised 'time-out culture', while flags can also take part in the 'time-in culture' that is an integrated part of ordinary everyday life.[340]

Music thus has a strong potential for both collectively constituted and emotionally charged expression. Being a piece of music, the European anthem has the characteristic capacities for emotionally involving and bodily anchored community building, but these capacities are typically confined to ceremonial events rather than integrated in everyday life.

Introducing the European anthem

The European anthem is supposed to be that of Europe in a wider sense, including non-EU nations as well, and was first officially adopted by the Council of Europe in 1972. Its melody is the core theme of the fourth (final) movement of Ludwig van Beethoven's Ninth Symphony, composed in 1823. It was set to Friedrich von Schiller's 'Ode to Joy', expressing an idealistic vision of the human race united in brotherhood: 'Alle Menschen werden Brüder'. The poem was written in 1785 but published in slightly revised form in 1803, which Beethoven compressed and modified to suit his purposes (Figure 7.1). However, though the general melodic line and the name 'Ode to Joy' remain, the official hymn differs from its original source by being compressed to two minutes, selecting and reshuffling Beethoven's melodic elements, and also cancels the lyrics. (The reasons and signifying effects of this will be discussed below.) 'Without words, in the universal language of music, this anthem expresses the ideals of freedom, peace and solidarity for which Europe stands', says the EU website, where it can also be listened to as an audio file: 'It is not intended to replace the national anthems of the Member States but rather to celebrate the values they all share and their unity in diversity'.[341]

Aside from the name 'Europe' and the myth of Europa, and not counting various ancient star circles that might have inspired the flag emblem, the anthem has the oldest pre-history, as its music goes back at least to 1823 (and the lyrics to 1785), and highly different actors have almost ever since used it to celebrate common European endeavours. In the post-World War II unification process, many activists called for a unifying anthem to supplement the common flag. Many other songs were proposed through the years, or newly composed by various enthusiasts, but Beethoven's hymn came to be repeatedly used in this function, and seemed to have a resonance with at least how the European elites wished to define themselves.

Several pleas and proposals for European songs, often in several languages, were proposed by various citizens to the Council of Europe in the aftermath of the war.[342] Early examples from the autumn of 1949 were 'Chant de la Paix' by Mrs Jehanne-Louis Gaudet, and 'Hymne eines geeinten Europas/Hymne à une Europe unifiée' by Carl Kahlfuss. In 1955, the Paneuropean Union's President Richard Coudenhave-Kalergi, who in 1950 had proposed the Council of Europe to use the movement's sun-cross flag and also had recently pledged for a Europe Day, proposed 'the hymn from Beethoven's 9th Symphony'. This music had already from 1929 been used by that same movement.[343] It continued to be sporadically used at European events, for instance at the tenth anniversary of the Council of Europe in Strasbourg, 20 April 1959. An increasing number of European events created a need for joint ceremonial singing. In the following years, some favoured the last movement of Georg Friedrich Händel's *Music for the Royal Fireworks* (1749), while the Belgian section of he Council

Lyrics for Beethoven's Ninth Symphony

German original	English translation
O Freunde, nicht diese Töne!	*Oh friends, not these tones!*
Sondern laßt uns angenehmere anstimmen,	*Rather, let us raise our voices in more pleasing*
und freudenvollere.	*And more joyful sounds!*
Freude! (men's chorus: *Freude!*)	*Joy! (Joy!)*
Freude! (chorus again: *Freude!*)	*Joy! (Joy!)*
Freude, schöner Götterfunken	Joy, beautiful spark of divinity
Tochter aus Elysium,	Daughter of Elysium,
Wir betreten feuertrunken,	We enter, drunk with fire,
Himmlische, dein Heiligtum!	Into your sanctuary, heavenly (daughter)!
Deine Zauber binden wieder	Your magic reunites
Was die Mode streng geteilt;	*What custom strictly divided.*
Alle Menschen werden Brüder,	*All men become brothers,*
Wo dein sanfter Flügel weilt.	Where your gentle wing rests.
Wem der große Wurf gelungen,	Whoever has had the great fortune
Eines Freundes Freund zu sein;	To be a friend's friend,
Wer ein holdes Weib errungen,	Whoever has won a devoted wife,
Mische seinen Jubel ein!	Join in our jubilation!
Ja, wer auch nur eine Seele	Indeed, whoever can call even one soul,
Sein nennt auf dem Erdenrund!	His own on this earth!
Und wer's nie gekonnt, der stehle	And whoever was never able to, must creep
Weinend sich aus diesem Bund!	Tearfully away from this band!
Freude trinken alle Wesen	Joy all creatures drink
An den Brüsten der Natur;	At the breasts of nature;
Alle Guten, alle Bösen	All good, all bad
Folgen ihrer Rosenspur.	Follow her trail of roses.
Küße gab sie uns und Reben,	Kisses she gave us, and wine,
Einen Freund, geprüft im Tod;	A friend, proved in death;
Wollust ward dem Wurm gegeben,	Pleasure was given to the worm,
Und der Cherub steht vor Gott.	And the cherub stands before God.
Vor Gott!	*Before God!*
Froh, wie seine Sonnen fliegen	Glad, as His suns fly
Durch des Himmels prächt'gen Plan,	Through the Heaven's glorious design,
Laufet, Brüder, eure Bahn,	Run, brothers, your path,
Freudig, wie ein Held zum Siegen.	Joyful, as a hero to victory.
Seid umschlungen, Millionen!	Be embraced, millions!
Diesen Kuß der ganzen Welt!	This kiss for the whole world!
Brüder, über'm Sternenzelt	Brothers, above the starry canopy
Muss ein lieber Vater wohnen.	Must a loving Father dwell.
Ihr stürzt nieder, Millionen?	Do you bow down, millions?
Ahnest du den Schöpfer, Welt?	Do you sense the Creator, world?
Such' ihn über'm Sternenzelt!	Seek Him beyond the starry canopy!
Über Sternen muss er wohnen.	Beyond the stars must He dwell.
Finale repeats the words:	*Finale repeats the words:*
Seid umschlungen, Millionen!	Be embraced, you millions!
Diesen Kuß der ganzen Welt!	This kiss for the whole world!
Brüder, über'm Sternenzelt	Brothers, beyond the star-canopy
Muss ein lieber Vater wohnen.	Must a loving Father dwell.
Seid umschlungen,	Be embraced,
Diesen Kuß der ganzen Welt!	This kiss for the whole world!
Freude, schöner Götterfunken	Joy, beautiful spark of divinity,
Tochter aus Elysium,	Daughter of Elysium,
Freude, schöner Götterfunken	Joy, beautiful spark of divinity
Götterfunken!	*Divinity!*

Figure 7.1. The lyrics of Beethoven's Ninth Symphony; words written by Beethoven are shown in italics; Schiller's original had a handful of more verses inserted before and after the words 'Ihr stürzt nieder, Millionen?/Ahnest du den Schöpfer, Welt?/Such' ihn über'm Sternenzelt!/Über Sternen muss er wohnen'.

of European Municipalities in 1962 recorded a 'European song' based on Beethoven's music, which had the advantage of being quite well known, though the lyrics were felt to be a bigger problem.

Activities in support of an anthem were particularly lively in Belgium, the Netherlands and France. It was less surprisingly also often used in Germany, for instance as a national anthem in sporting events where the two States entered a joint team, for instance at the Oslo Winter Olympics 1952 and the Tokyo Games 1964. Germany's affection for the tune actually went back to the Third Reich, where it was played at the 1936 Berlin Olympics, for Hitler's birthday and in concentration camps.[344]

The year 1970 was a Beethoven anniversary year, as he was born in 1770, which contributed to putting his work the focus of the anthem discussions. Also, early in 1971, Stanley Kubrick's movie *A Clockwork Orange* was released. Like Anthony Burgess' novel from 1962, it placed the final movement of Beethoven's Ninth Symphony in a key narrative position, as the tune that the delinquent Alex first likes and then is tortured with by playing it together with extremely violent films from Nazi Germany. In spite of the very negative associations made with the theme in the story, it became immensely popular, not least when the film soundtrack with Wendy (formerly Walter) Carlos' arrangement of the music for Robert Moog's recently invented electronic synthesiser was released in 1972.

> Hence the huge popularity of the Ode to Joy, which is now a tune on everyone's lips, a tune, however, which has lost its power to involve and unite, having become a soundtrack for films, documentaries, advertising spots, sporting events and much else besides.[345]

Adding to the pressure from institutions such as the Council of European Municipalities and the Committee on Local Authorities of the Consultative Assembly, a 'Round Table for Europe Day' in February 1971 also concluded 'it would be desirable for a European anthem to be instituted to symbolise the faith of our peoples in the cause of European unity'. This was in April 1971 supported by the Consultative Assembly and the Committee of Ministers. A Consultative Assembly report in June 1971 considered a selection to be made from suggestions received by the General Secretariat, or a Europe-wide competition to be organised, but both these options were discarded.

> All members were against the idea of a competition for the purpose of 'producing' an anthem; on the other hand, it was agreed unanimously that Beethoven's music was representative of the European genius and was capable of uniting the hearts and minds of all Europeans, including the younger generation. Also, bearing

in mind that the tune of the *Ode to Joy*, from the last movement of Beethoven's Ninth Symphony, had frequently been performed as a European anthem by local communities in particular, the Committee considered it preferable to give official approval to this incipient tradition and to propose the prelude to the *Ode to Joy*.

An arrangement of the work was in fact made for the Belgian section of the Council of European Municipalities in 1961 and published by Schott Frères of Brussels; this could be used for reference purposes.

As regards the words for an anthem some doubt was felt, mainly with regard to the words of the *Ode to Joy*, which were in the nature of a universal expression of faith rather than a specifically European one.

Members also wondered whether any words acknowledged as 'European' could ever be translated into another language and accepted as such by the other linguistic groups of the European family.

The Committee therefore preferred, for the time being, to propose only the tune for a European anthem, without words, and to allow some time to pass. One day perhaps some words will be adopted by the citizens of Europe with the same spontaneity as Beethoven's eternal melody has been.[346]

While the melody was widely accepted, Schiller's lyrics were an obstacle. One objection was that any words would be bound to a single linguistic community and thus run into conflict with the unifying purpose of the anthem. The other main objection was even more fascinating, as it questioned the validity of a universalist text to identify Europe: Beethoven's version of Schiller's words was thus deemed to be too little European and too globally inclusive to signify a specifically European identity, whereas the music itself appeared to have passed the test as being specifically European enough to serve this purpose. Skipping the words altogether became the easiest way out.

The 10 June 1971 Report by the Consultative Assembly of the Council of Europe on a European anthem from which this long quote derives was thus of the opinion that 'it would be preferable to select a musical work representative of European genius and whose use on European occasions is already becoming something of a tradition'.[347] In a long 'explanatory note', the Assembly's rapporteur, Mr René Radius, gave a background to the anthem plans and confronted a counter-argument 'that to propose a European anthem is too bold an undertaking for politicians'. He argued that this was part of the key task of 'spreading the European idea', not least in face of the expected enlargement of the European Communities, where 'the Council of Europe is required by its Statute to propagate the ideal of European unity and thus to prepare the citizens of Europe to live together in a spirit of solidarity and fraternity', and 'to inspire the peoples of Europe, who are still divided in more than one respect, with a genuinely European spirit, compounded of generosity, of faith and of fellowship'. The Flag and Day of Europe had been steps to this goal, and it was now time to add an Anthem to this toolbox:

> At this crucial hour in Europe's search for her identity, the time has perhaps come to provide her with what she still lacks in the trilogy of symbols by which our States identify themselves: like them, she needs her Flag, her Day and her Anthem. These will give her the new impetus she needs in order to advance on the road to unity, and she will find therein a resounding expression of her driving force and of her faith.[348]

Curti Gialdino finds the political contextualising of the anthem in relation to the whole European project elucidative: 'Thus the feeling of identity associated with Beethoven's artistic heritage was to act as a means of filling the void in terms of a historical basis for European integration, which was still lacking, or at best precarious.[349] In resolution 492 of 8 July 1971, the Consultative Assembly of the Council of Europe decided to accept the report's advice and 'propose the acceptance by member countries as a European anthem of the Prelude to the *Ode to Joy* in the fourth movement of Beethoven's Ninth Symphony' and to 'recommend its use on all European occasions if desired in conjunction with the national anthem'. A few months later, the Committee of Ministers also supported this idea.[350]

The conductor of the Berlin Philharmonics Herbert von Karajan was asked to write three instrumental arrangements—for piano, for wind instruments and for symphony orchestra. He also conducted the performance for the official recording. The Council of Europe then announced the anthem in Karajan's arrangement on 19 January 1972, and launched an extensive information campaign on Europe Day 5 May 1972.[351] The 'Ode to Joy' theme became increasingly popular in many different settings. In the 1970s it even became the national anthem of Ian Smith's apartheid rule in Rhodesia (now Zimbabwe).[352]

In June 1984, the Fontainebleau European Council set up a Committee on a 'People's Europe', the so-called Adonnino Committee, which was a prime motor for establishing the European flag. Its second report on a 'People's Europe' to the European Council meeting in Milan 28–29 June 1985 argued strongly in favour of the adoption and use of a European anthem:

> The music of the 'Ode to Joy' from the fourth movement of Beethoven's ninth symphony is in fact used at European events. This anthem has also been recognized by the Council of Europe as being representative

of the European idea. The Committee recommends to the European Council that this anthem be played at appropriate events and ceremonies.[353]

The European leaders gathered at the Milan summit followed this recommendation and thus chose the same anthem for the European Community as that adopted in 1972 by the Council of Europe. Finally, Beethoven's music had become the official EU anthem in 1985. At the ceremony where the European flag was raised for the first time at the European Commission building in Brussels on 29 May 1986, a Flemish brass band played the arranged anthem, after which a choral society sang its original German setting with lyrics.[354] Since that time, the anthem continues to be played at official European events and ceremonies, and it is also released in many different versions on record and on the web, as sound files or ringtones, arranged in many different musical styles and with a variety of traditional and newly written lyrics. It continues to accumulate meaning by being used in highly divergent contexts, including the 1989 protests at Tiananmen Square in Peking as well as the Japanese New Year celebrations.[355]

Referring to translation problems and the vast number of languages in Europe, Schiller's words were thus again excluded in 1985, as they had been in 1971. Though the original German lyrics thus have no official status, the music's meaning remains indissolubly tinted by Schiller's poem and not least its title, 'Ode to Joy'. This immediate intertext has to be taken into consideration by any attempt to interpret the cluster of meanings that has come to surround this anthem.

Interpreting Beethoven's *Ode to Joy*

This is the only EU symbol that is so expressly derived from an existing work, picking out a small part of that work and revising it for the new format. Resolution 492 (1971) of the Consultative Assembly of the Council of Europe on a European anthem (8 July 1971) stated that 'it would be preferable to select a musical work representative of European genius and whose use on European occasions is already becoming something of a tradition'. A deliberate decision was thus not to look for a newly composed tune, but to go back in history to find a suitable classical melody that was already anchored in citizens' minds and that also had firmly established the solemn aura capable of bearing the overwhelming weight of expressing shared European values. No such provision was made concerning any of the other symbols. While they also leaned on inherited tropes, they still allowed for a contemporary treatment of these, not being content with inheriting something rather finished from the past. The flag may for instance have borrowed all its elements from tradition, but it was still presented as a unique and new design, rather than as an adherence to a pre-existing symbol. However, for the music, none of the proposed new compositions gave any hope of finding anything remotely as attractive as what the European canon of classical music had to offer. The implied signifying result was already by such a decision to devalue later developments in music and to instead inscribe the anthem in a rather conservative classicist tradition.

This also makes Beethoven's oeuvre a clearly privileged intertext, in particular his Ninth Symphony and Schiller's poem which he integrated in its final movement. I will therefore save comparative references to other intertexts until next section, in order to focus on the most obvious contexts for the European anthem, in a concentric set of circles from the European anthem, over Beethoven's Ninth's fourth movement, Beethoven's Ninth symphony as a whole, Beethoven's total oeuvre and Schiller's poem to early nineteenth century bourgeois culture and art music and post-revolutionary modern capitalism in general. As Esteban Buch has argued, the Anthem functions as a metonym for 'the whole fourth movement, the whole Ninth symphony, the whole work of Beethoven, or even the whole Western "great music", which, in this way, is appealed to in order to reinforce the ethical and political legitimacy of the European community as a whole'.[356]

The interpretive analysis could either start with the EU anthem as a separate work in its own right or approach it as a reworked excerpt from Beethoven's symphony. While only a minor group of art music specialists know the symphony context in any greater detail, many will associate the anthem to Beethoven and thus have some basic idea about some of those contextual aspects as well. The EU itself repeatedly makes it known that the anthem has precisely that origin. The European anthem as such is not yet sufficiently established to have full autonomous work status, even though this may possibly change in the future, should the anthem survive and become successful, in the way that for instance the Eurovision tune for most listeners has managed to cut off its ties to Charpentier's *Te Deum*, as will be discussed below. There are many different anthem versions of shifting length, sung or instrumental, so that it remains a bit uncertain how it goes as such, and in settings where it is used, it is repeatedly linked back to Beethoven, so that the melody's origin in Beethoven's symphony still tends to overshadow its independent existence as EU's anthem. Therefore, I will here start my analysis by relating the Anthem to its original Beethoven context, rather than treating it as a completely distinct work. I will first discuss how it has been understood in its original context within Beethoven's own work, and then in the following section listen closer to the arrangements of the Ode melody that have been presented as the European anthem. Though it may sometimes be difficult to keep them strictly apart, I will strive to reserve the term 'Anthem' for the EU version of the tune, while speaking of the 'Ode' when discussing the core melody as found in the symphony.

The *European Navigator* finds it crucial to contextualise Beethoven's work in relation to its original political, social and historic setting, as he 'straddled the end of one period of history and the beginning of another'.[357] In the aftermath of the French Revolution and the Napoleonic wars, a new bourgeois order was established in Europe. For Beethoven—'a musician of the internal world, the realm of the mind'—music 'was pregnant with meaning and almost always embodied an idea'. 'Seriousness is the predominant feature of Beethoven, but this very seriousness may, even fleetingly, be transformed into joy, as in the Ninth Symphony.'

> The melody of the *Ode to Joy* is simple, almost elementary, and of an approachable and clear musicality to which it is easy to listen. Beethoven's main concern was to strike a perfect balance between unity (and exact repetition) and variety, in a form which was readily memorable. In the verses singing of the values of truth, liberty, universal fraternity and human happiness, man emerges victorious over all his physical and moral oppressions. Throughout his life, and even in its happier periods, Beethoven was beset by the torments of his deafness, financial straits, unhappiness in love and the agonies of life. The Kantian ideals of the enlightenment culture of the time, which provided a focus for Beethoven's knowledge and internal life, are brought to life and sublimated through the interweaving of music and poetry. It is precisely this exhortation to fraternity and friendship, to love and to peace, of which the Ode is a highly figurative symbol, that explains why the Council of Europe and then the European Communities decided to take as their official anthem a hymn to fraternity going beyond the confines of nations and beyond the differences between peoples in order to bring about something more sublime and exceptional in European society.[358]

Efforts were made to construct Beethoven as European, for instance by mentioning his Dutch ancestors and his move from birth and youth in Bonn to mature achievements in Vienna.[359] However, these seem rather contrived, as it would have been easier to show how composers such as Georg Friedrich Handel, Joseph Haydn or Wolfgang Amadeus Mozart were considerably more cosmopolitan in their life trajectories as well as in their musical production—and in the latter respect, even Johann Sebastian Bach's oeuvre appears more obviously a melting pot of highly diverse European elements deriving from German, French and Italian sources. However, the choice of Beethoven had other causes. Much emphasis was put on his seriousness and the way he was engaged in the complex issues of his day: issues of progress and fate, emancipation and oppression, destruction and hope, war and peace. It was often argued that he was not just a skilled musician but also a socially responsible thinker, already by his contemporaries seen as a true 'genius' who regarded music as pregnant with meaning and embodying more abstract human values and allegedly universal ideas.[360]

It is thus no mere coincidence that Beethoven in several compositions used, developed and invented themes relating to topical ideas of his time, including expressions of universal humanism and heroic anti-authoritarian liberation, for instance in the ballet *The Creatures of Prometheus* (op. 43, 1801), the third symphony (*Eroica*, op. 55, 1803) or the opera *Fidelio* (op. 72, 1814; the original version *Leonore* was from 1805). He consciously linked himself to such leading ideas of what was to become classical European modernity, and thus lends himself well to being appropriated by those who later seek to express these ideas, either to hail or to problematise them. Beethoven is perhaps the most widely known European art music composer. No other composer is equally well known and above all respected all over the world, even though Mozart and Bach come close.[361] Chuck Berry's 'Roll over Beethoven' (1956) is but one example of how the serious composer has been used as a generalised symbol for traditional high arts, and Kubrick's *A Clockwork Orange* (1971) being another example.

There is an interesting homology between Beethoven's time and our own, in that his hopes for the Congress of Vienna to establish European peace after the Napoleonic wars parallel the intentions behind the Coal and Steel Union after World War II to finally put an end to the repeated catastrophic hostilities between France and Germany. Beethoven's words sung before Schiller's 'Ode to Joy', 'Freunde, nicht diese Töne', were precisely heard as a call against violence, silencing the preceding aggressive chaos. This process of civilising domestication of dark forces is also represented in the music itself, where chaotic strife is forced into reconciliation, not by expulsion of the brutes but through their disciplining integration and submission under a more peaceful and happy order, forging unity out of diversity. With the carnivalesque 'Freude schöne Götterfunken' sung by a mass ensemble to an elevated but joyful dance tune that fuses high and low culture, a kind of Promethean aura is established around a secular but transcendental humankind, upholding Enlightenment values of human rights and dignity. The music therefore is linked to both the Europa and the Prometheus myths, and not least to the founding myth of the EU, in which Europe's economic post-war reconstruction is defined as an empowering peace project.

Already before analysing the music as such, the Anthem is clearly placed within a classical European high culture tradition of elevation. Gerard Delanty argues that the bureaucratic form of EU institutions has 'a reifying effect', mirrored in the chosen anthem, with its 'reifying tone' through which 'the politics of European identity sought legitimation in bourgeois high culture'.[362] However, there are interesting complexities involved here as well. Using an already existing tune from the classical art music heritage, and specifically by Beethoven, has several implications that confirm the theme of elevation that is so consistently present in all EU symbols discussed so far.

The tune constitutes the climax in the final movement of a late Beethoven work that is generally understood as a high peak in his oeuvre. He was himself the last of the big three Vienna classics providing a transition from classical early modernity to the Romantics and later the self-critical fragmentation of the Enlightenment impulses. His mature period is often associated with seriousness and wisdom. The main tune of the final movement thus draws a great work to a conclusion. Romain Rolland regarded Beethoven's 'immortal *Ode to Joy*' as 'the plan of his whole life': 'All his life he wished to celebrate Joy; and to make it the climax of one of his great works.'[363] In many respects, the Anthem bears the mark of age, maturity, finality, rich experience and wisdom. However, this stands in opposition to some aspects of the musical composition—as well as of the lyrics—that have an almost revolutionary and almost naïvely youthful urgency.

The music itself is in the centre of the classical European art music tradition, using the twelve-tone equal temperament foundation of major/minor tonality and functional harmonics that underpinned new modes of modern musical narrative through structural progression and tension development, including verse/chorus transitions as well as the sonata form. These creative tools evolved from late sixteenth to early nineteenth century Europe and enabled a series of new modes of musical expression corresponding to the lifeworlds and outlooks of an emerging modern society, with the bourgeois public sphere as an important hub of civil society. Big changes took place in the period around the French Revolution, as the post-aristocratic ruling classes took over the initiative and strived to construct a more suitable sound organisation that emphasised individualised emotional development, but also lifted up popular expressions in sublimated and refined forms into a more elevated sphere of fine arts.

Nicholas Cook has succinctly pointed out that Beethoven's music is full of contradictions and ambivalences: between unity and fragmentation, energy and despair, Classicism and Romanticism, seriousness and ironic jokes, sorrow and happiness, solemn abstraction and physical force, high art and 'low' popular earthiness, and universality and subjectivity.[364] This music in many respects expressed and tried to come to grips with basic contradictions in emergent bourgeois society and culture.[365] Susan McClary describes this music as juxtaposing 'desire and unspeakable violence': 'The Ninth Symphony is probably our most compelling articulation in music of the contradictory impulses that have organized patriarchal culture since the Enlightenment.'[366] János Márothy has argued that the early nineteenth century bourgeoisie developed a kind of 'Dionysian complex', resulting from a basic contradiction of bourgeois society and art: an 'insoluble duality of the *citoyen-bourgeois*'.[367] Modern life had become abstract and private, creating a nostalgic longing for public collective experiences. The loss of public experiences of Dionysian mass collectivity of antiquity was recovered in romantic events, sparked off by the re-emerging mass experience in the French Revolution, and expressed in aesthetic ceremonial forms such as Beethoven's symphonies, displaying a heroism stylistically deriving from the mass dances and marches of the French Revolution.[368] Márothy shows how the melismatically lengthened rhythm of the 'Ode to Joy' melody has a sentimental declamation that is stylistically a subgroup of polka rhythm: a series of open-closed pairs with ancient roots, much used in medieval plebeian forms.[369]

Beethoven's introduction of a choir and sung words in the symphony genre was an innovation with immense influence on later generations.[370] Schiller's 'An die Freude' had since long interested Beethoven. It was written in 1785 but in 1803 published in a revised version where some political elements were softened. Beethoven went even further in the same direction, using only half of Schiller's lyrics and making considerable alterations and rearrangements to suit his purposes. He avoided the most overtly political attacks at the tyrant's power, for instance changing 'Bettler werden Fürsten-brüder' ('Beggars become Princes' brothers') to 'Alle Menschen werden Brüder' ('All men will become brothers'). This was not only in order to avoid Metternich's censorship but also to produce the more abstract, utopian and idealistic expression that Beethoven himself wished to convey, focusing on the all-embracing community rather than the political act of revolution. With the same idealistic purpose, he also omitted sections reminding of a drinking song, and reordered the choruses to create an unbroken line of development from the terrestrial to the divine.[371]

In its symphonic setting, the ode introduces a popular voice, a steady tune that could be heard as 'natural' and authentic in contrast with aristocratic forms: a song of the people or 'of the good human being' ('des guten Menschen') in a more universal sense. Like so many other commanding marches and fanfares, it starts with an upward movement, but instead of swinging rapidly to the sky, it walks steadily upwards, starting with two sturdy steps on the same spot before ascending step by step, and with even and steady beats reminding more of common people on the move than of gallant horses or flying angels. This fusion of highly advanced composition techniques with low popular tunes, inspired by democratic and revolutionary practices, has great potential for meeting EU's need for satisfying popular demands as well as the cultural and political elites.[372] But the further elaboration of this tune in the symphony movement has puzzled many listeners, as it enigmatically eludes any easy interpretation.

Musicologist Nicholas Cook describes the Ninth's finale as formally 'a cantata constructed round a series of variations on the "joy" theme', but it has also been analysed as a sonata form, a concerto form or 'a conflation of four symphonic movements into one' (the latter suggested by Charles Rosen).[373] The following outline of the main sections of this complex movement is constructed on the basis of Cook's analysis (Figure 7.2).

Part	Length	Function	Element	Length	Music	Lyrics
A	1-207 = 207 b. ≈ 6'20"	Instrume ntal intro d-D	Review & recitative	1-91 = 91 b.	Review & recitative d	-
			Joy theme	92-115 = 24 b.	Joy theme D	-
			Joy v. 1	116-139 = 24 b.	Joy variation D	-
			Joy v. 2	140-163 = 24 b.	Joy variation D	-
			Joy v. 3	164-207 = 44 b.	Joy variation D	-
B	208-330 = 123 b. ≈ 3'30"	Vocal expositio n d-D	Review & recitative	208-240 = 33 b.	Review & recitative d	R: "O Freunde…"
			Joy v. 4	241-268 = 28 b.	Joy variation D	V1: "Freude…"
			Joy v. 5	269-296 = 28 b.	Joy variation D	V2: "Wem…"
			Joy v. 6	297-330 = 34 b.	Joy variation D	V3: "Freude…"
C	331-594 = 264 b. ≈ 4'10"	Turkish march Bb-D	Intro	331-342 = 12 b.	Intro Bb	-
			Joy v. 7	343-374 = 32 b.	Turkish march Bb	-
			Joy v. 8 extended	375-430 = 56 b.	Turkish march Bb	C4: "Froh…"
			Fugato	431-542 = 112 b.	Joy-based fugato Bb	-
			Joy v. 9	543-594 = 52 b.	Joy variation D	V1: "Freude…"
D	595-654 = 60 b. ≈ 3'20"	Starry episode G-g	Episode	595-626 = 32 b.	Episode G	C1: "Seid…"
			Episode	627-654 = 28 b.	Episode g	C3: "Ihr…"
E	655-762 = 108 b. ≈ 2'30"	Double fugue & episode D	Double fugue	655-729 = 75 b.	Double fugue based on Joy & episode themes D	V1: "Freude…" C1: "Seid…"
			Episode	730-744 = 15 b.	Episode D	C3: "Ihr…"
			Episode	745-762 = 18 b.	Episode D	C1: "Seid…"
F	763-940 = 178 b. ≈ 4'00"	Coda D	Coda 1	763-831 = 69 b.	Joy-based coda D	V1: "Freude…"
			Cadenza	832-850 = 19 b.	Cadenza D	-
			Coda 2	851-903 = 53 b.	Coda D	V1: "Freude…" C1: "Seid…"
			Cadenza	904-919 = 16 b.	Cadenza D	V1: "Freude…" C1: "Seid…"
			Coda 3	920-940 = 21 b.	Joy-based coda D	-

Figure 7.2. Graphic overview of the Fourth Movement of Beethoven's Ninth Symphony.

A. Bar 1–207. The movement starts with a three minutes d-minor introduction that unfolds a frustrated dialogue between a review of the preceding three symphony movements and an instrumental string bass recitative. It is as if the motives from those previous movements or times were presented and all lead to strife and chaos, which the bass recitative has to interrupt with its rubato speech-like but still wordless voice. This leads up to bars 92ff. where the D-major 'Joy' theme is first presented by the string basses and developed in higher and fuller registers through three variations: first by the full string orchestra, then finally with full orchestra and much wind instruments on top. The last variation is extended in an exalted frenzy, which suddenly quiets down around six minutes into the movement.

B. Bar 208–330. The sounds from the d-minor introduction reappear for a minute, again with chaotic drums being interrupted by the same recitative as before, this time sung by a baritone on lyrics by Beethoven: 'O Freunde, nicht diese Töne! / sondern lasst uns angenehmere anstimmen, / und freudenvollere. / Freude! Freude!' ('Oh friends, not these tones! / Rather, let us raise our voices in more pleasing / and more joyful sounds! / Joy! Joy!').[374] At bar 241, this opens up the D-major vocal 'Joy' variations 4–6, with the Schiller lyrics of verses 1–3, starting with 'Freude, schöner Götterfunken, / Tochter aus Elysium, / wir betreten feuertrunken, / Himmlische, dein Heiligtum!' ('Joy, beautiful spark of divinity / daughter of Elysium, / We enter, drunk with fire, / into your sanctuary, heavenly (daughter)!'). The first time, a solo voice is accompanied by the choir in the last eight bars of the tune, like a chorus. Each of these variations adds voices, creating a climactic process. The second repetition involves a polyphonic solo song ensemble and a chorus in full choir like before; the third varies the melody so that it almost sounds like laughter. It ends with a transitory extension.

The introduction to the movement thus presents three different musical ideas that each time ends in chaos (A). They echo each of the preceding three movements, so that the finale starts by summing up what has come before, but it is also easy to interpret them as symbolising three failed efforts to live together or build a society. This interpretation is particularly invited by the words 'Oh friends, not these tones!', and not least by the following 'Ode to Joy' lyrics that immediately forces the listener to hear this melody as the only successful way out of the compositional impasse—as well as of the interactional impasse for humanity which it has signified (B). At this point, the 'Ode' tune has the role of a jubilant and in many ways is a simple solution after so many efforts to integrate deeply divided forces: a strong and accessible hymn which lifts the whole symphony to a new—higher and more solemn but also more basic and popular—level.

In Greek mythology, the virtuous heroes had the privilege to rest in the Elysian fields of the Underworld.[375] Schiller's 'Ode to Joy' constructed joy as a 'beautiful spark of divinity' and 'daughter of Elysium', that is happiness as a personification of a divine spark to humanity from the paradise of eternal rest. This is already a quite complex picture. On the one hand, this joy is described as an elevating energy from the gods, parallel to how Prometheus stole fire to humanity. This is reinforced by the next line that depicts how 'we enter, drunk with fire' into the holy place or 'sanctuary' of joy. On the other hand, the dimension of eternity also makes death and the dead present in this joy, and the fire-drunkenness is also not without its dangers: this joy is obviously sublime rather than just pleasantly relaxed. The joy could remind of the intense desire in Europa and the bull, but surviving fire may also recall the resurrection of the Phoenix. The cathartic release is further emphasised by the next lines that talk about how the magic of joy 'reunites what custom strictly divided', so that 'all men will become brothers'. The narrative goes from dark suffering to sparks of joy and from traditional division to brotherly reunion. Associations include heroes finally resting and rejoicing after wars, perhaps reunited with their beloved dead. This could be relevant to a post-war experience that was urgent for Beethoven as a new Europe was to arise from the battlefields of the Napoleonic wars, and was to become again actualised after the Franco-Prussian war of 1870–1 and the two twentieth century world wars, which propelled Robert Schuman and the other EU architects. The symbols add up to a kind of palimpsest of meanings on several historical levels.

The next verse invites 'whoever can call even one soul his own on this earth' to 'join in our jubilation', while those who were unable to build any kind of friendship 'must creep tearfully away from this band'. In verse 3, joy is depicted as a natural resource for 'all creatures', 'all good, all bad'. Indeed, 'pleasure was given to the worm' so virtually no living being seems excluded in this universal celebration.

C. Bar 331–594. This whole section starts in Bb-major and introduces a highly contrasting element, in tone and expression as well as in key, reminiscent of the second subject in a sonata form, so that the return to D major in bar 543 feels like a kind of recapitulation. The choir exclaims 'O Gott' ('Oh God!') in a prolonged fermata, and a march in Turkish style starts quite softly, with Glockenspiel and woodwinds, first instrumental, and then with increasingly loud instrumentation to the bass soloist singing 'Froh, wie seine Sonne fliegen / durch des Himmels prächt'gen Plan' ('Glad, as His suns fly / through the Heaven's glorious design') to an 'alla Turca' version in 'Joy' variation 7, followed by the Chorus 4 lyrics sung to 'Joy' variation 8, with extension leading to a fugato episode based on the 'Joy' theme, ending with the more straightforward 'Joy' variation 9 sung by the full choir in D-major. This 'Turkish' variation of the 'Ode' theme introduces a new and, to generations of listeners, often problematic perspective on its meaning, which will be further discussed below. Its chorus words talk about 'brothers' running 'joyful, as a hero to victory'. This introduces a male heroism that contrasts to the previous all-encompassing and more passive reception of the blisses of nature.

D. Bar 595–654. But the marching Turkish episode is a short parenthesis. The music halts and the choir gently sings 'Seid umschlungen, Millionen' ('Be embraced, you millions!') to Chorus 1 lyrics in G-major, partly performed in a kind of dialogue between male and female voices, embodying the idea of men and women embracing each other. This again ends in a fermata, after which Chorus 3 in g-minor sings 'Ihr stürzt nieder Millionen?' ('Do you bow down, millions?'), sounding as if angelic voices sail down from heaven to earth. The lyrics of this whole section offer a glimpse up to the heavens, as the human brothers are embraced by 'a loving Father' who is supposed to dwell 'above the starry canopy'. This is expressed more as a hope and conviction than as truth, formulating the religious dimension as a matter of faith rather than of fact. Cook hears the lyrics expressing a belief in 'the existence of a loving Father above the stars', set to music in 'a remote, hieratic style' that evokes ecclesiastical chant, sounding like 'a series of daydreams', where the repeated notes in bars 647–54 'are surely meant to depict the twinkling of the stars, it is as if time stood still'.[376]

E. Bar 655–762. This section opens with a D-major double fugue based on the 'Joy' and 'Seid umschlungen' themes, thus mixing lyrics from Verse 1 and Chorus 3, ending with the 'Ihr stürzt nieder' episode of Chorus 3 and finally the Chorus 1 lyrics, so that the symphony ends with repeating the frantic ecstacy of joy. Cook sees this double fugue as representing 'a reawakening, a return to reality', with a concluding, integrating and recapitulatory function but also serving as a transition to the next series of codas.[377]

F. Bar 763–940. D-major ending starts with Verse 1 lyrics sang to coda figure 1 based on the 'Joy' theme, followed by a cadenza and then coda figure 2 with Chorus 1 followed by Verse 1 lyrics, and finally coda figure 3 again based on the 'Joy' theme ends the work. These coda sections sound like a rather traditional operatic finale. The words 'Alle Menschen werden Brüder' are strongly emphasised, until in the final bars 920ff. everything is united in ecstatic harmony: choir and soloists, strings and wind instruments, solemn and military sounds—all joyfully united in diversity![378]

Commentators such as Romain Rolland have described the Ninth Symphony's finale as a climactic victory over deep misery: a joy of struggle transformed into transcendental ecstasy and finally a veritable 'delirium of love'.[379] Cook describes in detail how subsequent listeners have interpreted Beethoven's symphony differently, according to their own agendas. For instance, Wagner chose to read the baritone's words 'not these tones' ('*nicht diese Töne*') as referring 'to the horror fanfare, to the first three movements, ultimately to instrumental music as a whole', so that musical time is transformed into 'dramatic or ritualistic time', and 'what began as a musical event turns at this point into a social one'.[380]

Cook also shows that even quite recent twentieth century critics have generally been disturbed by the heterogeneity of the work, in particular having great problems with 'the most outrageously foreign element' of the 'Turkish' music in bar 331ff., finding it 'almost perverse' that Beethoven combined this music—with both military and popular associations—with lyrics speaking of God's angels in the sky.[381] In this frustration, Cook recognises a dominant Romantic strategy of 'creating meaning out of incoherence' that tends to domesticate Beethoven's music, reducing its excess of meaning.[382]

> Romantic interpretations reduce the contradictory elements of the Ninth Symphony to a narrative thread or a series of pictures; absolute-music interpretations reduce them to an architectural plan. And the result in each case is the same: the music is deproblematized, sanitized, shrink-wrapped.[383]

Beethoven's music is obviously an eminently open text, full of 'unconsummated symbols' says Cook, borrowing a term from Susanne Langer. He shows how this has tempted different listeners to interpret the Ninth in highly contradictory ways, letting it support universal peace, western democracy, Nazi rule or even Chinese communism.[384] Cook instead follows Theodor W. Adorno by stressing the inner contradictions in this music: 'its lack of organic unity, its fragmentary quality, its ultimate refusal to make sense'.[385] 'The work that symbolizes the pursuit of wealth in Hong Kong and communist orthodoxy in the People's Republic, that stands for Western democracy and forms part of Japan's social fabric—how can such a work be said to mean anything at all?'[386] This work is 'profoundly ambivalent': the music deconstructing Schiller's lyrics which in turn deconstructs itself, as the Turkish march clashes with lines such as 'And the seraph stands with God'.[387] Cook believes that Beethoven here detached himself from his own affirmative message.[388]

> Beethoven's last symphony proclaims the ideals of universal brotherhood and joy; that is unmistakable. But at the same time, and just as unmistakably, it casts doubt upon them. It sends out incompatible messages. And that is why, like *Parsifal*, the Ninth Symphony has the capacity to resist being wholly assimilated within any single, definitive interpretation; however it is interpreted, there is always a remainder that lies beyond interpretation. But this resistance can only be effective it we remain conscious of the incongruities, the incoherence, the negative qualities of the music.[389]

In spite of this, Cook does not at all *abandon* interpretation but on the contrary argues for the need for *continued reinterpretation*, as 'the only way to prevent the Ninth Symphony from being consumed by ideology'.[390]

The most scandalous obstacle to any straightforward interpretation of the symphony lies in how the 'Turkish' march music is positioned in the overall design of the work. As Cook has shown, it has been perceived as an 'outrageously foreign element'. It had since the late eighteenth century been common to play with 'alla Turca' elements in classical music, inserting exotic touches of rough marching rhythms and instrumentation of percussion and wind, inspired by the military march music of the Ottoman Empire's janissaries, which had existed since at least the fourteenth century and had a growing influence on Europe, as part of an Orientalising vogue for Turkish culture. These military bands originally had the function to make maximal frightening noise so as to rouse respect when Turkish troops came marching in. When tamed by classical composers, with Mozart's piano sonata no. 11 in A-major K. 331 (c. 1783) as the most famous example, the style was reduced to an exotic spice signifying a combination of popular and Oriental roughness and rage.

When such tones are suddenly heard in Beethoven's Ninth, they immediately ask for some kind of justification and interpretation, and critics have generally baulked at their alien character in relation to what has come before. One example of this alienated reception is when for instance Walter Riezler hears the Turkish music 'like a march from another world, war-like, but first almost incorporeal, as if it, hardly anymore audible to us, emerged from the most distant far of the universe'.[391] However, the main provocation of these sounds does not lie in the sounds as such, but in their structural position within the work as a whole. A contrasting element of otherness could well be accepted if it was in some way contained and made intelligible within a totalising meaningful narrative, but the first appearance of these noisy and unsophisticated rhythms is combined with angelic words that commentators have found inappropriate for it, creating an 'almost perverse' effect. And when it then returns in the concluding orgiastic feast at the very end of the work, this also has caused trouble for those who found it much too unpolished and uncivilised to live up to their ideas of heavenly joy in an Elysian paradise.

As Cook mentions, interpreters have used shifting strategies to deal with these apparent anomalies. For instance, the 'Turkish' music could either be understood to denote the revolutionary mass activity of the common people, or to signify some kind of eastern ethnic otherness in relation to the basic western classical idiom of the work as a whole, with radical effects on how to understand Beethoven's 'message'—if there is any to be understood, a fact which Cook's deconstructive analysis seems to question.

One interpreter has linked this issue to the European unification project. In a series of articles from 2006 and 2007, Slavoj Žižek saw the negative results of the EU constitutional referendums as expressions of political populism that refuses complexity and constructs simple bipolarities of us and them, where the enemies comprise Brussels bureaucracy as well as illegal immigrants. He argued that instead of dismissing these sceptical French and Dutch opinions as misled, one should dare to abandon the blind faith in Europe's technological modernity and cultural traditions in order instead

> to dispel the fetish of scientific-technological progress AND to get rid of relying on the superiority of its cultural heritage. [...] It is time for us, citizens of Europe, to become aware that we have to make a properly POLITICAL decision of what we want. No enlightened administrator will do the job for us.[392]

This was the context in which Žižek, leaning on Cook, exemplified with the European anthem, 'a true "empty signifier" that can stand for anything' and therefore can ideologically serve as a musical basis for forgetting all existing inequalities in an ecstatic moment of unification. Žižek's primarily focuses on precisely the problem with the 'Turkish' march:

The mode then becomes one of a carnivalesque parade, a mocking spectacle—critics have even compared the sounds of the bassoons and bass drum that accompany the beginning of the marcia turca to flatulence. After this point, such critics feel, everything goes wrong, the simple solemn dignity of the first part of the movement is never recovered.

But what if these critics are only partly correct—what if things do not go wrong only with the entrance of the marcia turca? What if they go wrong from the very beginning? Perhaps one should accept that there is something of an insipid fake in the very 'Ode to Joy', so that the chaos that enters after Bar 331 is a kind of the 'return of the repressed', a symptom of what was errant from the beginning.

If this is the case, we should thus shift the entire perspective and perceive the marcia as a return to normality that cuts short the display of preposterous portentousness of what precedes it—it is the moment the music brings us back to earth, as if saying: 'You want to celebrate the brotherhood of men? Here they are, the real humanity'.

And does the same not hold for Europe today? The second stanza of Friedrich Schiller's poem that is set to the music in 'Ode to Joy', coming on the heels of a chorus that invites the world's 'millions' to 'be embraced', ominously ends: 'But he who cannot rejoice, let him steal weeping away.' With this in mind, one recent paradox of the marcia turca is difficult to miss: as Europe makes the final adjustments to its continental solidarity in Lisbon, the Turks, despite their hopes, are outside the embrace.

So, when in the forthcoming days we hear again and again the 'Ode to Joy', it would be appropriate to remember what comes after this triumphant melody. Before succumbing to the warm sentiment of how we are all one big family, I think my fellow Europeans should spare a thought for all those who cannot rejoice with us, all those who are forced to 'steal weeping away'. It is, perhaps, the only way we'll put an end to the rioting and car burnings and other forms of the Turkish march we now see in our very own cities.[393]

Žižek thus links Beethoven's composition to an argument about contemporary obstacles for unifying Europe, particularly on its eastern border:

The main sign of today's crisis of the European Union is precisely Turkey: According to most of the polls, the main reason of those who voted 'no' at the last referendums in France and Netherlands was their opposition to Turkish membership. The 'no' can be grounded in rightist-populist terms (no to the Turkish threat to our culture, no to the Turkish cheap immigrant labor), or in the liberal-multiculturalist terms (Turkey should not be allowed in because, in its treatment of the Kurds, it doesn't display enough respect for human rights). But the opposite view, the 'yes', is as false as Beethoven's final cadenza. [...]

So, should Turkey be allowed into the Union or should it be let to 'steal itself weeping away' from the EU's circle? Can Europe survive the Turkish march? And, as in the finale of Beethoven's Ninth, what if the true problem is not Turkey, but the basic melody itself, the song of European unity as it is played to us from the Brussels post-political technocratic elite? What we need is a totally new main melody, a new definition of Europe itself. The problem of Turkey, the perplexity of European Union with regard to what to do with Turkey, is not about Turkey as such, but the confusion about what is Europe itself. The impasse with the European Constitution is a sign that the European project is now in search of its identity.[394]

Žižek uses what he hears in Beethoven to reinforce his critical opinions on the EU project. His specific reading seems to contradict the 'empty signifier' thesis he borrowed from Cook, but may also be regarded as an example of Cook's request for continued reinterpretation to prevent the music from being appropriated by ideology.

Interpreting the European anthem

This whole argument is based on the larger symphony context of the 'Ode', but its relevance to the European anthem is questionable, as the latter silences all the lyrics as well as the Turkish sounds. The European anthem is thus at a significant distance from the text that Žižek and Cook analyse. It is possible that the Beethoven context remains an absent but still somehow remembered intertext, but one must also consider what the anthem expresses as such, in order to see how relevant these echoes from its original setting may still be.

It should first be noted that the uses made of the 'Ode' melody are not equally divorced from the original symphony context. Beethoven's Ninth Symphony is the most significant context in which the 'Ode to Joy' melody is embedded, and from which any interpretation of the European anthem necessarily fetches at least some elements. But to what extent is it its location in this context that has enabled it to have so many different uses, or is it on the contrary its isolation from this context that has opened up such an interpretive span? This is not easy to assess. The expressive force of the 'Ode to Joy' melody certainly cannot be fully explained without considering its original link to Schiller's lyrics as well as its place in the Ninth Symphony. It has been praised as a humanist credo to universal brotherhood but also been loved by the German Nazis who performed it at big celebrations, including Hitler's birthday; it was the national anthem of Rhodesia during apartheid but has also continued to inspire left-wing revolutionaries as well as peace-loving romantics.[395] It has been invested with immense positive value, but also with suspicion, on the verge of becoming an 'empty signifier', but precisely in this general function, it at least seems to have a capacity of signifying a wish for universal unification between humans in spite of divisions and strife: a suitable musical expression of the European motto of 'united in diversity'. In order to get to grips with more of its signifying range, it is time to have a closer look at the instrumental anthem as a separate text.

The anthem is not just an excerpt taken directly from Beethoven's symphony, but rather a transformed abstraction of a section from it. There are several versions of this anthem itself available at different websites, including a main instrumental version composed, recorded and copyrighted by Karajan, but also a vocal variant of this. A search through various websites of the EU and the Council of Europe shows that a whole range of different versions are available, several claimed to be to some extent official. Some build on Karajan's 1972 arrangement, others on a reworking from September 2000 by the French composer Christophe Guyard, 'specially commissioned to illustrate documentaries, news and other programmes covering the Council of Europe'.[396] 'A Council of Europe CD, including the first hip hop version of the European anthem world-wide, was put on sale to the public in April 2004. Entitled "Variations", it includes other adaptations of the "Ode to Joy", in particular symphony orchestra, organ, piano (classical and jazz), rock guitar, jazz violin, techno and trance versions.'[397] Some versions boosted by the Council of Europe are instrumental, others vocal, and with lots of different instrumentations, musical styles as well as lengths, tempos and formal compositions. There is for instance a piano version, a hip-hop version with a rapper and excerpt from famous politicians' speeches, as well as four Romani variations also released on CD (one with famous singer Esma Redzepova). The choice of presenting rap and Romani styles is interesting. While the hip-hop versions testify to a will to reach out to young generations, both of these stylistic offers also have an ethnic twist, associating the anthem to mobile, migrant people and to immigrant populations not least from the south and east. This is in line with the 'Turkish' sounds in Beethoven's original setting, and on a musical level seems to respond to Žižek's criticism, as it expresses a willingness to include those 'foreign' (stylistic as well as cultural and demographic) elements into the larger European 'we'.

However, no such reworked version—with or without lyrics—has any official status at all. The original decision to adopt 'the prelude to "The Ode to Joy", 4th movement of Ludwig van Beethoven's 9th symphony' was not crystal clear, and more recent EU presentations instead just describe the melody as 'taken from' Beethoven's work. It is really not in the symphony a prelude to the Ode, but rather that melody itself, and could be described as the first, instrumental version of this 'Ode to Joy': the 24 bars 92–115 in Beethoven's Ninth Symphony finale, following the recapitulating introduction and the instrumental recitative. Together with those 91 introductory bars, the subsequent three other variations on the same tune (bars 116–207) and a following second introduction with vocal recitative (bars 208–240), it comprises a very long (240 bars ≈ 7 minutes) 'prelude' to the vocal rendering of the Ode melody, but it is not all this 'prelude' that is included in the anthem.

The core of both the symphony movement and the anthem is at any rate the 'Ode to Joy' theme (Figure 7.3). Nicholas Cook describes it as both simple and complicated: 'The key to the finale is the "Joy" theme. It sounds as effortlessly natural as a folk song. But it gave Beethoven an enormous amount of trouble; there are literally dozens of versions of the last eight bars in the sketchbooks.'[398] Arguments for choosing this melody for the anthem often stress that it is a catchy song, easy to sing and remember, almost with a ESC quality. Its stylistic characteristics in terms of melody, rhythm and formal structure have roots in revolutionary French songs and marches such as the 'Marseillaise', 'Ça ira' or 'La Carmagnole'.[399]

The theme comprises 24 bars in 4/4 rhythm, with a straightforward song structure: AA'BA'BA'. In the symphony, when the solo voice first sings the ode (AA'BA'BA'), the choir joins in for the last eight bars (BA'). Also in instrumental versions, the last BA' repetition is often performed louder with more instruments. This makes this section

Figure 7.3   The European anthem melody.

work like a chorus or refrain, reinforcing the impression of a folk ballad or street song, and the repetition itself creates an insistent expression. The melody moves in a number of arcs. Each odd bar in the A (and A') sections climbs up four tones while each even bar climbs down three or four tones again, so that a full four-bar A (or A') section consists of two two-bar arcs. In the B parts, each bar instead presents an arc-formed motif with three or five tones, adding up to four one-bar arcs. Two syncopations are characteristic even in the simplest standard versions. First, the last bar of each A (and A') section starts with a dotted crotchet note (♩.♪ ♩). This little dance-like swing breaks off the steady 4/4 walk (♩ ♩ ♩ ♩), lending emphasis and energy to each phrase conclusion. Second, a syncopation is always made as the first note of the A' section following after a B section starts one unit earlier and is thus prolonged (♩ ♩ ♩ ♩|♩ ♩ ♩ ♩). This twist at each transition from B to A' sections help lending the tune a certain restless and eager energy that avoids the otherwise threatening stomping character.

Rhythmically, Beethoven presents several varieties, some solemnly hymn-like, other syncopated, energetic and march-like. Similar variations are made in instrumentation and harmonisation. In the symphony, its various settings explore its wide range of expressive potentialities, from the simple and steady folk-like hymn singing, reminding of the Lutheran Reformation tunes that Bach turned into high art, to the more urgent march of struggle and optimism in the 'Turkish' variation, as well as a series of complex fugato treatments. In the symphony movement's coda, there is also a version that is reminiscent of the operatic anthem type, so that Beethoven himself in his symphony suggested at least three of Boyd's main anthem varieties: hymn, march and opera.[400] The various rap and Roma variations mentioned above have a similar function of exploring the signifying potentials of the core melody. But certain modifications are made already in the standard versions presented as the European anthem at various EU websites.

The French composer Christophe Guyard's September 2000 arrangement of the anthem, supported by the Council of Europe, has roughly the same tempo as in Beethoven's symphony movement (140 bpm).[401] Lucidly performed by a small orchestra, its 41 seconds just include the main theme without any introduction or ending, nor any repetition. It avoids the ceremonial as well as the march-like character of other versions and appears more like a kind of relaxed cinematic background than a hymn. It is drawn from Guyard's 6'34" long 'Rhapsodie sur l'Hymne Européen', where it is surrounded by a fluid rhapsody of intertwined voices. It does not interrupt a chaotic torture like in Beethoven, but rather with light hand evolves from a playful mix of musical ideas that gently crystallise into the hymn tune and ends with some elegantly shimmering brass chords. This arrangement does not at all invite any singing or explicitly reminds the listeners of the hidden lyrics, but may perhaps be heard as a purely musical illustration of joyful happiness in the merging of different musical voices.

The more well-known original arrangement made by Herbert von Karajan in 1972 is much more solemn, dark and dense than Guyard's, with a Romantic nineteenth century feel, and definitely leaning towards the hymn type rather than the mid-tempo march that is more prominent in Beethoven's original setting.[402] Karajan recorded one vocal version and one with wind orchestra; the latter is in focus here. The tempo is also considerably slower (115–128 bpm) than in Beethoven's original version (140–160 bpm).[403] The total time length of 2'14" (in some versions 2'07") includes four introductory bars with the five first notes of the melody performed twice, rising up against a G major chord; then the 24-bars anthem melody twice in C major, first *piano*, then *forte* with full winds and percussion; and finally a 4 bars coda. The first hymn performance is presented with soft and quiet woodwinds, the second with louder percussion and brass instruments added as well. There is no transition in between, but they follow immediately after one another. The second repetition has some very slight echoes of Beethoven's alla Turca version, in the celebratory triangle and flute, but not at all in any noisy or rough way, rather adding festivitas to the solemn joy this arrangement expresses. The whole arrangement signals an almost sacrally serious, ceremonial, officious and pompous art music that seems to invite a reverential procession and/or communal hymn singing. Karajan's arrangement thus effectively downplays the Dionysic element, reinforcing the effect of omitting Schiller's lyrics.

Some existing 1'00" versions of Karajan's arrangement only have one verse plus the coda. There are also other versions with Karajan's sound, for instance a 2'27" vocal one where the hymn is after a slightly different introduction repeated three times in different keys, resulting in a forward-oriented progression with a stepwise release of tension (F#→B→G→C), and with shifting transitions between each part, probably intended to increase the climactic progression effect.[404]

Different sources thus offer shifting versions of the anthem, but some elements remain roughly constant, compared to its original symphony setting.

1. All of them place the tune in completely different context, either without any introduction and ending at all, or sometimes with just a couple of bars of brief intro and fade-out. Esteban Buch laconically notes that Karajan has made a kind of cut and paste exercise from Beethoven's movement, adding a clear beginning and end to keep it within a strictly confined two minutes format.[405] This *decontextualisation* cancels every hint of the ode as rising from the ruins of chaotic aggression that was so crucial for Beethoven as well as for the EU founding myth discussed in relation to Europe Day above.

2. The musical narrative is *linearised*, as all musical parameters are accumulated and heightened with each repetition, leading up to a unique moment of apotheosis where the anthem simply ends.[406] While Beethoven went through a series of

175

grave challenges into a carnivalesque celebration uniting highly contradictory musical elements, the EU anthem simply builds up a climax effect, reducing the implicit meaning to one of growth and increasing strength.

3. The anthem is normally performed in a considerably slower tempo and with a simplified instrumentation, texture and timbre compared to the symphony, resulting in a conventional ceremonial or even *sacralised* hymn feeling, lacking the vivid energy that Beethoven inherited from the late eighteenth-century French revolutionary music.

4. All anthem versions perform the tune in the *simplified* and more straightforward form it had in the first parts of the symphony movement, with no real polyphonic counterpoint and very faint traces, if any at all, of the wilder and noisier arrangement Beethoven used for the contrasting 'Turkish' section. In one way, this aspect tends to diminish the relevance of Žižek's comments for the anthem as such, but on the other hand it verifies that the Oriental representation is repressed by official EU policies.

5. The *devocalising* decision to omit the lyrics silences the original narrative element and paves the way for the much more simple formal arrangement mentioned above. Some European citizens will remember fragments of the lyrics, at least the word 'Freude' ('Joy') that is included in the title of the anthem. Still, the avoidance of words has important repercussions on what the anthem signifies.

The symphony movement analysis above showed how Beethoven's music together with Schiller's lyrics depicted war-like chaos being silenced by a gathering of forces, first in tranquility and then developing into a climactic dance: from chaos to harmonic union and then carnivalesque joy. The original lyrics and music thus combined to give the communion a Dionysian twist of ecstatic happiness. The orgiastic happiness of the Promethean 'fire-drunk' brothers is much more in line with the self-forgetting desire expressed in the Europa myth than with Captain Euro's perfect efficiency—it actually is reminiscent more of the Captain's main enemy Dr D. Vider's carnivalesque circus. Schiller's and Beethoven's praise of universal brotherhood that knows no boundaries also hints at the hybridity of the classical myth as well as of the egalitarian theme of the European flag and the motto 'united in diversity', though here more as a momentary—liminal or subliminal—ritual than in any permanent institution-building. But all this is silenced in the official instrumental version.

It should be remembered that the initial motivation for at all adopting an anthem was to get a basis for communal ritual activity on solemn occasions such as Europe Day. When the anthem was finally adopted without lyrics, this gave rise to a strange paradox that seriously limited its signifying potentials. Who sings an anthem without words? Are citizens supposed to whistle or hum? In practice, the use of an identificatory anthem lies in using it, and in particular for crowds to sing it jointly, which becomes so much more difficult when there are supposed to be no lyrics to the song! It seems obvious that the repressed lyrics will still contribute to how the anthem is perceived and interpreted.

While the anthem was selected to celebrate shared values of freedom, peace and solidarity, Beethoven found Schiller's words necessary to adequately express precisely these values. Music historians agree that instrumental music did not suffice to express Beethoven's ideas at this specific point in the Ninth Symphony.[407] The path-breaking decision to introduce a choir and sung words in a symphony was a necessary step in order to express the ideas he wished the work to embody. Beethoven himself made that very clear, by taking the extraordinary measure to add vocals to a symphony, and also by the way he constructed the musical texture of the finale movement. In the 6 minute instrumental introduction to the finale, fragments from the preceding movements are presented and each time stopped by an increasingly impatient double bass. The 'Ode to Joy' melody then appears as a kind of alternative solution in a hopeless situation, a final rescue in a cul-de-sac of humanity. The melody is first tentatively presented by woodwinds that are interrupted again by 'negotiations' with the sceptical bass, but then the strings start playing it with growing confidence, building up a dramatic crescendo. However, this is not the whole story: it is here that the composer seems to betray his respect for the necessity of words and human voices to convey his core message. There is a new stop, and that is where the bass voice recitative enters ('Oh friends, not these tones!') to introduce the singing of the 'Ode to Joy' lyrics. The melody itself does not seem sufficient to stop the chaotic tragedy: human verbal expressivity is a necessity. This makes the omission of lyrics in the European anthem even more problematic. When the music was adopted as anthem without words, the German lyrics having no official status and not being used by the EU, then it remains an open question how the music in itself could manage to have that function in the absence of the lyrics that Beethoven himself could not manage without. One may seriously doubt if Beethoven could ever have agreed with the EU website: 'Without words, in the universal language of music, this anthem expresses the ideals of freedom, peace and solidarity for which Europe stands'.[408] If so, that would probably be just because those who use the anthem will always also remember at least some parts of the original lyrics to which it is sung in its original symphony context.

To briefly sum up this last discussion, the omission of the lyrics thus has two main consequences. (1) On the semantic level, it represses an element of signification that even Beethoven himself found necessary, hiding the verbal narrative away and reducing the total expressive force of the anthem. (2) On the pragmatic level, it contradicts the original motivation for adopting an anthem by reducing it from a basis for communal singing that could interactively help forge an emotionally supported sense of co-presence with others to a kind of cinematic soundtrack as a backdrop for other activities where citizens participate more as consuming audiences than as members of a European community.

The words were left aside by a combination of reasons.

First, though rarely acknowledged, there seems to have been a reluctance to adopt a *German text* that had been loved by Adolf Hitler—and which yet has no really established and attractive English (or French) translation either. In any case, it was explicitly argued that Europe could not just have a *monolingual* anthem. Just as the motto immediately got translated into all main European languages, the song lyrics perhaps also should. This would then however be a much more difficult task than for the short motto, and would also risk causing confusion when the anthem is sung by transnational congregations. Doubts were expressed whether the words could at all be satisfactorily translated to all European languages and accepted by all parts of the continent.

The choice of a German tune with German lyrics had a controversial subtext that was sharpened by in 1972 letting the famous Austrian conductor Herbert von Karajan make the official arrangement and recording, which was released by Deutsche Grammophon and broadcasted on Eurovision on 5 May that same year, together with a message in 30 languages on images of Karajan, Berliner Philharmoniker and the European flag.[409] Karajan was skilled in marketing himself in the media and had conducted a series of admired recordings of Beethoven's symphonies. As Buch points out, there was also a certain logic in letting the new hymn of universal peace and brotherhood be sung from the heart of Europe, on the ruins of the *Third Reich* terrors.[410] Yet, the choice was highly problematic, as he had been a member of the Nazi party, which Buch feels compromises the humanist ethical claims of the EU and its anthem.[411] Buch also notes that contrary to national anthems and also to Beethoven's Ninth, which is in the common domain, the European anthem legally remains Karajan's work, for which he receives copyright fees.[412] The same applies to Guyard's more modern arrangement. It certainly is paradoxical that the EU has agreed to let an anthem that is supposed to belong to the whole of Europe remain the private property of living individuals who actually have 'only' arranged a song taken from Beethoven!

A different argument was also explicitly made when the anthem was to be decided. There were sincere doubts that Schiller's lyrics were actually *too universal and not specifically European*. This is a very interesting objection. One may well argue that universal human rights are a key European invention, with the Enlightenment and the French 1789 bourgeois revolution as milestones. But if Europe today needs something more specific to define itself and distinguish itself from other continents, must then universality be avoided and replaced by some kind of regional uniqueness? Is this in fact—tending to contradict the 'united in diversity' motto—a step back to exclusionary self-identification of the traditional kind that leans heavily on differences between Fortress Europe and its surrounding others, the West and the rest?[413] The conflict of interpretations has not reached any firm conclusion in this respect.

Beethoven's modification of Schiller's lyrics was thus deemed to be both too specific (German) and too general (universal). Many European officials and politicians expressed a hope for some future 'genius' to be able to provide a new and acceptable, more properly European text in the main European languages. This will remain highly difficult due to linguistic and cultural differences within Europe. Meanwhile, in order to at all get the tune accepted by all European states, the compromise was to have it without words, which makes it difficult to actually sing it jointly, thus paradoxically annulling the original motivation behind an anthem in the first place: to occasion communal singing. The instrumental anthem silences the collective human voice that Beethoven found essential to introduce to convey his intended meaning of the ode, and which the whole idea of having a European anthem in many ways continues to be dependent upon in order to function as a ritual marker of collective identity.[414]

Esteban Buch concludes: 'Thus, the European anthem will not be vocal music, nor instrumental music, but well a song where the lyrics is missing, an unfinished symbol.'[415] This critical formulation may perhaps open up for a partial rescue of the anthem, as the lack of words gives the music a chance to transmit its message across linguistic barriers, in a kind of 'universal language', which is a widespread (though highly problematic) presupposition about music's innate capacity.[416] It was previously argued that the open circle of the European flag also in a sense presented an unfinished symbol, inviting other actors to step in and fill it with shifting contents. The textless tune could likewise be used for karaoke, opening up a sonar space for singers to fill with expressive activity.[417] What from a critical perspective is an empty void may then simultaneously imply an invitation for participation. In any case, the original lyrics linger in the background for those who know a little bit about Schiller's poem or Beethoven's symphony, and at least the anthem title hints at happiness as a core value, coinciding with the desire and pleasure of the Europa myth.

Even though the anthem has excluded so much of its original context in Schiller's and Beethoven's works, it is still full of tensions, paradoxes and contradictions, which Buch clearly points out.[418] First, the anthem is a musical translation of the universal values of joy and brotherhood, but is forced not to explicitly express those same values. Second, it is supposed to express collective European democratic principles but is the work of a former Nazi. Third, the anthem illustrates the rootedness of the EU symbols in the nation-state tradition, but also the wish to be different from this tradition and develop truly late modern and transnational symbols. Fourth, it is to incarnate the 'voice of the Europeans' but with its silenced lyrics is impossible to sing. Only the music but not the lyrics have official status:

The hymn confirms the emblematic position of the 'Great Composer' Beethoven within a mythology of 'Great Europeans'. But by excluding Schiller's lyrics from its performance, the hymn refuses the ritual, established since the first modern national hymns, of using a single voice to express a community of citizens. This paradox has sometimes been felt to represent a failure, a sign of the 'unfinished' character of the symbol. But at the same time it may be taken to suggest the openness of Europe. In this sense, the hymn signifies Europe's refusal to adopt a fixed identity, and marks a deliberate break with nationalist discourses.[419]

Buch sees two possibilities. Either Europe copies national symbols in defining European identity through a gesture of excluding all others: 'strangers, immigrants, other states, other continents, the excluded of all sorts—all that "whole world" that was united in the universal brotherhood Schiller and Beethoven sang of'. Or else, Europe could be faithful to the unfinished anthem in striving to remain a land of hospitality and openness.[420] The whole discussion about this anthem thus links back to central and unresolved dilemmas for renewing a transnational European identity. There is a great political problem in how to integrate the experience of brutal wars and of Nazi genocide in Europe's historically anchored identity. Beethoven's Ninth can be heard to do precisely that, as did in a way the Europa myth. Whether Karajan's anthem manages to do the same is open to debate.

With Foucault or Adorno, one may perhaps want to step out of the interpretive entanglement and refrain from offering any new meaning for this tune, but rather respond to it with silence. Cook and Žižek walk another way and instead offer new and critical interpretations as their method to go against ideological uses of the music. This is also in line with Paul Ricoeur's recurring hermeneutical argument that the only way to react to problematic readings of a text is by proposing better ones, and thus to contribute to the unstoppable conflict of interpretations. This is precisely what I have strived to do here as well.

A brief look at how the anthem has been received indicates that some voices have really found it difficult to accept a song that was venerated by Nazi Germany as well as by apartheid Rhodesia under Ian Smith. In 2008 European Parliament, Jim Allister (NI, UK) was one of the few who went against both the anthem and the flag:

> Ode to Joy which we are going to purloin may be a very nice tune, but so is Jingle Bells and like Jingle Bells it heralds a fantasy, the fantasy that the EU is good for you. But unlike Jingle Bells, it will damage your national sovereignty and the right to control your own destiny. More, like code to destroy, than Ode to Joy.[421]

A brief mention of the European anthem in the web newspaper *Telegraph.co.uk* in 2009 immediately attracted more than 100 comments from predominantly British readers, most of them hostile towards the idea of substituting national anthems with a European one, for instance at sports events.[422] One example was Darby Allen: 'The Franco-German Empire is not a nation, so cannot aspire to a national anthem'; another Balor Bericks: 'the British people are not part of Europe and never will be' (both 2009-11-16). John from Finland suggested: 'If you hate Europe so much then move your island to the pacific' (2009-11-19), to which signature 'midenglander' responded: 'We Brits cannot accept an EUSSR, a successor to Napoleon's Continental System or Nazi Germany's Europe' (2009-11-21). A more balanced view was expressed by John Morgan (2009-11-18): 'A European anthem would have its place in pan-European affairs where a national anthem would be inappropriate. It could also be used as a salute to the European president on a state visit outside his or her home country, followed by the national anthem of the host nation.' An interesting proposal came from tony (2009-11-17): 'How about changing the anthem every year and using the winning entry from the Eurovision song contest as the anthem.'

The many lists of comments to YouTube recordings of the European anthem mainly contain political debates, but there are also some views on the choice of music. For instance, 'timpani112': 'the most prominent reason why I hate the EU so much is probably this freaking anthem. It's originally from Beethoven's 9th symphony where it is played in d. Here however, it's played in b, dragging the reputation of the song in the mud. Why did they have to ruin such a beautiful song?' Some find it awful ('Who wrote this shit?'), others love it ('I dont like the eu much but it has a good anthem'). 'Waranoa' is surprised: 'That's Beethovens 9th! I didn't know that was our anthem! Harray for Europe, the silliest and most wonderfull place on earth!' Several also comment on the missing lyrics, some finding the German text 'just beautiful', others like 'UnbirthXXI' suggesting to 'use sentences from several european languages, it would contribute to the "european" feeling of this song'. Unintentionally highlighting a tension between Schiller's lyrics and the European motto, 'vlamara123' thinks 'this piece expresses the beautiful thought of Europe: together without differences!'

In sum, it is hard to find outside the EU hard kernel any great enthusiasm over the anthem, but neither has it stirred up any overwhelming opposition.

Comparisons

Comparisons may fruitfully be made with (1) anthems for other nations or supranational unions, including alternative tunes proposed for Europe; (2) tunes for European organisations; (3) other pieces of music identifying Europe, mainly through lyrics.

(1) In the discussion at the 'What Story Should Europe Tell' website mentioned in Chapter 6, it was the anthem that sparked the whole debate. The administrator initiated the debate by asking if the anthem could be played at European sports events such as the EuroCup or Champion's League. The critical user Gheryando found this idea 'ridiculous' since this is 'an artificial anthem' that may well be used at political 'meetings, or celebrating important EU dates', but not otherwise.[423] He argued that 'a symbol must mean something to people', but people have little attachment to European symbols since they have not through a long history been anchored in public consciousness and memory and thereby linked to collective identity: 'Most EU symbols are empty'. His counter-examples were the Portuguese National Anthem 'A Portuguesa' and the French 'La Marseillaise', both of which were linked to historical events of great and continued importance to the citizens of each country. By comparison, the European anthem seemed irrelevant to him: 'What does the "anthem" of EU mean…?' Therefore, it should not be imposed 'in all events in Europe', though it may be useful to just celebrate important EU dates.

Like 'Ode to Joy' in its slow Karajan adaptation from 1972, the British national anthem 'God Save the Queen/King' is of the hymn type, though in triple time. It has been widely used in other works as well: for instance by Beethoven who in the early 1800s developed it into a set of piano variations (WoO 78, 1803) as well as in his battle symphony *Wellington's Victory, or The Battle of Vitoria* (op. 91, 1813). Even if the British and European anthems belong to the same main category of rather slow and solemn hymns, Beethoven's 'Ode to Joy' actually has more melodic and rhythmic similarities with the French 'La Marseillaise', which is an anthem of the more energetic march type (and which in turn is also related to the socialist 'The Internationale'). The melodic structure is more similar, with a rising arch ending in a fall back to a stable level, as is the march-inviting 4/4 time. This is not surprising, given its inspiration from songs and marches of the French Revolution. In the symphony context, it is also performed in a steady quasi march-like tempo, though its melodic contour is considerably more calm and limited than the bolder 'La Marseillaise'. In comparison to many European national anthems, 'Ode to Joy' seems to present a kind of common denominator: a strict basic melody of folk-like character, avoiding extravagant embellishments that would bind it to any specific nation or region. This way, in line with its composer's intentions, it makes itself available for representing transnational humanism, and thus for pan-European unity, even aspiring to universality.

There are various ways for national anthems to solve the linguistic problems that caused the European anthem to be deprived of its lyrics. There are of course always immigrant populations that problematise the idea of a dominant national language everywhere, but also prominently bi- or multilingual nation states such as Belgium, Finland, Spain or Switzerland still have sung national hymns with lyrics, with varying degrees of acceptance. The original French lyrics of the Belgian 'La Brabançonne' (The Song of Brabant) from 1830 has continuously been revised to avoid anti-Dutch elements, and of course also has a version in Flemish. Given the internal tensions between the Vallonians and the Flemish, it is no surprise that the lyrics have no official status, but still the song is actually used in practice. Finland's 'Maamme/Vårt land' (Our Land) from 1848 was written in Swedish but has a Finnish translation. It is again not officially legislated but used in practice. Switzerland's official anthem 'Schweizerpsalm' from 1841 has its text in all four official national languages, that is, translated from the German original to French, Italian and Romansch. Only the Spanish 'Marcha Real' (Royal March), going back to the mid-eighteenth century, is mostly performed without words, and its link to the royalty makes it problematic for semi-autonomous regions like Catalunya and the Basque countries. In Kosovo, the European anthem is also often played, as an act of respect for EU's role in assisting the process of national independence. Since 2008 it has a conventional national anthem named 'Europe' that has no lyrics, in order to avoid discrimination of any of its ethnic groups, while neighbouring Bosnia and Herzegovina has chosen to have an anthem with lyrics available in both Bosnian and Serbian language.

There is no officially established anthem for the whole of Asia, North or South America, but the African Union has in 2010 adopted an official African Union anthem, 'Let Us All Unite and Celebrate Together'.[424] It is on various websites played by a wind orchestra in a classical European-French slow military march style, but there is also a set of lyrics presented both in English and in French:

> Let us all unite and celebrate together
> The victories won for our liberation
> Let us dedicate ourselves to rise together
> To defend our liberty and unity
>
> O Sons and Daughters of Africa
> Flesh of the Sun and Flesh of the Sky
> Let us make Africa the Tree of Life

The next verses speak of joint singing for fighting together 'for lasting peace and justice on earth' and of joint working for Africa as 'the cradle of mankind and fount of culture'. The tune thus seamlessly inscribes itself in the European anthemic tradition, but the lyrics recontextualise it into a postcolonial context. Africa is not so much elevated to a supreme position (as is the case with Europe) but rather described in terms of roots and origins of mankind and culture, with political liberation, cultural creativity and unbroken ties to nature as main values, and with a union seemingly (and unrealistically!) unthreatened by any internal divides.

From the end of the war in 1945 to the adoption of the 'Ode to Joy' in 1972, a large number of alternative anthems have been proposed for Europe. Here, just one example will be scrutinised. On 9 May 1948, at the Hague Congress that was the cradle of much of the following European unification measures, a municipal brass band supported the participants singing in several languages the anthem 'Europa Één!' ('Europe Unite!'), specially created by Dutch composer Louis Noiret and Dutch lyrics by H. Joosten, translated also to English, French and Italian.[425] The first verse lyrics paint a gloomy picture:

> The world of today is overshadowed and grey
> her people have suffered much sorrow.
> And after the tears of the past bitter years
> they pray for a brighter tomorrow;
> But from distant shores there are rumours of wars
> that threaten all Europe's foundations,
> So this is our call to one and to all,
> Unite! Just as one mighty nation.

Precisely two years before the Schuman Declaration, uniting is here depicted as a safeguard against new dividing wars. The verse melody is in f minor, gently oscillating up and down, but the mood slowly evolves into more optimistic sounds, in particular when the F major chorus breaks in, with a fanfare-like figure reminding the listeners of the opening of 'La marseillaise'. The call for Europe to unite 'as one mighty nation' expresses a federalist perspective that would not be supported by the more sceptical voices that remain against all efforts to fuse the EU into a new supra-level nation state, and also tends to contradict the 'united in diversity' motto and other policies later developed to safeguard against such a melting-pot strategy. The chorus then defines the leading values for this union: 'Europe unite for happiness and freedom! / Europe unite to win enduring peace!' Echoing the 'Ode of Joy', happiness, freedom and peace demand a union that is also a matter of 'strength' and 'might'. The second verse calls for Europeans to 'save all our glorious tradition' in a central position, squeezed between 'the East' and 'the West'—reminding of west and central Europe's political wish to uphold some kind of sovereignty between the Communist Bloc and the United States. The third verse focuses on welfare issues: 'There are riches to spare for all peoples to share', calling for 'good, honest labour' to provide new wealth. Thus, the song illustrates precisely the agenda of the formation of modern European unification, combining peace and brotherhood with joy and happiness as well as with strength and expected new riches. While hybridity is not openly focused in this song, there is obviously an expression of desire and pleasure in joining forces. There is also a clear sense of elevation both in talking of Europe's 'glorious tradition' and in the image of union as a means to 'win throught to the light' after so long suffering in darkness. If there is any sense of dislocation here, it is not in geographic terms, but rather an image of Europe as not having been at home or at ease with itself, as deeply disturbed but now finally wanting to find peace.

(2) Besides the anthems of other nations and continents, comparisons may also be made with songs linked to other and more specific European organisations.

Figure 7.4. A theme from Georg Friedrich Handel's Coronation Anthem *Zadok the Priest*, the basis for the UEFA Champions League anthem.

The heroic 'Grand March' from Giuseppe Verdi's opera *Aida* (1871) and other famous tunes of classical music have through the years been used at European sports events, not least in football with its particularly strong link to Europe. However, the associated sports clubs of UEFA have selected an anthem of the hymn type. This may sound surprising for an organisation that deals with such physical practice, but it may well be precisely that which motivates the choice of something more elevated, in order to add necessary dignity and gravity. Händel's dignified Coronation Anthem *Zadok the Priest* is always performed at the key moment of British coronations (Figure 7.4). Händel himself was German but in his music heavily influenced by the innovative and effective Italian styles of his time, and he spent his last and most productive years in London. There, his four Coronation Anthems were composed for the coronation of King George II and Queen Caroline in Westminster Abbey in 1727. Both of them were like Händel also Germans in today's terms—George belonged to the House of Hanover. Like with Beethoven for the EU, this transnational identity is eminently suitable for a pan-European association such as UEFA, and considering the old English roots of the football game, and the continued strength of English teams, the choice of British coronation music has an evident symbolic value.

Händel's original work had biblical lyrics: just a brief excerpt from the First Book of Kings (1: 39–40), which had been sung on every English coronation since King Edgar in 973 AD. The song lines do not immediately present any very clear melodic or rhythmic figure, and the setting is simple. In the beginning, a sharply rising violin arpeggio over repeated low chords sets the tone, before the choir enters after one and a half minute or so, singing 'Zadok the priest and Nathan the prophet anointed Solomon king and all the people rejoiced'. A dramatic suspense effect is created by a continuous crescendo from the gentle beginning up to a full climax with timpani and trumpets as the choir sings: 'And all the people rejoic'd, and said: God save the King, long live the King, may he live forever! Alleluia, Amen.'[426] These words are then repeated in shifting combinations with musical motifs.

Whereas Händel's *Zadok* lasts for more than 5 minutes with a 90 seconds instrumental introduction and a contrasting middle section, the UEFA anthem is 3 minutes long, with just 25 seconds introduction. Its final 1-minute chorus is played before matches and television broadcasts. It is an adaptation made by Tony Britten in 1992, as part of the symbol package mentioned in Chapter 6, commissioned by TEAM. The music makes use of several elements from Handel's original composition, but reshuffles and transforms them to suit the new context. The UEFA anthem thus differs in melodic detail from *Zadok* much more than the EU anthem diverges from Beethoven's original work. It was performed by the Royal Philharmonic Orchestra and the Academy of St Martin in the Fields chorus, while a remixed version called 'Victory' has also been used, released by Polish trance/dance duo Kalwi & Remi in 2006.[427] Its choir sings simple, disjointed and heavily repeated phrases, alternating in UEFA's three official languages: French, German and English. This multilingual montage exemplifies another way of dealing with heterogeneous situations than when lyrics are constructed in several parallel translations. The words express the strength of the teams and of the sports events: on the one hand 'These are the best teams', 'The masters', 'The biggest teams' and 'The Champions', on the other hand 'The main event', 'A big gathering' and 'A big sports event'. Together they designate the greatness of the national sports teams that fill UEFA with specific competence, and of the pan-European Champions League that is organised for them by UEFA. The climactic moment is set to the exclamations 'Die Meister! Die Besten! Les Grandes Équipes! The Champions!'

It is no coincidence that the German words in the hymn include the word 'Mannschaften', which is the standard synonym of 'teams', belonging to the many words that tend to link sports to a masculine sphere, mirrored by the persistent privileging of male football also in this traditional context. Anthony King's analysis of UEFA's visual and musical symbols hears the *Zadok* anthem reinforcing the required aura of 'tradition and quality'.

> The majestic music which rises to an impressive major key crescendo signifies the installation of a new head of state. The baroque music of the Zadok anthem associates the Champions League with the monarchies of Ancien Regime Europe. The baroque music also interconnects with the silver house colours, for the aristocratic connotations evoked by the silver are reflected and affirmed in this noble music.[428]

King points at a clear homology between the televised images and the musical jingle: 'Music and colours merge together as one dense signifier, communicating a concept of silver in both sound and vision.'[429]

> Handel's music involves a series of lesser chords symbolizing a diverse subject population below the monarch but, at its climax, the music reconciles these lower chords into a single major key fanfare; a sovereign nation is unified beneath a supreme monarch. The Champions League Anthem communicates the same message of diverse subordinate elements unified beneath a sovereign body; the clubs are represented by the lower chords which are brought together in a majestic union under UEFA.[430]

A couple of *Zadok* clips on YouTube have attracted a lot of discussion where royalists and football fans join in expressing their love for Händel's music, even though the two groups sometimes clash, as when 'bulked' exclaims: 'its been reduced to as lowly and classless as a football anthem'. 'PremiumUnleaded' jokingly finds it 'appropriate that the first part of a piece for a coronation forms the basis for the theme of the world's most prestigious annual sporting competition'. But otherwise the discussion is more about monarchy and democracy than about the tune itself or its use by UEFA.

Figure 7.5   The Marc-Antoine Charpentier theme used as anthem for the European Broadcasting Union EBU and its Eurovision.

Whereas UEFA has anthem of the solemn hymn type, the televisual EBU has favoured a march (Figure 7.5). The Council of Europe radio broadcasts used excerpts from Georg Friedrich Händel's *Music for the Royal Fireworks* and the *Water Music*, but the EBU for its Eurovision transmissions instead selected a jingle consisting of the instrumental 'Prélude' to the grand motet *Te Deum* in D major (op. 146), composed in Paris in the early 1690s by Marc-Antoine Charpentier (1643–1704).[431] In 1953, the French-Belgian musicologist Carl de Nys rediscovered this *Te Deum*, whose opening

'Marche en rondeau' was in 1954 adopted by the EBU as a jingle for its newly launched disseminations. There seems never to have been any serious discussion of adding any lyrics, nor any such need, since nobody expects any viewer/listener to join in singing such a televised jingle.

Charpentier composed his most famous *Te Deum* in D (one of total six) in the Jesuit Saint-Louis church in Paris. In the late seventeenth century, the Jesuits were suspected of supporting Spanish interests in France. Charpentier had studied with Carissimi in Rome, and he brought modern profane sounds into the conservative church music, with straightforward and symmetric melodies and charmingly sonorous choruses. The only 1.5 minutes long *Te Deum* prélude is an anthem of the march type, and the composer himself characterised it as 'bright and very warlike'. It starts with an upward swing closely reminiscent of 'La Marseillaise'. However, while the latter continues with fanfare motifs calling people to rise against authorities, the former instead continues with neatly rounded melodies to conciliatory harmonies. While 'La Marseillaise' has radical or liberal republican and universalist associations, Charpentier's march instead seems to attract rather conservative and nationalist French royalist fans, judging from the many comments like 'Vive la France!' and 'Vive le roi!' found under recordings at various YouTube sites, where for instance 'darlingelf' says 'I wish that when I die my soul is magically transported to the time of the Grand Monarch!' and gets support from 'Sallieri1': 'Heil to the Old Europe! Beautiful! Anthem of christian, strong world! Nowadays our civilisation is dead … R.I.P.'[432]

A reviewer has described it as 'a rousing bit of splendor out of which we moderns have constructed a musical icon of Louis XIV's France', combining 'martial, dance-like, and intimate' aspects into a piece that 'evokes the close unity of church and state'.[433] In the twentieth century, the media, headed by television, can be said to have taken the place of religion, recontextualising the same music to now instead evoke public service's close unity of media culture and nation states.

With the EU, UEFA and EBU anthems, a wide range of west and central European influences balance each other. EU selected the German-Austrian-Dutch Beethoven, UEFA opted for Händel with his English basis while importing also German and Italian styles, and EBU chose the French Charpentier with some Spanish and Italian tints. Together they significantly cover the most influential of the original EU national traditions, though less relevant for the eastern and also northern part of Europe. All of them manage to symbolically elevate the bodies they represent, but while the European anthem has a republican, almost plebeian and modern ring, uplifting not by ceremonial brilliance but by quasi-natural, balanced perfection, the two others are firmly anchored in a traditional aristocratic and royal context. EU's hesitation to the 'Ode to Joy' lyrics for being 'too universal' has no counterpart for the other two anthems, and it may well be that the republican spirit of Beethoven is less bound to Europe than the monarchist mentality found in Charpentier and Händel, though modern elites cannot make this official EU policy. Except for all three having been recontextualised from their original uses to their respective new uses, in musical or lyrical terms none of them induce any strong sense of dislocation. There are no obvious associations to hybridity except maybe in the way the UEFA arrangement modifies the baroque style to a rather different expression, but all three may perhaps be said to embody some kind of pleasure and desire, at least in a general sense of musical luster, and to some listeners even provide sublime shivers of enjoyment.

(3) There are hundreds of other musical symbols of Europe, if counting not only tunes representing various European organisations but also programmatic art music and popular songs with lyrics that characterise Europe and Europeanness. I will here focus on the latter kind, and in particular songs presented in EBU's ESC. Among the more than one thousand songs performed in the ESC finals 1956–2010, five had 'Euro' in their titles and a lyrical topic that explicitly thematised Europeanness—the Belgian Telex: 'Euro-vision' (1980), the French Cocktail Chic: 'Européennes' (1986), the Irish Liam Reilly: 'Somewhere in Europe' (1990), the Italian Enrico Ruggeri: 'Sole D'Europa' (1993) and the Spanish Rosa: 'Europe's Living a Celebration' (2002). To these should be added the winner of 1990, Italian Toto Cotugno's 'Insieme 1992' with its repeated chorus line 'Insieme, unite, unite, Europe'.[434]

In 1980, Telex's 'Euro-vision' (by H. Dirks = Jacques Duvall = Eric Verwilghen) gave Belgium a seventeenth position (third last) in the Dutch Hague finale. Three men in black suits, blue shirts and white scarves—the singer surrounded by two synth players performed a kind of comic song, the singer ending by pouring out golden confetti (apparently symbolising the European stars, in a double sense) from his pockets and then taking out a mini camera to take a photo of the audience/camera, while the first two bars of Charpentier's Eurovision theme is heard played with a thin, plastic sound. Both the performance and the (French) lyrics are distanced, ironically mocking the whole event in which they take part. The first verse talks of beautiful singers nervously getting ready: 'May the best win / The borders are open.' The chorus just monotonously repeats 'Eurovision, Eurovision'. The link between stars and media is tight: 'Old Europe cheers the country that wins'; 'The eyes of the whole world are waiting, impatiently / for news flashes / that are going to announce / by satellite and by shielded cables / what's happening in their regions'. The song thus depicts the ESC itself as an artificial media event, with only one clear hint towards identifying Europe, namely that it is 'old', which links to a tradition of seeing Europe as endowed with a mature civilisation but can in retrospective also be seen as confirming the western confines of how it was then defined.

In 1986 in Norwegian Bergen, France also stood as number 17 (of 20) with Cocktail Chic's 'Européennes' (by Michel and Georges Costa). The quartet of female singers were dressed in much gold and typical 1980s' outfit (poodle hairstyle, long wide sweeping coats) and made simple, synchronised gestures. The lyrics talk of 'European girls' who 'feel like going away / when there's no more sunshine in the house'. This celebration of holiday trips first stays within Europe's borders, mentioning Amsterdam, Copenhagen, Capri, London and Paris as destinations. However, there is then an allusion to the globally connecting force of US music culture: 'We're European girls / and the things we love / we find them here, from London to Paris / even if the music is connected / live from Radio L.A.' Yes, 'We like the old continent / with background music USA', and to the global outlook is then also added images of 'Indian summer' and 'African sunsets'. In fact, there is an increasing ambiguity opening up a rift in the initial Eurocentrism, when at the end the words 'The weather is nice in California / but Saint-Tropez is also good' seem to place Europe as the second best. The song describes Europe as a united but diverse site of pleasure, and compares it as an old continent with the youthful United States as a given centre of the modern universe.

These two songs thus propose popular music, television media and tourism as uniting tools. This unification still only included the good 'old' western half of the continent. It was no mere coincidence that it was in Zagreb, Slovenia 1990, the year after the breakdown of the Communist Bloc, that no less than the two most successful tunes explicitly thematised European fraternity. It was evidently a moment where good music makers, artists and producers agreed with the wide audience that the European project had a renewed urgency. Still none of these two tunes explicitly widened the concept of Europe to include also the part that had for so long been confined behind the iron curtain.

On a joint second position (with equal votes as France) was Ireland's Liam Reilly with his own 'Somewhere in Europe'. Singing from his grand piano, dressed in shirt and tie but a loose brown jacket and trousers, and backed by two female singers, Reilly sang as an 'I' to a 'you' about having been separated but wanting to reunite: 'We should be together, and maybe we just might / if you could only meet me somewhere in Europe tonight'. The text mentions a wide range of European destinations—Paris, Rome, Amsterdam, German Black Forest, the Adriatic Sea and Seville—all of which are firmly located in the old, western part of Europe, and again focuses on tourist destinations and leisure-time practices. Such nostalgia for happy memories of lazy nightlife may be interpreted as a conservative lament for old Europe's lost innocence, rather than a celebration of the recent developments.

Italy won that same year of 1990 with Toto Cotugno's own composition 'Insieme 1992'. It was characteristic that this year the old West European nations favoured Ireland while Italy got more high points from the comparably few East European countries that had at that time entered the competition. Cotugno was a popular singer, performing here in all white, in front of five mixed-gender backup vocals. The song has a typical Italian pop sensibility, with melody hooks that are easy to remember and sing, and the song builds up an increasing pressure as it rolls along; a real popular hit with a symphonic sound on a steady walking beat. 'Insieme' means 'together', and the song is strongly focused on its repeated chorus 'Together, unite, unite, Europe', sung in English while the rest of the text is in Italian. Its central lyrics much more explicitly relate to current EU policies, though of course with the more intimate and personal double meaning needed to make it a real hit:

> With you, so far and different
> With you, a friend that I thought I'd lost
> You and I, having the same dream
> Together, unite, unite, Europe
>
> And for you, a woman without borders
> With you, under the same flags
> You and I, under the same sky
> Together, unite, unite, Europe
>
> We're more and more free
> It's no longer a dream and you're no longer alone
> We're higher and higher
> Give me your hand, so that we can fly
> Europe is not far away
> This is an Italian song for you
> Together, unite, unite, Europe
>
> For us, in heaven a thousand violins
> For us, love without borders
> You and I, having the same ideals, mmm …
> Together, unite, unite, Europe[435]

The title's '1992' was the year when the European Communities' 1986 Single European Act planned to launch the EU; in practice the EU was established with the Maastricht Treaty in November 1993. Phrases such as 'We're uniting more and more' and 'Our stars, one single flag / We're stronger and stronger' directly links the textual universe to the EU's vision of 'love without borders', which in turn echoes ideas from the European anthem and even back to the Europa myth, as the male Italian 'I' flies away with the woman to a dream-like Europe in a manner that may well remind of how Europa was abducted to Crete by Zeus-as-bull. The union called forth here is borderless, but like in the previously mentioned songs, an element of hybridity and diversity remains in initially describing the 'you' as 'so far and different'. The several times repeated declaration of the song as 'Italian' also adds situated particularity that affirms the persistence of national differences within this union.

In Irish Millstreet the same year that the EU was established, Enrico Ruggeri—perhaps in an effort to follow up on Italy's success three years earlier—only managed to place 'Sole D'Europa' at the twelfth position in the final. Ruggeri, dressed in black and white, stood alone with the microphone, singing his own emotional and rather melancholic ballad, accompanied first acoustically and in the end by rock drums and an electric guitar that gets a brief concluding solo. The Italian lyrics present a poetic reflection on the effects of war, with rather complex metaphors and a stretched-out narrative instead of concise political hooks. 'Sole D'Europa' means 'Sun of Europe', and the song is like a prayer to the sun to return to a war-stricken and forgotten Europe. A sad picture is given of a rather hopeless situation where 'the days never change' but also 'the dreams never change', and the chorus lines beg the sun to finally return: 'Wake up, sun, so we can feel you / Today nobody asks for you / Cover Europe with light, do you remember where it is? / Come with me, fly with me, warm me up again.' An undefined 'they' is said to 'change their uniform and colour / but their tired souls wait for the sun', and the final chorus repeats its prayer, but this time collectively: 'Wake us up, sun, make us understand [...] Rise for us, come up with us, warm us up again.'[436] There are many echoes here of the Schuman Declaration and even of Schiller and Beethoven, but the hope for a redeeming sun as a dues-ex-machina has a religious feel that differs from the dominant political tradition where Europe's awakening is instead supposed to derive from its own determination.

A kind of religious awakening spirit returned to Tallin, Estonia in 2002 when Rosa from Spain performed 'Europe's Living a Celebration', getting an honourable seventh position in the ESC competition. The song had lyrics by Xasqui Ten and music by Toni Ten, and sounded like disco with gospel influences, underlined by Rosa's steady voice and energetic performance in sweeping black dress, and with five backing vocalists. The song leaves a strong impression, with syncopated call-and-response polyphony that creates a sense of an ecstatic congregation. The title words in English are often repeated, but all other words are in Spanish and contain no specific reference to Europe; instead they celebrate an abstract feeling of togetherness. The 'I' feels a thrill as a new dream (or illusion; the Spanish term can have both meanings) is born inside her, opening a way from 'me' to 'you': 'All together, let us sing / Europe living a celebration / Our dream—our reality'. The song is about trusting passion and love in the heart, singing together and never saying goodbye again. This may of course signify again the unified European peoples, but is abstract enough to also cover more personal love unions, in the tradition of gospel and soul music where the line between spiritual and profane love was always thin.

So far, there seems to be two main topics involved in the ESC songs of Europe. One theme that rings in all the songs is a kind of touristic celebration of Europe's cultural density and historical heritage, with urban culture in the traditional western part of the continent in focus. A second topic that is most prominent since 1990 is a celebratory depiction of expanded and intensified European integration. Other topical Europe songs have also competed in the ESC's national qualification competitions as well as in the ESC semifinals. Let me just mention two interesting examples.

In the 2008 Swedish finals the ESC included a hit by the popular dance music veteran Christer Sjögren, 'I Love Europe', composed by Torgny Söderberg and Magnus Johansson, with lyrics in English by the veteran Swedish hit author Ingela 'Pling' Forsman. The song title is a melodic hook that is insistently repeated, often by the female chorus in a call-and-response fashion. The song is like a glimmering pastiche or parody of traditional German-Austrian Schlager, and the visual performance is full of kitschy elements, starting with the flirting interplay between Sjögren (dressed in black suit with dark blue shirt), the camera and the can-can choir-dance girls with small hats who generously lift their blue skirts and happily dance around the singer (Figure 7.6). Sjögren has a deep and warm masculine voice that contrasts with the almost metallic voice of female background singers who remind somewhat of the ABBA sound. Metallic carillon shimmers reminding of Christmas seem to place the tune in the north, but the rhythms of an acoustic guitar and a shining trumpet instead add a sunny Spanish spice to the mix, illustrating the love of Europe 'from the sun in the south to the ice in the north'. The trumpeter is a bald musician in white suit that contrasts Sjögren's dark colours, and he also adds several funny gestures to illustrate turning points in the music. At a key moment when there is an upward chord lift (in fact the second one in this), the women fold their skirts and magically transform them into a mix of European flags, completing the symbolism in a combined verbal, musical and visual climactic moment of ecstacy. The words speak of dancing and romancing in an enchanted Europe where 'a party's going on, and we are invited'. Being together is what creates the excitement, and it is fun to hear the EU described in so enthusiastic terms:

> This is magic! C'est magnifique!
> And all our people are together
> Ciao! Buenos dias! Que tal? Wie geht es dir?
>
> In Paris or in Rome, the same good vibration
> It's just like coming home, in all of our nations
> I feel it all around, this groovy sensation
> I love Europe, we're a part of one big family
> Yes, this is the place for you and me, we're a part of one big family

Again, only 'old' West Europe is mentioned, in a touristic approach that had obviously already become a strong but also somewhat outmoded tradition, as it did not manage to even get a chance to represent Sweden internationally that year. This comically naive song is in a way in line with the EU motto as well as the social democratic 'People's Home' ideology, where there is room for 'everyone'. The distance is actually not that great from the Europe anthem, except that the moment of high culture elevation is totally absent. However, a slight hint of the elevation theme may be heard in the talk of a party going on to which only true Europeans are invited. Like some of the other songs mentioned above, 'I Love Europe' can be heard as an example of how the European motto of 'united in diversity' has been illustrated, while the desire of the Europa myth has here been transformed to just pure happiness, and the diversity factor reduced to highly superficial aspects of style, instead emphasising the natural unity in terms of being 'one big family'. With his deep voice and firm body, Christer Sjögren is like the Zeus bull enjoying the company of the smiling nymphs, and the falling out of the flags could then signify the dislocation resulting in the establishing of Europe. The absence of any trace of past wars and pain may be typical for a country that has not since 200 years on its soil experienced such fearful destruction.

In 2010, the Lithuanian InCulto's own 'Eastern European Funk' only made it to the semifinal, but made an explicit symbolic statement on EU's controversial expansion to the east, in stark contrast to the previously analysed song. Five boys in checkered brown trousers, white shirts and black ties, and playing with colourful plastic mock instruments, sang and danced on the stage (Figure 7.7). The music was a funky modern dance tune with a few Balkan brass elements lending it a mildly eastern sound. Let me quote the whole English lyrics, presenting a fresh perspective on unification seen from the 'new' part of the continent:

> You've seen it all before
> We ain't got no taste we're all a bore
> But you should give us chance
> Cause we're just victims of circumstance
> We've had it pretty tough
> But that's ok, we like it rough
> We'll settle the score
> We survived the reds and two world wars
>
> Get up and dance to our Eastern European kinda funk!
>
> Yes Sir we are legal we are, though we are not as legal as you
> No Sir we're not equal no, though we are both from the EU
> We build your homes and wash your dishes,
> Keep you your hands all soft and clean
> But one of these days you'll realize Eastern Europe is in your genes

Until that moment, only West European entries (Belgium, France, Ireland, Italy and Spain) had presented songs with an explicit focus on Europe. Here, Baltic Lithuania made a very clear statement that somehow repeats the Schuman Declaration idea of rising from war disasters to glory, but transposed onto the post-Communist experience and adding an East–West tension to the equation. This had almost two millennia old roots back in the division of the Christianised Roman Empire into a western and an eastern half. InCulto's song made explicit the mutual distrust that has surfaced both on the general political level and within the ESC, where there has since the early 1990s been a recurrent debate on how to balance the taste structures of East and West Europe, that came to disturb the already precarious balance between north and south European preferences.

Other songs outside the ESC and from other genres of popular music than mainstream pop add shifting flavours to the identification of Europe. Some join the ESC chorus by giving a positive image of Europe's historical richness and beauty, often with a kind of nostalgic memories of experiencing inter-European encounters.

German electronic band Kraftwerk's 'Trans-Europe Express' and 'Europe Endless' were released on the group's album *Trans-Europe Express* (1977), with one complete version in English and another in German. The imagery of transcontinental trains revives futurist and modernist themes of the 1920s' avant-garde. Typical for Kraftwerk, both these songs have minimalistic lyrics, with short catch phrases endlessly repeated. Repetitions excluded, the complete lyrics of 'Europe Endless' is thus: 'Life is timeless / Europe endless […] / Parks, hotels and palaces […] / Promenades and avenues […] / Real life and postcard views […] / Elegance and decadence […]'. The central element of urban civilisation links to the theme of aristocratic elevation, while the initial and concluding combinatory pairs are highly ambivalent: eternity and repetition, reality and image, elegance and decadence. The resulting meaning is deliberately evasive, except for the linkage of Europe to classical aristocratic city culture that is problematised by the synthetic and repetitive sound structure, transforming infinite grandiosity into almost unbearable boredom. 'This song makes me feel good about being a European', writes a fan on a website for interpreting songs, but is contradicted by another: 'This song is not an ardent ode to Europe. Life is not timeless and Europe is certainly not endless, that's the point.'[437] In a way, the two do not directly contradict each other, and both readings may well be challenged, as the song's evaluation of Europeanness is far from unequivocal and it is hard to say if timelessness is in this case good or bad.

The same album's lead song had a similar structure: 'Trans-Europe Express […] / Rendezvous on Champs-Elysees / Leave Paris in the morning on T.E.E. […] / In Vienna we sit in a late-night café / Straight connection, T.E.E. […] / From station to station / back to Düsseldorf City / Meet Iggy Pop and David Bowie'. 'Station to station' is an intertextual reference to Bowie's song and album from 1976, and to his and Iggy Pop's collaboration in Berlin, where they were influenced by Kraftwerk's experimental style. In spite of esoteric avant-garde references and advanced musical expression, the lyrics share many thematic elements with the ESC and other popular tunes that depict cosmopolitan travels between the streets and cafés of west and central European cities.

Ex-lead singer of the English electronic synthesiser rock band Ultravox!, John Foxx (real name Dennis Leigh) in 'Europe after the Rain' (1981) speaks of a kind of archaic love reunion story: 'It's time to walk again / It's time to make our way through the fountained squares'; 'Your smile is glimmering when I say you've hardly changed / in Europe after the rain / when the nights are warm and the summer sways / in Europe after the rain'. British pop band Suede in 'Europe is Our Playground' (1997) declares that 'Europe is our playground, London is our town / so run with me baby now'—'let's take a chance / from Heathrow to Hounslow, from the Eastern Bloc to France' and 'let's make a stand / from peepshow to disco, from Spain to Camber Sands'. Terms differ from Sjögren's 'I Love Europe', but there is a celebration of diversity here too. Even more programmatic is German heavy metal band Bonfire's 'Thumbs Up for Europe' (1999) whose EU-celebrating lyrics remind of 'I Love Europe' and Captain Europe:

> There's a new kind of challenge
> Its colours are gold and blue
> It's got a circle of stars
> shining for me and you
>
> Let's all give it a shot
> ready or not
> it's our destiny
>
> Human blood is one colour
> so let's make history
>
> It's just a little step
> in mankind's dream
> One world united—in liberty [...]
>
> Thumbs up for Europe—you and me
> Thumbs up for Germany

This energetic rock tune was released on the album *Fuel to the Flames* that also included tunes like 'Proud of My Country' and 'Ode an die Freude' (simply a slow instrumental version of the anthem for electric guitars). However, most other tunes are less apologetic and straightforward. Some are indeed very difficult to interpret coherently. The UK rock band Psychedelic Furs' 'Sister Europe' (1979) never actually mentions 'Europe' except in the title, and is a poetic allusion to some kind of decay and decline, with sailors drowning, talking, drinking and falling, a broken radio playing Aznavour out of tune, and new cars falling to dust. Echoing the song title, the chorus line 'Sister of mine, home again' may perhaps hint that this is a depiction of a gloomy continent where 'even dreams must fall to rules' and 'words are all just useless sound'—a suitable phrase to characterise this song itself. A listener thinks the song 'is about the continent of Europe', and offers a quite complex reading of it:

> Europe is seeing all these people doing stupid things and acting out their petty, futile dramas. Europe is there the whole time through many generations and sees the same mistakes being made over and over and how everyone dies with nothing to show for it and everything eventually falls to dust. I think the person is calling Europe 'sister of mine' because he sometimes steps back and sees the big picture and starts to identify with things that are less transitory like the land which could represent the eternal witness or something. When he does this he feels like he's home.[438]

The lyrics of American indie rock band R.E.M.'s 'Radio Free Europe' (1985) are hard to understand or even hear. The 'I' seems to get off a ship in Europe (presumably from America) and expresses some kind of media critique: 'Raving station, beside yourself / Calling on in transit / Radio Free Europe / Decide yourself, calling all of the medias too fast'. Most listeners seem to agree that while the song touches upon Cold War radio propaganda, its precise meaning is deliberately vague and open.[439]

The meaning of Australian post-punk Birthday Party's 'Dumb Europe' (written by Nick Cave and Christoph Dreher, 1983) is equally hard to pinpoint, as it alludes to an intoxicated and dizzy state of mind: 'On this European night out on the brink / the cafes and the bars still stink / The air is much too thick for seeing / but not thick enough for leaning'. It then talks of utopia and destruction, catatonia and death, possibly referring to Australia's history of participation in twentieth century European wars, but it is far from clear what is meant by the chorus words 'we could all just die of shame / dumb Europe'.

In 'Fortress Europe' (2003), British electronica band Asian Dub Foundation offers one of the rare examples of a direct critique of European migration policies. From the initial 'Keep bangin' on the wall / of Fortress Europe' to the concluding 'Break out of the detention centers / Cut the wires and tear up the vouchers / People get ready it's time to wake up / Tear down the walls of Fortress Europe', the song takes a clear stand for free movement and against boundary controls: 'We're the children of globalization / No borders, only true connection / Light the fuse of the insurrection /

This generation has no nation / Grass roots pressure the only solution / We're sitting tight / 'cause asylum is a right'.

Outside the mainstream pop field represented in the ESC, the topics of war, division and death stand out as a dominant thematic cluster in songs with 'Europe' in their titles, at least in indie rock, metal and singer-songwriter styles. To some extent, this supports the previous interpretation of Europe Day, the EU motto and the EU anthem. Just to pick an example, Roxy Music's melancholic 'A Song for Europe' (1973) depicts how the 'I' walks alone in Paris and Venice, remembering lost moments without any hope for future redemption: 'There's no today for us / Nothing is there / for us to share / but yesterday.' At the end of this truly melancholic song, words are also sung in Latin and French. This was written at a time when Europe was still caught between the superpowers, with a serious atomic threat looming large. British post-punk band Killing Joke's 'Europe' (1985) expresses a deep anxiety over the history and threatening future of war: 'Take up your arms pick up your courage / A black sun is rising as the gods of Europe sleep'. Catastrophes and atrocities are mentioned: 'What have they done, what are they doing? / The place I love so butchered, scarred and raped / The years have passed us, still we're fighting'. The song is desperately pessimistic: 'Glory glory how we watch in Europe / the day humanity is over / Let nations east and west tremble at the sight' until 'reason dead forever—god let it be soon'.

'Europe after the Rain' is the title of a song by John Foxx that has been reused with a completely different tune by the German thrash metal band Kreator (1992). It also spans a temporal narrative with a problematic past, a paralysed present and an even more frightening future. Today's 'indecisive government' with bizarre 'perversion' has created confusion concerning good and bad: 'Can't remember who we are', 'Emotions paralyzed', 'Terrifying industry protect departed nations / Can't get back together again / Leaving Europe after the rain / Acceptance of neo-fascist / Persecuting anarchists / Put the wrong ones on the list'. Meaninglessness and hopelessness rule in a capitalist Europe run by 'materialistic parasites'.

The Swedish melodic heavy metal band Europe was founded as Force in 1979 but changed its name in 1982, allegedly inspired by the Deep Purple live album *Made in Europe*.[440] The band has never released any song with 'Europe' in its title, though it had one called 'America' (2004), indicative of the direction of identification of the band, in spite of its chosen name. However, some 1980s Swedish singer-songwriter tunes paint a similar picture as the previous ones. Jan Hammarlund: 'Jag vill leva i Europa' ('I want to live in Europe', 1981), Anders F. Rönnblom: 'Europa brinner' ('Europe's burning', 1982) and Björn Afzelius: 'Europa' (1984) all relate not to the wars left behind in the past but to a persistent war threat with missiles accumulating on both sides of the iron curtain. Hammarlund's song combines this with the other main theme, that of enjoying romantic visits to key continental cities, but in a nostalgic light, expressing the risk of loss through nuclear war. This depressing feeling lifted after 1989, and for instance in the Swedish rock artist Tomas Ledin's 'Genom ett regnigt Europa' ('Through a rainy Europe', 2006—probably inspired by John Foxx's 'Europe after the Rain'), there is consolation in that 'I' and 'you' at least can walk together in love even though the sun is not always shining.

However, 9/11 and the subsequent challenges posed by radical Islamists have continued to fuel rather dark narratives of a Europe caught in mortal combat on its east frontier. Some songs use a dark and violent imagery to defend Europe's mission to stand up against all external threats, thus giving voice to more or less openly fascist sentiments. One example is the Belgian black/folk metal band Ancient Rites with 'Mother Europe' (1998) and the rather similar '(Ode to Ancient) Europa' (2001). 'Mother Europe' is a phrase often used in white supremacist debates on European issues. This song points out 'the proud Hellenic civilisation' as 'the cradle of Europe where it all began', then adds a series of brave and gallant regions that have added to its glory: Flemish, German, French, English, Scandinavian, Italian, Slovenian and Celtic contributions are mentioned and each briefly characterised. These 'knights' are summoned up to stand reunited and proud: 'Mother Europe born from your womb / Mother Europe on Your soil shall be my tomb'. This is reminiscent of Captain Euro's mission, but the song never explicitly clarifies if a new war is expected and who is in that case the new enemy.

The British Nazi punk band Skrewdriver's song with the same title 'Mother Europe' (1994) explicitly expresses a xenophobian creed. It mentions how 'Mother Europe's sons / faced so many tragedies at the barrel of a loaded gun' but are now protected by her 'guardian angel', 'with a flag held high': 'Mother Europe stands by our side / Mother Europe, we all live for you now.' 'So many martyrs', 'honest men' and 'warriors' have been sacrificed through history: 'For keeping Europe sacred, will be our fateful quest'. This fascist imagery shares certain aspects with the European flag's symbolism of sacredness, and Skrewdriver continues by summoning to a new war against Europe's enemies.

> For far too long now we've sat in apathy
> But just be warned now, before the coming tragedy
> For the power and the glory stand within our reach
> We must prepare the struggle for the victory we seek
>
> Mother Europe stands by our side
> Mother Europe we will die for you now

Here, the enemies are never specified, but it is not difficult to fill in the blanks by thinking of the usual Nazi combination of homosexuals, Muslims and atheist Communists as intended targets of this forthcoming battle. And in some ways a more problematic example is the song 'Europa' by Globus—a band, or rather a commercial project propelled by the lead composer Yoav Goren's 'passion for dramatic, epic, cinematic music'.[441] Goren is also the co-founder of an LA-based production company for film trailers, Immediate Music, and Globus's music has an orchestral and epic tone and structure. 'Europa' appeared on their debut album *Epicon*, first released in 2006 in the United Kingdom. It has a fast but steady ground beat, with a rock sound, supplemented by a large choir and orchestra, and with short melodic phrases with a British or Nordic folk-ethnic quality that is also found in some heavy metal and black metal music. The song is organised in a dramatic flow that reminds the listeners of an emotionally dense cinematic experience, with war imagery projected on the walls behind the artists. The first verse enumerates a series of historical 'battlefields of blood and tears', including Agincourt, Waterloo, Gallipoli and Stalingrad: 'The cruellest of atrocities / Europa's blood is borne of these.' The second verse prolongs the list:

> Bolsheviks and feudal lords
> Chivalry to civil wars
> Fascist rule and genocide
> Now we face the rising tide
> of new crusades, religious wars
> Insurgents imported to our shores
> The western world, gripped in fear
> The mother of all battles here

The choir chants 'Heaven help us in all our battles' and in the chorus longs for 'glory', 'honour' and 'victory'. The new 'rising tide' soon locates the new threats coming from the east:

> Descendants of the dispossessed
> return with bombs strapped to their chests
> There's hate for life, and death in hate
> emerging from the new caliphate
> The victors of this war on fear
> will rule for the next thousand years

The message is ambiguous and may be interpreted either as a call for peace ('Europa, Europa / Find better days before us / In kindness, in spirit / Lead us to a greater calling') or for a final blow against the Islamic menace: 'Drop the bomb, end this fight!' In a similar double reading, the concluding exclamation 'Never again!' may remind of Käthe Kollwitz's famous 1924 pacifist drawing 'Nie wider Krieg' ('Never again war') but is also the slogan of the Jewish Defense League, which has been characterised as a right-wing terrorist group for its violent actions against Muslims. A YouTube site where 'Europa' is published had also by June 2010 attracted 3000 comments that mostly express fear and hate against alleged enemies: 'islam is a danger to Europe', 'russia&putin will fuck europe', etc.[442] The dramatic song succeeds in stirring up strong emotions, as when 'ayrond091' sighs 'I'm asian but tottaly love this song and dream of being a european I hate asia', or when 'Mordercabrudasow' ominously declares: 'I mean there should never again be a war in europe, but there will be, a fight of christs an muslims, an We christs will win. But it will be a Fight of Brothers. One european against another, not beacouse of Land but religion!! I will fight on the front an cleanse Europe!!' Others protest that 'religion only brings war and hatred betwen nations', while many post short lines like 'Proud to be German [or French, Finnish etc.] and European'. The song's ambiguity is sensed by many, including 'borsza2' ('it's very contradictory, ranging from utter extremism to total pacifism'), 'cptfursten', who sharply pinpoints why it is so 'confusing' and even 'false', and 'CountArtha': 'Epically xenophobic ...'. The confusion clearly manages to spark off substantial debate, as the song itself can evidently be interpreted in highly contradictory ways, expressing very strong emotions but leaving the question of how they are to be directed open-ended, thus inviting a racist and 'Islamophobic' reading.

The musical styles and expressions of these songs cannot be reduced to any common denominator. Traits either from European ethnic folk music or from the European art music tradition are often used to hint at a shared legacy, just as is the case with the European anthem. However, within these wide frames, the songs can make considerably diverging statements. Like the ESC entries, the other most 'mainstream' tunes express a joyful pleasure of sharing happy experiences across borders, which is close to the message of the official EU symbols. The more artistically ambitious ones tend instead to focus on painful memories and fears of alienation, strife or even destruction, constructing Europe as something deeply problematic and filled with unresolved tensions. Many tunes are quite open in their interpretations, merely pointing at the risks of new conflicts, but some are more politically explicit: either problematising the ongoing developments from leftist positions that question the new power structures that marginalise various weak others, or a right-wing position of traditionalist nostalgia for strong nations, emanating in xenophobic, tending towards even racist and fascist discourse. What most have in common is an idea that Europe is selected for a particularly important task and challenge, again confirming the centrality of the theme of elevation.

Conclusions

The flag analysis in the previous chapter ended by underlining how the different visual symbols proposed indicate an ongoing conflict of interpretations of what Europe means. Adding an auditory symbol to the previous verbal and visual ones, the European anthem further widens but also to some extent narrows the symbolic polysemy of officially defined Europeanness. The complex relationship between the wordless anthem, Beethoven's symphony and Schiller's poem gives ample evidence of an ongoing conflict of interpretations in this symbolic sphere, involving a confusing (palimpsestic) superimposition of different historical layers. Comparisons with other explicitly European songs further underline the ambiguities and contradictions apparent in this identification process.

1. Beethoven's composition is full of *dislocating* elements. Its introduction moves the listener restlessly between unbearable remembrances of the preceding movements, and then follows a breathtaking journey through sharply contrasting moods, from the rumbling Turkish march to the crisply glimmering stars and finally the mixing of all these seemingly disparate elements in the operatic finale. In contrast to this, Karajan's EU anthem manages to delete almost every trace of such mobility, instead presenting a fixed world of solemnity. Even the mixed roots of the 'Ode to Joy' tune itself, having transferred a melody with a popular and French revolutionary aura to become the backbone of a quasi-sacral hymn within the highest of the high arts, have effectively been played down by the slow and even tempo and the majestic arrangement. Several of the other official anthems have a similarly fixed and stable character, while the popular songs expectedly vary in this respect.

2. There are plenty connotations of desire in Beethoven's and Schiller's fused works. Many agree that Beethoven's Ninth represents a contradictory 'combination of *desire and destruction*'.[443] A similar tension may actually be traced all the way back to the Europa myth, where violent rupture and erotic lust were closely intertwined in both the main actors. It is this destructive side of Europe's history that has led to the quest for control and security that supplements and is meant to protect the living out of joint desires, but also tends to threaten these same desires, in a negative dialectics. However, the anthem makes a deliberate move away from this ambiguity, by removing all hints of the initial chaos as well as of the Turkish march noises blurring the final apotheosis. Instead, it chooses to conform to the flag's expression of harmonious balance and thus control. Some of the analysed songs, not least Christer Sjögren's 'I Love Europe', stand closer to Beethoven in this respect, whereas others tend more to express the destructive aspect of the European heritage, as a kind of desire for disaster, often wedded to a mortally magnified desire for control.

3. Both the music and the (repressed) lyrics of 'Ode to Joy' strongly contribute to the previous symbols' emphasis on some kind of *elevation*. On the one hand, the choice of classical music, borrowed from the ultimately high-ranked composer Beethoven, and taken from one of his most mature and complex works, clearly

states a will to define Europeanness as having top quality and status. Also, both the lyrics and music contain several markers of uplifted, solemn or even divine attributes. On the other hand, they both also present a temporal narrative moving through initial troubles upwards towards a jubilant climax—and this applies to the short anthem versions as well as the full symphony movement. The same is true for several of the other examples, including the Eurovision and the UEFA anthems, as well as for some of the popular songs with European titles, where Europe is described either as a particularly happy and lovable place, or as selected for a fateful world battle against evil forces. The few dystopic songs that instead describe Europe as a particularly nasty and doomed place are critical exceptions to the by now well-established rule, but even they tend to define Europe as something special (even if bad), that is, they reproduce the trope of selectedness.

4.   Finally, there are plenty of *hybrid* structures in Beethoven's original work— so much that Nicholas Cook and others have concluded that all its internal contradictions make it impossible to interpret it in any coherent fashion. Schiller's reference to humanity as becoming 'brothers' in combination with that to 'daughter of Elysium' immediately combines the two main genders, and the music then also adds different ethnic flavours, particularly the Oriental flavour of the central march section. Here again, the EU anthem carefully avoids all such complications and presents a sanitised version of Europeanness as white and (with the brass instruments) male. *Uniform homogeneity* rules, with only faint traces of any kind of diversity. This is also true for the other organisational anthems, while it is impossible to draw any firm conclusions from the popular songs. However, EU authorities' parallel release of anthem variants in a wide range of styles, from rap to romani, have again opened it up for recognising diversity, in a similar manner as the barcode has supplemented the official flag with its missing element of vital pluralism and difference.

All in all, the anthem basically confirms the main message conveyed by the flag, with a certain affinity to that from Captain Euro, depicting Europe as a rather controlled, fixed and unitary entity. However, its various contextual neighbours provide contesting identifications, and in particular the anthem's origin in Beethoven's Ninth Symphony, which still remains hard to repress as even the omission of the lyrics is not always respected when the anthem is performed at EU-related events, casts a shadow reminding the listeners of the heritage expressed by the Europa myth of a Europe full of dislocation, desire and diversity. As with all other official symbols, the idea of some kind of selectedness and elevation remains a constant element that in a naturalising way places Europe in the centre of its own universe, as if its status as the first geocultural world region was completely self-evident.

8

CURRENCY

The final, most recent and also in many ways the most effective and important official European symbol is monetary: the euro.[444] Money is an economic tool but also a cultural medium, reaching deep into citizens' pockets and circulating in everyday life—in a unique manner among the symbolic modes discussed here. It is truly a kind of banal symbolism of time-in culture, fully integrated in ordinary practices rather than isolated in any separate ritual sphere. Crucial to its function as identifying symbol is the way it is used but also the way it is designed, since it is this visual and material design that links Europe to yet another set of multiple meanings.

What's in a currency?

American industrialist Henry Ford is credited for declaring: 'I am not interested in money but in the things of which money is the symbol'. He probably meant a combination of economic wealth and social bonds, but real money signifies more than that, or perhaps it signifies in other ways than just through serving as a means of exchange of economic values. Money is also a medium of symbolic communication of meanings, not only of value.

Since the thirteenth century, the term 'money' referred to mint, coinage or metal currency, but from the early nineteenth century it also included paper money. In ancient Rome, money was coined by the temple of Juno, who bore the title *moneta*, possibly deriving from *monere* (advise, warn, monitor). 'Currency' derives from Latin terms for running and flowing, and is since the seventeenth century used for the circulation of money, divided into specific monetary systems that are often linked to nation states.[445] Money is a system of material tokens used for facilitating the distribution of commodities among private owners, divided into currencies that with the rise of nation states became guaranteed and organised by them, in a smilar way that verbal language was differentiated into specific languages that much later became adopted by nations. The institution of money, in general, is virtually universal in today's globalised world, but the national currencies invite specific sets of money to be linked to some kind of national identification practices.

As a means of value measurement and exchange, money abstracts from the peculiar use-values of individual commodities. In Karl Marx' terms, money is a 'real abstraction', a general equivalent that levels all other differences in interhuman exchange than those of economic value.[446] It has been suggested that this practical abstraction may have been instrumental in the contemporaneous development of abstract thinking, for instance in the general use of personal pronouns.[447] At the same time, money always has some kind of physical existence, as pieces of metal or paper, or at least as electronic configurations in banking networks. The design of those tokens tend to carry an excess of meaning, by not only signifying an amount of value but also necessarily contextualising that sum by denoting for instance the issuing country which guarantees that value as well as the year of issue. Actually the material money citizens have since centuries used in everyday life also includes many other aspects that serve to identify the community whose state authorities guarantee its validity. A difficult balance needs to be kept in order for money to function well as such, since if for instance coins are too specific they may become collector items and be withdrawn from money circulation too early. The current transfer to electronic money marks a decisive step in the direction of abstraction, but it appears coins and paper money will remain in use yet for a while.[448] The dialectics of abstraction and concretion remains crucial to an understanding of how money functions in society, and their successful combination enables money to serve to support the formation of communities across both geographic and social distances.[449]

These etymologies and characteristics remind that the functioning of money relies on a precarious combination of trust and stability with mobility and fluidity. Georg Simmel has suggested that the roundedness of coins that make them roll symbolises the rhythm of movement required for money to function in society as a means of exchange and thus of communication binding trading communities together. While stressing that money is the most transient thing, both symbolising and effecting movement (comparable to Marx' real abstraction), Simmel at the same time saw money as embodying the most enduring content of value.[450] Money is therefore the focal point of a dialectics of mobility and stability, linked to that of abstraction and specificity.

A third contradiction or at least tension is that between individuality and community. On the one hand, money is typically used by individuals (persons or companies) for transferring private ownership. Much economic theory begins with the individual human being who needs to exchange goods with other individuals, and where the macroeconomics of corporations or even states are treated as aggregations of such intraindividual relations. But, as Marx, Simmel and others have all agreed, money is on the other hand at the basic level a social relation; an institutionalised social mechanism for binding collectives together. The explicit purpose of the euro has been from the start to serve as both a practical means of and a symbol for the identification of Europe as a common good, at the same time as the monetary discourse continues to stress its role for individual users, reflecting the basic tension in the market economy between individual and collective interests. The dialectics of abstract/concrete, mobile/stable and collective/individual are mutually interlinked in ways that affect money's role in the formation of identities and communities. In the words of Suzanne Shanahan,

> identities and currencies share a set of logical parallels that make the agency of money particularly powerful in forging identity. [...] Currencies are the daily, ritualistic expression of popular trust in the political regime. To use money is to pay homage to community.

At the same time 'money, like identity, invariably takes on a different meaning for each individual', opening a scope for diversity to develop across unification. Money's power as a real abstraction makes it able to socially forge the same collective identities that it symbolises through its very usage and design.[451]

The institution of money is an organising and regulating tool for the circulation of goods and services, for mediating exchange values and binding society together. Coins and banknotes can only fulfil these economic functions of signifying and transferring exchange value if they have clearly identifiable material traits that ensure their authenticity and univocally represent their value, nationality and date of issue. They are means of communication intended for the combined use as unit of account, means of payment and store of value. In order to function as such, they must contain texts, images and patterns that make them interpretable as money. They thus not only signify 'frozen desire', but also forms of identification. Symbolic functions are extra-economic use values of money, indispensable if the primary functions of coins and notes as means of exchange are to be fulfilled. Many British pound notes and coins carry the inscription 'Decus et tutamen'—'An ornament and a safeguard', from Virgil's *Aeneid*. This is emphatically true of all money designs: they are at once aesthetic and economic, carriers of meaning as well as of financial value. Money has a secondary function as media texts, and issues of currency design therefore deserve to be taken more seriously by those who seek to understand the meaning of money.[452]

In *One-Way Street*, Walter Benjamin described letters and postcards as windows to the world—magical connections forged between daily life and the big world outside—and stamps as 'calling cards that large states leave behind in the nursery'.[453] Coins and banknotes share these connective capabilities, functioning like calling cards that large states and supra-states place in each little citizen's purse. But, as Hymans argues, currencies have the advantage of being at the same time universal (issued by every state), selective (focusing a more narrow number of designs compared to stamps) and regularly updated (unlike flags or anthems), making them a preferred case for studying the dynamics of national identification.[454]

The economic, social and cultural aspects of money are interwoven, and presuppose each other.[455] Monetary functions are increasingly often carried out digitally, but the use of the specialised artefacts of coins and banknotes still remains remarkably stable, since they are free of cost and relatively simple for the individual user.[456] They communicate a certain amount of abstract exchange value, but also introduce other meanings into daily life circulation. The ways in which to display and safely guarantee their value can be varied and elaborated in response to a wish to make them more visually appealing, or add other layers of meaning that reflect how economic values and the country of origin are understood by its monetary authorities and ordinary citizens. Produced by the international system of state national banks, they circulate condensed images of national identities and sociocultural value hierarchies through their carefully chosen design. Thus, they are widely spread media communicating collective identifications when being used by virtually everyone on a daily basis. Their design and thus semantic content is heavily regulated by political state institutions, making them communications media under strict control by the cooperating state and market systems of modern societies. However, as with other mass media, the mostly unconscious interpretation of their symbolic meanings by the citizens who use them is not fully contained by those systemic institutions, and is to a certain degree an object of negotiation and transformation. There is always a surplus of meaning in all kinds of textual production, as texts are open to imaginative interpretation.

Though money is an economic tool, it is also a cultural phenomenon: a vehicle for constructing and sharing meanings. George Herbert Mead has compared money to language and other forms of communication:

> As taught in economics, money is nothing but a token, a symbol for a certain amount of wealth. It is a symbol for something that is wanted by individuals who are in the attitude of willingness to exchange; and the forms of exchange are then the methods of conversation, and the media of exchange become gestures which enable us to carry out at vast distances this process of passing over something one does not want, to get something he does, by means of bringing himself into the attitude of the other person. The media of these tokens of wealth are, then, in this process of exchange just such gestures or symbols as language is in other fields.[457]

Money is thus a symbol and a means of communication—perhaps even a 'medium', in a double sense. First, its economic function is itself a kind of strategic coordinating action, mediating between people. Second, besides this kind of mediation, money also through designs mediates symbolic forms and meanings among users. If media are broadly conceived as mediating agents between humans, money certainly fulfils such a function already as a purely economic instrument, and has been discussed as such a systemic medium.[458] Matthias Kaelberer points out that 'the European Monetary Union itself establishes something of a European public space' where the euro 'serves as a tool of Europe-wide communication'.[459] However, the sense of 'communication' and 'medium' here need to be qualified in order to distinguish money from telephones or television. Jürgen Habermas differentiates between on the one hand money and power as media of coordination and steering which substitute for language, and on the other hand those forms of generalised communication effected by mass media technologies that do not substitute but rather condense face-to-face interaction.[460] While the latter are inseparably integrated in the lifeworld, the former are organised as differentiated systems by the market and the state. Their autonomy still remains relative, as it is still based on an element of loyalty and trust among citizens, and thus can never be fully cut off from the signifying practices that weave the nets of culture. According to Habermas, the historical trend towards increasing systemic differentiation has induced a late modern crisis of legitimation for the social order of state and market. Sociologists like Ulrich Beck and Anthony Giddens have in similar terms diagnosed a late modern problem of upholding trust in societal institutions, including state authorities as well as markets. The recurring crises in the monetary systems, including that of the euro and the EMU, may be seen as typical for what Beck has called the 'risk society'.[461]

Kaelberer underlines that 'money is based on trust', but also that modernisation processes have made this cohesive trust increasingly 'abstract and institutionalised', so that 'identity does not necessarily have to rest on deep affective feelings of belonging in order to support a modern relationship of trust'. Therefore, the trust needed for the euro to work needs only to be of the diffuse and polydimensional type typical of late modernity. The euro cannot rest on any naturalised deeply affective sense of shared belonging, but only on a constructed, diffuse and hybrid pan-European identity that is always combined with other (including national) identifications. But this may still well suffice, and Kaelberer does conclude that with reference to some elements of a shared history of cherishing welfare-state values of social solidarity, 'there is a sufficient level of Europeanness—as part of evolving hybrid identity structures—to support an effective functioning of the euro'.[462] Also, what unites a collective entity is often more evident from the outside than from within, and some European analysts may be blind to common traits since internal differences make it hard for them to see the wood for the trees. Based in his historical study of European banknote designs, Jacques Hymans argues that elements of a European commonality may not be out of reach, for the content of collective identities in Europe has been both more changeable across time and more uniform across space than identity scholars typically assert. [...] European national currencies at any one point in time have expressed a remarkable commonality of values.[463]

In Ferdinand Tönnies' terms, Europe may well function as primarily a Gesellschaft (a complex association built on instrumental and institutional processes of indirect mediation) rather than a Gemeinschaft (like a family or a kinship, based on mutual bonds and deep feelings of togetherness).[464] The euro has survived its phase of establishment, and if EU's monetary crisis does not lead to a total breakdown—in which case the money designs are not to blame—this functioning seems to indicate that Kaelberer might be right.

Introducing the euro

Money thus has an advantage over the previously mentioned symbols, namely to be present in every citizen's daily life, serving as the basis for an 'unflagged' or 'banal' (supra-) nationalism enacted by unfocused 'time-in' rituals that underpin imagined community, at the opposite end of the scale of for instance commemoration days or anthems.[465] Almost everyone deals with money on a daily basis, but few ever think much about it or have a closer look at the coins and bills they touch. The tangible immersion of money in everyday life is in this particular case limited by the boundaries of the EMU area, since not even all of the EU countries use the euro, and also by the gradual transition from cash to electronic means of payment.[466] The other EU symbols have at some point also been acknowledged by the Council of Europe, which makes them more easily acceptable as general European signifiers. It is in economic terms only valid for a core group of European states, but little is yet known about how the euro has been perceived and interpreted as a symbol of Europe at large, within or even less outside of the EMU area. Still, many people both inside and outside of Europe do encounter the euro, whether as visiting tourists or when in various contexts encountering the € sign, the word 'euro' or images of euro coins or banknotes.

The euro was installed as a materially effective mechanism that could simultaneously be designed in a symbolically striking way, in order to further strengthening identification of and with Europeanness. In general, this new identity is not intended to substitute for national identifications, but just to add a new, transnational level, as the EU is not intended as a federation that would replace nation states. All the other key symbols mentioned were never intended to replace the corresponding national days, mottos, flags or anthems, but to be added as yet another facet of citizens' complex identifications. However, this is slightly different with the euro, as it actually must replace the previous national currencies. This makes it more controversial, and can be seen as one factor limiting its use to the EMU area that is only a part of the whole EU. This lends to the euro an exceptional status among these symbols.

A presentation text on 'The Currency of the European Union' in *European Navigator* acknowledges that 'money has always been a powerful means of communication':

> Money talks, and its message is federating, as it is the lowest common denominator of the group using it. This makes it a highly effective and important instrument of identity which has become so customary, through its continuous use for 2400 years, that its role has been more or less forgotten. [...] Money is also a strong symbol of social ties. It carries with it faith, solidarity and expectations of guarantees; every currency reflects the trust of citizens in the role of the state as a guarantor of national cohesion, of the protection of citizens and of the improvement of their standard of living.[467]

The currency is explicitly treated by the EU itself (for instance in the draft constitution from 2003) in terms of an identifying symbol, and not only (or even primarily) as a practical tool for economic value transfer.[468] Indeed, the euro does signify one of the four fundamental 'free movements' of the EU—goods, services, people and money— but none of the other three has in any similar way been transformed into a key symbol. On the one hand, this testifies to a certain 'commercialisation' of the European project: an explicit acknowledging of the central role of capitalism and the market economy in the union, not a hidden linking mechanism but a cherished and almost sacralised idol of worship—a currency that has a declared role in signifying the shared identity of the European nations. On the other hand, it may simultaneously also be seen as an expression of a parallel culturalisation of the economy, acknowledging the fact that even money as aestheticised material objects (coins and banknotes) become part of an 'experience industry', while they do to some extent lose part of their traditional economic importance due to the increasing role of e-money.

On 1 January 2002, the seven different values of euro banknotes and eight values of coins were introduced in twelve of the EU member states, to be daily used by some 300 million Europeans in Austria, Belgium, Finland, France, Germany, Greece, Ireland, Italy, Luxembourg, the Netherlands, Portugal and Spain. Through a special agreement, Monaco, San Marino and Vatican City connected to the euro and issued their own coin designs, in spite of not being EU members. Other countries have continued joining EU and the eurozone: Slovenia in 2007, Cyprus and Malta in 2008, Slovakia in 2009 and Estonia in January 2011, so that the 'eurozone' has then grown to seventeen official EU member states, with Iceland and others expected soon to join.

Outside the EU five territories also use the euro: the British colonial fragments of Akrotiri and Dhekelia plus four French areas—Clipperton, the French Southern and Antarctic Islands, Mayotte, and Saint Pierre and Miquelon. Andorra, Montenegro and Kosovo also use the euro without any formal arrangement. Neither of all these issue their own money, but use the euros that are produced by the seventeen member states of the inner eurozone.[469]

The introduction of the euro had been prepared by a concerted information effort, including for children the Captain Euro superhero website analysed in the myth chapter above. The first coins were actually already minted back in 1999, when the currency was formally established, even if they weren't released for use until 2002, when in all 50 billion coins and 14.5 billion banknotes were released, with a total value of over €664 billion.

The banknotes look the same throughout the EMU area, while the coins have the front side (obverse) common to all euro countries and a rear side (reverse) specific to each country (but no less valid in all other euro nations). Each national set dominates the circulation of money in its respective country, but through travel and tourism, the national circuits leak into each other, so that even though most citizens will mainly see coins from their own countries, they will from time to time in their daily life also encounter images from elsewhere. Measuring how national euro coins mix in various countries would thus indicate dominant patterns in international contacts.

The name 'euro' (official three-letter abbreviation EUR) for the monetary unit of the pan-European currency was adopted in 1995 as a successor of the previous 'ecu' which was both an abbreviation of 'European currency unit' and the name of a currency used in France and Italy from 1260.[470] For Germans, the ecu sounded like 'ein Kuh' (a cow) and therefore was hard to take seriously. The euro has a strikingly variable pronounciation in different languages, compared for instance to the dollar. In Greek it is 'ev'ro', in French 'ø'ʁo', in German ''ɔʏʁo', in English: ''jʊəːrəʊ', while for instance Swedes tend to waver between the Greek and the English variants, reflecting a contested anglification of its national language, which especially in the introductory phase induced some confusion. After all, the name is unique, short and clear, and with an evident link to the name of the continent.

The € symbol is based on the Greek epsilon letter, according to all official sources meant to refer to both the word 'Europe' and ancient Greece as 'the cradle of European civilisation', and with the two horizontal bars symbolising the intended stability of this new currency.[471] One may also compare it with the famous signs for the pound (£) and the dollar ($), both of which include such (horizontal or vertical) strokes across some kind of letter. (The 'libra sign' £ derives from the Roman weight unit 'libra', a Latin word for balance or scales. The $ sign was first used for the peso and may derive from some Spanish coat of arms engraved on silver coins.) The € sign has also rapidly become acknowledged and integrated into the global core of monetary symbols. On the banknotes, the € sign only appears hidden within the vertical security bands, while it is altogether absent from the coins. This is not unique to the euro, as for instance US$ bills do not prominently feature the $ sign. However, the € sign is of course very common elsewhere, wherever the euro is mentioned in texts or images and used in practice.

In 1995 the European Monetary Institute (EMI), forerunner of the European Central Bank (ECB), selected two themes for the euro banknotes, based on the preparatory work of an advisory group of art historians, graphic designers and marketing experts: 'Ages and styles of Europe' and a broader theme of 'abstract/modern design'. For the first theme, the features to be depicted on each of the seven banknote denominations (€5, 10, 20, 50, 100, 200 and 500) were to represent a specific period of European cultural history: Classical, Romanesque, Gothic, Renaissance, Baroque and Rococo, the age of iron and glass architecture, and modern twentieth century architecture. It was also decided that the designs should incorporate the European flag as 'a universally accepted symbol of Europe'. A Europe-wide competition followed in 1996, with a jury of experts in marketing, design and art history, selected by EMI from candidates proposed by the national banks. The jury selected five versions of each theme, based on criteria of 'creativity, aesthetics, style, functionality, likely public perception and acceptability (in particular the avoidance of any national bias and the achievement of a proper balance between the number of men and the number of women portrayed on the banknotes)'. The latter problem was in the end solved by excluding all humans from the designs, and by letting the motifs be completely abstracted from any geographical location. Efforts were then also made to test their 'public perception' by making qualitative interviews with 1896 individuals throughout Europe: professional cash handlers and members of the general public. In 1997, the revised banknote designs could then be created (Figure 8.1).

It was the Austrian graphic designer Robert Kalina of the Österreichische Nationalbank who designed the banknotes.[472] Apart from basic information such as the value and the name of the currency in the Latin and Greek alphabet, they include a value-specific combination of the twelve EU stars with a set of windows and gateways from seven architectural periods: Classical (€5), Romanesque (€10), Gothic (€20), Renaissance (€50), Baroque and Rococo (€100), iron and glass style (€200) and modern twentieth century architecture (€500). All these architectural elements have been deliberately designed in order not to signify any particular building from any specific country, but are meant to synthesize features that unite the whole continent. They are scrupulously presented in official EU sources, explaining that the windows and gateways are intended to symbolise 'the European spirit of openness and co-operation', while the twelve stars represent 'the dynamism and harmony between European nations'. To complement these designs, the reverse of each banknote features a bridge, symbolising 'the close co-operation and communication between Europe and the rest of the world'. There is also a map of Europe, including tiny dots for the large-enough extra-European colonial territories of France, Portugal and Spain that also use the euro.[473] The visual representation of Europe as a spatial territory is thus complicated by its colonial past.

The obverse sides of the eight values of euro *coins* have a motif created by Mr Luc Luycx of the Royal Belgian Mint, who won a Europe-wide competition (Figure 8.2). They depict the value, the name 'EURO' and different variants of the EU map and twelve stars linked by parallel lines. The one, two and five cent coins supposedly show 'Europe's place in the world', by having a map of the entire globe with Europe in the centre. The ten, twenty and fifty cent coins depict 'Europe as a group of individual nations' by showing each country as a separate island (including also the EU member states who did not join the eurozone: Denmark, Sweden and the United Kingdom, but excluding all others, even those who soon were to become members). 'A united Europe without frontiers' is represented on the one and two euro coins, with an ordinary EU map. These three variants are also clearly differentiated in colours and general design, so that the coin series consists of three different value groups with three, three and two sizes in each.

Reflecting the EU enlargement, a new design was introduced in 2007, retaining the key elements as well as the three lowest denominations, but modifying the others so that the interpretation was totally changed. The three mid-values no longer show 'individual nations' but rather roughly the same map as the highest coins, only (as before) placed to the left of the value figures. This means that all the five highest coins now show Europe as a rather unified continent. Efforts were also made to normalise Europe's contour on all these five high-value coins by including the non-EU member Norway, extending the continent to the east and adding Cyprus (though it had to be radically moved to the north-west in order to become visible). The Council of Europe rejected the European Commission's proposal to include Turkey on the map.[474]

The three original design variants together thus told a narrative starting with entering Europe from afar, noting its place in a global context, then focusing on its internal diversity, and finally watching it unite into a coherent entity. In the later version, the second step was eradicated, resulting in a less elaborate story, moving from the globe to the continent and then just shifting it from the left to the right hand of the surface (Figure 8.3). The lines between stars imply a kind of unique and holy 'star quality' of each state with an emphasis on the linking work of their union. This interpretation is supported when both sides of the coin are acknowledged. Romano Prodi, President of the European Commission, has explained the coin sides as expressing the EU motto of 'united in diversity'. In this 'preferred reading', the common obverse side symbolises the unity of the European Commission, whereas the national reverse sides represent the diversity of the European Parliament. The two sides thus together symbolise the centre of economic and political power versus the nationally divided periphery. The obverse sides symbolically also emphasise pure financial value (a number for the euro amount in question), whereas the rear sides present symbolic and cultural aspects of identity.

The national reverse sides have to be framed by a twelve star circle and give the year of issue, but are otherwise pretty free for each country to design, and the countries have indeed made quite varying choices (Figure 8.4). New issues must also add the issuing nation's name. All 'national' coins may be used in all EU countries, resulting in a circulation of national signs between the EU states as well as to all other countries where the euro may be used, for instance through tourism and other travel. This means that a whole range of national symbols will possibly be found in any single EU citizen's wallet, reminding of the coexistence within the boundaries of this union of regions that might feel rather exotic.[475] These complexly evolving sets of euro designs will be further specified and discussed in the following section.

Interpreting the common euro designs

As explained above, each banknote and coin clearly presents the respective monetary value and the name of the currency, together with various other identifying security codes needed for it to serve as a trustworthy currency. The rest of the common designs are consciously abstract, in order to avoid the internal envy and competition that might have occurred if localisable and nationally biased motifs had been used. It was decided early not to depict people (in order to avoid the tricky identity politics of fair representation) or specific buildings (so as not to marginalise any non-selected region). Kaelberer regards this deliberate abstractness of the euro bill designs as typical of the 'process of abstraction and dematerialisation' that is inherent in the monetary system, with the transition to electronic money as the latest step.[476] The harmonious twelve interconnected stars and the map emphasise the cohesion of the union, but in an abstract and unspecific manner. The whole set of bridges, doors and windows on the notes likewise have a deliberately abstract character, in an effort to avoid any specific national bias, and also to steer clear of the androcentrism that so predictably dominated the national coin faces. That kind of abstract unity may well be problematised as an ideological or magical re-enchantment of a continent that is in reality little more than a purely instrumental economic project, and whose symbols are void gestures that contribute little to a possible future European identity formation. The abstract symbolic patterns and architectural details shown on the euro confirm this tendency, possibly testifying to a failure to anchor the EU project in deep-seated popular sentiments. On the other hand, it may also be argued that the abstractness is a necessary and positive trait: 'Successful symbols need to be vague and multi-layered, so they can appeal to and act as signifiers for all kinds of different groups and opinions.'[477] This is for instance also true for much of popular culture that is popular because the relative abstractness of its plots and characters make it possible for different audiences to invest them with shifting meanings, filling the signifying gaps with aspects relevant to one's own life, and thus invite rather than repel identifying readings.

There is an explicit continuity between the euro and the flag, since a small version of the latter is depicted in the upper left corner of all banknote fronts, and both banknote sides also integrate a section of a larger *star circle* into their main motifs. On the coin fronts, the stars are instead presented in two groups of six stars each, forming two tilted bows along the perimeter, with parallel straight lines connecting them two by two: vertical to the right on the two highest denominations (€1 and 2), to the left on the three middle ones (¢10, 20 and 50), and diagonally on the three smallest coins (¢1, 2 and 5). An interpretation may be to signify how money transfers normally are between two individual actors, and that the common European market is constructed out of a dense network of such bipolar transferences. All the national coin reverses are further framed by a more or less symmetric version of the star circle, and as the edge of the €2 coins are nationally determined, they sometimes also include the star circle. The euro is therefore a prime example of how the basic logo is reused and integrated in new contexts, to ensure European identification and transfer to such new contexts the same values that were analysed in Chapter 6.

Secondly, all banknote rears include a standard *map* of Europe, which as mentioned earlier also includes tiny representations of the colonial territories that still are controlled by EU member states. No national boundaries are visible, and the eastern border of the continent is characteristically diffuse, including the western half of Turkey, the Black Sea region and Russia. (This differs from the coins, as explained above.) Together with the value figures and the stars, maps are also the focal motif on the coin fronts. The three smallest denominations depict a whole globe showing Europe surrounded by west Asia and almost all of Africa. This is supposed to refer to 'Europe's place in the world'. In the original series, the three medium values show 'Europe as a group of individual nations' by having pulled each of the 2002 EU member states slightly apart from each other. The two € coins have a similar 'ordinary' map as on the banknotes, supposedly representing 'a united Europe without frontiers', which is thus by extension the highest stage of Europe's development, in accordance with the leading EU narrative as expressed by the Schuman Declaration, as well as Europe day and the anthem, where the current unification crowns a teleology in which Europe passed through disastrous division to achieve the present will to integrate. All in all, these maps present a bird's eye view of the European territory from above, offering a sense of control and perspective by drawing boundaries that combine protective outer limits with respect for internal national differences.

Besides these elements that confirm the core imagery interpreted in previous chapters, the banknotes' main motifs contribute important new aspects for identifying Europe, in the form of *doors*, *windows* and *bridges* from seven architectural periods, from the classical period to modern twentieth century. Together, these 'ages and styles of Europe' tell a 'money-story' (a term used by Vida Zei), of two millennia of architectural styles from Roman antiquity to a future-oriented present.[478] This story is meant to symbolise dynamism and progress, in constructing a linear hierarchy typical of western modernity and Enlightenment thinking, where history is conceived as future-oriented progression rather than as retrospective continuity or decay. The reliably progressing continuity makes a solid impression that anchors the current EU in a long line of cultural history. Skipping periods of chaotic decay reinforces an image of Europe as always improving and developing, but also respecting its traditions and varying its rich heritage into the future. A variant of this trustworthy progressivism is inherent in the EU project since the Schuman Declaration, for which World War II was an ultimate crisis and catastrophe from which all roads must lead to improvement, if the collected achievements of western culture is finally to be applied in a peaceful manner. Matthias Kaelberer has acknowledged the ideological force of such storytelling:

> The imagery on the euro banknotes attempts to establish links to a common European tradition. It refers back to the classical ancestry of Europe and deliberately constructs a common European historical memory. [...] The chronological ascent in artistic styles also reads history in conventional European teleological fashion as the story of progress. While German banknotes visibly emphasised historical discontinuities, the euro can conveniently 'forget' uncomfortable aspects of European history—such as war and imperialism—in the name of an optimistic and progressive vision of Europe. It 'romanticises' history as easily as national currencies do.[479]

Chris Shore likewise concludes that all the architectural banknote motifs symbolise 'transition, mediation, movement and the promise of a brighter future'.[480] It is true that the paper money-story does not explicitly allude to Europe's colonial past, nor to any of those wars that through centuries have continued to violently damage those same buildings that are here shown as almost eternally solid. The former forgetfulness adheres to the leading EU foundation myth, while the latter deviates from its narrative of resurrection after internal strife. Rather, the chronological narrative here is one of steady progress through the centuries, which is a form of historical consciousness that may itself since at least the eighteenth century Enlightenment be understood as typically European.

The precise choice of architectural styles offers more signifying cues, besides their teleological succession in general. The other continents—North and South America, Africa, Asia and Australia—would certainly have made different choices. The time span would for instance have differed: only in Europe could precisely the last two millennia be accepted as a reasonable historical totality. It is significant that the Classical motifs chosen for the lowest (€5) notes happen to be Roman rather than Greek. Whereas the € sign is based on a Greek epsilon supposed to refer to the cradle of European civilisation in classical Greece, the banknotes instead place Europe's narrative origin in Rome around year 0. The signifying effect of this choice is at least twofold. Spatially, it avoids placing the origin of Europe to its southeast corner. Temporally, it implies a start around the point zero of modern chronology. Taking a step back behind the magic year 0 would contradict a recurring trope of Europe as a Christian continent, and open the gate to a possibly endless series of previous Neolithic civilizations. Starting with Rome places the birth more in the centre of the continent, and coincides reasonably well in time with the emergence of its dominant religion, which still retains a focal point in papal Rome. The effect is to place the cradle of Europe centrally in Rome and contemporary with Christianity, thus bracketing Greek and other 'previous' cultures as pre-history. Its potentially decentring connections to the Middle East, Athens and Ancient Greece appear to imply an ambiguous identity as both European and Oriental, potentially destabilising the East/West polarity and endangering the self-sufficient idea of Europe as its own product. It is true that the euro symbol € with its basis in a Greek epsilon retains that liminal origin, but in a more hidden and general form, elevating this pre-Christian Greek culture above the mundane flow of history into a kind of universal sphere of pure and eternal origins and foundations for European civilisation. The € sign thus places the Greek origin outside of the historical narrative itself, in pre-history, in line with the idea of European civilisation as 'eccentric' as well as with the Europa myth's theme of dislocation. It is also significant that only some of the Greek coin motifs go further back than Christian times, reconfirming that the symbolisms of all the other member states agree to situate the birth of the European project in the year 0 AD and the Roman Empire, which is geographically ideally positioned, with its great land areas may seem more appropriate for the claims of a continent than the seafaring group of islands and coastlines that constituted the aquatic network formation of ancient Greece.

Roman culture also fits better with the fusion of engineering technology and humanist ideas that underpins the whole money-story on the banknotes. The choice of depicting buildings (rather than for instance people or artworks) has several implications. The architectural metaphor of 'building Europe' is often used to describe European unification in terms of planned political construction rather than for instance organic growth, revolutionary leaps or free market forces.[481] Choosing hard and stable human-made buildings further implies an emphasis on the accumulable (rather than ephemeral) aspects of human culture (rather than nature): fixed rather than variable capital, heritage rather than the fleeting present, products rather than processes, collective rather than individual works, combinations of harmonic aesthetics and practically useful engineering technology rather than any other artefactual genres or human faculties. The construction metaphor may be seen as a tribute to gradual reforms and also to the modern ideal of makeability: the omnipresent possibility of re-creation. A *European Navigator* introductory text on 'The Currency of the European Union' argues that these monumental motifs signify the stability of the currency and 'the capacity of human labour to create great works and to improve them over time'. This would then indicate that the unification process can always be further improved and redesigned, and that nothing is ever given once and for all. On the other hand the stability of the depicted monuments (and hopefully of the euro itself) would according to the same source testify to a 'desire to construct a solid and lasting whole, of stone and iron, which is not dependent on economic and political contingencies and mirrors the eternity linked to the motifs of classical culture'. Even the 'absence of people and geographical references' is in this sense read as expressing a money economy allegedly 'based on universality and intertemporality'.[482]

The specific choice of building elements—bridges, doors and windows—prioritises infrastructural frameworks rather than meaningful contents, practices of vision among the senses, and movement over stasis (e.g. habitation). The latter creates a certain tension to the stability of the constructions themselves, but this is more of a dialectics than a paradox, since it is this very stability that ensures the confidence that enables mobility. Again, this imagery confirms the perception of Europe as a fundamentally land-based entity in the tradition of the Roman Empire. Instead of ships and harbours, airplanes and airports, or modern media technologies, there are archetypical windows and doors for people to look and walk through, and bridges for people and land-based vehicles to cross. But this focus on infrastructures for communication at the same time harks back to Europe's traditional strength in mobility, travel and intercultural interaction, sharply distinct from the fixity of for instance the older high cultures around the Pharaonic Nile, the Mesopotamian (Sumerian, Akkadian, Assyrian and Babylonian) Euphrates and Tigris, the Indian Ganges or the Chinese Yellow River. While those were relatively static, Europe was always more dynamic, historically unstable, and crisscrossed by mobile populations. The very wish to mediate, link and communicate may therefore possibly itself be interpreted as typically European. The doors and windows supposedly symbolise 'the European spirit of openness and co-operation', while the bridges stand for 'the close co-operation and communication between Europe and the rest of the world'. In one sense, values such as openness and cooperation are extremely unspecific and would presumably be universally suitable for any kind of association in the world.[483] Still, there is something specific in how this imagery is developed here. These motifs are in a sense homological with the 'united in diversity' motto, as they depict architectural resources that serve to connect while also respecting difference.

Bridges, doors and windows are classical symbols for a deep-seated European dialectics of unity/difference, closure/opening and border/transgression. The focus on separation involved in the drawing of boundaries as well as in border struggles, the transitions over thresholds in passage rites and liminal phenomena, the current interest in borderlands, hybridity, third spaces and intermediarity—all this testifies to a deep-seated obsession with communication across boundaries that might possibly be universally human but where European thought and political practice have been at the forefront—for better and for worse. For Georg Simmel, analysing the metaphorical dialectics of bridge and door, 'the human being is the connecting creature who must always separate and cannot connect without separating'—'the bordering creature who has no border'; to Gaston Bachelard, 'man is half-open being'.[484] This aspect of European self-identification can on the one hand be understood in Habermasian terms as a capacity for communicative action, but on the other hand also in Foucauldian terms as a power/knowledge effect related to panoptical supervision and a constant urge and coercion to communicate and be open, in line with late modern capitalism's demand for flexibility and with the surveillance trends fuelled by terrorist movements and states.

The *European Navigator* text mentioned above also associates the euro to Simmel's metaphor of bridge and door, adding that this is valid for every man-made institution. In its own impersonal and abstract way, the euro offers European citizens a 'sense of belonging' within a common border but also opens out to 'an unknown world, an uncertain future'.[485]

The dominant image of Europe as a unity tends to be that of something deeply divided, but striving to overcome internal divisions by conscious efforts of mediation and communication, with a capitalist market system, democratic forms of governance, civil society and an open public sphere as implicit—but often contradictory—tools. 'United in diversity' may thus truly imply unity through and by difference. The internal differentiation of this continent may be its perhaps most distinguishable characteristic. This conforms to the Schuman Declaration and recent debates, according to which the historical experience of mutual extinction has resulted in a possibly abstract but still to some extent efficient will and ability to develop forms and models for mediating between opposites, enabling exchange without forging unitary identifications. This is one way to read the bridge and door symbols on the euro banknotes. According to the Dutch writer Cees Nooteboom, 'national identity is itself a melting-pot of cultural influences that transcend nationality and Europeanism consists simply in the recognition of unity in difference'.[486]

The bridge motif can be interpreted in two directions. On the one hand, it does construct Europe as open to the surrounding world, on the other hand, it also contains expansionist potentials. The inclusion of Turkey in the EU is a relevant example. With cosmopolitan Istanbul as prime symbol, Turkey is often depicted as a crossroads between Asia and Europe: a bridge between the East and the West. If such a bridge is left outside the EU, Europe's borders may be defended as a fortress wall around a relatively unitary Christian mainland. But homogeneity is then bought at the cost of losing control over this particular bridge, leaving its interface between Europe and the East outside the control of the EU. There are many—including leading politicians—who prefer this purist solution, in order to reinforce Europe's cultural unity. Others instead argue for integrating Turkey, as a way of increasing the richness and openness of the European project. This clearly supports a politics of multiculturalism or hybridity, but there may also be an aspect of control in this wish. Including such 'bridges' implies a certain control of them, reflecting many Europeans' wish for the border regions to become modernised or civilised according to a European grammar, for instance in terms of human rights, welfare provisions, democratic institutions and free markets. The choice of the bridge motif on the euro banknotes may thus imply both communication and control.

It is instructive to consider absences. Potential signs of division are consistently avoided, such as subcultures of all kinds or religious and political symbols, except for the most general and vague ones (like the Celtic harp). There are maps over the EU area, but the decision not to include any flags of member states on the notes or indeed on any of the national coin sides may perhaps be read as a post-national commitment.[487] Nowhere is there any representation of specific countries outside the EU, except for the indirect Greek reference to Turkey as adversary. Norway, Switzerland and the Eastern bloc, now gradually integrated into the EU, remain invisible on this first set of coins and notes, as do the surrounding continents as well as the transatlantic relations that have had such impact on the formation of Europe. The map on some coins are said to show Europe's place in the world, but this external world remains vague and hidden. There is a general talk of openness to other parts of the world, but no specific symbolisation of east/west or north/south relations, of European colonialism or American imperialism, besides the microscopic traces of colonial territories left as strangely placed dots on the maps. National symbols are downplayed to some extent (there are no flags for example), but so are specific regions, including those that cross intra-European national borders (like the Basque countries). Women remain marginal, and there is no representation of children or of the working classes. One key feature of modern Europe is particularly absent: mass migration. There are some possible references to border-crossings in the Finnish swans, the Greek independence men, the pilgrimage site of Santiago da Compostela and the pan-European class of royalties, but no clear symbol for the movements of refugees and workers into Europe and between its regions. The euro imagery does not care to represent the new Europe, by excluding any reference both to its recently integrated eastern half and to the many new immigrants from the Middle East, Asia, Africa and South America.

Think of possible alternatives. Natural motifs (plants, animals or landscapes) would be either too specifically bound to one place or too vaguely confined to Europe, and, more importantly, they would not enable a narrative of civilization and progress. Human portraits or situations would again be too specific, but the selection of infrastructural artefacts has the advantage of hinting at a parallel with the EU as an infrastructural project for communication between nations. Artworks would lack that technological and utilitarian aspect that architecture offers, and which applies so well to the EU, being a tool and a mechanism as well as a work and a symbol. Unlike human beings and some other art forms, the selected buildings are enduring artifices that seem to stand for the stable and trustworthy quality that the Union itself also strives for.

There is also an inherent parallelism between money and the kinds of buildings depicted on the banknotes, as both are means of communication, circulation and mobility; at the same time both are also leaning on fixed infrastructures that guarantee a sense of solidity, stability and trust that is needed for these dynamic exchanges to take place.

The historical progress told by the paper money-story is thus traced through monumental but utilitarian public buildings, bearing witness to a harmonious combination of aesthetics and technology, with a practical use for communication purposes. The identifying narrative of the banknotes declares Europe to be a western, Christian unity focused on historical progress, enduring stability, a seamless fusion of aesthetics and technology, boundaries and the processes of communication that cross them. There are aspects of identity, community and unity in this imagery, but more dominant are themes of transport, communication and diversity. So, again, diversity remains the basis also for the unity that can be discerned here: as with the EU, the unity of the euro is constructed out of differences. Europe has many historical experiences in common, but is one of the most internally differentiated world regions, with its old and established nation states, its many divergent languages and its many national and regional myths. Since the end of the Cold War and the fall of the wall, it does not appear as deeply internally divided as many other continents. It has all kinds of minorities but no longer any clear bifurcation, partly due to the EU project of uniting north and south, east and west. This project joins forces with parallel unifying efforts, such as the ecumenical rapprochement between the Christian churches. Christian religion is a unifying factor, but its role in political and economic life is held back by secularising counter-forces and by the efforts to better integrate non-Christian minorities, in particular the growing Muslim populations in many states.

Precisely how these new collective identifications of the euro designs will change over time, with the inclusion of more member states and the addition of later editions, is another question. More studies are also needed of how these money signs are read by those who use them, make them or regulate them. The emphasis on abstract forms in a high art formalist style and on images of technocratic infrastructures is typical of the increasingly problematic EU project from above. The Union needs to reconnect to popular images of more specific histories of interhuman and trans- rather than supranational encounters. Some such potential might lie hidden in European football and in the Eurovision Song Contest, or more importantly in transnational currents of everyday civic communication and a long history of movements for social justice. But similar traces of interhuman relations and transgressive identifications remain absent in the euro designs yet, both on banknotes and coin fronts. The former do display resources for communication but offer few hints of concrete diversities of content. Their dehumanised abstractness rather suggests universal uniformity, in line with the inseparable flag stars. It is up to the users of these symbols to imagine how communication across borders could be concretised—or in living practice populate the anonymous communication resources with meaningful contents.

Interpreting the national euro coin designs

Specific contents only appear on the national coin reverses, which circulate tiny illustrations of the plurality that Europe unites and that move through its symbolic doors and windows. The decision to let each country design its own set of national coin sides is in line with the motto. In the whole euro area, one may encounter coins that express values of any other EMU member state, which offers a tangible illustration of how Europe is both united and diverse. Both by its contrast to currencies elsewhere and by its multiple coin reverses, the euro currency is a way of 'symbolising boundaries'.[488] The national coin sides aim to make national populations feel a sense of belonging to Europe while at the same time showing how Europe is internally differentiated. Thus, they express a similar core idea as the motto of 'united in diversity', namely that European identity can only exist as a hybrid and multi-layered one.[489]

In order to see the patterns of difference between the twelve initial euro nations, it is necessary to scrutinise the coins designed in each country. In order to get hold of the historical dynamics, these will for the original twelve eurozone states also be compared to the currencies that circulated in the EU immediately before the introduction of the euro in January 2002.[490] The associated euro designs and the ones added after 2002 will be more briefly presented after the initial twelve sets.

Immediately before the introduction of euro, Austria had banknotes primarily depicting great composers, artists and scientists, while old coins had a vast range of motifs, including heraldic eagles, coats of arms, horsemen and flowers, buildings, towns and regions, images of phases of Austria's history or of its various peoples, cultural personalities, Olympic sports and the House of Hapsburg, but also symbols of Europe and the Wiener Secession. For the euro, Austria decided to produce a complete series of different coins, dedicated to plants, architecture and historical personalities, all designed by one artist (Josef Kaiser). The smallest coins contain typical flowers: an Alpine primrose (¢1), an edelweiss (¢2), and a gentian flower (¢5)—with the purpose to remind of ecological issues concerning Austria's contribution to a shared policy for protecting the natural environment. St. Stephen's Cathedral in gothic style (consecrated 1147) is a tourist must-see (¢10). The Belvedere Palace (1714–23) is a beautiful baroque building that is synonymous with Austria's freedom, since the treaty of its sovereign constitution was signed there in 1955 (¢20). The Wiener Secession building (1897–8) is an exhibition house signifying the birth of the art nouveau style in Austria, as a symbol of the dawn of a new era (¢50). The composer Wolfgang Amadeus Mozart (1756–91) was already on the old coins (€1). So was the pacifist Bertha von Suttner (1843–1914), a symbol of Austrian peace efforts (€2). Austria euros thus form a money-story moving from nature (plants) through material artefacts (buildings) to living human spirit (celebrities), in line with a secularised view on historical progress. Plants may be geographically located and culturally identified with a certain region or even nation, but are still not strictly limited to them. Whereas nature is presented as timeless, the cultural motifs point specifically at four periods: the twelfth and the eighteenth centuries, c. 1900 and 1955. The buildings chosen are associated with religion, politics and the arts—three key spheres of modern societies. As such, they have a universal touch, while still being anchored in a national context and in European culture: the cathedral is visited by tourists from anywhere, the constitution was a product of European negotiations after World War II, and art noveau was a widespread style. Mozart as cultural personality travelled a lot to Paris and to German, Italian and Czech cities, and his work soon became a keystone of 'universal' art music heritage. Bertha von Suttner secures an even gender balance and adds a political aspect that again emphasises international cooperation in Europe. The transition to the euro made no sharp break with the previous schilling motifs, but the selection clearly seems to imply Europeanness as a transnational endeavour, evolving from natural resources depicted in the lower denominations up to cosmopolitan culture and politics, echoing core values of mobility, enjoyment and elevation.

In Belgium, pre-euro banknotes depicted artistic creators or the royal couple, with coins mainly having royal motifs.[491] The Belgian euro coins opted for continuity with pre-euro money, and all the coins were designed by the director of the Turnhout academy of arts, Jan Alfons Keustermann. As a monarchy, Belgium presents on all its coins the face of King Albert II, with a monogram 'A' with a crown above, placed between the European stars. These coins focus on a very traditional aspect of the present: monarchy, in continuity with the past—an aristocratic form of rule that today has more representational than political functions. An international network of monarchies ties the royal families together by marriage and other relationships, and since monarchies are today a primarily European tradition, this could be seen to confirm European integration. Still, leaning just on royalty is a very narrow and conservative identification. Sticking to the ancient tradition of letting an image of the sovereign ruler guarantee the money value is a strikingly anachronistic, quasi-feudal practice in today's democratic parliamentary Europe. The fact that kings nowadays are more personas of popular culture than any real rulers gives an extra twist to that symbolism. The same royal portraits that two centuries ago represented real political power today rather stand for media fame, in an anachronistic marriage between premodern aristocracy and late modern commercialism. The single design also halts any narrative progress through the coin values, strengthening the impression of ahistorical stasis. These kinds of coins may therefore be placed in a similar category as for instance the Eurovision and UEFA anthems discussed in the previous chapter, emphasising hierarchic stability and uniformity more than anything else.

Finland's preceding mark banknotes fronted Finnish cultural celebrities from the last centuries, each surrounded by a suitable environment, while the coins had motifs from nature. The three different Finnish euro coin motifs were built on these older designs. A heraldic lion was placed on all the six smaller values. Two swans flying above a lake are found on the €1 coin; cloudberries and cloudberry flowers adorn the €2. The Finnish euro motifs do not explicitly denote any particular historical period, though a Finn may well connote them to specific tales and myths of Finland, for instance the coat of arms to the independence from Russia in 1809. The lion as such is far from a Finnish animal, but a traditional heraldic exoticism, common all over Europe, thus with a transnational edge to it, even if it is also integrated in an aristocratic or royal heritage of power symbols which is somewhat at odds with Finland's republican constitution and absence of domestic aristocracy. Cloudberries are specific to the northern hemisphere, and Finland is sometimes called a land of thousand lakes, frequented by migrating birds, which can be seen as a kind of border-crossing nomads. There is thus continuity with the past, but also an amount of transnationalising Europeanism, especially if one regards the narrative sequence from mythic nation symbols to a kind of 'natural communication' where the local is wedded to the translocal and transcontinental mobility is again acknowledged.

In France, the last edition of franc banknotes also depicted famous Frenchmen from arts and science. Coins contained the words 'République Française' (or 'RF') with the the motto 'liberté—égalité—fraternité' and one of the stock republican symbols: an ear of corn, a branch with leaves, a tree and a hexagon, the symbolic Républic woman in profile, the Spirit of the Bastille, the Mont St-Michel or the Panthéon. A national competition chose the euro designs, all of which are based in the traditional republican symbols from the French Revolution. A young and determined Marianne is embodying the desire for a strong and lasting Europe in the smallest coins (¢1, ¢2, ¢5). A sower in modern and timeless design, symbolising France integrated in Europe but remaining independent, adorns the next level (¢10, ¢20, ¢50). A tree symbolising life, continuity and growth, inscribed in a hexagon and surrounded by the republican motto 'liberté, égalité, fraternité', is found on the highest level (€1, €2). All these universalist and classicist motifs go back to the late eighteenth century French Revolution. Mythical (but not religious) and human figures, a tree and a verbal motto point towards France's role in planting the seed of Enlightenment, in which the EU project often inscribes itself. Its dissemination has universalistic pretensions but also conceals a darker side of Eurocentric imperialism. Other motifs, such as cultural and scientific personalities, have been excluded in favour of this thematic sphere, strongly favouring unity, not diversity. The sequence from low to high values reinforces this impression by telling the story of a youthful newborn nation who then disseminates its message like a missionary of reason and democracy, resulting in the organically tree-like growth of a global society where all have their fixed positions. This reconciliation or fusion of nature and culture is typical of modernity, where the new is permeated by the archaic: 'the new in the context of what has always already been there', that 'is always citing primal history', to quote Walter Benjamin.[492]

Germany's last series of mark banknotes showed cultural personalities in front of historical buildings of particular cities, with related objects on the rear sides. In order to express West Germany's integration into (western) Europe, almost as an invitation to the Schuman Declaration two years later, a 1948 5 DM note actually featured Europe and the bull.[493] The lower values of the old coins had a girl planting a tree and an oak twig, while the highest showed the Bundesadler and ex-Bundeskanzler Willy Brandt, with the inscription 'Einigkeit und Recht und Freiheit' ('Unity and Justice and Freedom') on the edge. On the German euro coins, the oak twig echoes a motif from the old Pfennigs (¢1, ¢2, ¢5). Brandenburger Tor is a symbol of the split in and but also the reunion of Germany—the view through the arch is meant to underline the unification of Germany and of Europe (¢10, ¢20, ¢50). The federal eagle (Bundesadler) is a traditional symbol of German sovereignty (€1, €2). Like several other countries, Germany has thus maintained a clear continuity, with a widespread plant with traditional national connotations, the frightening bird that is reminiscent of authoritarian periods of German history (Bismarck or the Third Reich) and, more interestingly, the building that has such a complex history. It was ordered by Frederick the Great and built by Carl Gotthard Langhans, inspired by the Propylaea of Athens. At first it was called the 'Gate of Peace', but after its topping quadriga was stolen and taken to Paris by Napoleon in 1806 and returned in 1814, it became a 'Gate of Victory', and established as a symbol of Prussia. As such it was the site for celebrating the victory over France in 1871, and used in similar ways during World War I and by the Nazis. In the Cold War, it became part of the Berlin wall and a symbol of divided Europe, but after the 1989 reunification, its opening on the Unter den Linden avenue has made it a symbol of the reuniting of Germany and of East and West Europe at large. It is thus a traditional symbol of Berlin and of unity across deep divides, thus a suitable symbol for the European project, too.[494] As a whole, however, the coin series embeds this split/reunion dialectics in a rather conservative and authoritarian story by starting with nature and ending with the eagle as both naturalised and mythified symbol of national power, making the German euro series rather ambiguous and open to contradictory readings.

In Greece, the last drachma banknotes each developed a specific theme that tended to link ancient mythology with historical heroes and societal spheres. For instance, on the lowest note value, 'Letters—Education and their contribution to the nation's independence' was the idea behind Goddess Athena, backed by the translator and educator Adamantios Korais, who went to Paris in 1788 and was important in the Greek struggle for independence, while the highest value note thematised 'health', with twentieth century pathologist George Papanicolaou and the God of medicine Asclepius. The watermarks showed either a charioteer of Delphi or Alexander the Great's father, King Philip of Macedonia of the fourth century BC. Coin motifs included ships, an olive tree branch, sports championships, classical gods, Homer, Democritus and Aristotle, as well as more recent national heroes, political activists and intellectuals. The three lowest Greek euro coins are devoted to ships: an Athenian trireme from the time of Komon, fifth century BC, for more than 200 years the largest warship afloat (¢1); a corvette, used in the Greek War of Independence 1821–7 (¢2); and a modern seagoing tanker, reflecting the innovative spirit of Greek shipping (¢5). The next three show heroes in the Greek struggle for independence, mainly from the Turkish empire: Rigas Velestinlis-Fereos (1757–98, national hero and poet during the Ottoman occupation, exile in Constantinople, Bucharest and Austria, inspired by the Enlightenment, French Revolution and Napoleon, martyr in the war for independence 1789) (¢10); Ioannis Capodistrias (1776–1831, Greek political leader in independence struggle and prime minister, striving to get general European support, assassinated in 1833) (¢20); and Eleftherios Venizelos (1864–1936, modernising Cretan liberty leader against the Turks, head of Crete 1899 and first prime minister of Greece in periods from 1910 to 1933) (¢50). The highest values carry mythic motifs: the owl as a symbol of wisdom, from an ancient Athenian 4 drachma coin, fifth century BC (€1) and a Spartan mosaic of the myth of the abduction of Europa by Zeus in the shape of a bull (€2), directly linked to the European myth discussed earlier. Greece thus has a focus on its long history and its myths based in classical antiquity. The historical periods referred to are the fifth century BC, the struggle for independence during the decades around 1800 and in the early twentieth century, and the post-war period of economic expansion and oil trade. The ships both connect to Greece as a traditional seafaring nation and to the inherently transnational or even global character of the seas and of trade in general, and thus to the euro and the EU as transnationalising forces. The three freedom fighters refer to Greece as an independent nation, but also connect with other European forces in their struggle for this autonomy, confirming the 'united in diversity' concept. If Turkey ever finally becomes an EU member, it will appear somewhat remarkable that Greece has chosen to identify through men who mainly fought against that future union partner.[495] It is also notable that all three historical persons are male, while women are instead represented by the abducted Europa, who connects the EU to a Greek myth, but in a rather passive and not so glorious manner, since Europa is shown as mastered by the potent male Greek god. Many motifs connect back to the previous drachma coins, but the mythic ones imply a renewal that is meant to link up with Europe but in a way that at the same time confirms Greek macho pride. As a narrative whole there is a progress from artefacts and persons to mythical symbols with natural elements. Nature thus does not come first in Greece, and the highest level cannot refrain from returning to classical antiquity, even though the temporal progress in each of the two first subseries move the ordinary modern way from past to present.

Ireland before 2002 had banknotes depicting great Irish historical figures, from Catherine McAuely who founded the Sisters of Mercy to James Joyce and heroes from the Irish struggle of independence, each combined with relevant houses, writings and artefacts. The Celtic harp was the standard element on Irish £ coins, matched by various animals from traditional Irish inscriptions (bull, fish, horse, deer). The Irish government decided to let all euro coins have identical design: the Celtic harp as a traditional symbol of Ireland, with the word 'Éire'. This mythic and national motif stresses Celtic specificity, though popular fantasy fiction has spread such symbols widely. A musical instrument is in itself a peaceful aesthetic symbol, but with complex levels of association added through the violent Irish history. The lack of change between value levels resonates with the choice of the harp as a musical instrument, as music (and in particular folk music) is so often regarded as an eternal and universal language binding people together across all historical, geographic and social distances. Even though such ideas are in reality often false when it comes to existing musical genres, this harp may well in a general way invite being interpreted as an elegant visual shape linked to a mild and pleasant sound that many would easily appreciate.

In Italy, the lire banknotes had historical cultural heroes from science and arts, while coins mainly reproduced classical subjects in the shape of rather unspecific bodies and faces. For the Italian euro coins, the viewers of RAI television programme chose between a series of design proposals. Each value got its own motif, all related to key Italian artistic works: Castel del Monte castle near Andria in Ampulia, built in 1240 as residence for Emperor Fredric II (¢1); Mole Antonellina tower in Torino by Alessandro Antoeli (1863; originally conceived as a synagogue but built as the largest tower of Italy and now the key symbol of the town) (¢2); the Flavius amphitheatre Colosseum in Rome, begun by Emperor Vespasian c. 75 BC, inaugurated by Emperor Titus in 80 AD (¢5); Sandro Botticelli's *The Birth of Venus* (c. 1485) (¢10); sculpture of forms of movement by leading Italian futurist Umberto Boccioni (1882–1916) (¢20); Emperor Marcus Aurelius equestrian statue at Piazza Capitolium, Rome (1538) (¢50); Leonardo da Vinci's *Vitruvian Man*, Italian Renaissance (1513): human body, harmony between man and the universe (€1); Raphael's portrait of Dante Alighieri (1508–11): symbol of virtues, goodness and beauty (€2). Italy is thus the country whose coins are most dedicated to cultural history, with subjects from the first century BC to the thirteenth, fifteenth, sixteenth, nineteenth and early twentieth centuries AD. They are lined up in no particular chronological order, but the three highest coins all have sixteenth century motifs, hinting at a rather backward-looking view of that golden Renaissance era, thus evading or even contradicting the progressivist banknote story. Buildings come first, then visual arts, and the most symbolically charged motifs in the end. The only female subject is the goddess of beauty, whereas the final male figures stand for grand human values, significantly with the more 'physical' Vitruvian man placed slightly lower than the universal mind of Dante—all reinforcing conservative dichotomies of male/female and soul/body. Compared to before the euro, Italy has developed a new set of subjects with a wide scope and with a sharper focus on supposedly universal values, with the sphere of aesthetics in focus, avoiding the more divisive associations to politics.

Luxembourg franc banknotes depicted the Grand Duke Jean in front of various palaces, while the modern European Centre of Luxembourg-Kircherg or the cities of Luxembourg and Echternach on the reverse. The old franc coins also depicted the Grand Duke. Luxembourg's euro coins have identical motifs but in three variants, following the obverse groups. All depict Grand Duke Henri, who inherited the throne from his father in October 2000, with the domestic country name 'Letzebuerg'. These coins can be interpreted in the same way as those of Belgium, though there is more continuity here in that even the previous notes were equally narrow in focus.

In the Netherlands, the guilder banknotes did not depict the Queen but instead had themes related to nature and were designed in a rather modern, abstract style: kingfisher, robin, sunflower, owl, lighthouse and lapwing. The immediate pre-euro Dutch coins had Queen designs with geometrical patterns, but there had also been various commemorative coins, as well as a final 'goodbye to the guilder' coin issued in 2001, with a funny troll-like figure drawn by a twelve-year-old school boy. For the euro, the Netherlands also chose to have an almost identical design on all coins: Queen Beatrix, in two variants (the €1 and €2 with a different layout than the rest), with the words 'Beatrix, Koningin der Nederlanden', and framed by the twelve stars. This third Benelux nation has chosen the same coin genre as its two neighbours, but only with a more contemporary artistic design that speaks of a wish to be stylishly 'modern'. These coins are similar to the pre-euro coins, while the wider and more artistic themes of the old banknotes have been lost completely.

Portugal's last escudo banknotes celebrated the great world explorers and colonisers, together with sailing ships or warrior knights, while the last pre-euro coins had the royal coat of arms on one side—the word 'escudo' (like 'schilling') actually means shield and refers to that coat of arms. Euro designs were chosen in a graphic competition, won by Manuel Fernandes dos Santos with three seals of the first Portuguese King, Dom Afonso Henriques: the first royal seal from 1134 with the word 'Portugal' (¢1, ¢2, ¢5); the royal seal from 1142 (¢10, ¢20, ¢50); and the royal seal from 1144 surrounded by some of the country's castles and coats of arms within the European stars, supposedly symbolising dialogue, value exchange and the dynamics of the EU (€1, €2). In continuity with its past coins, the set of Portuguese images is very narrow, with its three hardly distinguishable seals deriving (in chronological order) from a span of ten years in the twelfth century. It is the birth of the nation state that is celebrated, though the highest value coins add some elements that possibly signify some kind of opening up to the world. Portugal has thus refrained from the old exploration motifs, thus bidding farewell to references to an era of brave but violent efforts to go around the world in the name of capitalist trade and imperial power.

The last pesetas banknotes of Spain depicted the (in)famous conquistadors, explorers and scientists who helped Spain colonise the Americas. Earlier coins had the King or the royal couple, with coat of arms, stylized flame with branch of leaves, man and bull, castle, church doorway or water wheel. The last series of pesetas had a great variety of motifs, changing every year, and dealing with different topics related to the autonomous regions, personages from the Spanish culture and history, or commemorating important events. Spain divided its euros into three main series: the Romanesque cathedral of Santiago de Compostela (eleventh century), world famous pilgrimage destination (¢1, ¢2, ¢5); author Miguel Cervantes (1547–1616), father of Spanish literature (¢10, ¢20, ¢50); and King Juan Carlos I de Borbón y Borbón (€1, €2). Like Italy, Spain is a deeply subdivided nation with many regions that have a large degree of autonomy. This may be an explanation why the king alone has not been allowed to dominate all coin sides—and this was true also before the euro. Basque and Catalonian subjects have also been left aside. Instead, it is the relatively less controversial Galician outpost and the central area of Madrid and La Mancha that is represented. Read in a sequence, the coins go from past to present, from national periphery to centre, from buildings to people and from religion and literature to politics. The choice of the world-famous tourist and pilgrimage site of the cathedral, as well as of Cervantes whose *Don Quixote* is regarded not only as a literary point of origin for Spain but also as the global birth of the novel, indicates a willingness to emphasise transnational links in each dimension. The dynastic and the religious institutions were dominant organisers of political power before the era of the nation state, and both of them tend to transgress national borders: through the pan-European network of royal houses and through the global network of churches.[496] The same is true of culture, not least literature and the novel, which is today a global genre. Spain's royal face and cathedral façade, as well as its knight-errant of the woeful countenance, can all therefore be said to transcend Iberic boundaries. And even more so than with Portugal, the abandoning of the conquistador era may be interpreted either as forgetfulness of the colonial past or as a true step beyond and away from it. Desire, border-crossing mobility and in Cervantes' case also a kind of hybridity are therefore apparent themes found in these Spanish euro coins.

Non-EU members Monaco, San Marino and the Vatican State have issuing rights too.

Monaco has on its euro coins the coat of arms of the Sovereign Princes of Monaco on all six lower values, topped by a double portrait of HSH Prince Rainier III and HSH

Hereditary Prince Albert (€1) and HSH Prince Rainier III (€2). Its generic choice thus remains close to that of the Benelux monarchies.

San Marino features three towers on the low level coins: first tower La Guaita (¢1), Statue of Liberty (¢2) and third tower Il Montale (¢5). The mid-series presents the Basilica of San Marino (¢10), *Saint Marino* on a canvas of the Guercino school (¢20) and the three towers La Guaita, La Cesta and Il Montale (¢50). The republic's official coat of arms is on the €1, the Palazzo Pubblico government building on the €2 coin. Being a republic, this tiny nation has avoided the head of state and instead chosen old buildings, a combination of art and city, and a national symbol.

The State of Vatican City has let its sovereign, His Holiness Pope John Paul II, reign on all its five coins (only ¢1, ¢2, ¢5, ¢20 and €1 were issued). This connects to the most traditionalist monarchies. When the Pope died his portrait was replaced also on the coins by that of his successor, Benedict XVI. The religious theme of course is not surprising here.

During 2007–11, five more countries joined EU and the eurozone, all issuing their own euro coins. Cyprus joined in January 2008 with three motifs: two wild sheep of the old mouflon species (¢1, ¢2, ¢5); the fourth-century BC Greek merchant Kyrenia ship, uniquely preserved since classical Greece and a symbol of lost home for many refugees (¢10, ¢20, ¢50); and the *Idol of Pomos* from sometime around thirtieth (!) century BC—a female fertility figure that strangely enough holds out her hands in cross shape and with a little cross amulet hanging around her neck (€1, €2). The ship combines with the Greek coins to reproduce their underlining of an old history of mobility and exile, linking today's migration with those transformed into the Europa myth, while the ancient amulet offers an even much older reference to what European culture might have been long before the classical Greek "cradle of civilisation" had been formed.

Estonia issued its euro in January 2011—all of them showing a map contour of Estonia.

Malta in 2008 started using its three motifs, divided in the same way as Cyprus: the megalithic Mnajdra temple altar from the fourth millennium BC; the coat of arms of Malta; and the Maltese cross, used by the Knights of Malta from the fifteenth century AD, but with roots back to the eleventh century crusades. Again, there is thus a combination of very ancient roots with the much later and quite aggressive Christian frontier to the Muslim world.[497]

Slovakia issued in 2009 likewise three motifs: Kriváň, a High Tatras mountain with great significance for ethnic and national movements since the early nineteenth century; Bratislava Castle with its long and winding history; and the coat of arms of Slovakia, showing a double cross on three hills. The Christian topic goes back to Slovakia's historical role as border to the Byzantine Empire.

Slovenia in 2007 came up with a unique design for each value. The lowest ¢1 coin has a stork, which as a migratory bird connects Europe to Africa. The ¢2 represents the

Prince's stone, a Roman column base that was in the Middle Ages used for installing Carinthian dukes. Some Austrians questioned this coin, since Carinthia was divided after the World War I. The ¢5 coin shows Ivan Grohar's painting *A Sower* sowing stars, which of course nods at the EU flag as well as the famous sower reproduced on French coins. On ¢10 is found Jože Plečnik's draft for a national parliament looking almost like the tower of Babel, with the inscription 'Cathedral of Freedom'. ¢20 shows a pair of Lipizzaner horses; and ¢50 has the Triglav mountain, the constellation of Cancer and lines from Jakob Aljaž's song 'O Triglav, My Home'. On the €1 coin is Primož Trubar, Slovenian Protestant reformer, and the inscription 'To Exist and Persevere'. The highest €2 value represents Romantic poet France Prešeren and the first line of the seventh stanza of Slovenian national anthem 'Zdravljica'. Both Slovakia and Slovenia thus introduced mountains as a motif, strongly suggesting stability and fixity, in opposition to ships and other motifs of mobility.

To this overview should be added that each eurozone state may each year release one commemorative €2 coin, which almost all have also done. Some for instance celebrate the European Constitution, the 2004 EU extension, the 2007 Portuguese and 2008 French EU presidencies, the Olympic Games, the United Nations, the Universal Declaration of Human Rights, as well as a large number of individual celebrities or national events and buildings. Germany will from 2006 to 2021 each year issue one coin for each of its 16 *Bundesländer* (states), while Spain will from 2010 to 2050 honour UNESCO World Heritage sites, thus having determined its commemorative coins for a longer period. There have also been made two joint commemoration issues for all eurozone countries (Figure 8.5). One such coin in 2007 celebrated the 50 years anniversary of the Treaty of Rome, depicting the treaty signatures as an open book under the word 'EUROPE', surrounded by Michelangelo's geometrical paving on the Piazza del Campidoglio in Rome where the treaty was signed in 1957 (and which also forms the background to Italy's own ¢50 coin). In 2009, another commemorated the tenth anniversary of the euro itself. Its design was selected by electronic voting and was made by a sculptor at the Bank of Greece. It depicts some kind of primitive (or childish) man in cave art style, united with the € sign, almost like a shield or a bow and arrow, thus underlining the euro's role as an extension of man and something to trust for the individual citizen. These special issues are produced in a limited number, but may on the other hand receive increased attention as collector items. This applies even more to gold and silver coins (with a face value between ¢25 and €100 000, with €10 as a common level) that are not so much intended for circulation as means of payment as for collecting.

The detailed investigation of this plethora of euro designs could expand indefinitely, as their number and variety expand at an accelerating pace. In this context however, it seems more fruitful to start looking for dominant patterns in the main designs mentioned above, focusing on the original set of common sides plus the main twelve sets of national reverses.

Overall, there is no uniformity in how the countries have divided the coins into sub-series. Austria, Greece and Italy (as well as San Marino) have eight different designs, though often grouped in internally related subsets in parallel to the obverse groups. (Monaco presents four designs, following the obverse groups but also differentiating between the one and two euro coins.) The most common solution, chosen by France, Germany, Luxembourg, Portugal and Spain, is to create three back designs, one for each main type of obverse design (though Luxembourg is a border case since all its coins have the same Grand Duke, only in three variants). Finland also has three types, but with individual designs on the one and two euro coins and the rest identical with each other. The Netherlands has two main designs (one and two euros differentiated from the lower values). Belgium and Ireland (as well as the Vatican) have only one design each. One might say that the common obverse designs tend to favour a '3+3+2' tripartition, which a majority of the nations have decided to break away from in one way or the other, though the largest ones have followed the main rule. It is hard to see any clear trend when it comes to the motifs chosen for lower or higher currency values. Different countries have made very different 'money-stories', based on contrasting hierarchies, but a common story goes from a basis in nature and technology up to culture, myth and ideas on the highest values, reflecting a possibly typical European dualist hierarchy of body/soul or base/superstructure, which has both materialist and idealist versions, depending on whether the low material basis is seen as founding or subordinated.

Motif statistics vary depending on whether all twenty euro countries are counted, or just the seventeen EMU member states, or the original twelve; and also whether one counts the total number of coins (in all 8 x 20 = 160) or just the number of genuinely different motifs (in all 74 designs). Classification is also difficult since several motifs fill double functions. This said, around 40 per cent show human figures, 2/3 of which are male. Buildings, human artefacts and natural motifs are three categories with each a roughly equal share of the remaining designs. Some general patterns appear, forming main genres and country groups.

Summarising the national coin sides, some main iconical genres may be distinguished:

1. Rulers are shown by Belgium, Luxembourg, the Netherlands and Spain, but also the three affiliated states. (The three yet non-euro nations Denmark, Sweden and the United Kingdom also belong to this category, but none of the later added euro states Cyprus, Estonia, Malta, Slovakia or Slovenia.) All the monarchies—and only these—display their rulers, leaning towards an ancient tradition of authorising money values by showing the ruling head of a clan, empire or nation.[498] In modern republics, that practice has become less useful, due to a combination of recurrent shifts of power and perhaps also to some

little degree an egalitarian spirit of democracy that shuns displaying such clear symbols of state power as national symbols. (However, the fact that presidents may well appear on stamps contradicts this somewhat optimistic interpretation.) Hereditary monarchies have stable heads of state, at the cost of stripping these anachronistic institutions of all essential instruments of real political power. It is slightly paradoxical that these monarchs nowadays have almost no political power, being reduced to purely symbolic signs for their nation states. But precisely this makes them doubly useful as money motifs, and perhaps the most easily accessible and in a way uncontroversial choice. Faces of state rulers are symbols of power and one of the few undisputedly nationalist symbols. They fuse aristocratic historical roots with late modern entertainment business and popular culture, and offer a simple solution for countries to avoid the work of finding other ways to signify their relation to the world. If the specific monarch depicted has had no personal role as transnational bridge-builder, this motif is bound to the old European system of nation states out of which international systems like the UN and the EU were once born, but else contains no other, more innovative or up-to-date transnational significance. However, a kind of transnational bridging is inherent in the monarchic institution, as the royalties of different countries, particularly in Europe, have always tended to blend through intermarriage, thus contributing a key force of unification that may partly explain why the royal symbolisms (think of the royal blue colour of the flag or the EBU and UEFA hymns discussed in previous chapters) continue to be attractive in today's European contexts as well, even within republics.[499]

2. National symbols are selected by Finland, France, Germany, Ireland and Portugal. (This is also true for Malta, Slovakia, Monaco, San Marino and probably also Sweden if it ever issues a euro.) Heraldic animals, coats of arms and other traditional symbols that have been monopolised by certain states have similar functions as the rulers' faces, and are equally old as money symbols. They do avoid the anthropomorphisation of power that inheres in the royal face, instead showing the nation state in a more abstract and superhuman form. But again, they also tend to reproduce feudal roots of the narratives of nation building that became so popular as a way to legitimise and historically anchor the imagined communities born in the modern, bourgeois nationalist movements of the nineteenth century. Again, all national symbols to some extent do have transnational roots and routes: they have travelled and branched off in various directions, and are never undisputedly local. Benedict Anderson (1991) has pointed out that being much older than nation states, churches as well as royal houses remain particularly promiscuous in that respect, even when the latter are subsumed under national authorities and bound to their names—the King of X

is often closely related to the Queen of Y. Such interconnections are generally successfully suppressed within each national context, but may come out into the open as these coins circulate also in other regions where similar symbols may well be used with a completely different sphere of meaning. For an Irish citizen, the Celtic harp probably is a univocal and deep-rooted image for the Irish nation, but in Wales, Britanny or Galicia it might well intersect with other local traditions, in Jewish tradition it rather is reminiscent of King David of the Old Testament, and for a Greek or a Finn who gets such a coin in her purse, it may well be understood as just a nice old instrument that shows the universal reach of music. The question is which kinds of such lines are drawn through the choice of such symbols: political, military, commercial, cultural, etc. Whereas the harp implies harmony and communication, crowns and seals signify power and authority, eagles and lions like coats of arms connote violence and military force, and plants have naturalising meaning-effects of growth, care, boundedness to the soil, etc. In some cases, notably France, national symbols also have explicitly universalistic overtones—at least for the inhabitants of the countries in question. In the classical French imagination, 'liberté, égalite, fraternité' is a truly universal motto, as it has also to some extent become due to the combination of colonialism and the global spread of republicanism, emphasised by the US constitution and later the UN declaration of human rights.

3. History, in the form of cultural or political artefacts and individuals, appears on coins from Austria, Germany, Greece, Italy and Spain. (This also holds for San Marino, Cyprus, Malta, Slovakia and Slovenia.) There are many subtypes in this category, as history contains many things with highly divergent implications. Political events, leaders or buildings may of course relate to key moments of nation-formation, in which case the signification of such motifs come close to the previous ones. Social, scientific or aesthetic heroes or works mostly have a more crossover status, as they tend to move across borders and become important all over the world. They are chosen because they have some special connection to the country in question, and they do of course bring honour to this specific country, but they tend to stress its positive links to the surrounding world rather than its separation from others. A range of other differences appears depending on whether persons, events, buildings or other kinds of artefacts are depicted. Buildings are more fixed to a place than paintings or people who can travel across boundaries, but they may on the other hand easily be visited by many and become widely known and loved, not least through modern mass tourism. Historical motifs tend to be selected to represent various regions within the nation, ages of national splendour and kinds of achievement, so that they taken as a whole represent the moral, intellectual and cultural strength of a country.

Euro coins display two political freedom fighters (the Greeks Capodistrias and Venizelos), one peace activist (the Austrian von Suttner), who also is the sole woman honoured in this way by the EU, three literary authors (the Greek Velestinlis-Fereos, Italian Dante and Spanish Cervantes) and one composer (Vienna's Mozart). This slight dominance of the cultural domain is increased when buildings are added, with three mainly political (the Austrian Belvedere Palace, the German Brandenburger Tor, the Italian Castel del Monte) against five cultural—mostly religious—ones (the Austrian St. Stephen's Cathedral and Wiener Secession building, the Italian Mole Antonellina and Colosseum, and the Spanish Santiago de Compostela cathedral).[500] Greece's three ships express economy and trade but also transports of other kinds, military as well as civil. Adding other human artefacts further emphasises the cultural face of Europe, with Italy's wide range of monuments and artistic works (Botticelli's *Birth of Venus*, Boccioni's futurist movement forms, Marcus Aurelius equestrian statue, Da Vinci's *Vitruvian Man*, Raphael's Dante). It should also be noted that the Spanish Santiago da Compostela cathedral as well as Cervantes are of course as much rooted in specific Spanish regions as is the king, and thus may well be less relevant to other Spanish regions. A Basque nationalist in Bilbao might feel them to be irrelevant to his agenda, or even despicable symbols of what he wants to dissociate himself from. On the other hand, that cathedral is a site of pilgrimage for all of Spain and its surrounding countries, thus lending itself well to symbolise transnational connections, and Don Quixote is after all no particularly heroic figure. Also the Italian series of great artworks makes certain definite choices: there are for instance no motifs located in Palermo or Sicily. On the other hand, their beauty have historically to a large extent come to transgress geographic borders and been appropriated as national artistic and intellectual treasures—or even keystones in a pan-European heritage of the type that proponents for a shared European identity tend to applaud. (Estonia is alone in showing a national map, which does not clearly fall into any of these categories, but may perhaps be seen as a result of political history.)

4.   Myths are used by France and more obviously Greece. There might well be mythical elements in many of the motifs discussed so far, as nation can be regarded as a kind of myth, and local myths and tales may well be implicitly evoked in many disguises. Myth is thus ever-present, but only in a few cases is this presence obvious as the main aspect. The French republican figures of Marianne and the sower are modern myths, once deliberately constructed in order to break with previous traditional ones. They refer back to a classical antique heritage that is explicitly invoked on the two highest Greek coins. The owl of wisdom seems to emphasise the character of the EU project as an

intellectual construction, a wise decision for cooperation instead of conflict that has some way to go before it gets anchored in the emotive sentiments of its populations. The abduction of Europa by the bull may be interpreted as kind of a national wet dream, as this animalistic Greek god with his virile force conquers his beautiful female loot, object of his male erotic lusts. Had a comparatively influential nation like Germany chosen a similar symbol, this might have awakened some hostility among its neighbours, but as Greece does no longer seem to pose any real threat to its north-western partners, such an allusion can only produce a smile. After all, as a goal for millions of EU charter tourists, Greece has already since long won the hearts of us all. Still, as the name 'Europe' means 'the West', and this bull myth connects to a historical process of culture imported from the East, there is a potential decentring element in such a self-identification of this continent.[501] The relative scarcity of explicitly mythical subjects on these coins might partly be caused by the reluctance to found the union in the only reasonable narrative: that which acknowledges its deep debt and sustained links to its great Asian neighbour.

5.   Nature is depicted in Austria, Finland and Germany. (Cyprus, Slovakia and Slovenia also use such motifs.) Plants and animals like the Austrian gentian, edelweiss and alpine primrose, the Finnish flying swans and cloudberries, and the German oak twig all offer ambivalent implications. On the one hand, they may contribute to a naturalisation of nationalist constructions by illustrating a kind of Blut-und-Boden philosophy of people, nations and cultures bound to the very soil of a specific geographic area. On the other hand, nature rarely respects fixed boundaries—at least not political ones. Swans are eminently migratory birds, and such nomadism can hardly be contained within the confines of a single region, be it Finland or even Europe. Plants do thrive in certain conditions, and may culturally be associated with some specific region, but even such identifications are notoriously unreliable. *Sound of Music* famously made the song 'Edelweiss' a prototypical symbol for the Alpine region, but not only is it hard to distinguish Austria from Switzerland in this respect (though one is and one is not at all in the EU), the film was also a typical Hollywood product and the plant can be found in lots of places, and not only in botanical gardens. A German coin tradition has used the symbolism of oak groves as ancient places of Germanic worship, but oaks are holy symbols also for Zeus, Jupiter and Kybele, as well as in Christian, Jewish, Indian and Chinese myths.

In practice, the boundaries between these main generic types are fleeting and permeable. National symbols may integrate natural or mythic elements, and the balance between separation and connection in each kind of symbol varies between contexts. Strong national symbols may or may not have clear transnational or even globalising aspects, whereas plants or animals are also shiftingly bound to a specific national soil.

One may further tentatively discern four main groups of countries, depending on the general and dominating patterns in their euro coinage.

A.   Nationalists: Half of the initial twelve euro countries clearly lean towards the national side, representing themselves by symbols that primarily point out their specificity in relation to European neighbours. (This is also valid for the three associated members, the three non-euro EU members, and for Estonia and Slovakia.) It is the monarchies that have generally taken this road, showing the faces of their kings and queens, but there are a few exceptions—in both directions. The three BeNeLux monarchies (as well as Monaco) all depict their monarchs on all their national coin sides.[502] The Vatican State with its Pope also fits in this category, and it seems as if the remaining EU nations of Denmark, Sweden and United Kingdom will eventually make a similar choice. It might be no coincidence that the populations of these latter monarchies have felt it particularly difficult to take the full step into the EMU.[503] The Iberian Peninsula offers interesting exceptions. The Spanish monarchy has its king only on the largest value coins, and I will therefore place it in another category. On the other hand, Portugal is nowadays a republic, but still has gone the nationalist way and chosen to use the old royal seal and coat of arms used since the birth of Portugal as a nation in the twelfth century—not a royal head but still a royalist form of national symbol.

B.   Universalists: France and Ireland have national symbols that invite global interpretations of a much less separatist kind than the previous nationalist ones. Republican symbols are parts of a universalistic discourse and practice, expressly appealing to supposedly universally applicable human values. The figure of the sower associates to divine creativity and human culture in general, perhaps also to the Christian Sermon on the Mount and thus to missionary activities, but primarily secularised ones in the spirit of Enlightenment, with its own reverse side in form of colonialism. Anti-imperialist, postcolonial and postmodernist critiques today have attacked and relativised any such claims, but the EU project itself is only one example of the many renewed efforts to accept their specific location while still defending their universalistic potentials. The harp makes a non-verbal claim of a similar kind, building on the force of instrumental music to move hearts across linguistic and national boundaries. Again, this can be criticised as an ideological illusion, covering the fact that musical life fuels the divisive borders between people or cultures, only along different lines than those of verbal culture. Still, the harp does at least not have a fixed semantic link to any particular territory or state apparatus, at least not to those EU citizens who are not very well informed about Irish mythology, and it may therefore be seen as a kind of universalist statement.

C. Culturalists: On Austrian and Italian coins, cultural history clearly dominates. This may be a way to boost one's own grandeur by claiming copyright for the treasures of cultural creativity in historical heritage. Anyhow, the effect is one of historicisation and culturalisation. Human artefacts from various epochs are lifted up as crucial for collective identification, implying at least a potential for relativisation of values. Pointing at aesthetic perfection as the ultimate key to values puts more dangerously divisive political issues in the background, in favour of taste issues that may certainly be controversial but usually less violently so. This is particularly true for the most classical of subjects, but due to the way that art history tends to de-politicise and universalise artworks, even for instance the Boccioni movement image is easily appropriated as a kind of UN-protected 'world heritage', in spite of the somewhat problematic nationalist war cult of some of the proponents of Italian Futurism. Also the more political persons and buildings chosen by these two countries tend to emphasise peaceful and cooperative efforts rather than national separatism, notably Bertha von Suttner. A curious exception is the Marcus Aurelius statue, since it originally stood on the column in Rome that was inaugurated in the year 193 to commemorate the victory of this emperor over the Germans. However, even this and all his other martial deeds are today easily forgotten in favour of the rumour of his being a noble and self-reflecting secular thinker, depicted in that famous statue as a prince of peace. Another one may be the Colosseum, where many European slaves to the Roman empire were once mercilessly slaughtered. Yet none of these motifs are tightly knit to any particular national project, since they mostly predate the birth of Italy's modern nation state. Many artefacts and buildings have been created by exploitation of foreign workers or cultures, but the ones chosen in these cases today seem not to exclude transversal identifications. Being included in heterogeneous series, they show artefacts from different historical epochs as a rather arbitrary chain of gems that could be wilfully extended by others, with a slightly different meaning, adding to the historicity and thus secularising relativity of culture.

D. Chameleons: As has been argued here, most motifs have potential for ambiguity— being interpretable in different and sometimes oppositional directions. Some nations present themselves in series of images of highly divergent kinds, combining the previous positions and adding yet others. Thus, Finland, Germany, Greece and Spain use similar national symbols as the first groups (royalties, heraldic animals and coat of arms), but mixed with efforts to transcend borders by adding consciously transnational motifs, either culturalist or naturalist ones. (Something similar may be said of Cyprus, Malta and Slovenia.) Many of their chosen motifs are often also in themselves ambiguous. Take for instance the Greek Velestinlis-Fereos, who was an intellectual and a creative poet but also an activist of national liberation, and all the three Greek individuals associated national liberation from some foreign powers (that is, from Ottoman Turkey) with coalitions with other European countries. If Turkey will eventually join the Union, this separatist symbols will seem to some extent to run against the main rhetoric of peaceful collaboration between the member states. Likewise, the Greek ships combine many different functions, from classical Mediterranean trade cosmopolitanism through warfare vessels to global oil distribution. And with the mythical subjects on top, Greece certainly presents a quite open and ambivalent series. Finland and Spain likewise combine national symbols with cultural or natural themes with transnational implications, as has already been discussed. Germany is an equally divided case, with the dark heraldic eagle and the oak twigs framing the intermediary motif of the Brandenburger Tor which is itself an extremely ambiguous one. It is a symbol of German unity, from Prussia to the reunited Bundesrepublik of today, but it also serves as a reminder of first the struggles between Germany and France and then the Cold War divide between East and West Germany (and Europe). The official explanations of this motif repeatedly stress this tension, emphasising that from having been a celebration of anti-French war and then a heavily fortified point of division, it has today become a gate for intense crossings. This is said to be underlined by the specific pictorial perspective used on the coins, emphasising the road through the gate rather than the wall in which it once was a closed door. As Gerard Delanty optimistically states, 'Berlin is no longer the symbol of a divided Europe but the capital of a united Germany'.[504]

It is not only the 'chameleons' that offer ambiguous identifications. The categories often blend, as for instance even the most innocent flower is apparently chosen for its associations with a national identity, and the boundary between mythology and nature is permeable. Many of these multifaceted national symbols have historically developed in fierce struggles against other (surrounding) nations, though in some few instances there are implications of some kind of inter-European cooperation.

In all, there is a slight tendency to a north/south division line with wider sets of images down south than in the Lutheran and possibly more iconoclastic north.

This pattern is superimposed on and partly coincides with a political differentiation between constitutional systems—monarchies and republics—most of the remaining monarchies today being found in the north. The respective age of each national formation, as well as other and more specific historical experiences, also contribute to the numismatic style developed in each state. Simple generalisations are hard to make, however. For instance, Maurice Roche argues that societies 'based on immigration', on 'acts of revolution' or on 'science-based technological production and/or risk-taking capitalist markets necessarily locate and explore their collective identities in terms of their common presents and futures rather than their pasts'.[505] This seems mainly to serve as an explanation for the United States, but the diagnosis halts when comparing EU members. It is not quite evident whether this is confirmed by the euro or not, since many nations are awkward mixtures. UK money tended to cling on the ancient royal past even under neoliberal Thatcherism, as does the Swedish krona in spite of its strongly science-and-technology based production. Another line of interpretation is suggested by William Johnston, who argues that national differences between European countries in terms of forms of celebration can be related to a kind of 'civil religion' used to justify and legitimate the various regimes. Different European countries celebrate different kinds of memories. In France, the French Revolution is almost always the focal point. In Germany, there is a 'civil religion of *Kultur*', with cultural personalities in focus: artists, philosophers, musicians and writers. Austria relies heavily on the culture of the Hapsburg empire, with music and theatre as important elements. Italy is said to have a weaker national identity, instead leaning towards city or regional identifications, in addition to the persistent role of the Catholic Church and its saints. Britain's civil religion circles around the monarchy. Johnston sums this up in a main dichotomy between a French and a German model, stressing either political ramifications or apolitical creativity.[506]

The Brandenburg Gate thus expresses a historical transition from division to unification. However, most countries have chosen stability rather than innovation in their euro designs. There are few examples of notable shifts with the introduction of the euro, as most nations lean heavily towards their pre-euro traditions.

Spain and Portugal both gave up the usual themes from their old colonial history, which might have been problematic in relation to the European project. Classical colonialism was a violent competition between European states, which contradicts the present efforts of peaceful cooperation. The colonial imperialism in the Third World certainly resulted in strengthened global interconnections, but in an extremely unequal and coercive manner that hardly is good marketing for Europe in relation to Africa, South America or Asia today. Their old motifs showed men who opened up the world for Europe's exploitation, undoubtedly with many civilisational gains but at the cost of so much blood, human suffering and uneven economic exploitation that it must be considered as one of Europe's most problematic contributions to world history.

While Portugal retracted to a more inward-looking nationalist stance, Spain—singular among traditional monarchies—dared to expand its image in transnational and even self-ironical directions, including artistic, architectural, literary and religious themes in its self-image. On the other hand, this modernising tidying-up effort conceals the colonial aspect of Europe's history that has been essential to its very formation and self-understanding as a continent in contrast to its others.

Most other nations have stuck to their respective conventional range of symbols, but in some cases made selections and minor refinements that underline common European values and international links, thus showing how each country contributes with its own voice, while interplaying with the surrounding others. The Austrian, German and Finnish plants have some regional specificity but may also allude to the issues of global ecology that are one of the reasons for transnational cooperation. Finland lets aggressive heraldic lions be accompanied by migratory birds that know no boundaries and may symbolise the late modern age of mobility. Buildings and artworks have been crucial to the history of each country, but also for international relations and visiting foreigners. Many of the depicted individuals have been cosmopolitan in their lives and work, and are well known across the continent. The French republican themes intend to unify the world, and da Vinci's *Vitruvian Man* has a similarly universal intent in signifying the Renaissance focus on humanity abstracted from all characteristics—except gender, where masculinity continues to rule.[507] And while the German Brandenburg Gate has a painful history of division, the reopened road running through it gives hope for new encounters between the East and West. The BeNeLux and other monarchies have given more meagre contributions to this process, reducing their collective identifications to one single and in many ways marginal aspect.

The recently added EU member states east of the old iron curtain have tended to use the occasion of introducing their new currency to stage efforts to develop a greater awareness of their role and function in pan-European cooperation. For instance, already in autumn 2004, Estonia let its citizens vote among ten coin designs, more than half a dozen years before it finally entered the eurozone in January 2011. A spokesman of the National Bank of Hungary has declared that they will choose 'symbols that are near to the heart of Hungarians and are interesting', and that they 'would like to put them for social discussion in as wide circles as possible', through the several competitions that have been launched, as a kind of 'social dialogue'.[508] In this way, the euro transition is made to resonate with wider processes of societal change. In comparison, in a country like Sweden, with considerably more 'euro-skepticism', the National Bank has declared that it will only place the royal portrait and the symbol of three crowns on its euros, should there ever be a Swedish one.

Comparisons

The 'What Story Should Europe Tell' website discussion on European symbols has already been mentioned, and it is interesting to note that the only EU symbol that was accepted by the critical voice was that of the euro: 'The only true EU symbol that means anything is the € symbol'.[509] Unfortunately, no explicit argument was given for this position, except for telling how it can be typed on a computer keyboard, which links to the web chat context, but that opinion supports the many other indices of the relative success of this symbol.

One of the most oddly shaped coins ever was the 2002 issue of a $10 silver coin from the Republic of Nauru, a minor island republic in the Pacific Ocean, mainly known in Scandinavia for its profitable Internet suffix '.nu' ('now') (Figure 8.6). It was shaped as a map of West Europe, in order to celebrate the 'first issue of the euro'.[510]

Three EU member states decided not to introduce the euro in 2002. There is on the web considerable speculation about their possible future euro designs, with images of 'concept coins' or 'what-if coins', and even proposals from the national banks.

Denmark chose not to join the EMU and has thus kept its old krona currency. Banknote motifs include author Karen Blixen (1885–1962); composer Carl Nielsen (1865–1931); actress Johanne Luise Heiberg (1812–90); atom physicist Niels Bohr (1885–1962) with yin-and-yang vignettes from his coat of arms: and painters Anna and Michael Ancher (1859–1935 and 1849–1927). Rear sides show various old stone reliefs from Danish churches. Their coins show royal motifs: the Queen's monogram and an abstract pattern inspired by Viking age decoration styles on the lower values; the Queen and the national coat of arms with three lions and nine hearts under a crown on the higher ones. Rumours on the Internet assume that as Denmark will sooner or later enter the EMU, their euro coins will most probably also depict their Queen, thus lining up with the traditional monarchies and leaving out the cultural personalities they now have on banknotes.

Sweden also stuck to their old krona, and their national bank (Riksbank) offers detailed information on its website. Since this is my home country, I will therefore also present it in a somewhat more detailed manner. The 20 krona depicts the author Selma Lagerlöf (1858–1940) in front of her home region Värmland landscape (forest and lake), with the manuscript introduction to her first novel *Gösta Berling's Saga* and a horse carriage with Lagerlöf as passenger, plus a microtext from same novel ('The lake has its sources far up in the north, and the country is a perfect country for a lake. The forest and the mountains are always collecting water for it; tiny rivers and brooks stream into it the whole year around. It has fine white sand.'). On the back appears a passage from Lagerlöf's *Nils Holgersson's Wonderful Journey through Sweden*, with Nils and Mårten goose flying over the flatlands of Skåne, in southern Sweden. Next, the 50 krona shows the 'Swedish nightingale' Jenny Lind (1820–87) with notes from

Vincenzo Bellini's opera *Norma*, Stockholm's old opera house and microtext quotation from composer Arnold Schoenberg ('Music conveys a prophetical message, which reveals a higher life form towards which humanity is developing. And it is because of this message that music appeals to people of all races and nationalities'). On the rear is a silver harp, its tonal range and an excerpt from the score of modern composer Sven-David Sandström's *Pictures for Percussion and Orchestra* over a stylised Swedish landscape. The 100 krona displays the famous naturalist Carl von Linné (Linnaeus, 1707–78) with pollinating plants from his early work *Præludia Sponsaliarum Plantarum* and botanical gardens in Uppsala, where he was director, plus his motto in microtext: OMNIA MIRARI ETIAM TRITISSIMA ('Find wonder in all things, even the most commonplace'). On the rear is a bee pollinating flower (which Linné himself never realised the role of), pollen grains, the lobes of a stigma and the result, a germ and a reconstruction of how a flower looks through the multifaceted eye of a bee—all motifs taken from pictures by photographer Lennart Nilsson. The 500 krona has Karl XI (1655–97), King of Sweden 1672–97, during whose reign Sveriges Riksbank was founded in 1668, in front of the first Riksbank building in Stockholm, with the Riksbank's motto HINC ROBUR ET SECURITAS ('From here comes security and strength') in microtext. On its back is the engineer Christopher Polhem (1661–1751) in front of the large gear wheel from his industrial plant at Stjärnsund in Dalarna, with mathematical calculations from his notebooks and Falu copper mine with one of his ore hauling plants. The lesser values leave the royalties behind. The highest value, 1000 krona, shows Gustav Vasa (1496–1560), who founded the Swedish hereditary monarchy and united Sweden into a state with a central government. Following the reformation in 1527, he also incorporated the young Lutheran church, making it into a Swedish state church. He is depicted with oil painting in the Stockholm Cathedral showing an atmospheric phenomenon 1535 (the parhelion picture) and a microtext quotation from Gustav Vasa: SCRIPTURAM IN PROPRIA HABEANT LINGUA ('Let them have the holy scripture in their own language'). The rear shows *Description of the Northern Peoples* from 1555, written by Olaus Magnus (1490–1557), who was the last Swedish Catholic archbishop and a scientific author on Swedish geography and cultural history, together with an image of harvest being gathered and threshed in radiant sunshine. Swedish coins are consistently royalistic, with various combinations of the King Carl XVI Gustaf, his crowned monogram, the lesser national coat of arms and the King's motto 'For Sweden—with the times'.

The Swedish national bank has on various occasions expressed an intention to stick to the royalist tradition, thus confining their euro designs to only the Swedish King and possibly the lesser national coat of arms, deriving from the fourteenth century and consisting of three crowns, deriving from medieval times and supposedly inspired by the three New Testament kings (or holy men) in combination with more or less mythical conceptions of the foundation of the Swedish nation through some kind of merger with three older kingdoms, though this is highly uncertain. The Swedish monarchy is like all others in itself, in a way, transnational, since the king's ancestor was a French general who immigrated in the early nineteenth century, and since it has had marital ties with other European nations, including the present queen who met the king when she worked as a kind of tourist hostess in Germany. This transnational interpretation is not the dominant or preferred one, since the king as a formal head of state—a ceremonial symbol without real political power—is one of the very few possible choices that undisputedly point towards the Swedish nation state, neither more nor less. As for the three crowns insignia, they might perhaps also be read as a vague sign of 'united in diversity': plurality and diversification but also synthesis and totality. However, the similarity of the crowns strongly favours the unity side, avoiding any real sign of diversity. After all, three crowns may also be at least thrice as strong as one, implying a very strong and united central state authority where all constituents are made equal and have to conform to the overarching rule. According to the will of the national bank, the Swedish euros will thus side with those of the most traditionalist other monarchies, stressing an anachronistic symbol of the nation state as the only, meagre face of Sweden to the outer world, though there have been voices (including mine) asking for a more Spanish solution, adding some other motifs as well.

Britain's banknotes all have Queen Elizabeth on the obverse side, while the rear sides depict social reformer Elizabeth Fry (1780–1815) with a group of women and children (£5); naturalist Charles Darwin (1809–82) with a humming bird (£10); and composer Sir Edward Elgar (1857–1934) with patron saint of music St. Cecilia and Worcester Cathedral (£20). Almost all coins are related to the history of the United Kingdom. Lower values have the seated figure of Britannia, the badge of England in form of the royally crowned Tudor Rose, part of the Crest of England with a crowned lion, the Scottish crowned thistle badge, the Prince of Wales badge comprising three ostrich feathers enfiling a coronet of crosses pattee and fleurs-de-lys with the motto 'Ich dien' ('I serve'), and a porticullis with chains royally crowned—an adaption of King Henry VII's badge. A series of ten different £1 coins all have on the front three lions—heraldic symbol for England, and the edge inscription 'Decus et tutamen' ('An ornament and a safeguard'). On their backs are a series of ten different designs with symbols for Scotland, Wales, Northern Ireland, England and the United Kingdom, different heraldic symbols (thistle, leek, flax plant or oak tree with royal diadem, UK shield of royal arms with crown, Scottish lion royal arms, Welsh dragon badge, Celtic collar with cross and pimpernel flower or three English lions) and inscriptions: 'Nemo me impune lacessit' ('No none provokes me with impunity'), 'Pleidiol wyf I'm gwlad' ('True am I to my Country'), 'Decus et tutamen' ('An ornament and a safeguard', from Virgil's *Aeneid*). The £2 coin is an exception, with its symbolic representation of the development of British Industry from the Iron Age to the modern computer age, with the inscription 'Standing on the shoulders of giants' on its edge. The design of possible future British euro coins is a strict secret, though most web sources seem to bet on the monarchist choice of Queen faces there, as well.

In *A Flutter of Banknotes* (2001), Brion and Moreau survey the motif history of European paper money. Dominant motifs have been antique gods or predominantly female allegorical figures representing human virtues or aspects of activity related to the idea of progress: commerce, industry, agriculture, science and art. Symbols of permanence or vigilance were meant to inspire confidence: anchors, hives, towers, open eyes, lamps or cocks. Other banknotes depicted national symbols: coats of arms, heraldic beasts, portraits of monarchs, or more indirectly motifs relating to folklore, local landscapes or place-bound mythology. Portraits in a realist style have dominated since the World War II, and national figureheads from art, philosophy and science became prominent features from the 1960s. In general, banknotes tend to reflect main values of the issuing societies: 'faith in progress, the virtue of work, social harmony, the greatness of a nation', offering an insight into 'the great founding myths of Western society'.[511]

A study by Jacques E. C. Hymans investigates currency iconography as indicator of collective identities in Europe since the early nineteenth century, using a database of 1368 notes from all the fifteen member states. Its main finding is that time (period) appears more decisive than space (nationality) for paper money images, indicating that states express a transnational spirit of the times rather than unique national identities. Inspired by Ronald Inglehart's theories of cultural shifts, Hymans discerns in these fifteen countries an overall trend for the social focus to move from state through society to the individual and of basic norms to move from tradition through material goods to post-materialist values.[512] Hymans sees the paper euro as confirming these trends, but in this case the focus on banknotes hides away the national differences that may only appear on coins. It is also in practice often difficult to decide whether a specific symbolic motif should be understood as a state, societal or individual actor, or reflecting traditional, materialist or post-materialist values.

Currencies on other continents of the world to some extent share similar iconographic traits, but affected by the specific national history and context. It is for instance instructive to compare the euro with money from the United States, Russia and South Africa who all have a history as federations. Each of them also has a size and a degree of global influence that can be compared to that of Europe, which is also true of mainland China (Figure 8.7).

The US dollar coins show the Statue of Liberty in New York: a well-known national symbol that was a gift from France and links classical myth and heritage to secular and universalist republican Enlightenment values. US dollar bills front past presidents, while reverse sides have the motto 'In God we trust' together with historic federal buildings (Lincoln Memorial, White House, the Capitol etc.). This raises the question why the euro does not show the European motto, since that would have increased coherence between the symbols and boosted the fame of the 'united in diversity' slogan. There is no single existing artefact that may stand for all of Europe in the same way as does the Statue of Liberty for the US, nor any given and limited set of key figures who could have been honoured to represent European history. No wonder thus that Europe and the United States differ so much in their respective currency iconography.

Almost the same goes for the People's Republic of China (PRC), where the yuan banknotes of the renminbi currency have on the obverse side Chairman Mao Zedong, the founder and first president of the PRC. On the reverses are various landscapes, parks or buildings with symbolic importance for China. A centralised dictatorship nation like the PRC is even farther removed from European diversity than the ethnic melting pot of the United States.

Russia is both geographically and historically a closer neighbour, and its rubles have been continuously revised to reflect recurrent political shifts. Coins front either Russia's national protector Saint George or the two-headed eagle emblem. Ruble banknotes show various constructions (a fortress, a hydroelectric plant, a stock exchange and a theatre, monuments, sculptures, churches, monasteries, bridges and ships) from different Russian cities and referring to different historical periods. While identifiable personalities are not as prominent as before, in line with the euro banknotes, the identification of key cities and buildings invites contestation from excluded ones, which was precisely what the EU wanted to avoid by not allowing specific buildings or people on euro banknotes.

In South Africa, rand coins show coat of arms and animals, while banknotes obverses have heads of the Big Five game (rhinoceros, elephant, lion, buffalo and leopard), all confirming a traditional image of natural African wildness. Banknote reverses either show smaller animals or images of new constructions in science, technology and industry, in an effort to show a way forward to modern development. The latter remind of the high-value euro bridges and windows, but wildlife species as key money icons is peculiar to Africa and could never have been chosen for the euro—not even if one could imagine certain other species as typical for this northern continent.

In sum, the euro imagery seems pretty original compared to these competitors. The star circle remains unique, even though China and the United States have (differently configured) stars in their flags and coats of arms and the Chinese also depict them on their money. While some Russian rubles also happen to show a bridge and a ship, these do not systematically build up any lead motif of communication constructions as with the euro banknotes. None of the others mentioned here have a particular focus on doors, windows or bridges—on the contrary, they tend instead to display mountains or monumental buildings of a closed and closing kind, perhaps to emphasise the solidity of their state rule. It is also interesting to note that territorial maps play a much more central role in Europe than elsewhere, possibly reflecting a need to explain and underline the (expansive) boundaries of this relatively new geopolitical entity. Russia's way of displaying key places in various cities may to some extent be compared to the national euro coin reverses, in that they also give space for showing off internal diversity, but Moscow does this with much firmer stress on unity than on diversity.

The euro design seems so far to have been favourably received. There are certainly many critics against the euro as a payment instrument, even though fewer and fewer argue for returning to the previous national currencies. However, the look of the banknotes and coins has rarely been seriously criticised, even though there have been caricatures and ironic alternative designs. For a G20 meeting in spring 2009, *Freaking News*—a website for comic photoshop manipulation—organised a competition for creating a new global currency by combining existing currencies. One entry, 'Bilderberg Note', mixed a $100 with a €100 bill and with Henry Kissinger's portrait in the middle. The 'Doleur' looked a bit like the €500 but US dollar green and with a $10,000 denomination. The 'Pooro' fused $20 and €20 with a bag man in the centre, and on the back side a peek under a bridge where homeless people squatted, unveiling the coarse realities beneath all lofty slogans.[513]

Conclusions

The euro currency is a potent symbol of this economically anchored new community. It is present everywhere in private and public life, as key part of and tool for the inter-European circulation of values and exchanges between people in everyday life. The symbolisms selected add to the more abstract one of the flag by specifying the kind of connections conceived between the states/stars.

Currency symbolisms often intertextually link to other symbols, mostly to flags. The common euro images explicitly refer to the star circle but not clearly to any of the other EU symbols. The national coin reverses also integrate the stars and also implicitly thematise the 'united in diversity' motto, whereas the day and the anthem are not evidently present anywhere, perhaps reflecting the dividing lines between time-in and time-out culture and between visual and aural symbols. Only one Greek euro coin nods to the Europa myth, whereas geopolitical maps are prominently present everywhere. On US banknotes, the motto is also boosted, but else it is mainly flag symbols that are given space in money designs, no doubt because of their immediately recognisable visual character that make them serve as prime identifiers.

Once more, the four main identity themes are further developed in the pan-European money facets.

1.   The networking need may be seen as an effect of previous *dislocation*, adding a new dimension to that theme. In a sense, the many wars have dislocated populations and given birth to mutual distrust and alienation, which in turn has bred a longing for re-unification through communication rather than through violent force. In a more specific sense, the constructions for communication form a synthesis between stability and mobility, which is also in line with the previous symbols. The functioning of money in general is built upon an ideal conjunction of stable trust and free mobility, and the European project demands a similar balance to be stricken. The banknote motifs do their best to illustrate this dialectic.

2.   The theme of *desire* is likewise not immediately apparent in the currency design. Any stylish layout can of course communicate a sense of aesthetic pleasure, but it is at first difficult to find any obvious representation of joy or attraction in the content of these designs. Nor is there any clear alternative presence of control or destruction, which were found in some of the previous symbols. The euro instead has a rather cool appearance, avoiding any strong emotional impact, which may be one reason why it has also not provoked any reactions of intense distaste. However, one may well interpret the communicative constructions as inviting communication. In this sense, windows, doors and bridges could be seen as expressing a desire for opening up and connecting to the other: to interact among member states as well as with the surrounding world. This would further support the flag symbolism where the circular void was seen as an agora inviting communicative action between citizens. Indeed, a desire for contact is central to the European unification process, and the invitation to member states to design their own coin sides to participate in this economic public space is another confirmation of this quest for networking and communication.

3.   The theme of *elevation* is at first sight not as prominent as with the other EU symbols. It returns through the star circle with its sacred and stellar connotations, but not as clearly in the building motifs. It is true that the money-story of historical progression does indicate a movement from primitive, low and heavy stone edifices to the high-rising contemporary style, promoting an understanding of history as an elevation from dark origins to the brightly shining present. Still, this is the symbol where this theme is weakest.

4.   The construction of the two coin sides again implies *hybridity*, where the common obverses stand for coherent unity while the national reverses add a strong element of diversity—the whole serving as almost a materialisation of the European motto.

9

Projecting Europe

All official EU symbols strive to promote an image of Europe as strong, united and beneficial for all. A closer interpretation, guided by comparing these symbols with other and sometimes oppositional symbols, has disclosed a series of inner tensions and contradictions in this signifying process. The cumulation of interpretations has resulted in a rich symbolic web of signification with a number of main themes that point at key facets but also tensions in European identity. One such tension runs between the strong hopes that shared symbols would strengthen the European project and their striking lack of success so far. In view of Europe Day 2010, in the midst of the turbulent eurozone crisis, EU President Herman van Rompuy published an article defining the core essence of the EU in 'welfare, security and a shared fate', but at the same time demanding nobody 'to be enthusiastic and wave EU flags or join the peace choir'.[514] It is not uncommon for officials to downplay the importance of the same symbols that were originally motivated by a wish to reinforce the public awareness of precisely the shared values that they at other times are felt to problematise.

No symbols stand for themselves. They are interpreted in contexts of use bringing them together in intersymbolic interaction. The anthem is sung and the flag colours are publically displayed on Europe Day, while the € sign is sometimes used not only to identify money but also other things that are European. The symbols sometimes cooperate, and there is also a transfer between some of them, notably from the flag to the currency.[515] To further complicate things, the neat set of five EU symbols is just a rather arbitrary selection from a much wider and fuzzier cluster of different symbolic realms of relevance for how to symbolise European identity.

Additional symbolic realms

Lots of other symbol genres could also be investigated, even though they have no equally official EU legitimacy. Some of them have actually been discussed and even institutionalised by European authorities, though have not entered what might be called Europe's 'Big Five' league.

Maps are as such very important tools of identification, in particular for geopolitical units such as this one. They are also eminently present on all euro currencies. Europe has notoriously slippery geographic borders, not least to the east where the borders to Asia have never been quite clear. The history of Europe's visual mapping is highly intricate and informative in relation to the issue of identification.[516] This map has been continuously redrawn according to both changing inner divisions and global power balances, and the choice of cartographic projection method, colouring and ornamentation will inevitably also have signifying impact. For instance, the Council of Europe has always defined Europe very widely, reaching into what otherwise is often seen as West Asia and the Middle East, whereas the EU countries are fewer and also exclude central nations such as Switzerland.

Vehicle number plates have already been mentioned as locations for flagging the star circle. The EU does not issue passports, though this would have been a strong symbol for a pan-European citizenship. There are only common rules for member states' national passports, which have to be burgundy red and contain the words 'EUROPEAN UNION'. European stamps have at least since 1956 been issued jointly by larger sets of European countries, often celebrating anniversaries or events with motifs referring to peace and welfare. Still, they have not in the last decades been added to the core set of official symbols, and remain of secondary importance in this respect, as even fewer people than those who are familiar with the Big Five would remember to have seen any such stamp or even know them to exist.

Buildings such as those of the European Parliament and the Council of Europe in Brussels and Strasbourg, or more generally buildings of a 'European' character, have also sometimes been discussed as of symbolic importance. Just like the modernist UN building in New York once was a well-known icon of political globalisation, efforts are made to make these buildings attractive as concrete and functional emblems of international cooperation. Still, few can actually recognise any of these buildings, and they play little role in identifying Europe. It is often hard to find even any images of these houses on the websites of their respective organisations. No single building seems yet able to stand for the whole of Europe, even though several nations certainly have easily identifiable constructions such as the Eiffel Tower in France or the Brandenburg Gate in Berlin—and it is no coincidence that the latter also appears on German euro coins, and that many other national coin motifs also include buildings, just as is the case with other national currencies.

A whole city may well also serve as a symbol standing for a nation or a continent. In Europe's case, it was once suggested that the coat of arms of Strasbourg could serve as a European flag, but this never got sufficient support. Today, since the 2001 Treaty of Nice formally made Brussels the capital of the EU, it is that city that is—both as a name and as a real material city—often used as a metaphor for the EU, in particular by sceptics who wish to express how EU power is located far away from 'common citizens' in their home countries. 'It is decided in Brussels' is then a way to locate Europe at a distance from oneself, implicitly stating that the speaker is not really European or that the EU is just a matter for distant elites. The AMO firm that created the EU barcode also had been asked for ideas of how to enhance the visual profile of Brussels, from architecture to graphic design on documents etc.

Again, Europeanness may of course also be signified by combinations of other cities, and again the euro coins offer ample evidence. In a more organised manner, this has been institutionalised as the 'European Capital of Culture' (first named 'European City of Culture'), as conceptualised by Greek Minister of Culture Melina Mercouri in 1983, and with Athens as the first such city 1985. Until 2000, there was just one cultural capital each year, but since then the number has varied. This is an occasion for cities to market themselves internationally, but further research would be needed to discern in what way these activities have perhaps contributed to the symbolic identification of Europe.

A Europe Prize 'for the best, and most inspired, literary work and film of the year, outstanding in form and furthering the idea of European unity' was proposed to the Council of Europe in 1951 but failed to be adopted.[517] It was then instead taken up as an encouragement to the local municipality that had 'done most to propagate the ideal of European unity', and has been annually awarded since 1955.

As for languages, English is most commonly used as a lingua franca within Europe, in spite of the fact that most native English speakers live outside Europe—in Australia, Canada, South Africa and the United States—and also the great majority of European citizens do not have English as mother tongue. It is therefore difficult to describe English as signifying Europeanness any more than French, German or Finnish. Perhaps what signifies Europe most is the polyglot diversity that is so central to the self-understanding in the EU motto.

As was seen with both some national euro coins and South African banknotes, animals can be used for identifying a community, and so can plants, landscapes or other natural phenomena. Many countries have national animals, plants and trees that are sometimes more beloved, recognised and used than the pompous national personifications, and used in parallel to them, without any specific regard to their mutual coherence. For instance, the Irish have Hibernia but more importantly the shamrock; France has the fleur de lis and the Gallic rooster (representing the history and culture of the nation rather than the state); Switzerland the edelweiss; Russia the bear; and a whole range of European countries make use of various heraldic designs of eagles or lions—even though the latter were always exotic rather than domestic phenomena. Inanimate objects used for national identification include the Irish Celtic harp, Sweden's three crowns and several nations' manifold varieties of crosses. Some such symbols are incorporated in flags or depicted on stamps and coins, as will be discussed in later chapters. Finally, there are also a series of national patron saints such as the Irish St Patrick or Norwegian St Olav, but these have several disadvantages: they are linked to the Catholic Church which makes them problematic for secularised political purposes and not least in predominantly Protestant countries, and there are often also several different saints of prominence in each country.

A Californian blog discusses the issue of iconography and asks why it is so hard to think which animal could represent Europe, compared to the easiness with which this may be done for the other 'superpowers': the US eagle, the Russian bear, the Chinese dragon and the Indian elephant.[518] The blogger suggests a number of possibilities. A lion is common in European national iconography but there are no wild lions in Europe since Roman times. An eagle is also common, but it is already used by the United States. A griffin—half eagle, half lion—could be a compromise, but there is then again a competition with cities or countries that already use it. This is also true for other national symbols containing animals such as roosters, horses, owls or rams. Another blog mentions that 'a French newspaper' has found two most popular candidate animals among EU politicians: the dove and the bull, where one connotes Europe's intended 'soft power' (the ability to obtain a goal not by coercion or payment but by attraction, making others 'want what you want') and love of peace, while the bull has stronger historical connotations, thanks to the Europa myth.[519] However, a problem with the bull is that it is Europa and not Zeus who symbolises Europe. Another website jokingly suggests that a chameleon might be a suitable animal for the undefinable aspect of Europe, and the satirical proposal of a flying duck was mentioned in the flag chapter, meant as an ironic comment to European soft power in contrast with the tougher US eagle.[520]

It appears impossible—and politically hazardous—to select one single animal or plant to fairly represent the whole of this heterogeneous continent. Animals are mobile creatures and there is no species that is limited only to Europe while also existing in all European countries and regions, and roughly the same also holds for plants and inanimate objects. It might be easier for the relatively more coherent Australian or Antarctic continents, but Europe's biological diversity effectively prevents any such effort. One might perhaps try and select some species that has been particularly important to European culture and history, but even that is difficult, and as animal symbolisms are rarely officially sanctioned anymore, and play no particularly strong role compared to other symbolic realms, the will to invest energy and work in such a project is limited. Future will tell if popular signifying practices will ever result in such a choice of animal or plant symbol for Europe, but given the great differences between climate, flora and fauna across the continent, this may be seriously doubted.

One could also add dances, cinema, artworks, culinary cultures and so much else where there is some kind of discourse around what is typically European. However, there are yet no fixed and officially recognised symbolisms in any other sensory mode than those discussed in previous chapters, and they are all bound to verbal, visual and aural communication: motto, flag, anthem etc. Some perfumes or food dishes may for instance commonly be identified with a region or a country, and individuals may associate a smell, a taste or any other bodily experience with a collective belonging. One might for instance imagine that it might in a distant future become common to eat a special cake or some other specific dish on Europe Day, so that a culinary taste becomes articulated with European identity. Still, these associations remain quite fluid and are not officially acknowledged and organised in the way that the symbolisms in words, images and music analysed here are.

Things are a little bit different with saints, where the Vatican has given St Benedict of Nursia official status as Europe's main patron saint. The Italian San Benedetto da Norcia lived during 480–547, was the founder of western Christian monasticism and was canonised in 1220 by Pope Honorius III. He founded twelve monasteries but no religious order: the Order of St Benedict is a later construction. On the fourteenth centenary of St Benedict's death, Pope Pius XII in 1947 called him 'the father of Europe', and Paul VI in 1964 officially declared him 'Patron Saint of all Europe'. Sharing his papal name, Benedict XVI in April 2008 argued that 'with his life and work St Benedict exercised a fundamental influence on the development of European civilization and culture' and helped Europe to emerge from the 'dark night of history' that followed the fall of the Roman empire.[521] The Carolingian Empire some 250 years later was an evidence of this new importance of Christianity for European reorganisation. Among existing saints, the choice of St Benedict as Europe's patron saint was thus not far-fetched. However, the series of post-WWII activities by the Vatican to construct a 'Vatican Europe' that would resurrect a kind of Medieval Holy Roman Empire elicited fear and condemnation among socialists, and with the lesson learnt, the EU has chosen to rather consistently avoid such overtly Christian elements in its symbolic policy. No serious discussion seems to have taken place for recognising the Vatican's initiative on a formal EU level, but this has remained the expression of a special interest of the Roman Catholic Church, with no particular influence even on the other main Christian confessions in Europe.

Pope John Paul II almost caused inflation in naming patron saints for Europe. The Greek brothers St Cyril (Constantin, 826–69) and St Methodius (815–85), who had mainly been active in East Europe, were in 1980 declared co-patrons of Europe, together with St Benedict. On 1 October 1999, the same Pope went on to name three female patron saints of Europe, to match the previous three male patrons: St Bridget of Sweden (Birgitta, 1302–73, canonized by Pope Boniface IX in 1391); Catherine of Siena (1347–80, canonised in 1461 by Pope Pius II); and St Teresa Benedicta of the Cross (St Edith Stein, 1891–1942, canonised in 1998—she came from a Jewish family in Poland and was gassed in Auschwitz). The same John Paul II had in 1997 also canonised St Hedwig (Jadwiga, 1374–99), who had been Polish monarch, and described her as a patron saint of a 'United Europe'. This would imply that there are actually at least seven Catholic patron saints for the whole of Europe, headed by St Benedict. However, none of these saints is venerated by Protestants or other non-Catholic confessions, and outside their home countries and congregations they are little known among the general public.

Four facets

It is not possible to present a comprehensive inventory or cultural map of symbolic motifs, since there are too many dimensions to consider, since each symbol relates to too many others, and since this symbolic field continually and subtly changes on all levels. Still, some comparative observations may be made of intermedial homologies and other patterns of similarity and difference between these symbolic genres, summarising some main interpretive directions of European identification today.

The symbols favoured by the EU are modelled upon national standards, but strive to add some transnational twist. All nation states have established national flags, often inscribed in their constitutions. Official mottos are less common for nations, but almost all countries have national anthems, and most also a national day and a characteristic currency with similar symbolic status. Flags and money are involved in vernacular contexts where they are seen and used by ordinary citizens, as integrated in time-in culture. Mostly unfocused, they engage in a kind of 'banal Europeanness'. Anthem and day, on the other hand, demand a deeper engagement in order to function at all, and have so far therefore also been less successfully integrated in Europeans' lives, even though such ritual practices of time-out culture may well anyway be important to identification. The flag easily lends itself to continent branding, whereas the anthem is considerably less suitable for such purposes. The motto has a kind of mid position: rarely used in everyday life but underlying much policy discourse, as a leitmotif of how integration is to be organised the European way. The symbols used by other organisations, individual activists or artists, presented as serious alternatives or as critical comments, likewise circulate through various channels, some in the vernacular underground, others framed by museums or other specialised institutions.

All such symbols have to be polysemic and ambiguous, charged with a surplus of meaning, in order to be capable of recontextualisation and articulation with endlessly new sets of values in new contexts. It is therefore no surprise that none can therefore be pinned down to one single line of interpretation: they simply must have multiple meaning potentials in order to fulfil their functions as key identifying symbols, since the identities they are meant to signify are also multifaceted and in flux. In the hermeneutic spiral movement of conflicting interpretations, there is no fixed starting point, as collective identities are always in the making, while each symbolic design is at the same time also understood in relation to a transient set of other symbols that co-determine its meaning. A star circle may for instance in one moment be seen as respectful veneration of a suprahuman power but in the next moment understood instead as a bold declaration that worldly humans dare compete with the old gods; an empty circle, for some, signals a shameful void while to others serves as a stage inviting actors to enter. In this way, symbols present a set of structural and formal frameworks that are then in shifting contexts through history filled with varying or even contradictory contents by actors who represent different interests. This makes it so hard to pinpoint the precise significance of each such symbol.

In vaguely recalling the Europa myth and unreflexively using its own name, Europe links up to an imagined origin in a transgressive union between gods, humans and animals, and of adventurous and forced dislocation and mobility from east and south towards west and north. Based on historical experiences, it has in the motto made a promise to make its own inner diversity the basis for its unified integration. By performing an anthem and organising joint activities on a special annual day, it strives both to reflect upon its past and future trajectory and to explore ways of being European in the present. The values extracted from the oldest, mythic symbol are developed in different directions by the others: the official as well as the unofficial ones.

In a more qualified sense, many of these symbols construct Europe as lifted up to a higher level, in a historical movement marching through the greatest difficulties towards a privileged destiny. Europe's centrality is not an innate condition but a result of development, of *rising from disaster*, through suffering to greatness. This may ring of sacral overtones, from Zeus disguised as bull to the star circle as saintly nimbus, but it also has a secular interpretation, from the Prometheus myth to Schiller's and Beethoven's dance on the Elysian fields, which would be almost blasphemic if taken literally, but making more sense as metaphors of the Kantian dictum of *sapere aude*, the pledge for humanity to make use of its own reason rather than rely on divine authorities. There is a difficult ambiguity in this imagery. What was here described as the EU founding myth can for instance be regarded in at least two different ways. Either Europe is seen as primarily a suffering victim of its own destruction, temporarily occupied by evil forces but finally released to rise to true grandiosity and wealth, or Europe is at least as much a guilty perpetrator of those historic atrocities, in which case the final elevation is more of an ethical quest for finally abandoning hatred and evilness. In one case there are dreams of heroic revenge and competing for world power, in the other, dreams of forgiveness and peace with itself and the surrounding others. Traces of both these readings may be found in the Schuman declaration as celebrated on Europe Day, making the theme of elevation difficult to assess, as it has both authoritarian and critical potentials.

1. The geopolitical and demographic *origin* and positioning of Europe is since the beginning haunted by a sense of horizontal *dislocation*. This is most clearly expressed in the Europa myth, but, as noted by Todorov, Brague and others, there are faint echoes of this original eccentricity elsewhere too, balancing the initially noted theme of elevation. Europe derives from elsewhere and has a deep-seated desire for reaching out to its imagined point of origin and to the whole world, while its centrality is conceived as the result of its own achievements rather than a given essence. Stability and fixation is thus a task more than a starting-point, and a strong element of mobility and transience remains at the core of European identifications. Europe once was a marginal outpost but is now the centre of its symbolic universe, and far from being easily granted, this centrality needs to be continually deserved by intensifying efforts of global communication. The United States has in a much later and shorter time-span also understood itself as rising from a peripheral colony to the world-leading empire of science, wealth and entertainment, and today Asian regions signal their readiness to take over the initative.

    However, several of the later symbols tend to fix Europe, evoking a stability, fixity and rootedness that more or less desperately tries to counteract the sliding and fragmenting that always threatens such unified solidity, from internal as well as from external pressures. This centring effort may be understood as a kind of response and reaction to continuing decentring historical events, from the Renaissance through the Enlightenment to the great twentieth century geopolitical shifts. This results in an unresolved competition between centrifugal and centripetal forces.

2. The main *driving force* behind this collective movement is depicted in terms of *desire*. The moment of desire was particularly evident in the Europa myth and in the original Beethoven-Schiller version of the anthem, but could also be found in the more recent symbols. It is possible to find secret streams of desire also underneath the metaphors of control, stability and harmony. Europe seems driven by a precarious combination of two key desires. One is the *desire for perfection*, linked to the next theme of elevation, and particularly prominent in the flag's star circle, but also lurking here and there among the other symbols as well. The other is the *desire for contact with others*, across boundaries, running all the way from Europa to the euro, and linked to the previous theme of dislocation and eccentricity. Such a wish is also ambivalent. There was an

irresistible mutual curiosity between Europa and the divine bull, and a similar communicative urge drove the great explorers to discover 'new' continents in order to accumulate knowledge, power and wealth. In the crusaders' desire for the Oriental region or colonial imperialism, selfish exploitation and oppression initated a spiral of destruction, but also contributed to build bridges not only for troops and goods but also for people and ideas, in a dialectic where the evil aspects dominated but where there was also a kind of emancipatory potential hidden, which even Karl Marx acknowledged. While Michel Foucault has highlighted the close interdependence of knowledge and power, this does not imply that *all* communication is always a kind of violence. Postcolonial critics have sharply problematised the Eurocentric tendency to conflate universal values with European interests, 'grounded in egocentrism, in the identification of our own values with values in general, of our *I* with the universe'. In Todorov's formulation:

> Since the period of the conquest, for almost three hundred and fifty years, Western Europe has tried to assimilate the other, to do away with an exterior alterity, and has in great part succeeded. Its way of life and its values have spread around the world.[522]

Still, Todorov insists that 'it is possible to establish an ethical criterion to judge the form of influence: the essential thing, I should say, is to know whether they are *imposed* or *proposed*'.[523]

> We need not be confined within a sterile alternative: either to justify colonial wars (in the name of the superiority of Western civilization), or to reject all interaction with a foreign power in the name of one's own identity. Nonviolent communication exists, and we can defend it as a value.[524]

This is in line with Habermas' distinction between strategic and communicative action. The European desire for communication has repeatedly been married to a will to power and domination, but at the same time also contains germs of self-critical openness to others. This quest for communication is far from an innate essence of Europe, since European history is equally full of non-communicative acts of violence and oppression. Still, the many formulations of communication and translation as a key theme—from euro banknotes to scholars like Todorov, Ricoeur and Balibar—indicate that this has developed into an increasingly focal orientation, deriving from specific historical experiences combining universalising communication with self-critical reflection.

Focusing on the concept of 'European cultural identity' Jacques Derrida also insists on the acknowledgement of difference and alterity for a 'Europe still to become', while Étienne Balibar gives Europe the task of being 'the *interpreter of the world*, translating languages and cultures in all directions'.[525] In the article 'Reflections on a New Ethos for Europe', Paul Ricoeur discusses 'the future of Europe in terms of imagination', outlining a series of models for a 'post-national state' to combine identity and alterity at different levels.[526] His first model is that of *translation*, where he argues for a 'translation ethos' of hospitality that would be capable of mediating between different cultures. His second model is that of the *exchange of memories*, whereby people take responsibility for 'the story of the other' in mobile identifications through readings that constitute narrative identities. Here, he warns that a 'rigid and arrogant conception of cultural identity' makes it difficult to revise inherited stories:

> What really prevents cultures from allowing themselves to be recounted differently is the influence exercised over the collective memory by what we term the 'founding events', the repeated commemoration and celebration of which tend to freeze the history of each cultural group into an identity which is not only immutable but also deliberately and systematically incommunicable. The European ethos which is sought does not of course require the abandonment of these important historical landmarks, but rather an effort of plural reading.[527]

It is necessary to allow different recountings of the past, from different standpoints, and to open up communicative space for such dialogical or contesting counter-narratives. Europe needs not only a linguistic hospitality but also a 'narrative hospitality' in order for its traditions to develop their 'dialectical dimension', where transmission allows for innovation. Ricoeur puts this in terms reminding of Walter Benjamin and Ernst Bloch:

> Indeed the past is not only what is bygone—that which has taken place and can no longer be changed—it also lives in the memory thanks to arrows of futurity which have not been fired or whose trajectory has been interrupted. The unfulfilled future of the past forms perhaps the richest part of a tradition. The liberation of this unfulfilled future of the past is the major benefit that we can expect from the crossing of memories and the exchange of narratives. It is principally the founding events of a historical community which should be submitted to this critical reading in order to release the

burden of expectation that the subsequent course of its history carried and then betrayed. The past is a cemetery of promises which have not been kept.[528]

Ricoeur's third model is that of *forgiveness*, understood as a form of mutual revision of entangled life stories, resulting from the exchange of memories. Europe's violent history makes such forgiveness (that is not the same as forgetting!) necessary, as a form of charity, a shattering of debt and 'lifting the burden of guilt which paralyses the relations between individuals who are acting out and suffering their own history'. This is only indirectly applicable to the political sphere 'whose principle is justice and reciprocity, and not charity and the gift', but the boundary between these spheres is not quite impermeable, and Ricoeur talks of 'some wonderful examples of a kind of short circuit between the poetical and the political'. Like the founding fathers of the EU, Ricoeur thus finds forgiving and compassion necessary between Europe's peoples.[529] 'From beginning to end we have held to the blueprint of "mediations". In this sense, the proposed models may be seen as contributing to the crucial ongoing debate between the right to universality and the demand of historical difference.'[530] Europe Day, the European motto and anthem as well as some of the euro designs at least offer faint glimpses of such a communicative ethics of translation and forgiveness, though there are also opposite examples in other symbols.

3.   There is a *direction* of vertical *elevation* in a great majority of these symbols. The European flag is a good example, with its symmetric star circle pulling Europeans up among the skies in perfect mutual harmony. In one sense this is trivial, since any European symbol of course puts Europe in focus, lifting it up from the stream of the ordinary that temporarily steps back and serves as its context. But other symbols such as the barcode, where the theme of elevation is at least insignificant, show that the theme of elevation is more than trivial here. All regions tend to see themselves as the centre of their own local universes, but while Europe's symbols make her the unquestioned centre of the human world, other continents mostly have some sense of being positioned in a specific direction, for instance Latin America, Africa and Australia in the south, Asia as eastern or North America as a western frontier. There are of course European actors who see themselves as representing for instance the northern hemisphere, but it is striking how the symbols analysed here tend without hesitation to place Europe in the centre of their combined geopolitical and sociocultural universe. The Europa myth is the outstanding exception, but almost every later symbol tends to organise its worldview so as to distribute its others around its own hub. Europe thus remains the great One against all symbolic Others, the First region

of the human world, symbolically placed on top of the world. The Europa myth placed it in a dislocated position to the north and west of the world's centre, and this self-understanding has to some extent survived in the sense that Europe identifies itself as part of the global north and west: on top of the world rather than in its centre.

4.   The *resulting texture* of Europeanness is likewise repeatedly punctuated by *hybrid diversity*, even where efforts are made towards creating an integrated unity. The double-sided coins testify to this complexity that is also pointedly expressed by the motto. Some of its key aspects have already been discussed in relation to the desire of communication under the second point above, since there is an intrinsic dialectic between external and internal exchanges. An unresolved tension remains between diversity and equality. While the myth, motto and currency all have strong elements that support diversification and make plurality a main strength of Europe, the flag and several lesser symbols make a virtue of equality. This is no polarity, as equality may well be understood as a matter of equal value between those who are radically different, in spite of their difference. In fact, equality is a key value only for those who are strongly diversified, since between those who are from the beginning similar, mutual equality is no very significant goal. This dialectics is what the motto strives to express. In practice, however, it is not always that easy to deal with this balancing act, and the EU again and again tends to underestimate the importance of fully acknowledging its internal variety.

In conclusion

Symbols are hard to manage: they are unruly and always open to reinterpretion, for several reasons. On the one hand, that which they signify changes. In this case, Europe itself—as an idea and a community project—evolves: what it means today must therefore differ greatly from what it meant in the nineteenth century, before the final dissolution of the great colonial empires (the Ottoman as well as the European ones) and before the disastrous fascist rules. Another motor lies in the symbolic field itself, where signifiers can change meanings due to events that affect completely different phenomena that happen to use similar symbolic forms. Socialism has added a particular significance to the red colour, and the Nazis made it impossible to use swastikas as ordinary ornamental elements. The complex interrelations of all such transitions cannot be safely predicted, but result from evolving conflicts of interpretation. Symbols are therefore hard to use as tools for pre-defined goals. Their fate is the result of myriads of big and small acts of interpretation involving an unlimited number of actors and situations. Symbols are in this respect like a language. Precisely for that same reason, they are at the same time good for reading and understanding their times, just like with languages, artworks or lifestyles.

Standardised symbols can never by themselves constitute sufficient grounds for a shared civil society-based European identity of the kind that has been discussed as necessary to underpin the political, economic and institutional aspects of the EU. Such a collective identity project is emerging only slowly, perhaps too slowly, creating difficult tensions in the relations between citizens and the political establishment in Brussels. Jürgen Habermas, Dieter Grimm and others have repeatedly stressed that as a political community, Europe must express itself in the consciousness of its citizens in more ways than through the euro. They have stressed the role of media in shaping that public sphere that is the condition for democratic participation, as integral part of an intermediary area between parliaments and citizens, together with political parties, associations and social movements. Hitherto, this mediating process malfunctions in the EU, where such intermediary structures are to a great extent missing, though there are shifting views on the chances for such a Europeanised communication system to grow that could be the basis of a truly European political discourse, making the EU 'a sphere of publics' by letting national circuits of communication open up onto each other—united in diversity.[531] The modern European identity project has emerged from the bitter experience of not only great internal differences but also extreme violence. From this, Europeans claim to have gradually developed methods and institutions for dealing with conflicts by ritualising them, using them for social innovations in dialectical strategies for solving problems through acknowledging 'reasonable disagreements', in a history that has lead to increasingly abstract forms of 'solidarity between strangers'.[532]

The 2007 Lisbon Constitutional Treaty claims that European history has given rise to 'the universal values of the inviolable and inalienable rights of the human person, freedom, democracy, equality and the rule of law'; that the EU is 'founded on the values of respect for human dignity, freedom, democracy, equality, the rule of law and respect for human rights, including the rights of persons belonging to minorities', values that are 'common to the Member States in a society in which pluralism, non-discrimination, tolerance, justice, solidarity and equality between women and men prevail'; and that the union's aim is 'to promote peace, its values and the well-being of its peoples'.[533] This raises a series of questions that can only be answered by a critical examination of much more than only these symbols as such. One may on the one hand question the empirical and pragmatic truth of such declared values. Can Europe—and its union—in practice be said to live up to these values? If so, how are they operationalised in all policy domains? On the other hand, one may semantically ask whether these values are really expressed by prevailing representations of Europe. In what way do European symbols signify—or contradict—the dominant aims and ideas that are emphasised by official discourses?

Symbols alone are far from sufficient. Still, they do mean something. Flags, anthems, mottos and celebrations are used in rather specific places, but still have a certain effect on how people conceive of what Europe is about. European identifications emerge in everyday interactions among people, but are supported by specific public channels and symbols afforded official status. Each such symbol may in itself appear trifling, but in combination and context, they etch an image of what Europe is for its own politicians and citizens—and for those of other continents. The fact that the final chorus from Beethoven's Ninth—'Freude schöne Götterfunken' with its androcentric call for brotherhood and holy joy—is used as the musical Leitmotif of Europe does produce a meaning-effect, not necessarily as an immediate representation of what Europe is, but of how it wants to be. The European anthem has suppressed the original words of the theme, but their memory lingers on and resonates with the universal claims of uplifting human peace and solidarity, in the Schuman declaration and other EU texts. In this way, the chosen symbols cement Europe's self-assumed role as standard-bearer in the modern project of enlightenment, with its problematic as well as emancipatory sides. The symbols combine to keep alive the world wars memories as founding tales and myths of the EU. While erasing the colonial as well as the migration issues, they concentrate on the peace-loving praise of diversity and communication as the antidote to Europe's past guilt.

Two concluding reflections could be made.

First, there is a struggle going on over the identification of Europe and Europeanness. This means that there is yet no fully hegemonic identity construction, so that it is possible for oppositional voices to enter the ongoing negotiations with new symbols and new interpretations.

Second, there is a persistent ambivalence in how Europe is identified in all symbolic fields, and between the symbols analysed here. This tension is sometimes a hidden undercurrent opening for alternative readings, at other times an open tension or even clash between contrasting identifications. One may tentatively identify some dominant axes of tension and negotiation. One is the precarious combination of unity and diversity, with homogenous conformity on the one hand and on the other inner conflicts, fragmentation or even dissolution as threatening extreme cases. Another is stability versus mobility, with rigid stagnation and homeless alienation as dangers. Negative control and positive pleasure also need to be balanced in some way, in order to ensure justice, equality and efficiency as well as a sense of goal and direction, with uncreative boredom and sectarian Euro-fanaticism as the corresponding risks. New research is needed to refine contextualising interpretations of a wide set of circulating symbols, and to approach many different settings in which these symbols are made and used.

The Captain Euro comics and Černý's Entropa artwork represent two opposing extreme points, whereas most other current symbolisms are more ambiguous, reflecting a rather open situation where the identity—and boundaries—of Europe is yet far from permanently fixed. Neither Captain Euro nor Entropa covers what Europe means today. Both of them correspond to facets of Europeanness—the enclosed fortress on the one hand and the impossibly fragmented puzzle of discrete nation states on the other. But it is between them that the much more interesting symbols move and project contested and ambiguous identities: ambivalent and sometimes contradictory, dialectical or mediating identifications that continue to transform and challenge us who live (with and through) them.

There is not just one meaning of and for Europe. European identity is not fixed and not univocal. Instead, there are negotiations between various positions, full of inner tensions and ambivalences. Europe's identity is neither void nor totally arbitrary. Instead, historically and socially specific sets of meanings stretch out a field of polarities and polysemic interpretations and identifications. There is a struggle going on over the identification of Europeanness, a conflict of interpretations where different actors construct Europe differently, but with some emerging intersectional and intermedial patterns. Europe is an emergent, open and ambiguous project, which can neither be reduced to an ideological façade for the self-sufficient hegemony of a colonial superpower, nor to the celebration of values of peace, freedom and solidarity. Symbols are core nodes in the cultural field, whose role in constituting social identities and communities should not be underestimated. They are used in conflicts of interpretation to express a shifting balance between elevation and egality, unity and diversity, stability and mobility, and control and pleasure.

If I would, finally, make an effort to synthesise in one single formula the main identifying meaning the combination of all these symbols tend to construct for Europe, I would confirm the ideas of Europe as eccentric, decentred and translational: Europe is characterised by its *desire for elevating contacts with others*!

Notes

1. David Černý's website, www.davidcerny.cz/startEN.html (2010-10-18).

2. This analysis has gained from useful and inspiring feedback at various seminars, workshops and conferences, including the European Science Foundation ESF programme "Changing Media, Changing Europe" 2000-2004; the 6th "Crossroads in Cultural Studies" international conference at Bilgi University in Istanbul, Turkey 2006; the "Beyond Boundaries: Media, Culture and Identity in Europe" conference at Bahçeşehir University, Istanbul 2009; the "Nation, History, Media: Cultural Representations and Collective Identities" workshop at the Centre for Cultural Research CCR, University of Western Sydney UWS, Australia 2009; seminars of the Departments of Sociology and of Music at the University of Edinburgh 2010; the Communication seminar at the KTH Royal Institute of Technology in Stockholm 2009; a research workshop with media studies scholars from Karlstad, Malmö, Örebro and Södertörn Universities 2010; and the higher seminars of the Department of Culture Studies (Tema Q) at Linköping University and of the Department of Media and Communication Studies at Södertörn University—all these latter in Sweden. Many colleagues have offered valuable feedback, in particular Peter Aronsson at Linköping University. The basic ideas have further been enriched by research collaboration with European scholars including David Hesmondhalgh, Stephen Coleman and Giles Moss at the University of Leeds, UK; Mikko Lehtonen at the University of Tampere in Finland; Joke Hermes, Robert Adolfsson and Peter 't Lam at InHolland University in the Netherlands; Melanie Schiller at the University of Amsterdam; Süheyla Kırça Schroeder and Dieter Mersch at the University of Potsdam in Germany; Peter Csigo at Budapest University of Technology and Economics in Hungary; Maruša Pušnik at the University of Ljubljana in Slovenia; and Asli Telli Aydemir

at the Istanbul Bilgi University in Turkey. Limited parts of earlier text versions have been published in Fornäs (2007, 2008 and 2009). Maarten Vanden Eynde, Nicolas De Santis and other creators and copyright owners of images used in the book have generously provided both permissions and valuable information. The quality of publication has been enhanced by generous grants from the Sven and Dagmar Salén Foundation and the Publication Committee of Södertörn University. It has been great to collaborate with the wonderful publishing staff at Intellect Press, whose stylistic improvements transformed the manuscript into a real book. Finally, this book would never even had been written without the never failing encouragement of my most beloved companion, Hillevi Ganetz.

3.   William Shakespeare (1597): *Romeo and Juliet* (II, ii, 1-2).

4.   Lévi-Strauss (1962/2004) and Ricoeur (1975/1986) indicate some of the immense complexities involved in the symbolic, metaphoric and narrative practices of naming.

5.   See the entry 'Myth' in Williams (1976/1988: 210ff.), or the problem inventory in Cassirer (1925/1955).

6.   Ricoeur (1969/1974: 28–29); see also Armstrong (2005: 3–4).

7.   Lévi-Strauss (1949/1987, 1962/2004 and1978/2001).

8.   Armstrong (2005: 7).

9.   Ricoeur (1965/1970, Chapter 2).

10.   Barthes (1957/2000: 109ff.).

11.   Benjamin (1982/1999: 13; see also 388 and 884). Ricoeur (1965/1970) describes Marx, Freud and Nietzsche as three path-breaking masters of suspicion.

12.   Cassirer (1925/1955: 243ff.); Vernant (1965/2006).

13.   Ricoeur (1960/1969: 161–74).

14.   Stråth (2000: 20, 28).

15.   Though not mentioned by name, Europa was already present in Homer's *The Iliad* in the late ninth or the eighth century bc, where, in book 14, Zeus mentions his affair with the 'daughter of Phoenix', who bore him the sons Minos and Rhadamanthus. The following summary of the name and myth is compiled from Cotterell (1986: 157–8), Delanty (1995: 16–29), Passerini (2003) and the *Wikipedia* (entries 'Europa (mythology)' and 'Symbols of Europe').

16.   Wintle (2009: 105), whose chapter 3 provides a detailed overview of visual representations of Europe in the ancient world and her later uses in art and political cartoons.

17.   Europa is also the name of a daughter of Oceanys and Tethys, but this is the most widespread version.

18.   Cotterell (1986: 157).

19.   See for instance Hall (2003: 39ff.), Rice (2003), *NationMaster.com Encyclopedia* (www.nationmaster.com/encyclopedia/Placename-etymology: 'Europe'), *Online Etymology Dictionary* (www.etymonline.com: 'European') and *Wikipedia* ('Europa (mythology)') for references to such theories.

20.   Delanty (1995: 22). See also Delanty & Rumford (2005: 28ff.) and several elucidating chapters in Stråth (2000/2010) and Broberg et al. (2007).

21.   Delanty (1995: 16ff.).

22.   Delanty (1995: 27); see also Anderson (2009: 475ff.).

23.   Delanty (1995: 28, 47 and 82–3).

24.   'Europe in Bible Prophecy' (www.seekingtruth.co.uk/europe.htm, 2009-02-16).

25.   Delanty (1995: 114).

26.   Passerini (1999); compare also the stress on desire in Passerini (2000/2010).

27.   Rabier (2003: 71–4) offers some examples.

28.   Hall (2003: 39).

29.   Wintle (2009: 107).

30.   Rice (2003: 85).

31.   Rice (2003: 79) argues that 'the bull is properly to be seen as an archetype of power and domination', with sexuality in a secondary position.

32.   Passerini (2003: 30–1).

33.   Passerini (2003: 30) mentions that strikingly many artistic versions of the myth have been made by artists with non-European origin, which shows that it does not 'belong' solely to Europe, just like European identity is produced both from the inside and from the outside, in a continuous negotiation and sometimes conflict of interpretations.

34.   Rabier (2003: 68). Rice (2003: 81) sees the myth as 'implying the transfer of cultural apparatus from the east to the west'.

35.   Bernal (1991).

36.   Thomson (1949/1978: 124 and 376–7).

37.   Graves (1961: 173).

38.   Todorov (1982/1992: 109).

39.   Brague (1992/2002). Edgar Morin (1987/1990) is one among many others who have likewise described Europe as formed on the basis of deep divisions; see also Anderson (2009: 524ff.).

40.   Bauman (2004), referring to Lourenço (1991).

41.   Beck and Grande (2004), Beck (2006), Appiah (2006).

42.   Gilroy (1993).

43.   See for instance Cesarani and Fulbrook (1996), Delgado-Moreira (2000), Gowland et al. (2000/2006), Georgiou (2006), Meinhof and Triandafyllidou (2006) and Demossier (2007).

44.   Information on continent names derive from a wide range of standard encyclopaedias.

45.   Anderson (1983/1991); Hobsbawm (1983a).

46.   *Wikipedia*: 'National personification', http://en.wikipedia.org/wiki/National_personification (2010-10-20).

47.   Some more examples are presented by Burke (2000/2010: 116ff.).

48.   *Concise Oxford English Dictionary* (2006: 1077). Other sources suggest different life cycles, from a thousand years down to the three days from burning and resurrection that resonates with the death and resurrection of Christ in the *New Testament*.

49.   Heffernan (1998: 43).

50.   Phoenix Europe Express S.A. (www.phoenix-europe.fr, 2010-05-15).

51.   Horizon Phoenix Europe (horizonphoenixeurope.com, 2010-05-15); Phoenix Institute Europe (www.phoenixinstituteeurope.org, 2010-05-15).

52.   *Wikipedia*: 'Euro Gold and Silver Commemorative Coins (Belgium)' (en.wikipedia.org/wiki/Euro_gold_and_silver_commemorative_coins_%28Belgium%29#2005_coinage, 2010-05-10).

53.   The myth was in the late eighth century bc narrated in Hesiod's *Theogony* and *Works and Days*, and then in Aeschylus' fifth century bc drama *Prometheus Unbound*. Minor parts of the following analysis derive from Fornäs et al. (2007a: 11).

54.   For an analysis of Prometheus' strange mix of benevolent innocence and guilty hubris, see Ricoeur (1960/1969: 218ff.). Ricoeur (1955/2007: 85) also argues that in contrast to Greek ethics, 'Christianity does not condemn Prometheus and even recognizes in him the expression of a creative intention'.

55.   Shelley (1820/1930); Kant (1784/1997).

56.   Shelley (1820/1930: 41, 46).

57.   Examples include Brown (1992) and Bertilsson (1998).

58.   Landes (1969: 12).

59.   Landes (1969: 7).

60.   Shelley (1818/2001).

61.   Kant (1784/1997).

62.   *Wikipedia*: 'EUREKA Prometheus Project' (en.wikipedia.org/wiki/EUREKA_ Prometheus_Project, 2010-05-12).

63.   Prometheus Europe Ltd: 'Worldwide Brokers and Commerce Agents' (prom-europe.com, 2010-05-12).

64.   European Observatory on Health Systems and Policies: 'PROMeTHEUS— Health PROfessional Mobility in THe European Union Study' (www.euro.who. int/observatory/Studies/20090211_1, 2010-05-12).

65.   University of Tartu: 'Prometheus: European Union Studies' (www.ut.ee/192781, 2010-05-12).

66.   See for instance Tait (2001).

67.   Tait (2001) is one example on how the two have been juxtaposed.

68.   Spengler (1926–8).

69.   Hawkins (1920/1996: 262).

70.   Prometheus Asia (www.prometheus-asia.com, 2010-05-17).

71.   Bird and Sherwin (2006).

72.   Barthes (1957/2000).

73.   Barthes (1957/2000: 143).

74.   Hansen (2000) goes in this direction.

75.   Ricoeur (1960/1969: 19, 161, 237, 347ff.).

76.   Ricoeur (1960/1969: 162).

77.   *Captain Euro: Europe's Superhero* (www.captaineuro.com, 2009-04-20); see also *Wikipedia*: 'Captain Euro' (2009-04-20).

78.   The only reference to Central Europe is Helen's fondness for flamenco and waltz.

79. Ricoeur (1965/1970: 459ff.) analyses the dialectics between the archaeology and the teleology of the subject: between historical or developmental roots and tasks or projects.

80. HBO: *Carnivàle*, www.hbo.com/carnivale (2009-10-08).

81. De Santis, Nicolas: e-mail to the author 2011-04-12.

82. Glaister, Dan: 'Die, Europhobe Scum', *The Guardian*, 1999-04-06 (www.guardian. co.uk/business/1999/apr/06/emu.theeuro, 2009-04-20).

83. Aaron: 'Captain Euro to the Rescue!', *Free Will*, 2003-09-27 (www.freewillblog. com/index.php/weblog/comments/3626/, 2009-04-21).

84. Hannan, Daniel: 'Using Children to Sell the EU Message', *Telegraph.co.uk*, 2006-08-08 (www.telegraph.co.uk/comment/personal-view/3626882/Using-children-to-sell-the-EU-message.html, 2009-04-21).

85. Helen: 'Wham! Kerpow!', *EU Referendum*, 2007-12-28 (eureferendum.blogspot. com/2007/12/wham-kerpow.html, 2009-04-21).

86. A French example is the discussion initiated by Lottie, the Curse of Millhaven: 'Captain Euro, protège nous des tziganes et des financiers!', *fr.misc.finance*, 2008-08-08 (www.archivum.info/fr.misc.finance/2008-08/msg00280.html, 2009-04-21).

87. Lagerkvist (2005: 255).

88. Ricoeur (1960/1969: 14–15).

89. Peirce (1940/1955: 99).

90. The sub indexes $_{1,2}$, etc. will only be used sporadically below, in order to emphasise which symbol concept is being referred to.

91. Peirce (1940/1955: 102, 112).

92. Cassirer (1923/1955: 186); Langer (1942: 24).

93. Elias (1989: 369).

94. Mead (1934: 45–6).

95. Mead (1934: 146).

96. Segal (1957: 395–6).

97. Segal (1957: 397); Fornäs (1995: 146–7).

98. Wittgenstein (1953); Lorenzer (1971: 38–9).

99. Lorenzer (1986: 50).

100.   Lorenzer (1986: 60).

101.   Ricoeur (1975/1986: 319–20).

102.   Ricoeur (1976: 87).

103.   Ricoeur (1976: 58, 61 and 69).

104.   Ricoeur (1960/1969: 350).

105.   Ricoeur (1960/1969: 350).

106.   See Fornäs (1995: 154ff.; 1997) for further arguments in this direction.

107.   Peirce (1940/1955: 115).

108.   Geertz (1983: 118).

109.   Habermas (1981/1984).

110.   Stråth (2000/2010a: 15; 2000/2010b: 410ff.).

111.   Hall (1992).

112.   Ricoeur (1960/1969: 15).

113.   Ricoeur (1965/1970: 12).

114.   Ricoeur (1969/1974: 12–13).

115.   Ricoeur (1969/1974: 317).

116.   Fornäs (1995: 222ff.).

117.   Ricoeur (1990/1992: 116). This doubleness offers a welcome way out of the formal sterility of reducing identity only to sameness, as for instance in Stråth (2000/2010a: 13–14).

118.   Ricoeur (1991a: 33); see also Ricoeur (1991b).

119.   Ricoeur (1991a: 198).

120.   Ricoeur (1994: 130).

121.   Ricoeur (1990/1992: 297).

122.   Cohen (1985: 58).

123.   See for instance Young (1997), Yuval-Davis et al. (2006) and Wintle (2009: 6–7).

124.   Cohen (1985: 70).

125.   Cohen (1985: 12).

126.   Cohen (1985: 118).

127.   Anderson (1983/1991).

128.   Hall (1996: 4).

129.   Kristeva (1974/1984); Ricoeur (1990/1992).

130.   Malmborg & Stråth (2002: 5), see also Stråth (2000: 22ff.) on Europe as an incomplete construction process and Stråth (2000/2010: 14) on European identity as 'discursively shaped in a specific historical situation, [...] seen in the plural, always contested and contradictory'.

131.   For instance in Hall (1986/1996: 141–2), from where the following quotes derive.

132.   Cohen (1985: 21).

133.   Cohen (1985: 15, 20).

134.   Ortner (1973: 1339ff.).

135.   Ortner (1973: 1344).

136.   Ricoeur (1976: 64).

137.   Ricoeur (1965/1970: 504–3).

138.   Ricoeur (1976: 64).

139.   Lorenzer (1970: 93ff. and 1971: 40–1).

140.   Ricoeur (1976: 78).

141.   Ricoeur (1981: 193); see also Ricoeur (1969/1974).

142.   Ricoeur (2005: 137).

143.   Cohen (1985: 70).

144.   Cohen (1985: 117).

145.   Ricoeur (1955/2007: 278–9).

146.   Ricoeur (1955/2007: 280).

147.   Kaelble (2003); Lutz et al. (2006).

148.   Bruter (2003, 2004 and 2005).

149.   Shore (2000: 36).

150.   Shore (2000: 36).

151.   Delanty (1995); Habermas (2001).

152. Heffernan (1998: 233).

153. European Convention (2003: 3ff.). For a critical discussion of the EU constitution, see Eriksen et al. (2007).

154. European Convention (2003: 222). For further information on the EU and its symbols, see *European Navigator* (www.ena.lu), *The EU at a Glance* (europa. eu.int/abc) and *Wikipedia* (en.wikipedia.org/wiki/European_symbols).

155. On European citizenship, see Hansen (2000), Shore (2000), Bloomfield and Bianchini (2001), Ilczuk (2001), Roche (2001), Balibar (2004), Bruter (2004), Stevenson (2006) and Hintjens (2007). On Europe as identified by its oppositions to others, see Stråth (2000/2010), Levin (2007) and Gifford & Hauswedell (2010).

156. For general overviews and analyses of European history, politics, culture and identity, see also Nelson et al. (1992), García (1993), Tonra & Dunne (1996), Jacobs & Maier (1998), Mikkeli (1998), Jansen (1999), Andrews et al. (2000), Jönsson et al. (2000), Stråth (2000/2010), Sakwa & Stevens (2000/2006), Bussière et al. (2001), Cerutti & Rudolph (2001), Guerrina (2002), Meyer (2004), Karolewski & Kaina (2006), Sjursen (2006), Parker (2008) and Anderson (2009).

157. *Concise Oxford English Dictionary* (2006).

158. Wintle (2009: 7–8).

159. Heffernan (1998: 45).

160. Trausch (1999: 21).

161. Heffernan (1998: 9–10). Malmborg & Stråth (2002: 13ff.) also stress the role of religion in the interplay between national and European identifications.

162. Heffernan (1998: 11).

163. Heffernan (1998: 12–13, 17).

164. Hobsbawm (1990) offers a history of nations and nationalisms that however only in passing mentions European unification as a supranational threat (pp. 174–7) and has little to say about symbols except that religious icons 'represent the symbols and rituals or common collective practices which alone give a palpable reality to otherwise imagined community' (p. 71).

165. Much of the following builds on information and source material gathered by a web resource published with 'active support of the European Commission and the Luxembourg State' by Centre Virtuel de la Connaissance sur l'Europe (Virtual Resource Centre for Knowledge about Europe, CVCE), based at Château de Sanem in Luxembourg: *European Navigator* (www.ena.lu) (2009-02-19). This source will

often be used below, both as an archive of official EU-related documents and also as an informative source of documents that introduce and present key aspect of European unification.

166.   Heffernan (1998: 209–10).

167.   The main funding documents as well as summaries of the historical development are accessible through *European Navigator*, www.ena.lu (2009-02-19). For an overview over the development of the post-1945 European unification process and the role of pan-European movements, see also Delanty (1995), Heffernan (1998: 203ff.), Burgess (2000/2010) and Persson & Stråth (2007).

168.   This and the following quotes are from Robert Schuman (1950): 'The Schuman Declaration', reproduced in the *European Navigator*, www.ena.lu (2009-02-19).

169.   'Treaty constituting the European Coal and Steel Community', reproduced in the *European Navigator*, www.ena.lu (2009-02-19).

170.   On EU's tenacious colonial aspects, see Hansen (2000) and Tängerstad (2000/2010).

171.   This builds on documents and presentations published by *European Navigator*, www.ena.lu (2009-02-19).

172.   These will in later chapters be further analysed and compared to the EU symbols.

173.   EEC Foreign Ministers (1973): 'Document on The European Identity', reproduced by *European Navigator*, www.ena.lu (2009-02-19). See also Stråth (2000/2010b: 385ff.).

174.   EEC Foreign Ministers (1973): 'Document on The European Identity', reproduced by *European Navigator*, www.ena.lu (2009-02-19).

175.   The Lisbon Treaty can for instance be found at *European Navigator*(www.ena. lu).

176.   *Final Act*, Official Journal of the European Union, 2007 C 306-267, quoted from *Wikipedia*: 'Symbols of Europe' (en.wikipedia.org/wiki/European_symbols, 2009-02-16).

177.   Parliament committee draft recommendation quoted in 'MEPs legalise EU symbols through the backdoor', *EurActive.com* 2008-09-12 (www.euractiv.com/en/future-eu/meps-legalise-eu-symbols-backdoor/article-175323, 2009-02-16). See also Rickard Jozwiak: 'EU assembly embraces EU symbols', *European Voice.com* 2008-10-09 (www.europeanvoice.com/article/2008/10/eu-assembly-embraces-eu-symbols/62641.aspx, 2009-02-16); *Wikipedia*: 'Symbols of Europe' (en.wikipedia. org/wiki/European_symbols, 2009-02-16).

178. Miller (2008: 7–8).

179. *European Navigator* (www.ena.lu, 2009-02-19) credits Carlo Curti Gialdino, Professor of International Law in Rome and former Legal Secretary at the Court of Justice of the European Communities, for its sections on the symbols, and also republishes English translations of his book, Curti Gialdino (2005). For an overview over all EU symbols, see also Prisacariu (2007).

180. Anders Bruun Laursen: 'EU Wants Our Souls: Symbols of the Union to be Official', *Euro-Med DK* 2008-09-13 (euro-med.dk/?p=1718, 2009-02-16). Spelling mistakes have been corrected here.

181. Sam Leith: 'European Union symbols are a waste of time and public money', *Telegraph. co.uk* 2008-09-13, www.telegraph.co.uk/comment/columnists/samleith/3562125/ European-Union-symbols-are-a-waste-of-time-and-public-money.html (2009-09-25).

182. Kaelble (2003: 47ff. and 52ff.).

183. European Commission (2006). On European media policies as tools for developing a transnational public sphere, see also Bondebjerg & Golding (2004), Chalaby (2005), Williams (2005), Sarikakis (2007), Fossum & Schlesinger (2007) and Schlesinger (2008).

184. Wintle (2009: 11–12).

185. A larger and more comprehensive study would add considerably more materials, including interviews with individuals at both the top and bottom levels: producers, designers and politicians as well as citizens who encounter the symbols in everyday life. This task remains to be done.

186. Fornäs et al. (2007b: 130–44).

187. Ricoeur (1983/1984: 16); see also Ricoeur (1985/1988: 104ff. and 2000/2004: 131–2).

188. The literature is here too overwhelming to be summarised in a footnote, not least in social anthropology and studies of religion where a wide range of ritual theories have been developed.

189. Hobsbawm (1983a: 1).

190. Warring (2004: 10ff.).

191. Gillis (1994).

192. Hobsbawm (1983b: 265); see also Gillis (1994), Warring (2004) and Lindaräng (2007).

193. Johnston (1991: 69), Eriksen (1999: 16ff.), Lindaräng (2007: 37ff.).

194. Johnston (1991: x, 21ff., 63).

195. McCrone & McPherson (2009: xiii, also 212 and 220).

196. 'Europe Day', *European Navigator* (www.ena.lu).

197. The formulation is from the Schuman Declaration.

198. Some early proposers were Mrs Von Finckenstein and the President of the Pan-Europa Union, Count Coudenhove-Kalergi, who was a key lobbyist for adopting a full set of European symbols. See the overview in the 'Report by the Consultative Assembly of the Council of Europe on a European anthem' (10 June 1971; rapporteur: Mr Radius), accessible at *European Navigator* (www.ena.lu). The first quote is from Coudenhove-Kalergi's proposal in 1955, the following one from the 1971 report.

199. 'Report by the Consultative Assembly of the Council of Europe on a European anthem' (10 June 1971), reproduced by *European Navigator* (www.ena.lu).

200. Committee of Ministers meeting in Strasbourg, 7 May 1971, quoted in the 'Report by the Consultative Assembly of the Council of Europe on a European anthem' (10 June 1971), *European Navigator* (www.ena.lu).

201. The report and other relevant documents are accessible at *European Navigator* (www.ena.lu).

202. Curti Gialdino (2005: 178ff.), quoting a 2004 Monnet Working Paper by A. von Bogdandy.

203. Depoux' proposal is also published on the Internet (membres.lycos.fr/europ/, 2009-05-18).

204. *Wikipedia*: 'Symbols of Europe' (en.wikipedia.org/wiki/Symbols_of_Europe, 2009-05-28); similar formulations for instance also at Knowledgerush web community (knowledgerush.com/kr/encyclopedia/European_motto, 2009-05-28).

205. 'Europe Day', *European Navigator* (www.ena.lu).

206. 'Report by the Committee on a People's Europe submitted to the Milan European Council (Milan, 28 and 29 June 1985)', *European Navigator* (www.ena.lu).

207. This and the subsequent quotes in this paragraph are from a European Union information website presenting the EU symbols (europa.eu/abc/symbols/9-may/euday_en.htm, 2009-05-28).

208. EU symbols information website (europa.eu/abc/symbols/9-may/euday_en.htm, 2009-05-28).

209.   Johnston (1991: 36).

210.   Johnston (1991: 6, 19).

211.   Johnston (1991: 97–8).

212.   Johnston (1991: 100).

213.   Johnston (1991: 120–1).

214.   Geisler (2009: 10ff.); see also McCrone & McPherson (2009: 2–3).

215.   Billig (1995); Jensen (2002: 5).

216.   See *Wikipedia*: 'National Day' (en.wikipedia.org/wiki/National_Day, 2009-05-28).

217.   Warring (2004: 229); see also McCrone & McPherson (2009).

218.   *Wikipedia*: 'Australia Day' (en.wikipedia.org/wiki/Australia_Day, 2009-05-28).

219.   *Wikipedia*: 'Africa Day' (en.wikipedia.org/wiki/Africa_Day, 2009-05-28).

220.   EU symbols information website (europa.eu/abc/symbols/9-may/index_en.htm, 2009-05-28).

221.   This was proposed by the Consultative Assembly in 1962 and again by the Committee of Ministers in 1964; see 'Report by the Consultative Assembly of the Council of Europe on a European anthem' (10 June 1971), accessible at *European Navigator* (www.ena.lu).

222.   'Report by the Consultative Assembly of the Council of Europe on a European anthem' (10 June 1971), *European Navigator* (www.ena.lu).

223.   'Europe Day', *European Navigator* (www.ena.lu).

224.   'Probably very few people in Europe know that on 9 May 1950 the first move was made towards the creation of what is now known as the European Union', EU symbols information website (europa.eu/abc/symbols/9-may/euday_en.htm, 2009-05-28).

225.   Prisacariu (2007: 89–94).

226.   McCrone & McPherson (2009: 149).

227.   'Europe Day celebrations become a tradition in Ukraine, says premier', *Interfax-Ukraine*, 16 May 2009 (www.interfax.com.ua/eng/main/13933/, 2009-05-28).

228.   marky: 'Europe Day!', *European Lifestyle*, 9 May 2009 (www.european-lifestyle.net/magazine/?p=581, 2009-05-28).

229.   chris-eblana (Christos Mouzeviris): 'Europe's Day. 09/05/2009. My contribution to it', *Think about it*, 8 May 2009 (we.thinkaboutit.eu/profiles/blogs/europes-day-09052009-my, 2009-05-28).

230.   AriRusila: 'Europe Day Finnish way', *blogactiv.eu*, 10 May 2009 (arirusila.blogactiv.eu/2009/05/10/europe-day-finnish-way, 2009-05-28).

231.   'Marking Europe Day', *Monday Morning*, Issue 1899, 18 May 2009 (www.mmorning.com/ArticleC.asp?Article=6847&CategoryID=7, 2009-05-28).

232.   Kosmopolit (Andreas): 'Happy Europe Day!', *Kosmopolito: The Blog with the European perspective*, 9 May 2009 (www.kosmopolito.org/2008/05/09/happy-europe-day, 2009-05-28).

233.   Margot Wallström: 'The subtle pleasures of Europe Day', *The Local. Sweden's News in English*, 9 May 2009 (www.thelocal.se/19338/20090509/, 2009-05-28).

234.   The italicised words are written in English in the Swedish original. Bränteknuva is a tiny village with a funny name in south Sweden.

235.   This and the following quotes derive from georgd (2010-05-10): 'Weekly Report: Europe Day', *Oneworld Platform for Southeast Europe*, oneworldsee.org/Weekly-Report-Europe-Day (2010-10-27).

236.   georgd (2010-05-10): 'Weekly Report: Europe Day', *Oneworld Platform for Southeast Europe*, oneworldsee.org/Weekly-Report-Europe-Day (2010-10-27).

237.   Curti Gialdino (2005, note 8).

238.   Curti Gialdino (2005: 130ff.).

239.   See for instance *European Navigator* (www.ena.lu) and Curti Gialdino (2005: 130ff.).

240.   Toggenburg (2004: 2ff.).

241.   Delanty & Rumford (2005: 61ff.).

242.   Delanty & Rumford (2005: 64).

243.   Delanty & Rumford (2005: 65–6).

244.   Delanty & Rumford (2005: 68).

245.   Heffernan (1998: 220).

246.   *European Navigator* (www.ena.lu).

247.   *Wikipedia*: 'E pluribus unum' (en.wikipedia.org/wiki/E_pluribus_unum, 2009-09-29).

248. Curti Gialdino (2005: 131–2).

249. Kirshenblatt-Gimblett (1992).

250. Toggenburg (2004: 6).

251. Iclsleicester: 'EU relevant toBritain?' 2008-03-29, iclsleicester.wordpress. com/2008/03/29/eu-relevant-to-britain/ (2009-09-25).

252. Sam Leith: 'European Union symbols are a waste of time and public money', *Telegraph. co.uk* 2008-09-13, www.telegraph.co.uk/comment/columnists/samleith/3562125/ European-Union-symbols-are-a-waste-of-time-and-public-money.html (2009-09-25).

253. WSP Group website, www.wspgroup.com/en/WSP-Group (2010-08-28).

254. WSP Group (2010): *WSP at a Glance*, www.wspgroup.com/en/WSP-Group (2010-08-28).

255. Glocalisation has been theorised by Roland Robertson (1995).

256. Balibar (2004: 235).

257. This and the following derives from a wide range of sources, including the following: *Encyclopedia Britannica*: 'Flag' (www.britannica.com/EBchecked/ topic/209225/flag, 2009-09-28); *Nationalencyklopedin*: 'Flagga' (www.ne.se/lang/ flagga, 2009-09-28); *Wikipedia*: 'Flag' (www.wikipedia.org/wiki/Flag, 2009-09-28); the Flags of the World website www.allstates-flag.com/fotw/flags (2010-08-24); Elgenius (2007) and Eriksen & Jenkins (2007). A forthcoming overview is provided in Elgenius (2011).

258. Elgenius (2007), Prisacariu (2007: 57).

259. Billig (1995).

260. Eriksen (2007: 4–5).

261. *European Navigator* (www.ena.lu).

262. This memorandum and other relevant sources are published by *European Navigator* (www.ena.lu).

263. For summaries of the flag's history, see *European Navigator* (www.ena.lu), Curti Gialdino (2005: 80–5), Hersant (2003: 100ff.), Larcher (1995) and various articles in *Wikipedia* and other dictionaries.

264. Wintle (2009) offers a range of examples of how the flag design and other European imagery have been used, both in the official EU contexts and in alternative or critical practices such as political cartoons.

265.   Quotes from *The EU at a Glance*: 'The European Flag', europa.eu/abc/symbols/emblem/index_en.htm (2009-09-30).

266.   Wintle (2009: 439).

267.   *European Navigator*: 'The Flag of the European Union' (www.ena.lu, 2009-09-28).

268.   Pastoureau (2001).

269.   *Color Wheel Pro*: 'Color Meaning' (www.color-wheel-pro.com/color-meaning.html, 2009-09-30).

270.   Hersant (2003: 101–2).

271.   *European Navigator*: 'The Flag of the European Union' (www.ena.lu, 2009-09-28).

272.   *European Navigator*: 'The Flag of the European Union' (www.ena.lu, 2009-09-28).

273.   *European Navigator*: 'The Flag of the European Union' (www.ena.lu, 2009-09-28).

274.   *European Navigator*: 'The Flag of the European Union' (www.ena.lu, 2009-09-28).

275.   Hersant (2003: 103).

276.   Curti Gialdino (2005: 82ff.).

277.   *Wikipedia*: 'Flag of the United States' and 'Betsy Ross flag' (en.wikipedia.org/wiki/Flag_of_the_United_States; en.wikipedia.org/wiki/Betsy_Ross_flag; 2009-11-16).

278.   *End Times & Bible Prophecy*: 'Europe in Bible Prophecy' (www.seekingtruth.co.uk/europe.htm, 2009-09-29); the quote is from *Revelation* 12:1 in the *Bible*.

279.   *European Navigator*: 'The Flag of the European Union' (www.ena.lu, 2009-09-28).

280.   Kristeva (1974/1984).

281.   Hersant (2003: 104).

282.   *European Navigator*: 'The Flag of the European Union' (www.ena.lu, 2009-09-28).

283.   Vernant (1965/2006).

284.   Vernant (1965/2006: 206–11, 213–59).

285.   Vernant (1965/2006: 238).

286.   Larcher (1995: 4).

287.   Association for Asian Research AFAR (2006): 'Brief Introduction to Chinese Culture: Colors in Traditional Chinese Culture' (www.asianresearch.org/articles/2930.html, 2009-10-12).

288.   African Union website: 'AU Symbols & Anthem', www.africa-union.org/root/au/AboutAU/AUSymbols/ausymbols.htm (2010-08-13); *Wikipedia*: 'Flag of the African Union' (2009-09-28). See also for comparison Srirupa Roy (2006) on the development of the Indian flag.

289.   The new AU flag was the outcome of a competition open to all African citizens, including those in the diaspora; 106 received entries were evaluated by an expert panel chosen by the AU Commission (African Union: 'A New Flag for the African Union', Press release N024/2010, 31-01-2010, Addis Abeba: African Union).

290.   The latter was a reinterpretation offered in 1929 by Mohandas Gandhi, in an effort to escape the trappings of religious divisions, when Sikhs asked for their black colour to also be included (Roy, 2006: 501–6).

291.   Hernant (2003: 101).

292.   Published by *European Navigator* (www.ena.lu).

293.   Hersant (2003: 100); *European Navigator*; *Wikipedia*: 'Federalist flag'.

294.   The following overview builds on a wide range of publicly available sources, including *European Navigator* and standard encyclopaedic sources, of which only a selection will be referenced here.

295.   Website of the Central Commission for Navigation on the Rhine, www.ccr-zkr.org (2009-10-08); *Wikipedia*: 'Central Commission for Navigation on the Rhine', en.wikipedia.org/wiki/Central_Commission_for_Navigation_on_the_Rhine (2009-10-08).

296.   *Wikipedia*: 'European Coal and Steel Community', en.wikipedia.org/wiki/European_Coal_and_Steel_Community; and 'Flag of the European Coal and Steel Community', en.wikipedia.org/wiki/Flag_of_the_European_Coal_and_Steel_Community (2009-10-08).

297.   Website of the Western European Union WEU, www.weu.int; *Wikipedia*: 'Western European Union', en.wikipedia.org/wiki/Western_European_Union; and 'Flag of the Western European Union', en.wikipedia.org/wiki/Flag_of_the_Western_European_Union (2009-10-09).

298.   *Wikipedia*: 'Presidency of the Council of the European Union', en.wikipedia.org/wiki/Presidency_of_the_Council_of_the_European_Union (2009-09-25).

299.   Website of the European Broadcasting Union EBU, www.ebu.ch (2009-10-12); *Wikipedia*: 'European Broadcasting Union', en.wikipedia.org/wiki/European_Broadcasting_Union (2009-10-12). For a critical discussion, see Bourdon (2007).

300.   The information about the consecutive EBU logos derives from the EBU archives in Switzerland and has kindly been provided by Avril Mehon-Roberts at the EBU in Geneva.

301.   This interpretation is quoted in an e-mail from Avril Mehon-Roberts at the EBU office (2009-11-16).

302.   King (2004: 325).

303.   Website of the Union of European Football Associations UEFA, www.uefa.com (2009-10-12); *Wikipedia*: 'UEFA', en.wikipedia.org/wiki/Uefa (2009-10-12). For historical perspectives on the shifting relation of football to European identity, see Crolley & Hand (2006).

304.   King (2004: 333).

305.   The logo was after a competition designed by the London-based firm Design Bridge. See King (2004) for a fascinating and detailed analysis.

306.   King (2004: 327–8).

307.   King (2004: 329).

308.   King (2004: 331).

309.   King (2004: 334).

310.   King (2004: 334).

311.   King (2004: 334).

312.   King (2004: 335).

313.   King (2004: 335).

314.   King (2004: 335).

315.   Website of OMA, www.oma.eu (2009-10-12).

316.   *EU barcode*, www.oma.eu/index.php?option=com_projects&view=project&id=282&Itemid=10 (2009-10-12). See also the CRW Flags website www.crwflags.com/FOTW/flags/eu!cha.html (2010-04-30).

317.   Only 1512 voted, see BBC News 2002-05-08: 'Down with EU stars, run up stripes' (news.bbc.co.uk/2/hi/europe/1974721.stm, 2010-04-30). The single positive voice came from a Greek man; the negative ones were from France, Germany

and the United Kingdom.

318. Tom W. Bell: 'EU "Barcode" Flag Parody', 2002-05-10 (www.tomwbell.com/graphics/FlagParody.html, 2010-04-30).

319. *Picobelleuropa*, www.picobelleuropa.nl (2009-10-09); www.picobelleuropa.nl/uk_eurovlag.htm (2010-04-30).

320. The quote is from Maarten Vanden Eynde's website www.enoughroomforspace.org/projects/view/12; additional information in personal e-mail to the author (2011-01-25).

321. FOTW Flags of the World website: 'Gay European flags', flagspot.net/flags/eu_gay.html (2010-08-09).

322. All these variants are presented—in the edited versions shown here—at the FOTW Flags of the World website: 'European Union: Protest flags', flagspot.net/flags/eu%7Dant.html, and 'The European Union flag in cartoons', flagspot.net/flags/eu!cart.html (2010-08-09).

323. Kaelberer (2004: 177).

324. Anders Bruun Laursen: 'EU Wants Our Souls: Symbols of the Union to Be Official', *Euro-Med DK* 2008-09-13 (euro-med.dk/?p=1718, 2009-02-16).

325. Larcher (1995: 10–11).

326. Prisacariu (2007: 61–4).

327. *Spectrezine*: 'Alternative logo to mark 50 years of EU chosen', www.spectrezine.org/content/alternative-logo-mark-50-years-eu-chosen (2010-09-18).

328. European Story: 'What Story Should Europe Tell?' (europeanstory.net/forum/comments.php?DiscussionID=39, 2010-03-23).

329. Langer (1942: 78ff.); Lorenzer (1970, 1986); Kristeva (1974/1984).

330. *Concise Oxford English Dictionary* (2006: 55).

331. Martin (1995: 275).

332. Malcolm Boyd: 'National Anthems', hemingways-studio.org/dictionary/Entries/S19602.htm (2010-06-09); see also his entry on 'National Anthems' in *The New Grove Dictionary of Music and Musicians*, 2nd ed., vol. 17, New York: Grove's Dictionaries, 2001: 655. See also Maugendre (1996) and Bristow & Martin (2006), and for a montage of European anthems, listen to FuggedabouditNL: 'European Anthems' at YouTube, www.youtube.com/watch?v=uDoAr8VHLDI (2010-06-17).

333. Daughtry (2003: 44); see also Schiller (2009: 32). On music and local or national identity, see alsoConnell & Gibson (2003) andBiddle & Knights (2007).

334. The following summarises a wide range of literature on music and identity. See Fornäs et al. (1988/1995), Middleton (2006) and Tagg (2009).

335. Langer (1942).

336. See Fornäs et al. (1988/1995: 210–28) but also Rosolato (1974), Feder et al. (1990), Salomonsson (1991) and Middleton (2006).

337. Derrida (1967/1976).

338. Fornäs (1997 and 2003).

339. Anderson (1983/1991: 145); see also Daughtry (2003: 45).

340. Jensen (2002: 5).

341. *The EU at a Glance*: 'The European Anthem' (europa.eu/abc/symbols/anthem/index_en.htm, 2010-03-22).

342. No other source specified, this historical overview is based on Curti Gialdino (2005), Larcher (1995) and René Radius: 'Explanatory Note', *Report by the Consultative Assembly of the Council of Europe on a European Anthem* (10 June 1971), *European Navigator* (www.ena.lu).

343. Buch (2003: 89).

344. Curti Gialdino (2005).

345. Curti Gialdino (2005); see also *Wikipedia*: 'A Clockwork Orange', en.wikipedia.org/wiki/A_Clockwork_Orange_(film) (2010-03-24).

346. René Radius: 'Explanatory Note', *Report by the Consultative Assembly of the Council of Europe on a European anthem* (10 June 1971),*European Navigator*(www.ena.lu).

347. *Report by the Consultative Assembly of the Council of Europe on a European Anthem* (10 June 1971), *European Navigator* (www.ena.lu).

348. René Radius: "Explanatory Note", *Report by the Consultative Assembly of the Council of Europe on a European Anthem* (10 June 1971), *European Navigator* (www.ena.lu).

349. Curti Gialdino (2005).

350. Council of Europe: 'Flag, anthem and logo: the Council of Europe's symbols', www.coe.int/T/E/Com/About_Coe/emblems/emblemes.asp (2009-09-25).

351. *Wikipedia*: 'Symbols of Europe', en.wikipedia.org/wiki/Symbols_of_Europe

(2009-09-25).

352. Curti Gialdino (2005).

353. The Adonnino Committee second report to the European Council (1985), republished by the *European Navigator* (www.ena.lu).

354. Curti Gialdino (2005).

355. Cook (1993); Curti Gialdino (2005).

356. Buch (2003: 96; my translation).

357. All quotes in this paragraph are from the *European Navigator* (www.ena.lu).

358. *European Navigator* (www.ena.lu).

359. Larcher (1995: 13) and most of the official EU web sources.

360. This is seen in all the documents from the process of establishing the European anthem, as well as for instance in Curti Gialdino (2005) and Prisacariu (2007: 72–3).

361. Pettersson (2004) points at the centrality of Beethoven's persona for the nineteenth and twentieth century establishment of a male European art music canon.

362. Delanty (1995: 128).

363. Rolland (1903/2009: 42).

364. Cook (2003: 92ff.); see also Mayer (1978: 54ff.) and Nielsen (1978: 224).

365. Nielsen (1978: 233).

366. McClary (1991: 128, 129).

367. Márothy (1974: 552–3).

368. Márothy (1974: 68). On the musical links from the 'Ode to Joy' to the French revolution, see also Knepler (1961/1975: 582ff.) and Nielsen (1978: 224).

369. Márothy (1974: 63–4).

370. Among Beethoven's followers as composers of choral symphonies were Héctor Berlioz, Felix Mendelssohn, Franz Liszt, Gustav Mahler, Ralph Vaughan Williams, Sergei Rachmaninov, Igor Stravinsky, Dmitri Shostakovich and Benjamin Britten.

371. This paragraph builds on Solomon (1977/1980: 434), Nielsen (1978: 228) and Cook (1993: 106).

372. Buch (2003: 91).

373.   Cook (1993: 34).

374.   The (unknown) English translation is one of the oldest and most commonly used, but there are numerous others as well.

375.   The word has opaque origins, and may either refer to being struck by Zeus'/ Jupiter's lightning, or to an Egypt word that denotes the happy 'reeds' land of the resting dead; see *Wikipedia*: 'Elysium', en.wikipedia.org/wiki/Elysium (2010-06-02).

376.   Cook (1993: 37).

377.   Cook (1993: 37).

378.   Cook (1993: 37).

379.   Rolland (1903/2009: 44–5).

380.   Cook (1993: 89, 90).

381.   Cook (1993: 92).

382.   Cook (1993: 92–3).

383.   Cook (1993: 93).

384.   Cook (1993: 94ff.).

385.   Cook (1993: 98).

386.   Cook (1993: 99).

387.   Cook (1993: 101).

388.   Cook (1993: 103–4).

389.   Cook (1993: 104).

390.   Cook (1993: 105).

391.   Riezler (1951: 246–7; my translation).

392.   Quotes are from Žižek (2006); similar formulations are also found in Žižek (2007 and 2007a). See also Bohlman (2004: 30–3).

393.   Žižek (2007a).

394.   Žižek (2007).

395.   Cook (1993); Žižek (2006).

396.   The Council of Europe website at www.coe.int/t/dc/av/hymne_EN.asp (2010-05-05).

397. Council of Europe: 'Flag, anthem and logo: the Council of Europe's symbols', www.coe.int/T/E/Com/About_Coe/emblems/emblemes.asp (2009-09-25).

398. Cook (1993: 34). The concise anthem version is available at many EU sources, including the Delegation of the EU website, www.delidn.ec.europa.eu/en/eu_guide/eu_guide_4.htm (2010-05-05). A very simple electronic piano version also circulates on many websites, including the *Wikipedia*.

399. Recorded examples as well as lyrics and other relevant documents are published by the Center for History and New Media of George Mason University in Fairfax, VA, at the *Liberty, Equality, Fraternity: Exploring the French Revolution* website, chnm.gmu.edu/revolution/browse/songs/# (2010-05-27).

400. Malcolm Boyd: 'National Anthems', hemingways-studio.org/dictionary/Entries/S19602.htm (2010-06-09).

401. Council of Europe website at www.coe.int/t/dc/av/hymne_EN.asp (2010-05-05).

402. This version can be downloaded from *The EU at a Glance*: 'The European Anthem' (europa.eu/abc/symbols/anthem/index_en.htm, 2010-03-22) and at *European Navigator* (www.ena.lu).

403. Karajan's own 1962 recording lets the ode move around 140 bpm, while for instance Fritz Busch in 1950 even went up to 150–160 bpm.

404. European Travel Network: *EuropeanAnthem.eu* (www.etntalk.com/european_anthem, 2010-05-31).

405. Buch (2003: 95).

406. Buch (2003: 95).

407. See for instance Knepler (1961/1975: 582ff.) and almost all other analyses.

408. *The EU at a Glance*: 'The European Anthem' (europa.eu/abc/symbols/anthem/index_en.htm, 2010-03-22).

409. Buch (2003: 93–4).

410. Buch (2003: 93).

411. Buch (2003: 96–7).

412. Buch (2003: 95).

413. Hall (1992).

414. A similar situation occurred in Russia after the dissolution of the Soviet Union, when first a melody composed by Mikhail Glinka was adopted without lyrics,

which made many ask for words in order for instance for sports teams to have 'a "proper anthem" to sing at matches' (Daughtry 2003: 51).

415. Buch (2003: 92; my translations).

416. Buch (2003: 96; my translation).

417. 'Karaoke' is a Japanese invention, literally meaning 'empty orchestra' or pre-recorded tunes with song to be filled in by users themselves (Fornäs 1994 and 1998).

418. Buch (2003: 96 and 97–8; my translations).

419. Buch (2003: 97–8).

420. Buch (2003: 97; my translations).

421. Miller (2008: 8).

422. Andrew Pierce: 'Should Europe have its own anthem?', *Telegraph.co.uk*, 2009-11-16 (www.telegraph.co.uk/news/worldnews/europe/eu/6582221/Should-Europe-have-its-own-national-anthem.html, 2010-05-31). Compare Daughtry (2003) on the intense debates on the post-1989 Russian national anthem.

423. European Story: 'What Story Should Europe Tell?', europeanstory.net/forum/comments.php?DiscussionID=39 (2010-03-23).

424. African Union website: 'New AU Anthem', www.africa-union.org/AU symbols/ausymblos.htm (2010-08-13); *Wikipedia*: 'African Union', en.wikipedia.org/wiki/African_Union#Symbols (2010-08-13). One of the closest competitors was Chief Charles O. Okereke's 'God Bless Africa', sounding as a mixture of the British anthem and a solemn Christian hymn, and also talking of Africa as 'our family', united on its way away from slavery, colonialism and diseases (www.africamasterweb.com/AuAnthem.html, 2010-08-13).

425. *European Navigator*: 'The Proceedings of the Hague Congress' (www.ena.lu); sheet music with complete lyrics in Dutch, English, French and Italian electronically available as open access (www.geheugenvannederland.nl/?/nl/items/TIN01:NOI26).

426. Aylesbury Choral Society: 'Coronation Anthems', programme notes, www.choirs.org.uk/prognotes/Handel Coronation Anthems.htm (2010-06-16).

427. King (2004: 324); *Wikipedia*: 'UEFA Champions League Anthem', en.wikipedia.org/wiki/UEFA_anthem (2010-06-15); see also *Wikipedia*: 'Symbols of Europe', en.wikipedia.org/wiki/Symbols_of_Europe (2009-09-25).

428. King (2004: 330).

429. King (2004: 331).

430. King (2004: 333).

431. Curti Gialdino (2005); *Wikipedia*: 'Te Deum (Charpentier)', en.wikipedia.org/wiki/Te_Deum_%28Charpentier%29 (2010-06-14); see also *Wikipedia*: 'European Broadcasting Union', en.wikipedia.org/wiki/Ebu (2010-06-15) and *Wikipedia*: 'Symbols of Europe', en.wikipedia.org/wiki/Symbols_of_Europe (2009-09-25).

432. Compare for instance the comments listed at 94David's YouTube site: 'Charpentier—Te Deum', www.youtube.com/watch?v=mTaRVUIZXy8 (2010-06-14) with those at bursty13: 'La Marseillaise, French National Anthem', www.youtube.com/watch?v=4K1q9Ntcr5g (2010-06-14).

433. Steven Plank (2006): 'Charpentier: Te Deum and Grand Office des Morts', *Opera Today*, 17 May 2006, www.operatoday.com/content/2006/05/charpentier_te_.php (2010-06-16).

434. On the ESC, see Planeta (2005), Wolther (2006), Raykoff & Tobin (2007), Bohlman (2008) and the ESC homepage at www.eurovision.tv. All song lyrics and other information can easily be found on the Internet.

435. Translation from the *Lyrics Translations* website, lyricstranslations.com/eurovision-lyrics/toto-cutugno-insieme-1992 (2010-06-17).

436. Translation by Martin Maillot and Carlos Martinez from *The Diggiloo Thrush* website, www.diggiloo.net/?1993it (2010-06-14).

437. HCN 2007-06-10 and StephenDaedalus 2008-01-02 on *Song Meanings*: 'Europe Endless Lyrics', www.songmeanings.net/songs/view/123303 (2010-10-15).

438. Signature thebodiesobtained 2008-04-30 on *Song Meanings*: 'Sister Europe Lyrics', www.songmeanings.net/songs/view/ 3530822107858570248 (2010-10-15).

439. *Song Meanings*: 'Radio Free Europe Lyrics', www.songmeanings.net/songs/view/ 43916 (2010-10-15).

440. Europe's website: 'Joey Tempest', finalcountdown.freehostia.com/member_joey.htm (2010-10-15).

441. *Globus* website, www.globusmusic.com (2010-06-18).

442. Uwakimono's YouTube clip 'Globus—Europa', www.youtube.com/comment_servlet?all_comments=1&v=Fc56moy0poA (2010-06-18; all spelling mistakes in the original).

443. McClary (1991: 130).

444. Kaelberer (2004: 162) states that 'the euro is certainly the most important symbol of European integration and identity beyond the individual EU member states to date'.

445.   'Money' and 'Currency', *Online Etymology Dictionary* (www.etymonline.com, 2010-08-17). For the history and meaning of money in general, see Simmel (1896/1991 and 1900/1989), Withers (1909/1947), Zelizer (1994/1997), Buchan (1997), Rowe (1997), Smithin (2000), Ferguson (2001) and Johansen (2001).

446.   Marx (1867/2001 and 1939/1993).

447.   Sohn-Rethel (1970/1973), Müller (1977).

448.   OECD (2002).

449.   Marx (1867/2001), Simmel (1900/1989: 714ff.), Shanahan (2003: 162f and 176), Waswo (2003: 156), Kaelberer (2004: 167–8).

450.   Simmel (1900/1989: 708 and 714ff.).

451.   Quotes are from Shanahan (2003: 166–7). See also Heinemann (1969) and Zelizer (1994/1997) on the social functions of money, and Shanahan (2003: 162–3 and 178), Servet (2003: 132 and 136), and Kaelberer (2004: 162 and 171) on the links between money, identity and social relations of trust.

452.   'Understanding money is a matter of understanding ourselves', writes Rowe (1997: xxiii), without bothering to waste words on what coins and banknotes actually look like, and the same goes for Withers (1909/1947) and Buchan (1997). An exception is Hörisch (1996), who is acutely aware of the materiality of money. Zei (1995) interprets maps, Tito portraits, heraldic symbols, flags, stamps and currencies as representations of the nation state in Slovenia before and after the dissolution of the Yugoslavian federation.

453.   Benjamin (1955/1997). See also Hörisch (2001: 190ff.).

454.   Hymans (2004: 7).

455.   In the preface to Brion & Moreau (2001), the Belgian Minister of Finance Didier Reynders states that the banknote fulfils a double role of symbol: for the sum it represents, 'but also for the economic and political states of the nations'. Pierre Bourdieu's theory of economic, social, symbolic and cultural capital likewise notes their complex interrelations (see for instance Bourdieu 1993: 29ff.). 'The purely economic cannot express itself autonomously but must be converted into symbolic form' (Swartz 1997: 90).

456.   An expert report on the future of money leaves the impression that traditional cash will for a long time remain side by side with electronic, digital money forms (OECD, 2002). A possible future global currency—a 'geo'—will probably also become embodied in tangible, visible and interpretable shapes. According to Brion & Moreau (2001: 120), the role of banknotes 'has been remarkably stable', even in spite of the growth of e-money. Johansen (2001: 331, 338, 349ff.) mentions

that cash is the only 'forced' form of payment in Norway, where a specific law paragraph states that state coins and banknotes must always be valid means of payment. While cash payments actually increased in the 1990s, he still regards banknotes as degenerating and declining.

457.   Mead (1934: 292).

458.   See for instance Thyssen (1991) on Parsons', Luhmann's and Habermas' theories of the symbolic generalised media of money, power and love.

459.   Kaelberer (2004: 176).

460.   Habermas (1981/1987).

461.   Beck (1986/1992).

462.   All quotes from Kaelberer (2004: 162; see also 172ff. and 177–8).

463.   Hymans (2004: 24).

464.   Tönnies (1887/1988).

465.   Billig (1995: 41) includes coins and banknotes with flags as normally unnoticed symbols of modern national states, forming an everyday 'banal nationalism' that is naturalised and hidden away so that the label of 'nationalism' can be projected only onto 'others'. See also Risse (1998) and Passerini (2003) on symbolic constructions of European identity. The concept of 'in-time' culture derives from Jensen (2002: 5).

466.   OECD (2002), Kaelberer (2004: 68), Prisacariu (2007: 85).

467.   'The currency of the European Union', *European Navigator* (www.ena.lu).

468.   Earlier versions of the euro analysis have been published in Fornäs (2007 and 2008).

469.   On aspects of power and economy in the history of the EMU and other international money regimes, see Ferguson (2001: 332ff.).Ludes (2002) discusses the social meaning of money and describes the media debates on the launching of the euro in various countries, with a rich material attached on a dvd/cd-rom, but no interpretation of visual designs. Brion & Moreau (2001: 119ff.) has information and images of all euro and immediate pre-euro banknotes.See also Kaelberer (2004).Facts on the euro designs and launching process derive from the European Monetary Institute: 'Selection and further development of the Euro banknote designs' (www.ecb.int/emi/press/press05d.htm); the German Bundesfinanzministerium's website (www.bundesfinanzministerium.de/); the ECB website (www.euro.ecb.int/en/section.html); Burak Bensin: 'Euro Money!' (www.angelfire.com/on/fifa/).

470. Curti Gialdino (2005) and Shore (2000) outline the birth of the euro. When explanations of the designs are quoted here without naming any source, they are standardised formulations that may be found in a wide range of official EU websites and publications.

471. Brion & Moreau (2001: 117 and 120).

472. The banknote designs contain the number corresponding to the value of the note in question, the name of the currency in the Latin (EURO) and Greek alphabet, the initials of the European Central Bank in the five linguistic variants (BCE, ECB, EZB, EKT and EKP) covering the eleven official EU languages, and the signature of the President of that bank. The letters in front of the serial numbers on the euro banknotes indicate in which country they are printed: L = Finland, M = Portugal, N = Austria, P = The Netherlands, R = Luxembourg, S = Italy, T = Ireland, U = France, V = Spain, Y = Greece, X = Germany, Z = Belgium.

473. French Guiana, Guadeloupe, Martinique, Réunion, the Azores and the Canary Islands are thus represented on the map. Mayotte, Saint-Pierre and Miquelon also use the euro but are regarded too small to figure on the notes, and the French Southern and Antarctic Territories have also been excluded from visualisation.

474. This information derives from *Wikipedia*: 'Euro Coins', en.wikipedia.org/wiki/Euro_coins (2010-09-15), but is also found on many other websites, including those of the EU itself.

475. Hörisch (1996: 13ff.) notes the ambivalence or double face of money as 'heads and tails': one side with some portrait of a legitimizing sovereign (*Kopf*, head) and the other specifying the monetary value (*Zahl*, number). He goes on to present a fascinating analysis of the relation between money and poetry (economy and literature, numbers and letters).

476. Kaelberer (2004: 168).

477. Wintle (2009: 442).

478. Zei (1995: 337–8).

479. Kaelberer (2004: 170).

480. Shore (2000: 115).

481. Shore (2000: 112).

482. 'The Currency of the European Union', *European Navigator*, www.ena.lu (2009-02-19).

483. Shanahan (2003: 172).

Notes

484. Simmel (1909/1994: 10, see also 5); Bachelard (1958/1994: 222–3). See also Arnold van Gennep (1909/1960), Walter Benjamin (1982/1999: 494, 836) and Victor Turner (1969).

485. 'The Currency of the European Union', *European Navigator*, www.ena.lu (2009-02-19).

486. Quoted from Delanty (1995: 129). Brion & Moreau (2001: 119) likewise state that the choice of architectural styles of Europe as banknote design theme 'made it possible to evoke the cultural heritage common to all the Union's member states, thereby fulfilling one of the dreams of Robert Schuman, who had longed to base a European Union on cultural foundations'.

487. Brion & Moreau (2001: 120) note that while national symbols were often found on coins, only Finland, Austria and Germany have previously included any national emblem on their own banknotes.

488. Shore (2000: 87ff.).

489. Shanahan (2003: 173–4), Kaelberer (2004: 172).

490. A more detailed analysis is presented in Fornäs (2007).

491. According to Brion & Moreau (2001: 51), Belgium has like Spain and Italy favoured artists rather than other professions on their banknotes. In 2003, Belgium released 10€ silver coins (costing 31€ each), only valid in Belgium, to celebrate Georges Simenon, author of the Maigret detective novels. Early 2004, similar coins were launched to honour Hergé's comic heroes Tintin and his dog Millou. Similar commemorative editions have been released by other countries as well.

492. Benjamin (1982/1999: 544 and 10).

493. Brion & Moreau (2001: 118).

494. Ladd (1997: 72ff.). Hörisch (1996: 78ff.) analyses the German banknotes, including the gendered sequence of portraits, where the male figures are always worth the double of the female ones, and where science is shown as male and art as female.

495. Brion & Moreau (2001: 53) also comment how the strained relations with Turkey have continually been apparent on Greece's banknotes, which 'since the Second World War have carried portraits of heroes of national independence, or scenes of combat between Greece and the Ottoman Empire'.

496. Anderson (1991).

497. On efforts of Christianisation in the construction of Malta's founding myths, see Gerber (2000/2010).

498. The Vatican belongs here, too, as its pope shares important formal traits with kings.

499.   Uricchio (2009: 19).

500.   San Marino's buildings are also of a mixed kind.

501.   Hall (2003), Rice (2003).

502.   Brion & Moreau (2001: 53) find that Great Britain and Luxembourg have regularly had their reigning monarchs on banknotes, while Belgium, Sweden and Spain have only done so sporadically, while republics rarely depict their presidents (Finland twice being an exception, in 1955 and 1975). Hardt and Negri (2000: 345-7) list three means of global control: the bomb as ultimate means of violence, money as means to control the market, and ether as the final and dominant medium of managing communication: 'The bomb is monarchic power, money aristocratic, and ether democratic.' This fascinating model is hard to apply on the euro, which seems to combine features of all three aspects.

503.   Hymans (2004: 16ff) notes that 'images of monarchs and national leaders have endured to a greater extent' than Inglehart's model might anticipate, locating 'the fiercest resistance to the cultural trends' in the later joiners to the EU.

504.   Delanty (1995: vii).

505.   Roche (2001: 76).

506.   Johnston (1991: 52ff.).

507.   Brion & Moreau (2001: 51) mention that all famous persons ever selected for banknotes in Belgium, Finland, Spain and Portugal have been male, whereas German and Scandinavian countries have offered women more space, in particular women from literatures, the arts or women's liberation movements. The German notes also strived to balance religious convictions and regional origins of persons represented.

508.   Gábor Misssura interview broadcast February 2004 by the European Association of Regional Television Circom Regional (www.circom-regional.org/enlargement/SL/SL15-the-euro-and-hungary.pdf).

509.   European Story: 'What Story Should Europe Tell?' (europeanstory.net/forum/comments.php?DiscussionID=39, 2010-03-23).

510.   Fleur de Coin: 'Unusual coins', www.fleur-de-coin.com/articles/unusualcoins.asp (2010-09-13).

511.   Brion & Moreau (2001: 28–9, 34, 43, 51 and 110; the direct quotes are from p. 55).

512.   Hymans (2004).

513.   *Freaking News* (2009): 'Global Currency Pictures', www.freakingnews.com/Global-Currency-Pictures--2359.asp (2010-09-18). Kissinger was active in the powerful Bilderberg Group conference in 2008.

514. Published in Swedish by *Dagens Nyheter*, 2010-05-08 (my translation).

515. On intermedial relations, see Fornäs et al. (2007b: 127).

516. Uricchio (2009).

517. From a December 1951 Council of Europe report, quoted by M. Radius (1971): 'Report by the Consultative Assembly of the Council of Europe on a European anthem', published by *European Navigator* (www.ena.lu). Information on the other symbols are found at many different websites.

518. 'Iconography Issue', *Not a Potted Plant* 2007-12-19 (notapottedplant.blogspot.com/2007/12/iconography-issue.html, 2009-02-16).

519. LP: 'EU Symbols', *International Law Prof Blog* 2009-01-18 (lawprofessors.typepad.com/international_law/2009/01/eu-symbols.html, 2009-02-16). On the concept of 'soft power', and Europe as 'the closest competitor to the United States in soft power resources', see Nye (2004: 5–18 and 75–83).

520. *Picobelleuropa!* website, www.picobelleuropa.nl/www.picobelleuropa.nl/uk_ideebus.php?id=01 (2009-10-12); *Spectrezine*: 'Alternative logo to mark 50 years of EU chosen', www.spectrezine.org/content/alternative-logo-mark-50-years-eu-chosen (2010-09-18).

521. These and the following descriptions are based on a wide range of encyclopaedic and EU sources.

522. Todorov (1982/1992: 42–3 and 247–8).

523. Todorov (1982/1992: 179).

524. Todorov (1982/1992: 182).

525. Derrida (1991); Balibar (2004: 235).

526. Ricoeur (1992/1995: 3). A more extensive treatment of the underlying models is made in Ricoeur (2000/2004).

527. Ricoeur (1992/1995: 7).

528. Ricoeur (1992/1995: 8–9); compare Benjamin (1950/1999 and 1982/1999) on the suppressed and unfulfilled potentials of the past, or Bloch (1959/1995) on hope and potentiality.

529. Ricoeur (1992/1995: 9ff.).

530. Ricoeur (1992/1995: 12).

531. Grimm (1995); Habermas (2001a); Kaitatzi-Whitlock (2007); Nieminen (2009); Salovaara-Moring (2009). Habermas' ideas on a 'sphere of publics' explicitly

derive from an analysis by Philip Schlesinger and Deidre Kevin. Peter van Ham (2000) is one of those who doubt if the European symbols so far will generate the feeling of common historical roots and belonging needed for an emergent European identity, which needs to be an identity in non-identity, acknowledging diversity.

532.   Habermas (2001a); see also Habermas (1992). This has been discussed in terms of tolerance by Habermas, while Jacques Derrida prefers the concept of hospitality (Borradori, 2003; Habermas & Derrida, 2003). See also Amin (2004).

533.   Lisbon Treaty, Articles I:1 and I:2, *European Navigator* (www.ena.lu).

References

Amin, Ash (2004): 'Multi-Ethnicity and the Idea of Europe', *Theory, Culture & Society*, 21(2): 1–24.

Anderson, Benedict (1983/1991): *Imagined Communities: Reflections on the Origin and Spread of Nationalism*, 2nd edn, London: Verso.

Anderson, Perry (2009): *The New Old World*, London/New York: Verso.

Andrews, Joe, Malcolm Crook & Michael Waller (eds) (2000): *Why Europe? Problems of Culture and Identity* (2 volumes), Basingstoke: Palgrave Macmillan.

Appiah, Kwame Anthony (2006): *Cosmopolitanism: Ethics in a World of Strangers*, New York/London: W.W. Norton.

Armstrong, Karen (2005): *A Short History of Myth*, Edinburgh: Canongate.

Arslan, Savaş, Volkan Aytar, Defne Karaosmanoğlu & Süheyla Kırca Schroeder (eds) (2009): *Media, Culture and Identity in Europe*, Istanbul: Bahçeşehir University Press.

Bachelard, Gaston (1958/1994): *The Poetics of Space*, Boston: Beacon Press.

Balibar, Étienne (2004): *We, the People of Europe? Reflections on Transnational Citizenship*, Princeton/Oxford: Princeton University Press.

Barthes, Roland (1957/2000): *Mythologies*, London: Vintage Books.

Bauman, Zygmunt (2004): *Europe: An Unfinished Adventure*, Cambridge: Polity Press.

Beck, Ulrich (1986/1992): *Risk Society: Towards a New Modernity*, London: Sage.

Beck, Ulrich (2006): *Cosmopolitan Vision*, Cambridge: Polity Press.

Beck, Ulrich & Edgar Grande (2004): *Das kosmopolitische Europa. Gesellschaft und Politik in der Zweiten Moderne*, Frankfurt am Main: Suhrkamp.

Benjamin, Walter (1950/1999): 'Theses on the Philosophy of History', in Walter Benjamin (1969/1999): *Illuminations*, London: Pimlico.

Benjamin, Walter (1955/1997): *One-Way Street and Other Writings*, London: Verso.

Benjamin, Walter (1982/1999): *The Arcades Project*, Cambridge MA/London UK: The Belknap Press of Harvard University Press.

Bernal, Martin (1991): *Black Athena: The Afroasiatic Roots of Classical Civilization. Volume I: The Fabrication of Ancient Greece 1785–1985*, London: Vintage.

Bertilsson, Margareta (1998): *Prometheus Unbound? On the Relation between Knowledge and Power: A Research Proposal*, København: Sociologisk Institut, Københavns Universitet.

Biddle, Ian & Vanessa Knights (eds) (2007): *Music, National Identity and the Politics of Location*, Aldershot: Ashgate.

Billig, Michael (1995): *Banal Nationalism*, London: Sage.

Bird, Kai & Martin J. Sherwin (2006): *American Prometheus: The Triumph and Tragedy of J. Robert Oppenheimer*, New York: Vintage Books.

Bloch, Ernst (1959/1995): *The Principle of Hope*, Cambridge MA: MIT Press.

Bloomfield, Jude & Franco Bianchini (2001): 'Cultural Citizenship and Urban Governance in Western Europe', in Nick Stevenson (ed.): *Culture and Citizenship*, London: Sage, 99–123.

Bohlman, Philip V. (2004): *The Music of European Nationalism: Cultural Identity and Modern History*, Santa Barbara CA: ABC-CLIO.

Bohlman, Philip V. (2008): 'On Track to the Grand Prix—The National Eurovision Competititon as National History', paper for a NHIST Carpathian Workshop.

Bondebjerg, Ib & Peter Golding (eds) (2004): *European Culture and the Media*, Bristol: Intellect Books.

Borradori, Giovanna (2003): *Philosophy in a Time of Terror: Dialogues with Jürgen Habermas and Jacques Derrida*, Chicago/London: The University of Chicago Press.

Bourdieu, Pierre (1993): *The Field of Cultural Production: Essays on Art and Literature*, Cambridge: Polity Press.

Bourdon, Jérome (2007): 'Unhappy Engineers of the European Soul: The EBU and the Woes of Pan-European Television', *The International Communication Gazette*, 69(3): 263–80.

Brague, Rémi (1992/2002): *Eccentric Culture: A Theory of Western Civilization*, South Bend IN: St. Augustine's Press.

Brion, René & Jean-Louis Moreau (2001): *A Flutter of Banknotes: From the First European Paper Money to the Euro*, Antwerpen: Mercatorfonds.

Bristow, Michael Jamieson & Philip Neal Martin (2006): *National Anthems of the World*, 11th edn, London: Orion Publishing.

Broberg, Gunnar, Jonas Hansson, Sten Högnäs, Rebecka Lettevall & Svante Nordin (2007): *Europas gränser. Essäer om europeisk identitet*, Nora: Nya Doxa.

Brown, Richard (1992): *Economic Revolutions in Britain 1750–1850: Prometheus Unbound?*, Cambridge: Cambridge University Press.

Bruter, Michael (2003): 'Winning Hearts and Minds for Europe: The Impact of News and Symbols on Civic and Cultural European Identity', *Comparative Political Studies*, 36(10): 1148–79,

Bruter, Michael (2004): 'On What Citizens Mean by Feeling "European": Perceptions of News, Symbols and Borderless-ness', *Journal of Ethnic and Migration Studies*, 30(1): 21–39.

Bruter, Michael (2005): *Citizens of Europe? The Emergence of a Mass European Identity*, Basingstoke: Palgrave Macmillan.

Buch, Esteban (2003): 'Parcours et paradoxes de l'hymne européen', in Passerini (2003), 87–98.

Buchan, James (1997): *Frozen Desire: An Inquiry into the Meaning of Money*, London: Picador.

Burgess, J. Peter (2000/2010): 'Coal, Steel and Spirit: The Double Reading of European Unity (1948–1951)', in Stråth (2000/2010), 421–55.

Burke, Peter (2000/2010): 'Foundation Myths and Collective Identities in Early Modern Europe', in Stråth (2000/2010), 113–22.

Bussière, Eric, Michel Dumoulin & Gilbert Trausch (eds) (2001): *Europa: The European Idea and Identity, from Ancient Greece to the 21st Century*, Antwerp: Mercatorfonds.

Cassirer, Ernst (1923/1955): *The Philosophy of Symbolic Forms. Volume 1: Language*, New Haven/London: Yale University Press.

Cassirer, Ernst (1925/1955): *The Philosophy of Symbolic Forms. Volume 2: Mythical Thought*, New Haven/London: Yale University Press.

Cerutti, Furio & Enno Rudolph (eds) (2001): *A Soul for Europe: On the Political and Cultural Identity of the Europeans. Vol. 1: A Reader*, Leuven: Peeters.

Cesarani, David & Maria Fulbrook (eds) (1996): *Citizenship, Nationality and Migration in Europe*, London/New York: Routledge.

Chalaby, Jean K. (2005): 'Deconstructing the Transnational: A Typology of Cross-Border Television Channels in Europe', *New Media & Society*, 7(2): 155–75.

Cohen, Anthony P. (1985): *The Symbolic Construction of Community*, Chichester/London: Ellis Horwood/Tavistock.

References

Concise Oxford Dictionary (2006), 11th edn, Oxford/New York: Oxford University Press.

Connell, John & Chris Gibson (2003): *Sound Tracks: Popular Music, Identity and Place*, London/New York: Routledge.

Cook, Nicholas (1993): *Beethoven: Symphony No. 9*, Cambridge: Cambridge University Press.

Cotterell, Arthur (1986): *A Dictionary of World Mythology*, Oxford/Melbourne: Oxford University Press.

Crolley, Liz & David Hand (2006): *Football and European Identity: Historical Narratives through the Press*, New York: Routledge.

Curti Gialdino, Carlo (2005): *I Simboli dell'Unione Europea, Bandiera—Inno—Motto—Moneta—Giornata*, Rome: Istituto Poligrafico e Zecca dello Stato S.p.A. (partly translated into English, at the *European Navigator* website, www.ena.lu; accessed 2011-06-02).

Daughtry, J. Martin (2003): 'Russia's New Anthem and the Negotiation of National Identity', *Ethnomusicology*, 47(1): 42–67.

Delanty, Gerard (1995): *Inventing Europe: Idea, Identity, Reality*, Basingstoke/London: Palgrave Macmillan.

Delanty, Gerard & Chris Rumford (2005): *Rethinking Europe: Social Theory and the Implications of Europeanization*, London/New York: Routledge.

Delgado-Moreira, Juan M. (2000): *Multicultural Citizenship of the European Union*, Aldershot: Ashgate.

Demossier, Marion (ed.) (2007): *The European Puzzle: The Political Structuring of Cultural Identities at a Time of Transition*, New York: Berghahn Books.

Derrida, Jacques (1967/1976): *Of Grammatology*, Baltimore/London: Johns Hopkins University Press.

Derrida, Jacques (1991): *L'autre cap, suivi de La démocratie ajournée*, Paris: Minuit.

Eco, Umberto (1980/1994): *The Name of the Rose*, San Diego: Harcourt Brace.

Elgenius, Gabriella (2007): 'The Origin of European National Flags', in Eriksen & Jenkins (2007), 14–30.

Elgenius, Gabriella (2011): *Symbols of Nations and Nationalism: Celebrating Nationhood*, Basingstoke: Palgrave Macmillan.

Elias, Norbert (1989): 'The Symbol Theory: Part Two', *Theory, Culture & Society*, 6(3): 339–83.

Eriksen, Anne (1999): *Historie, minne og myte*, Oslo: Pax Forlag.

Eriksen, Erik Oddvar, John Erik Fossum & José Agustín Menéndez (eds) (2003): *En författning för Europa?*, Göteborg: Daidalos.

Eriksen, Thomas Hylland (2007): 'Some Questions about Flags', in Eriksen & Jenkins (2007), 1–13.

Eriksen, Thomas Hylland & Richard Jenkins (eds) (2007): *Flag, Nation and Symbolism in Europe and America*, London/New York: Routledge.

European Commission (2006): *White Paper on a European Communication Policy*, Brussels: Commission of the European Communities, COM(2006), 35.

European Convention (2003): *Draft Treaty Establishing a Constitution for Europe*, Brussels: The European Convention (CONV 850/03).

European Navigator, Château de Sanem, Luxembourg: CVCE (Centre Virtuel de la Connaissance sur l'Europe (Virtual Resource Centre for Knowledge about Europe)) (www.ena.lu).

Feder, Stuart, Richard L. Karmel & George H. Pollock (eds) (1990): *Psychoanalytic Explorations in Music*, Madison: International Universities Press.

Ferguson, Niall (2001): *The Cash Nexus: Money and Power in the Modern World, 1700–2000*, London: Allen Lane.

Fornäs, Johan (1994): 'Karaoke: Subjectivity, Play and Interactive Media', *Nordicom Review*, 15(1): 87–103 (urn.kb.se/resolve?urn=urn:nbn:se:liu:diva-15602).

Fornäs, Johan (1995): *Cultural Theory and Late Modernity*, London: Sage (books. google.co.uk/books?id=HzNu27pkijkC&pg=PP1&dq=johan+Fornäs#PPP1,M 1).

Fornäs, Johan (1997): 'Text and Music Revisited', *Theory, Culture & Society*, 14(3): 109–23 (urn.kb.se/resolve?urn=urn:nbn:se:liu:diva-15570).

Fornäs, Johan (1998): 'Filling Voids along the Byway: Identification and Interpretation in the Swedish Forms of Karaoke', in Tôru Mitsui & Shûhei Hosokawa (eds): *Karaoke around the World: Global Technology, Local Singing*, London: Routledge, 118–35.

Fornäs, Johan (2003): 'The Words of Music', *Popular Music and Society*, 26(1): 37–51 (urn.kb.se/resolve?urn=urn:nbn:se:liu:diva-15568).

Fornäs, Johan (2004): *Moderna människor. Folkhemmet och jazzen*, Stockholm: Norstedts.

Fornäs, Johan (2007): *Reading the €uro: Money as a Medium of Transnational Identification*, Norrköping: Department of Culture Studies (Tema Q Report 2007:1, www.ep.liu.se/ea/temaq/2007/001; accessed 2011-06-02).

Fornäs, Johan (2008): 'Meanings of Money: The Euro as a Sign of Value and of Cultural Identity', in William Uricchio (ed.): *We Europeans? Media, Representations, Identities*, Bristol: Intellect, 123–39.

Fornäs, Johan (2009): 'Between Captain Euro and Entropa: Symbols of Europe as Ambivalent Identifiers', in Arslan et al. (2009), 22–32.

Fornäs, Johan, Peter Aronsson, Karin Becker, Svante Beckman, Erling Bjurström, Tora Friberg, Martin Kylhammar & Roger Qvarsell (2007a): *Culture Unbound: Dimensions of Culturalisation*, Norrköping: Department of Culture Studies (Tema Q, Report 2007:5; also Linköping University Electronic Press, www. ep.liu.se/ea/temaq/2007/005; accessed 2011-06-02).

Fornäs, Johan, Karin Becker, Erling Bjurström & Johan Fornäs (2007b): *Consuming Media: Communication, Shopping and Everyday Life*, Oxford: Berg.

Fornäs, Johan, Ulf Lindberg & Ove Sernhede (1988/1995): *In Garageland: Rock, Youth and Modernity*, London/New York: Routledge.

Fossum, John Erik & Philip Schlesinger (eds) (2007): *The European Union and the Public Sphere: A Communicative Space in the Making?*, London/New York: Routledge.

García, Soledad (ed.) (1993): *European Identity and the Search for Legitimacy*, London: Pinter.

Geertz, Clifford (1983): 'Art as a Cultural System', *Local Knowledge: Further Essays in Interpretative Anthropology*, New York: Basic Books, 94–120.

Geisler, Michel E. (2009): 'The Calendar Conundrum: National Days as Unstable Signifiers', in David McCrone & Gayle McPherson (eds): *National Days: Constructing and Mobilising National Identity*, Basingstoke: Palgrave Macmillan, 10–25.

Georgiou, Myria (2006): *Diaspora, Identity, and the Media: Diasporic Transnationalism and Mediated Spatialities*, Cresskill NJ: Hampton Press.

Gerber, Gerold (2000/2010): 'Doing Christianity and Europe: An Inquiry into Memory, Boundary and Truth Practices in Malta', in Stråth (2000/2010), 229–77.

Gifford, Paul & Tessa Hauswedell (eds) (2010): *Europe and Its Others: Essays on Interperception and Identity*, Oxford: Peter Lang.

Gillis, John R. (ed.) (1994): *Commemorations: The Politics of National Identity*, Princeton NJ: Princeton University Press.

Gilroy, Paul (1993): *The Black Atlantic: Modernity and Double Consciousness*, London/New York: Verso.

Gowland, D. A., Richard Dunphy & Charlotte Lythe (eds) (2000/2006): *The European Mosaic: Contemporary Politics, Economics and Culture*, 3rd edn, Harlow: Pearson Education.

Graves, Robert (1961): *The White Goddess*, London: Faber and Faber.

Grimm, Dieter (1995): 'Does Europe Need a Constitution?', *European Law Journal*, 1(3).

Guerrina, Roberta (2002): *Europe: History, Ideas and Ideologies*, London: Arnold.

References

Habermas, Jürgen (1981/1984): *The Theory of Communicative Action. Vol. 1: Reason and the Rationalization of Society*, Cambridge: Polity Press.

Habermas, Jürgen (1981/1987): *The Theory of Communicative Action. Vol. 2: Lifeworld and System: A Critique of Functionalist Reason*, Cambridge: Polity Press.

Habermas, Jürgen (1992): 'Citizenship and National Identity: Some Reflections of the Future of Europe', *Praxis International*, 12(1): 1–19.

Habermas, Jürgen (2001): *The Postnational Constellation: Political Essays*, Cambridge: Polity.

Habermas, Jürgen (2001a): 'Warum braucht Europa eine Verfassung?', *Die Zeit*, 27/2001.

Habermas, Jürgen & Jacques Derrida (2003): 'Nach dem Krieg: Die Wiedergeburt Europas', *Frankfurter Allgemeine Zeitung*, 31 May 2003.

Hall, Stuart (1986/1996): 'On Postmodernism and Articulation: An Interview with Stuart Hall', in David Morley & Chen Kuan-Hsing (eds): *Stuart Hall: Critical Dialogues in Cultural Studies*, London: Routledge, 131–50.

Hall, Stuart (1992): 'The West and the Rest: Discourse and Power', in Stuart Hall & Bram Gieben (eds): *Formations of Modernity*, Cambridge/Milton Keynes: Polity Press/The Open University, 275–331.

Hall, Stuart (1996): 'Who Needs "Identity"?', in Stuart Hall & Paul du Gay (eds): *Questions of Cultural Identity*, London: Sage, 1–17.

Hall, Stuart (2003): '"In But Not of Europe": Europe and Its Myths', in Passerini (2003).

Hansen, Peo (2000): *Europeans Only? Essays on Identity Politics and the European Union*, Umeå: Department of Political Science, Umeå University.

Hardt, Michael & Antonio Negri (2000): *Empire*, Cambridge MA/London UK: Harvard University Press.

Hawkins, Walter E. (1920/1996): 'Thus speaks Africa' and 'To Prometheus', *Chords and Discords*, Boston: Richard G. Badger; reprinted in Nancy Cunard (ed.) (1970/1996): *Negro: An Anthology*, New York: Continuum, 262.

Heffernan, Michael (1998): *The Meaning of Europe: Geography and Geopolitics*, London: Arnold.

Heinemann, Klaus (1969): *Grundzüge einer Soziologie des Geldes*, Stuttgart: Enke.

Hersant, Yves (2003): 'Douze étoiles d'or', in Passerini (2003), 99–106.

Hintjens, Helen M. (2007): 'Citizenship under Siege in the Brave New Europe', *European Journal of Cultural Studies*, 10(3): 409–14.

Hobsbawm, Eric (1983a): 'Introduction: Inventing Traditions', in Eric Hobsbawm & Terence Ranger (eds): *The Invention of Tradition*, Cambridge: Cambridge University Press, 1–14.

Hobsbawm, Eric (1983b): 'Mass-Producing Traditions: Europe, 1870–1914', in Eric Hobsbawm & Terence Ranger (eds): *The Invention of Tradition*, Cambridge: Cambridge University Press, 263–307.

Hobsbawm, Eric J. (1990): *Nations and Nationalism since 1780: Programme, Myth, Reality*, Cambridge: Cambridge University Press.

Homer (9–8 century BC/1950): *The Iliad*, Harmondsworth: Penguin (see also publicliterature.org/books/iliad/xaa.php).

Hörisch, Jochen (1996): *Kopf oder Zahl: Die Poesie des Geldes*, Frankfurt am Main: Suhrkamp.

Hörisch, Jochen (2001): *Der Sinn und die Sinne. Eine Geschichte der Medien*, Frankfurt am Main: Eichborn Verlag.

Hymans, Jacques E. C. (2004): 'The Changing Color of Money: European Currency Iconography and Collective Identity', *European Journal of International Relations*, 10(1): 5–31.

Ilczuk, Dorota (2001): *Cultural Citizenship: Civil Society and Cultural Policy in Europe*, Amsterdam: Boekmanstudies.

Jacobs, Dirk & Robert Maier (1998): 'European Identity: Construct, Fact and Fiction', in Maria Gastelaars & Arie de Ruijter (eds): *A United Europe: The Quest for a Multifaceted Identity*, Maastricht: Shaker, 13–34.

Jansen, Thomas (ed.) (1999): *Reflections on European Identity*, European Commission Forward Studies Unit (ec.europa.eu/comm/cdp/working-paper/european_ identity_en.pdf).

Jensen, Klaus Bruhn (ed.) (2002): *A Handbook of Media and Communication Research: Qualitative and Quantitative Methodologies*, London/New York: Routledge.

Johansen, Øystein Kock (2001): *Fra stenpenger til euro: Betalingsmidlenes forunderlige verden*, Oslo: Den norske Bank.

Johnston, William M. (1991): *Celebrations: The Cult of Anniversaries in Europe and the United States Today*, New Brunswick NJ/London UK: Transaction Publishers.

Jönsson, Christer, Sven Tägil & Gunnar Törnqvist (2000): *Organizing European Space*, London: Sage.

Kaelble, Hartmut (2003): 'European Symbols, 1945–2000: Concept, Meaning and Historical Change', in Passerini (2003), 47–61.

Kaelberer, Matthias (2004): 'The Euro and European Identity: Symbols, Power and the Politics of European Monetary Union', *Review of International Studies*, 30: 161–78.

Kaitatzi-Whitlock, Sophia (2007): 'The Missing European Public Sphere and the Absence of Imagined European Citizenship: Democratic Deficit as a Function of a Common European Media Deficit', *European Societies*, 9(5): 685–704.

Kant, Immanuel (1784/1997): *Foundations of the Metaphysics of Morals and, What is Enlightenment?*, 2nd edn, Upper Saddle River: Prentice-Hall.

Karolewski, Ireneusz Pawel & Viktoria Kaina (eds) (2006): *European Identity: Theoretical Perspectives and Empirical Insights*, Berlin/Münster: Lit.

King, Anthony (2004): 'The New Symbols of European Football', *International Review for the Sociology of Sport*, 39(3): 323–36.

Kirshenblatt-Gimblett, Barbara (1992): 'Performing Diversity', in Åke Daun, Billy Ehn & Barbro Klein (eds): *To Make the World Safe for Diversity*, Stockholm: Swedish Immigration Institute and Museum/Ethnology Institute, 51–62.

Knepler, Georg (1961/1975): *Musikgeschichte des XIX. Jahrhunderts*, Århus: PubliMus.

Kristeva, Julia (1974/1984): *Revolution in Poetic Language*, New York: Columbia University Press.

Ladd, Brian (1997): *The Ghosts of Berlin: Confronting German History in the Urban Landscape*, Chicago/London: The University of Chicago Press.

Lagerkvist, Amanda (2005): *Amerikafantasier. Kön, medier och visualitet i svenska reseskildringar från USA 1945–63*, Stockholm: JMK, Stockholm University.

Landes, David S. (1969): *The Unbound Prometheus: Technological Change and Industrial Development in Western Europe*, Cambridge: Cambridge University Press.

Langer, Susanne K. (1942): *Philosophy in a New Key*, Boston MA: Harvard University Press.

Larcher, Aloïs (1995): *Le drapeau de l'europe et l'hymne européen. La genèse de deux symboles*, Strasbourg: Council of Europe.

Levin, Paul T. (2007): 'From "Saracen Scourge" to "Terrible Turk": Medieval, Renaissance, and Enlightenment Images of the "Other" in the Narrative Construction of "Europe"', Los Angeles: University of Southern California (diss.).

Lévi-Strauss, Claude (1949/1987): *Structural Anthropology*, New York: Basic Books.

Lévi-Strauss, Claude (1962/2004): *The Savage Mind*, Oxford: Oxford University Press.

Lévi-Strauss, Claude (1978/2001): *Myth and Meaning*, London/New York: Routledge.

Lindaräng, Ingemar (2007): *Helgonbruk i moderniseringstider. Bruket av Birgitta- och Olavstraditionerna i samband med minnesfiranden i Sverige och Norge 1891–2005*, Norrköping: Tema Kultur och samhälle, Linköpings universitet.

Lorenzer, Alfred (1970): *Kritik des Psychoanalytischen Symbolbegriffs*, Frankfurt am Main: Suhrkamp.

Lorenzer, Alfred (1971): 'Symbol, Interaktion und Praxis', in Alfred Lorenzer, Helmut Dahmer, Klaus Horn, Karola Brede & Enno Schwanenberg (eds): *Psychoanalyse als Sozialwissenschaft*, Frankfurt am Main: Suhrkamp, 9–59.

Lorenzer, Alfred (1986): 'Tiefenhermeneutische Kulturanalyse', in Alfred Lorenzer (ed.): *Kultur-Analysen*, Frankfurt am Main: Fischer, 11–98.

Lourenço, Eduardo (1991): 'De l'europé comme culture', *L'Europe introuvable. Jalons pour une mythologie européenne*, Paris: Éditions Métailié.

Ludes, Peter (2002): *Medien und Symbole: €UROpäische MedienBILDung*, Siegen: Universitätsverlag Siegen.

Lutz, Wolfgang, Sylvia Kritzinger & Vegard Skirbekk (2006): 'The Demography of Growing European Identity', *Science*, 314: 425.

Malmborg, Mikael af & Bo Stråth (eds) (2002): *The Meaning of Europe: Variety and Contention within and among Nations*, Oxford/New York: Berg.

Márothy, János (1974): *Music and the Bourgeois, Music and the Proletarian*, Budapest: Akadémiai Kiadó.

Martin, Peter J. (1995): *Sounds and Society: Themes in the Sociology of Music*, Manchester/New York: Manchester University Press.

Marx, Karl (1867/2001): *Capital: A Critique of Political Economy. Vol. I: The Process of Production of Capital*, London: Electric Book Co.

Marx, Karl (1939/1993): *Grundrisse: Foundations of the Critique of Political Economy*, London: Penguin.

Maugendre, Xavier (1996): *L'Europe des hymnes dans leur contexte historique et musical*, Sprimont: Mardaga.

Mayer, Günter (1978): *Weltbild—Notenbild. Zur Dialektik des musikalischen Materials*, Leipzig: Reclam.

McClary, Susan (1991): *Feminine Endings: Music, Gender, and Sexuality*, Minnesota/Oxford: University of Minnesota Press.

McCrone, David & Gayle McPherson (eds) (2009): *National Days: Constructing and Mobilising National Identity*, Basingstoke: Palgrave Macmillan.

Mead, George H. (1934): *Mind, Self and Society: From the Standpoint of a Social Behaviorist*, Chicago: The University of Chicago.

Meinhof, Ulrike H. & Anna Triandafyllidou (eds) (2006): *Transcultural Europe: Cultural Policy in a Changing Europe*, New York: Palgrave Macmillan.

Meyer, Thomas (2004): *Die Identität Europas. Der EU eine Seele?*, Frankfurt am Main: Suhrkamp.

Middleton, Richard (2006): *Voicing the Popular: On the Subjects of Popular Music*, New York/London: Routledge.

Mikkeli, Heikki (1998): *Europe as an Idea and an Identity*, Basingstoke: Palgrave Macmillan.

Miller, Vaughne (2008): *The European Union Symbols and Their Adoption by the European Parliament*, London: International Affairs and Defence Section, House of Commons (Standard Note SN/IA/4874, www.parliament.uk/commons/lib/research/briefings/SNIA-4874.pdf; accessed 2011-06-02).

Morin, Edgar (1987/1990): *Penser l'Europe. Edition revue et complétée*, Paris: Gallimard.

Müller, Rudolf Wolfgang (1977): *Geld und Geist. Zur Entstehungsgeschichte von Identitätsbewußtsein und Rationalität seit der Antike*, Frankfurt am Main: Campus.

Nelson, Brian, David Roberts & Walter Veit (ed.) (1992): *The Idea of Europe: Problems of National and Transnational Identity*, New York: Berg.

Nielsen, Poul (1978): *Musik og materialisme. Tre aspekter af Theodor W. Adornos musikfilosofi*, København: Borgen.

Nieminen, Hannu (2009): 'The European Public Sphere as a Network? Four Plus One Approaches', in Salovaara-Moring (2009), 19–34.

Nye, Joseph S., Jr. (2004): *Soft Power: The Means to Success in World Politics*, New York NY: Public Affairs.

References

OECD (2002): *The Future of Money*, Paris: OECD.

Ortner, Sherry B. (1973): 'On Key Symbols', *American Anthropologist*, 75(5): 1338–46.

Parker, Noel (ed.) (2008): *The Geopolitics of Europe's Identity: Centers, Boundaries and Margins*, New York: Palgrave Macmillan.

Passerini, Luisa (1999): *Europe in Love, Love in Europe: Imagination and Politics in Britain between the Wars*, London: Tauris.

Passerini, Luisa (2000/2010): 'The Last Identification: Why Some of Us Would Like to Call Ourselves Europeans and What We Mean by This', in Stråth (200/2010), 45–65.

Passerini, Luisa (ed.) (2003): *Figures d'Europe / Images and Myths of Europe*, Bruxelles: P.I.E.-Peter Lang.

Pastoureau, Michel (2001): *Blue: The History of a Color*, Princeton: Princeton University Press.

Peirce, Charles S. (1940/1955): *Philosophical Writings of Peirce*, New York: Dover Publications.

Persson, Hans-Åke & Bo Stråth (eds.) (2007): *Reflections on Europe: Defining a Political Order in Time and Space*, Bruxelles: P.I.E. Peter Lang.

Pettersson, Tobias (2004): *De bildade männens Beethoven. Musikhistorisk kunskap och social formering i Sverige mellan 1850 och 1940*, Göteborg: Göteborgs universitet.

Planeta, Katarzyna (2005): *Media Circle—Circle of Mediation: Eurovision Song Contest as a Symbolic Model of Common European Space*, Uppsala: Uppsala University (Master of Arts in Euroculture).

Prisacariu, Ioana-Sabina (2007): 'The Symbols Role in the Creation of a European Identity', Master Thesis in European Studies, Iași: University of Iași (www.angeloti.info/ioana_prisacariu_master_thesis.pdf; accessed 2011-06-02).

Rabier, Jacques-René (2003): 'Tradition et résurgences d'un mythe: le ravissement d'Europe', in Passerini (2003), 65–76.

Raykoff, Ivan & Robert Deam Tobin (eds) (2007): *A Song for Europe: Popular Music and Politics in the Eurovision Song Contest*, Aldershot: Ashgate.

Rice, Michael (2003): 'When Archetype Meets Archetype: The Bull and Europa', in Passerini (2003), 77–86.

Ricoeur, Paul (1955/2007): *History and Truth*, Evanston IL: Northwestern University Press.

Ricoeur, Paul (1960/1969): *The Symbolism of Evil*, Boston: Beacon Press.

Ricoeur, Paul (1965/1970): *Freud and Philosophy: En Essay on Interpretation*, New Haven CT/London: Yale University Press.

Ricoeur, Paul (1969/1974): *The Conflict of Interpretations: Essays in Hermeneutics*, Evanston: Northwestern University Press.

Ricoeur, Paul (1975/1986): *The Rule of Metaphor: Multi-Disciplinary Studies of the Creation of Meaning in Language*, London: Routledge & Kegan Paul.

Ricoeur, Paul (1976): *Interpretation Theory: Discourse and the Surplus of Meaning*, Fort Worth: Texas Christian University Press.

Ricoeur, Paul (1981): *Hermeneutics and the Human Sciences: Essays on Language, Action and Interpretation*, Cambridge: Cambridge University Press.

Ricoeur, Paul (1983/1984): *Time and Narrative. Volume 1*, Chicago/London: University of Chicago Press.

Ricoeur, Paul (1985/1988): *Time and Narrative. Volume 3*, Chicago/London: University of Chicago Press.

Ricoeur, Paul (1990/1992): *Oneself as Another*, Chicago/London: University of Chicago Press.

Ricoeur, Paul (1991a): 'Life in Quest of a Narrative', in David Wood (ed.): *On Paul Ricoeur: Narrative and Interpretation*, London/New York: Routledge, 20–33.

Ricoeur, Paul (1991b): 'Narrative Identity', in David Wood (ed.): *On Paul Ricoeur: Narrative and Interpretation*, London/New York: Routledge, 188–99.

References

Ricoeur, Paul (1992/1995): 'Reflections on a New Ethos for Europe', *Philosophy & Social Criticism*, 21(5/6): 3–13.

Ricoeur, Paul (1994): 'Imagination in Discourse and in Action', in Gillian Robinson & John Rundell (eds): *Rethinking Imagination: Culture and Creativity*, London: Routledge, 118–35.

Ricoeur, Paul (2000/2004): *Memory, History, Forgetting*, Chicago/London: The University of Chicago Press.

Ricoeur, Paul (2005): *The Course of Recognition*, Cambridge MA/London UK: Harvard University Press.

Riezler, Walter (1951): *Beethoven*, Zürich: Atlantis Verlag.

Risse, Thomas (1998): 'To Euro or Not to Euro? The EMU and Identity Politics in the European Union', *Arena* Working Papers 98/1 (www.arena.uio.no/publications/ wp98_1.htm; accessed 2011-06-02).

Robertson, Roland (1995): 'Glocalization: Time–Space and Homogeneity–Heterogeneity', in Mike Featherstone, Scott Lash & Roland Robertson (eds): *Global Modernities*, London: Sage, 25–44.

Roche, Maurice (2001): 'Citizenship, Popular Culture and Europe', in Nick Stevenson (ed.): *Culture and Citizenship*, London: Sage, 74–98.

Rolland, Romain (1903/2009): *Beethoven*, Charleston, SC: BiblioLife.

Rosolato, Guy (1974): 'La voix: Entre corps et langage', *Revue française de psychanalyse*, 38(1): 76–94.

Rowe, Dorothy (1997): *The Real Meaning of Money*, London: HarperCollins.

Roy, Srirupa (2006): '"A Symbol of Freedom": The Indian Flag and the Transformations of Nationalism, 1906–2002', *The Journal of Asian Studies*, 65(3): 495–527.

Sakwa, Richard & Anne Stevens (eds) (2000/2006): *Contemporary Europe*, 2nd edn, Basingstoke: Palgrave Macmillan.

Salomonsson, Björn (1991): 'Musikupplevelsen. Psykoanalytiska synpunkter', in Hans Reiland & Franziska Ylander (eds): *Psykoanalys och kultur. Uppbrott och reflektioner*, Stockholm: Natur och Kultur, 161–74.

Salovaara-Moring, Inka (ed.) (2009): *Manufacturing Europe: Spaces of Democracy, Diversity and Communication*, Göteborg: Nordicom.

Sarikakis, Katharine (2007): *Media and Cultural Policy in the European Union*, Amsterdam: Rodopi.

Schiller, Melanie (2009): '*Sonic Resurrections*': *Popular Music and National Identity in Post-War Germany*, Pilot Study, Amsterdam: ASCA, University of Amsterdam.

Schlesinger, Philip (2008): 'Cosmopolitan Temptations, Communicative Spaces and the European Union', in David Hesmondhalgh & Jason Toynbee (eds): *The Media and Social Theory*, London/New York: Routledge, 75–92.

Segal, Hanna (1957): 'Notes on Symbol Formation', *International Journal of Psycho-Analysis*, XXXVII(6): 391–397.

Servet, Jean-Michel (2003): 'L'euro: Fenêtres et ponts d'un nomadisme monétaire', in Passerini (2003), 127–46.

Shakespeare, William (n.d.): *The Complete Works of William Shakespeare*, Oxford: Clarendon Press.

Shanahan, Suzanne (2003): 'Currency and Community: European Identity and the Euro', in Passerini (2003), 159–79.

Shelley, Mary Wollstonecraft (1818/2001): *Frankenstein, or The Modern Prometheus*, London: Electric Book Co.

Shelley, Percy Bysshe (1820/1930): 'Prometheus Unbound: A Lyrical Drama in Four Acts', *Complete Works*, London: Benn.

Shore, Cris (2000): *Building Europe: The Cultural Politics of European Integration*, London/New York: Routledge.

Simmel, Georg (1896/1991): 'Money in Modern Culture', *Theory, Culture & Society*, 8(3): 17–31.

References

Simmel, Georg (1900/1989): *Philosophie des Geldes*, Frankfurt am Main: Suhrkamp.

Simmel, Georg (1909/1994): 'Bridge and Door', *Theory, Culture & Society*, 11(1): 5–10.

Sjursen, Helene (ed.) (2006): *Questioning EU Enlargement: Europe in Search of Identity*, Abingdon, Oxon/New York: Routledge.

Smithin, John (ed.) (2000): *What is Money?*, London: Routledge.

Sohn-Rethel, Alfred (1970/1973): *Geistige und körperliche Arbeit. Zur Theorie der gesellschaftlichen Synthesis*, Frankfurt am Main: Suhrkamp.

Solomon, Maynard (1977/1980): *Beethoven*, London: Granada.

Spengler, Oswald (1926–8): *The Decline of the West*, 2 volumes, New York: Knopf.

Stevenson, Nick (2006): 'Citizenship and the "Other": Europe's Democratic Futures', *European Journal of Cultural Studies*, 9(3): 385–96.

Stråth, Bo (ed.) (2000): *Myth and Memory in the Construction of Community: Historical Patterns in Europe and Beyond*, Bruxelles: P.I.E. Peter Lang.

Stråth, Bo (ed.) (2000/2010): *Europe and the Other and Europe as the Other*, 4th printing with changes, Bruxelles: P.I.E. Peter Lang.

Stråth, Bo (2000/2010a): 'Introduction: Europe as a Discourse', in Stråth (2000/2010), 13–44.

Stråth, Bo (2000/2010b): 'Multiple Europes: Integration, Identity and Demarcation to the Other', in Stråth (2000/2010), 385–420.

Swartz, David (1997): *Culture and Power: The Sociology of Pierre Bourdieu*, Chicago/London: The University of Chicago Press.

Tagg, Philip (2009): *Everyday Tonality: Towards a Tonal Theory of What Most People Hear*, New York/Montréal: The Mass Media Scholars' Press.

Tait, Joyce (2001): 'More Faust than Frankenstein: The European Debate about the Precautionary Principle and Risk Regulation for Genetically Modified Crops', *Journal of Risk Research*, 4(2): 175–189.

Tängerstad, Erik (2000/2010): "'The Third World" as an Element in the Collective Construction of a Post-Colonial European Identity', in Stråth (2000/2010), 157–93.

Therborn, Göran (1995): *European Modernity and Beyond: The Trajectory of European Societies 1945–2000*, London: Sage.

Thomson, George (1949/1978): *The Prehistoric Aegean: Studies in Ancient Greek Society*, London: Lawrence & Wishart.

Thyssen, Ole (1991): *Penge, magt og kærlighed. Teorien om symbolsk generaliserede medier hos Parsons, Luhmann og Habermas*, Copenhagen: Rosinante.

Todorov, Tzvetan (1982/1992): *The Conquest of America: The Question of the Other*, New York: HarperCollins.

Toggenburg, Gabriel N. (2004): "'United in Diversity": Some Thoughts on the New Motto of the Enlarged Union', paper for the II Mercator International Symposium: 'Europe 2004: A new framework for all languages?', Tarragona 27–28/2 2004.

Tönnies, Ferdinand (1887/1988): *Community and Society*, New Brunswick NJ: Transaction Publishers.

Tonra, Ben & Denise Dunne (1996): *A European Cultural Identity: Myth, Reality or Aspiration?*, Dublin: Institute of European Affairs.

Trausch, Gilbert (1999): 'Consciousness of European Identity after 1945', in Jansen (1999), 21–6.

Turner, Victor (1969): *The Ritual Process*, Chicago: Aldine.

Uricchio, William (2009): 'European Identity as Palimpsest', in Arslan et al. (2009), 13–21.

van Gennep, Arnold (1909/1960): *The Rites of Passage*, Chicago: University of Chicago Press.

Vernant, Jean-Pierre (1965/2006): *Myth and Thought among the Greeks*, New York: Zone Books.

Warring, Anette (2004): *Historie, magt og identitet—grundlovsfejringer gennem 150 år*, Århus: Aarhus Universitetsforlag.

Waswo, Richard (2003): 'The Fact (and Figures) of the Supreme Fiction', in Passerini (2003), 147–58.

Wikipedia (en.wikipedia.org/wiki).

Williams, Kevin (2005): *European Media Studies*, London: Hodder Arnold.

Williams, Raymond (1976/1988): *Keywords*, London: Fontana Press.

Wintle, Michael (2009): *The Image of Europe: Visualizing Europe in Cartography and Iconography throughout the Ages*, Cambridge: Cambridge University Press.

Withers, Hartley (1909/1947): *The Meaning of Money*, 7th edn, London: Murray.

Wittgenstein, Ludwig (1953): *Philosophische Untersuchungen/Philosophical Investigations*, Frankfurt am Main/Oxford: Suhrkamp/Basil Blackwell.

Wolther, Irving (2006): *'Kampf der Kulturen'. Der Eurovision Song Contest als Mittel national-kultureller Repräsentation*, Würzburg: Königshausen & Neumann.

Young, Iris Marion (1997): *Intersecting Voices: Dilemmas of Gender, Political Philosophy, and Policy*, Princeton NJ: Princeton University Press.

Yuval-Davis, Nira, Kalpana Kannabiran & Ulrike Vieten (eds) (2006): *The Situated Politics of Belonging*, London: Sage.

Zei, Vida (1995): *Symbolic Spaces of the Nation State: The Case of Slovenia*, Iowa: Communication Studies, University of Iowa.

Zelizer, Viviana A. Rotman (1994/1997): *The Social Meaning of Money*, Princeton NJ: Princeton University Press.

Žižek, Slavoj (2006): 'Against the Populist Temptation', *Lacan dot com* (www.lacan.com/zizpopulism.htm; accessed 2011-06-02).

Žižek, Slavoj (2007): 'The Disturbing Sounds of the Turkish March', *In These Times*, 2007-11-06.

Žižek, Slavoj (2007a): '"Ode to Joy", Followed by Chaos and Despair', *The New York Times*, 2007-12-24.

List of Figure Sources

0.1   en.wikipedia.org/wiki/File:Entropa-rectangular.jpg

1.1   commons.wikimedia.org/wiki/File:Europa_copy.jpg

1.2   commons.wikimedia.org/wiki/File:Europa_bull_Louvre_MNC626.jpg

1.3   Courtesy of the J. Paul Getty Museum, Los Angeles

1.4   commons.wikimedia.org/wiki/File:Carl_Milles_Europa_och_Tjuren.jpg

1.5   fr.academic.ru/dic.nsf/frwiki/1587951

1.6   imagewizardry.com/images/phoenix-bird-image.gif

1.7   Courtesy of the Liechtenstein Museum, Vienna

1.8   www.seeklogo.com/phoenix-satellite-tv-logo-108520.html

1.9   Courtesy of Nicolas De Santis

1.10 Courtesy of Nicolas De Santis

3.1   http://www.zonu.com/fullsize1-en/2009-11-04-10821/Europe-satellite-map.html

3.2   http://commons.wikimedia.org/wiki/File:Europa-mapa_polityczna.png

3.3   commons.wikimedia.org/wiki/File:European_Union_borders.png

3.4   commons.wikimedia.org/wiki/File:Council_of_Europe_(blue).svg

4.1   Courtesy of Sven-Bertil Bärnarp

6.1   commons.wikimedia.org/wiki/File:Flag_of_Europe.svg

6.2   wikipedia/commons/4/45/Pietro_da_Cortona_Allegory_of_Divine_
        Providence_and_Barberini_Power_(detail)_WGA17684.jpg

6.3   Courtesy of the Prado Museum, Madrid

6.4   Courtesy of Henri Adam de Villiers

6.5   commons.wikimedia.org/wiki/File:US_13_Star_Betsy_Ross_Flag.svg

6.6   commons.wikimedia.org/wiki/File:Anaximander_cosmology-fr.svg

6.7   commons.wikimedia.org/wiki/File:Anaximander_world_map-en.svg

6.8   commons.wikimedia.org/wiki/File:Flag_of_Kosovo_(yellow).svg

6.9   commons.wikimedia.org/wiki/File:Flag_of_Turkey.svg

6.10   commons.wikimedia.org/wiki/File:Flag_of_China.png

6.11   en.wikipedia.org/wiki/File:Flag_of_the_UNIA.svg

6.12   en.wikipedia.org/wiki/File:Flag_of_the_African_Union.svg

6.13   commons.wikimedia.org/wiki/File:Flag_African_Union.svg

6.14   commons.wikimedia.org/wiki/File:Triquetra-Cross.svg

6.15   commons.wikimedia.org/wiki/File:Former_Flag_of_the_International_
        Paneuropean_Union.svg

7.3   Transcribed by Johan Fornäs

7.4   Transcribed by Johan Fornäs

7.5   Transcribed by Johan Fornäs

7.6   http://lilianseurovision.blogspot.com/2010_08_01_archive.html

7.7   es.wikipedia.org/wiki/InCulto

8.1   Courtesy of European Central Bank, Frankfurt am Main (www.ecb.europa. eu/euro/html/hires .en.html)

8.2   www.eucoins.info/2008/12/19/euro-coins-and-pictures

8.3   en.wikipedia.org/wiki/Euro_coins

8.4   http://worldcoingallery.com/countries/circ_sets/index.htm

8.5   en.wikipedia.org/wiki/Euro_coins

8.6   www.fleur-de-coin.com/articles/unusualcoins.asp

8.7   Available at commons.wikimedia.org and http://www.chinatoday.com/fin/ mon/index.htm

For the license terms of all Wikimedia Commons sources please see: http://creative commons.org/licenses/by-sa/3.0/.

INDEX

A

The Abduction of Europa (Sotiriadis) 13
Adonnino Committee 89, 90-1, 119, 157-8
Adonnino, Pietro 78
Africa 17, 93
African Union (AU) 94, 129-30, 183
Afzelius, Björn 198
agency, and intentionality 104
Aida (Verdi) 185
Albania 74, 99
Algeria 73
Allister, Jim 180
ambiguity/ambivalence,
    in coin design 240-2
    Europa myth 41-2
    and symbols 264
America 18 *see also* USA
AMO 140-1
An die Freude (Schiller) 163
Ancient Rites 199
Andorra, and the euro 212
Andros, Adam 29 *see also* Captain Euro
animals, as symbols 145, 221, 234, 237-8,
    240, 247, 253-7 *see also individual*
    animal names

anniversaries, and community 87
Antarctica, naming 18
anthem 77, 78, 153-8, 264
    adoption 157-8, 172-3, 176-7
    alternative suggestions 181, 184
    arrangements 157, 174-6, 178
    and Captain Euro 176
    categories 150, 182
    comparisons 181-201
    contradictions 179-80, 203
    date 153
    decontextualisation 175
    defined 149-52
    desirability 155-6
    desire and destruction 202
    dislocation 202
    and diversity 203
    elevating effect 161-2, 202-3
    and Europa myth 176, 202, 203
    hostility to 180-1
    hymn types 182
    and identity 150, 156-7, 180
    and inclusion 172
    influences 188-9
    intepretation 171-81
    and language 178, 182-3
    linearisation 175-6
    lyrics 156, 158, 176-9, 182-3
    message 203

Figure 0.1. David Černý: *Entropa* in the European Council building in Brussels, 2009 (photo Marek Blahuš).

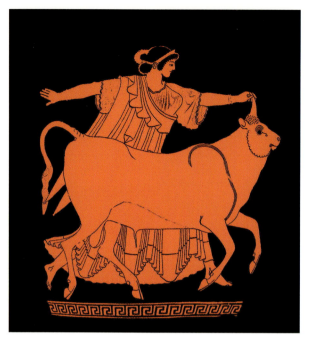

Figure 1.1. *Europa and the Bull*, Greek vase painting, Tarquinia Museum, c. 480 BC.

Figure 1.2. *Europa and Zeus Transformed into a Bull*, terracotta figurine from Boeotia, Musée de Louvre, c. 460 BC.

Figure 1.3. Rembrandt van Rijn: *The Abduction of Europa*, 1632, The J. Paul Getty Museum, Los Angeles.

Figure 1.4. Swedish sculptor Carl Milles: *Europa and the Bull*, Halmstad, Sweden, 1935 (photo Henrik Sendelbach).

Figure 1.5. Nikos and Pandelis Sotiriadis: *The Abduction of Europa*, sculpture outside the European Parliament building in Strasbourg, 2005.

Figure 1.6. Phoenix.

Figure 1.7. *Prometheus Brings Fire to Mankind*, Heinrich
Friedrich Füger, 1817 (Sammlungen des Fürsten von
und zu Liechtenstein, Vaduz – Wien).

Figure 1.8. Murdoch's Chinese
Phoenix Television logo (www.
seeklogo.com/phoenix-satellite-
tv-logo-108520.html).

Figure 1.9. *Captain Euro*, created by Joe Simon and Jack Kirby for the EU in 1998; here together with his partner Europa and Lupo the wolf. Captain Euro® and all related characters © Nicolas De Santis 1997–2011.

Figure 1.10. Captain Euro with Twelve Stars team members Pythagoras and Marcus to the right above 'baddie' Ninot, and to the left the evil D. Vider, Mala and Junior. Captain Euro® and all related characters © Nicolas De Santis 1997-2011.

Figure 3.1. Satellite image of Europe (zonu.com).

Figure 3.2. Polish map of Europe's countries.

Figure 3.3. European Union member states, 2007.

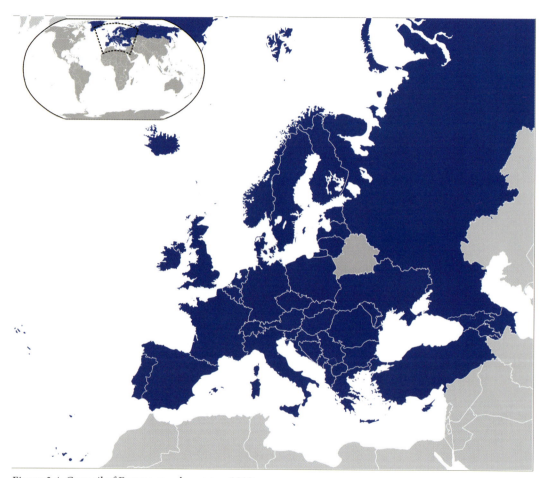

Figure 3.4. Council of Europe member states, 2009.

Figure 4.1. *Medelålders plus* ('Middle Aged Plus'), by Sven-Bertil Bärnarp, *Dagens Nyheter*, 9 May 2010. He: 'Nothing French, nothing Italian, nothing German, nothing Spanish or even Danish.' She: 'No, Europe Day is celebrated with *mother fucker*, *asshole*, *my God* and *high five* in Swedish public service television and all commercial channels.' © Sven-Bertil Bärnarp 2010.

Figure 6.1. The EU flag.

Figure 6.2. Pietro Berrettini da Cortona's fresco in the Grand Salon of Palazzo Barberini in Rome, 1639. Attribution: Sailko.

Figure 6.3. Giovanni Battista Tiepolo: *The Immaculate Conception*, 1767–69, The Prado, Madrid.

Figure 6.4. 'Our Lady of the Miraculous Medal', celebrating the apparition of St Mary on Rue du Bac in Paris, 1830. Photograph taken by Henri Adam de Villiers in la chapelle Notre-Dame de la Médaille Miraculeuse.

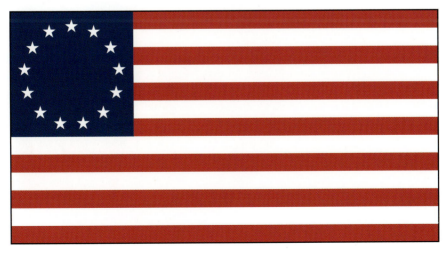

Figure 6.5. The US 'Betsy Ross flag', 1777–95.

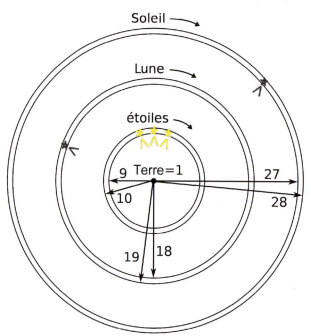

Figure 6.6. Greek philosopher Anaximander's circular cosmology, c. 610 BC–c. 546 BC.

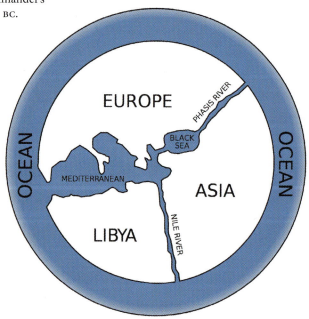

Figure 6.7. Anaximander's world map.

Figure 6.8. Kosovo flag.

Figure 6.9. Turkey flag.

Figure 6.10. Flag of the People's Republic of China.

Figure 6.11. Pan-African flag of the UNIA
Universal Negro Improvement Association
and African Communities League.

Figure 6.12. African Union Flag used until 2010.

Figure 6.13. African Union Flag used after
30 January 2010.

Figure 6.14. Carolingian Triquetra-cross.

Figure 6.15. Original Paneuropean Union flag.

Figure 6.16. Paneuropean Union flag in its recent version incorporating the EU stars.

Figure 6.17. European Movement flag.

Figure 6.18. Flag of the Central Commission for Navigation on the Rhine (CCNR).

Figure 6.19. Flag of the European Coal and Steel Community (ECSC).

Figure 6.20. Flag of the Western European Union (WEU).

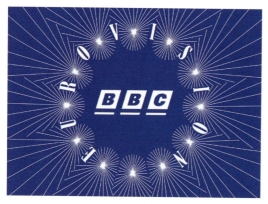

Figure 6.21. 1950s logo of the European Broadcasting Union (EBU).

Figure 6.22. 1990s logo of the European Broadcasting Union (EBU).

Figure 6.23. The Eurovision Song Contest (ESC) logo in Istanbul 2004.

Figure 6.24. Union of European Football Associations (UEFA) logo.

Figure 6.25. Champions League logo.

Figure 6.26. EU barcode.

Figure 6.27. Picobelleuropa, 2005.

Figure 6.28. Maarten Vanden Eynde's 2006 flag in *Europe 2006–2014*, 2005. Silkscreen flag, spun-poly (155 gr/m2 polyester cloth), UV proof and washable.

Figure 6.29. Gay European flag used in Gay Pride events since 2005.

Figure 6.30. Vlad Nancă: *I Do Not Know What Union I Want to Belong to Anymore*, 2003 (photo Johan Fornäs 2010).

Figure 6.31. Nemania Cvijanović: *The Sweetest Dream*, 2005 (photo Johan Fornäs 2010).

Figure 6.32. David Černý's *Entropa*, Brussels 2009 (photo Marek Blahuš).

Figure 7.6. Christer Sjögren, 2008 (lilianseurovision.blogspot.com).

Figure 7.7. InCulto, 2010 (Ane Charlotte Spilde).

front   back

5 euro

10 euro

20 euro

50 euro

100 euro

200 euro

500 euro

Figure 8.1. Euro banknotes, 2002.

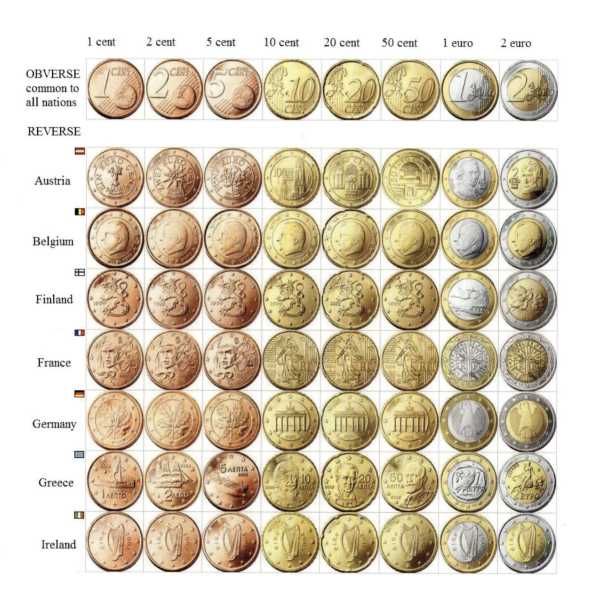

Figure 8.2 (This and facing page). Euro coins from the original twelve EMU member states Austria, Belgium, Finland, France, Germany, Greece, Ireland, Italy, Luxembourg, Netherlands, Portugal and Spain, and the associated countries Monaco, San Marino and Vatican City, 2002.

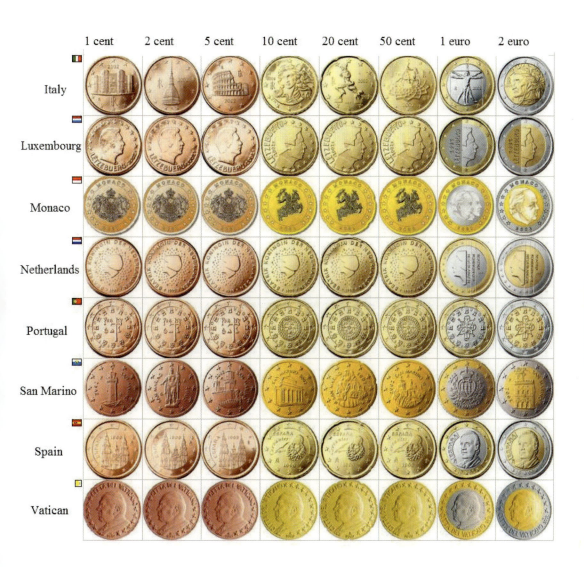

OBVERSE
new series
from 2007

10 cent   20 cent   50 cent   1 euro   2 euro

Figure 8.3. New Euro coins obverse, 2007.

Figure 8.4. Euro coins (reverse) from the five new member states Cyprus, Estonia, Malta, Slovakia and Slovenia, 2007–11.

2007   **2009**

2 euro
commemorative
coins

Figure 8.5. Commemorative €2 coins (reverses), 2007 and 2009.

Figure 8.6. Nauru's $10 coin from 2002.

front   back

US
5 dollar

China
100 yuan

Russia
50 ruble

South Africa
50 rand

Figure 8.7. US $5 banknote since 2006, Chinese 5 yuan banknote since 1999, Russian 5 ruble banknote since 1998 and South African 50 rand banknote since 1999.